Although known as a fighter airplane, the P38 was never created as a fighter and was never intended to combat other fighters. It was designed as an airborne anti-aircraft weapon to intercept and destroy enemy bombers.

But, astonishingly, the records show that the P38 shot down more Japanese aircraft in World War II than any other fighter plane and that it was a major factor in deciding the outcome of World War II.

The P38 is still shrouded in mystery and controversy. Martin Caidin and the men who flew this remarkable machine unravel the truth with an eyewitness account of the

FORK-TAILED DEVIL: THE P38

FORK-TAILED DEVIL: The P-38

Martin Caidin

BALLANTINE BOOKS • NEW YORK

ISBN 0-345-31292-9

Manufactured in the United States of America

First Edition: November 1971
Sixth Printing: September 1983

This book is for

Joe Wesley Dickerson
Arthur W. Heiden
Edward B. Giller
F. Val Phillips
Charles W. King
Tony LeVier
Milo Burcham
Bill Coleman
Revis Sirmon
and
Hey! The roll; call the roll!
Those who flew the Lightning . . .
Those gone.
Those still here. . .

Contents

1. Twilight Zone

We stood in a group beneath the four heavy machine guns and cannon clustered wickedly in the nose of the big fighter. To each side of the gleaming waxed surface shone a spinner and silvery propeller blades. From nose to tail the airplane glistened with the beauty only repeated hand waxing can impart to a winged machine. Colonel Revis Sirmon of the Confederate Air Force climbed into the cockpit. He strapped in, went through the checklist, looked out for the hand signal the props were clear. Sirmon hit the starter for the left engine. Never did a husky Allison turn over smoother or faster, never did one of those big engines purr more softly, a deep-throated growling rumble that astonished everyone with its low beat. Then the other set of blades whirled in the bright sun, the second engine rumbled with the same authoritative manner, and the machine was alive, dipping ever so gently on the nose strut as the power tried to ease her forward. There was an air of disbelief about it all. You had the feeling of standing somewhere in the Twilight Zone, the years stripped away like pages of a book turned backward, because this was the summer of 1968 and that beautiful winged creature trembling with restrained power was a twin-engine fighter of a war, an era of flight, long past.

In the midst of history, we stood on the flight line of the Confederate Air Force. The sun weighed on the concrete of Rebel Field with a heavy hand. Harlingen, Texas lies at the very bottom of the United States, and it is the

1

heat of Mexico and Texas, turning shirts and hair wet with perspiration. The big fighter before us rumbled with power, and I took the moment to scan the flight line. Beyond the Lightning waiting for flight, still parked near the edge of the runway, was the big Flying Fortress I had just landed after an hour of touch-and-go landings. And *that*, without power-boosted controls, guarantees a flight suit soaked from head to foot.

To the left of the B-17G, lined in a row before the main hangar, wing to wing, stood a Consolidated B-24J Liberator, the four-engined counterpart of the Fortress from the days of World War II. Its immediate companion was a true rarity, perhaps the only one of its kind still flying in the world, the Martin B-26 Marauder, the twin-engined medium bomber once infamous as "Martin's Miscarriage," or the "Incredible Prostitute" (the wings in the early models were so short the airplane had no visible means of support, cried its pilots). There was a Douglas A-26 Invader, the flat-bellied medium bomber transformed by the magic of postwar designation shuffling into the B-26; the change marked the loss from Air Force inventory of the Marauder, and the A-26 took up its new number. Further along the row of historical holdouts was a Beech C-45 Expeditor, the famed ship known world over as the D-18, or simply the Twin Beech. There was a venerable Gooney Bird, the Douglas C-47 Skytrain, courtesy of the original DC-3. Further down the line stood an ugly intruder, a Fairchild C-119 Packet with huge engines and booms. With the Packet there was a Boeing B-47E Stratojet and a Northrop F-89 Scorpion. These, however, were of the postwar breed and were more tolerated than appreciated by the pilots and ground crews of the Confederate Air Force fiercely loyal to the winged machines of the Second World War.

Behind us and to our right spread an air buff's wildest dream come true. Another Lockheed Lightning, this one a P-38H model rather than the husky P-38L ticking over before flight. Parked neatly in their slots could be seen a group of fighters fairly reeking with history—but every one of them in top flying condition. A Curtis P-40F

Warhawk in dazzling blood-red hue from nose to tail. A huge, deep-bellied Republic P-47D Thunderbolt, one of six being resurrected at the time. Two sleek North American P-51D Mustangs. A rare Bell P-63 Kingcobra, gleaming white, showing the flag of the Confederate Air Force. An even rarer North American P-82 Twin Mustang, the special breed of two P-51s fastened into a single twin-engine brute; this was the only one in the world still flying. A Spitfire Mark XIV commanded, as it must and always does, special attention and respect. Three Messerschmitt Me-109G fighters—the Gustav model that had been in service with the Spanish Air Force. There were still more —three Grummans, for example. An F4F-4 Wildcat, then the F6F Hellcat, and an F8F-3 Bearcat. We looked at a Goodyear FG-1 Corsair, manufactured under license as an almost-duplicate of the original Chance Vought F4U inverted-gull wing fighter. Still more wings of yesteryear: a Fairchild PT-19 and a Vultee BT-13, the ear-pounding Vibrator of basic training days. There were several North American T-6 Texans on the line, as well as a strange hybrid, an AT-6 (known today simply as T-6) modified with a single cockpit and some clever fuselage and wing work to resemble the Mitsubishi Zero fighter. There were all these and there would be more to come. To one side of the hangar, battered and seedy, was the only flying Douglas A-20G Havoc in the world; it was marked for complete restoration. The North American B-25J Mitchell was in the hangar getting new tail feathers. Plans were under way to bring in a huge Boeing B-29 Super-fortress. The machinery was already working to obtain a Douglas SBD Dauntless, a Grumman TBF Avenger; somewhere there was a Douglas B-23 Dragon, a breed of limited production quantity. We had our eyes on a Heinkel He-111 and a Junkers Ju-87 Stuka, and perhaps even a Ju-88. There were more, but then the sound of power growing throatily turned our heads and we stood back as Revis Sirmon nudged the beautiful Lightning forward and around in a wide turn to taxi to the end of the active runway. Few Lightnings—of the P-38L or any other model—have ever commanded the respect of the fighter restored by Revis Sirmon and the Paul Fournet Air Service of Louisiana. It wears gleaming camouflage, it carries its four heavy guns and single cannon in the nose, and painted on the sides of the engine nacelles, immediately behind and beneath the spinners, was its name, *Scatterbrain Kid*. The name has special meaning to Revis Sirmon, perhaps as much as the Lockheed Lightning itself. The man behind the controls of the big fighter taxiing to the active was doing more than fulfilling his personal dream of owning and flying his own Lightning. Revis Sirmon had been flying the P-38 for a long time. Long enough to go back to World War II when Sirmon was a young fighter pilot taking the Lightning on combat missions deep into Europe.

History caught up in a swift rush with itself as Sirmon turned onto the runway. For a moment the big fighter hesitated, nose wheel pointing straight down the long concrete strip. In the cockpit Revis Sirmon went swiftly through his final checks. Moments after his left hand advanced the twin throttles every eye on the field turned to watch. The Lightning demands and commands attention at such moments, and it was no different now. The expected thunder did not materialize as Sirmon released the brakes and the machine edged forward. No shattering roar, no racketing cry one expects and hears from the Thunderbolt or the Mustang. The sound was, well, smooth, powerful, muted . . . It refuted the reality of two great piston engines. It swelled and fell easily and smoothly over the field, building in volume but never crashing down and outward. Sirmon took her off quickly, easily. No more than ten feet high he held her there, accelerating quickly as the gear came up. For a moment the big fighter rocked her wings as first one main gear and then the other tucked away, passing through a brief imbalance. Then she was clean, and the same surprising view was shared by all. Studied from her side, the bigness of the Lightning fades away. The airplane becomes startlingly clean in this view, sleek, everything where it belongs, a bullet shape where there is none expected. The deep moan rose to a demanding cry as the Lightning picked up speed. Still Sirmon held her down. He was perhaps halfway down the long concrete ribbon when suddenly the Lightning burst into new life. The right wing lifted as the nose came up and the big P-38 in an astonishing display of power showed her twin-boomed plane form as Sirmon took her almost straight up, rolling gently as he did so. In moments, the quiet of the engines still unreal, the Lightning was beyond 2,000 feet, rolling out and down from the zoom climb from take-off, her direction reversed, grabbing quickly for speed. We watched, waiting for what must come next. Sirmon took her to the other end of the field, the right wing lifted, went through the vertical and she came down and around, beyond the vertical, dropping like a stone. With a booming moan of power the Lightning whipped past us at something better than 400 miles per hour, streaking along the runway, and then bidding her pilot, using her speed, disappeared in a swooping lunge for the sky that took her thousands of feet above us before Revis Sirmon rolled her out.

The Twilight Zone . . .

Well before this moment on the flight line of Rebel Field I had decided that a book, *the* book, on the P-38 must be written. Not simply a collection of combat reports of pilots interspersed liberally with technical details. This sort of book, often replete with photographs, is a valuable addition to any air combat library, for each such publication invariably makes its own special contribution to historical lore. But it lacks something, and that something is the machine itself, the winged machine of flight, the combat machine, the soul, if you will, of the airplane itself.

A book on the P-38 posed particularly thorny problems, especially if it were to be more than simply a compilation of details and the assembled quotes from pilot and combat reports. All too easy to do this, and all too inadequate. With some experience in writing air combat history behind me I could appreciate particularly the problems at hand. When, with Jiro Horikoshi and Masatake Okumiya, I wrote the book *Zero!* (which has been selling now for more than fifteen years), we prepared a vast spectrum of the Japanese naval air war as it was seen, understood, and lived from the industrial, military planning, and, combat viewpoints. *Zero!* was far more than the story of a fighter airplane and its employment; the Zero fighter was the very representation of Japanese naval airpower that enabled the Japanese to even think of committing themselves to war on a mass scale. Similarly, again with Horikoshi and Okumiya, we prepared the book *The Zero Fighter,* which was, in essence, a detailed technical development of Japanese aeronautical engineering always reflecting the long development period leading to the Zero, its many modifications, and its successors. The two books, basically, reflected the story of one machine, but they differed greatly in content and intent, and together formed much of the final story. But not completely. There was to be yet a third book, the story of Saburo Sakai, the leading ace of Japan (sixty-four kills air-to-air of American, British, Chinese, Australian and Dutch aircraft) as a Zero pilot. Fred Saito did a vast amount of research, much of it with Japanese pilots who had previously refused to discuss their air combat experiences, and together we wrote the book *Samurai!* We have been gratified, of course, with the fact that *Zero!* and *Samurai!,* both selling for fifteen years, have been reprinted in many languages throughout the world, to the extent of several millions of copies, and have become singular achievements for the areas they represent.

At the same time I hasten to add that these books, no matter how intimately they are involved with the Zero, represent only an element of the story of this one airplane. The story can never be complete without hearing the viewpoint of those who fought against the Zero, and in this area I wrote a number of books, including among them *Flying Forts, The Ragged, Rugged Warriors, The Mission, Air Force, Golden Wings,* and others, all of which included those men who were on the receiving end of the Zero fighter, or, who in their capacity as pilots or gunners managed to destroy a considerable number of the Japanese fighter.

Through all these various viewpoints we were able to receive a portrait of the machine that favored the decision of the Japanese to go to war. Sometimes, no matter how deeply one delves into a particular airplane, however, the complete picture is never gained and we are left with a cameo of the full story. The individual facet is of course invaluable for it is from the many horizons of historical tales that we gain depth. The book *Thunderbolt!* provides another example. It is the story not of the P-47 fighter, but rather that of Robert S. Johnson, who shot down twenty-eight German fighters in air-to-air combat over a period of but eleven months. Bob Johnson and I never intended specifically in writing this book to tell the story of the famed Jug, but it was impossible not to paint a portrait of considerable depth of the airplane, and the intimacy of relationship between Bob Johnson and the Thunderbolts he flew is a must for any historian seeking the grander view of this fighter.

An opposite to *Thunderbolt!* must be *Messerschmitt Me-109,* which I wrote as—how to put this?—a technical-personal-combat-historical portrait of the Me-109 fighter. In this area the primary interest centered about one of the greatest airplanes ever built, for more than anything else it could do in terms of flight capabilities or numbers of aircraft, the Me-109 in its many variants and through its long life dictated—quite literally—the fortunes of war that must affect, and so did, an entire world. This, too, was the particular signature of the Mitsubishi Zero fighter, more than any other individual Japanese aircraft. In this category we would find the Spitfire, B-29, the B-17 and B-24, the Lancaster and the Ju-88, and many more machines too numerous to list here. The point is, however, that aircraft reached the accolade of "great" only when they flew in sufficient number and affected severely the outcome of battles and wars. Thus the Curtis P-40, hamstrung by its own inadequacies, fought and clawed its way to immortality because of its singular availability at critical moments and, to a lesser extent, because its ruggedness assured its survival in unfavorable situations. The P-40s that *should* have fallen from the skies managed, somehow, to stagger back to home fields for repeated resurrection.

What, then, the role of the Lockheed P-38 Lightning in this same war? It is not that quick and easy an answer, and the very complexity of the answer has helped to sustain the shroud of mystery and controversy behind which the P-38 has remained so much the enigma.

To respond to the first question that must be asked there can be only one answer—the P-38 was a major factor in deciding the outcome, and the time frame of events, of the battles making up the Second World War. There can be no question if we involve one point only, and that is that the P-38 shot down more Japanese aircraft in World War II than any other fighter plane. As such it achieved primacy in its essential mission—the destruction of great numbers of the enemy while carrying out its combat assignments. If we wish to lean toward the viewpoint of the purist, we would find a grudging concession to judgment by numbers alone, since so many P-38 fighters were modified hastily into F-4 and F-5 photographic reconnaissance aircraft. The number ran into the many hundreds, and there is no question that had several hundred additional P-38s in the combat zone been available for the role of direct combat with the enemy, the final tally of P-38 pilots must have risen by an appreciable number. In the same vein, of course, must be included the P-38s that were modified to carry a bombardier and a Norden bombsight, those modified for special radar equipment as pathfinders, and other variants that were carried out on the production line and at modification centers.

But there is more than one kind of purist, and the value of an airplane can hardly be judged by the statistical totings on scoreboards, for then we must ignore aircraft usage as fighter-bombers and ground-attack machines, all of which are the factors for judgment in the overall success of the *weapon*. And it is the weapon we are considering. No one can appraise the aircraft of the Second World War and not consider the role of the Douglas C-47, and its variants, as a *weapon*. Logistic it might be, of course, but it was a means of utilizing a winged machine to apply military strength where and when needed.

These are elements indispensable in evaluating the P-38 for what it was—one of the finest *weapons* to be applied in the Second World War. The Messerschmitt Me-109 fought in diverse climates and under difficult conditions and it was one of the greatest weapons ever devised and used in mass numbers. But it *was* restricted to the European continent and to North African areas, and its element of greatness would have been sorely compromised had the Me-109 been required to fulfill the role of the P-38 in the Pacific. There range was God, and the Me-109, for all its outstanding characteristics, was grimly deficient in this area. Indeed, one of the critical factors that gave the edge to the British in the Battle of Britain was the comparatively short range of the Me-109E variant that bore the brunt of that fierce combat. Had the Germans been able to endow the Me-109E with greater range and endurance they might have cracked the thin armor of British defenses and history itself could well have taken a turn other than we know from past experience and our weighty tomes. Thus as outstanding as was the Me-109E as an airplane in fighter-to-fighter combat, this one failing was all-important. A tactical achievement that can only be considered as brilliant was, however, a disaster in the strategic sense.

There is the old saw that one man's meat is another man's poison, and the variables of personal preference, combat conditions, supply, logistics support, and many other factors, all contribute to final judgement. What better example of this element in judging aircraft than the Brewster F2A Buffalo? As a machine sold to the British and the Dutch, for use in the Pacific and Asia, it was a bitterly hated and much-maligned stubby beast. Its equipment demanded much modification and over-attention in the field. Its firepower was lacking. It wallowed in the sky. British pilots discovered they could not loop the airplane. That statement deserves a pause. Gregory R. Board, who shot down several Japanese aircraft while flying the Buffalo (and was himself shot down several times), reported that when receiving the fighter planes, the British and Australian pilots were dismayed to learn the thing could hardly get out of its own way.

American pilots flying the Buffalo in the Battle of Midway in June 1942 were flayed viciously by Japanese Zero fighters, and the few survivors of the uneven combats reported that to fly the Buffalo against the Zero was suicide and, further, that the Buffalo was fit only for training and never for combat.

One must conclude, then, that no one would want the keg-shaped Brewster. No one, that is, except the Finns, who utilized their export versions of the Buffalo in winter combat against the Germans. The Finnish pilots, instead of repeating the laments of the Brewster barrel, lauded the performance of the machine under the severe conditions of their bitterly cold winter operations and, indeed, achieved a number of fighter pilot aces with the Buffalo! However, it must be added that this episode of success with the Brewster has produced more head-shaking and wonder than the conclusion that the Buffalo was, perhaps, more than was indicated by its miserable performance against the Japanese.

We could continue in this vein for some time and hardly be in danger of exhausting the comparisons that leap to mind, as well as those that provide interesting speculation. What might have happened, for example, had there been large-scale figher-to-fighter combat between the superb Focke-Wulf FW-190 and the equally capable Grumman F6F Hellcat? But of all that one may consider most interesting, none can surpass the desire of the pilots who flew the big (28,000 pounds) Northrop P-61 Black Widow night fighter armed with four 20-mm cannon and four turret-mounted .50 caliber machine guns. The arguments of the most maneuverable fighter of the war? Remember these? No doubt the Spitfire Mk. IX was heavily favored, or even the FW-190, and who will question the Zero or Oscar (Hayabusa)? But even the Japanese admitted the Grumman F6F could turn inside a Zero, and to those experienced with these machines the F6F holds the laurels. Ah, but that huge P-61, heavier and larger than a medium bomber. Would the reader consider that *this* was the most maneuverable fighter plane of World War II? No? Even when you consider those full-span spoilers swifter and more efficient than any ailerons? Or that the AAF officially states that the P-61 "proved to be highly maneuverable, more so than any other AAF fighter." And that includes the P-51D Mustang which weighed *but a third* the combat weight of the Black Widow. Well, that's another book . . .

One further point must be made before getting into the thick of the P-38 story. Decisions made far from the skies of combat often determined the future development course of what would become "great" aircraft. Both the P-39 and the P-40 fighters were intended not for aerial combat, but for defensive operations against enemy invasions of the United States. As such their primacy was invested in low-level operations—more so against invasion forces than enemy aircraft. The result was the production of both machines without superchargers for their engines, and as poor as was the P-40 for altitude operations the P-39 was considerably more the dreary machine. When, in combat theaters, other aircraft were available in quantity to assume fighter operations at altitude, the P-39s were turned loose for ground attack and proved excellent machines. This in no way can sustain the record of the P-39 as a fighter plane, but it is interesting to note that its intended purpose was for ground attack and its secondary capabilities were for air combat—and secondary indeed the machine proved to be.

One wonders what might have been the record of the durable P-40 had that aircraft, from the outset of its career, enjoyed a supercharged engine that would have permitted high performance at high altitudes. The entire picture of this machine, the "foot-in-the-door" fighter of American air combat operations, might have been altered drastically for the better.

The wonder at this possibility is sustained in the reality of another aircraft—the brilliant design we know as the Mustang. With this machine, in its early days, there was often the query of *"What if . . . ?"* What if we could modify the Mustang into a fighter where it might be able to operate at high altitudes instead of being restricted only to the lower heights? Wouldn't *that* be something!

Thus we return to the original concept of the Mustang, designed by North American Aviation to British specifications as the company's NA 73 design. Two aircraft were required to be delivered to the Army Air Forces while production was being prepared for the British. Those two fighters, the XP-51 models, carried the AAF name of Apache—the Mustang title was bestowed upon the NA 73 version by the British, and overshadowed the AAF title until it disappeared and our own models also became known as Mustang. This airplane, as used by the British, was never intended for other than medium and low altitudes, and was designed, in fact, for rhubarb operations —low-level sweeps into enemy territory. Its primary mission, like that of the older P-39 and P-40, was ground attack and, as such, without supercharging for its Allison engine, it could no more slug it out with enemy fighters at 35,000 feet than could the creaking Airacobras and Tomahawks.

Then came the decision to mate the Mustang airframe with the Rolls Royce Merlin engine—and what was the greatest fighter airplane *of the second half of the war* was created. The reader will note the emphasis that it was for the second half of World War II that we regard the Mustang as the supreme machine of its type, combining all the characteristics fighter pilots desire—speed, maneuverability, climb, firepower, durability, ease of control, altitude performance, and so forth.

This is why, when I wrote my book on the Messerschmitt Me-109, through all its variants, I pleaded the case that the Messerschmitt must edge all other aircraft as the single "greatest" machine. It was there from beginning to end, and few will dispute that no worth can be attached to a fighter that simply was not there during the fighting, as is the case with the Mustang during the earlier years of the war.

Let us examine one of the more misleading premises concerning the P-38. Throughout most books concerned with the generalities of fighter performance and record during World War II there exists a singular glaring error. Because the ultimate combat role of the P-38, P-47 and P-51 was for long-range combat—the escort mission—as opposed to shorter-range performance of such fighters as the Spitfire, it has become accepted that these fighters were designed from the outset for such missions. Nothing could be further from the truth. The P-38 was designed as a fast-climbing interceptor of limited range. The P-47, emerging from the Seversky P-35/Republic P-43 designs (and the never-built XP-44), was intended as a high-altitude fighter. And the P-51, as a low-altitude penetration or rhubarb attack fighter. None were designed for anything even approaching the range at which ultimately they operated.

The very nature of the performance achieved by the Lockheed P-38 Lightning by the middle years of the Second World War is all the more astonishing when we realize the original mission assigned to this airplane and the manner of its design. Lockheed, which produced the P-38, was given its interceptor assignment, and was also led to believe that no more than a maximum of fifty aircraft would be procured by the Air Corps (later the AAF). Thus the internal tankage of the P-38 was kept to its minimum since weight was a major consideration. More important in the long run was the manner of design. Counting on only fifty airplanes as a maximum order Lockheed did everything but to design the P-38 for mass production. The airplanes were virtually to be hand-built. No facilities were prepared for any long production run and when demands for the P-38 exploded in the midst of Lockheed offices, one may imagine the shock and consternation. The production P-38, strange to say, was born in the midst of a converted brewery. But that is a point for future chapters, and this moment is taken to stress to the reader that to understand the nature of the P-38 it must be understood that the machine with which we are dealing was *never* intended for either long-range missions or mass production, and these facts serve only to enhance the wonder of this airplane.

As for the final decision to write this book, the writer must admit to considerable outside influence. In early February of 1970, Ballantine Books received in their New York office an unsolicited letter from a Mr. Arthur W. Heiden of Atlantic, Iowa. Since Mr. Heiden's letter is eloquently clear, it is reproduced for the reader:

Gentlemen:

I would like to see one accurate and authoritative book published that would be *the* historical work on the Lockheed P-38 fighter aircraft.

Since I have enjoyed many books published by your company and especially respect the aviation writing of Mr. Martin Caidin, this letter is an attempt to persuade you both to produce a book on this subject with the impact of *Flying Forts, Zero!, Me-109,* and others.

As a former Combat Fighter Pilot, Fighter Training Instructor, and Staff Combat Operations Officer with experience in P-38, P-40 and P-51 aircraft, I am continually provoked by the repetitive inaccurate writing that forms the history of the P-38. As the B-17 shaped Bomber Doctrine, I am convinced that the P-38 has had as great an impact on Fighter Doctrine

Considering the fragmented and inaccurate history on this great machine, I cannot express too strongly my feeling of urgency for this effort to be made.

If I may suggest:

1. The historic significance of the P-38 has been missed.

2. It was the first all-purpose aircraft in the military inventory.

3. It was able to adapt to all missions, without reservation, throughout World War II.

4. Vastly outnumbered in all combat theaters, it always held its own and advanced against all circumstances until production and training could overpower the enemy.

5. It was the direct lead-in to jet operations, including systems, problems, characteristics, and capabilities.

6. Several ocean crossings led to experiments that formulated post-World War II nuclear delivery and mobile Fighter Doctrine.

7. It was the stimulus to air leaders who were later to develop these doctrines. The result was the jet fighter's role as a deterrent with its nuclear and worldwide capability.

8. That P-51s replaced P-38s mostly for economical reasons and ease of production and training, not because of a significant difference of performance.

9. That operational problems were resolved to a highly satisfactory degree and gave the P-38 advantages that no other fighter of the time had.

10. That each problem, such as compressibility, supercharger regulators, single generators, cockpit heat, intercoolers, electric propellers, and others, were very interesting, previously unencountered, interrelated, and often suffered from production priorities and plain bad luck.

11. That pilot training was unusual compared with single-engine fighter training.

12. That Lockheed's close factory-support program has often been viewed out of context. Problems were magnified where in competitive cases there was no one around to freely admit to the problem and then attempt to solve it.

13. That those who write on the subject fail to counsel with Tony LeVier or even bother to read his fine book, *Pilot*.

14. That an in-depth combat evaluation seldom, if ever, appears in print.

I offer any aid at my limited means that this proposal be born.

ARTHUR W. HEIDEN

Well, how do you turn down a letter like *that*?

You don't, and we—Ballantine Books and myself—didn't.

The reader is informed here, and quickly, that Tony LeVier, Lockheed's great test pilot and one of the world's greatest fliers, and an old friend of the writer, has generously given his permission to refer freely to his experiences with the P-38 that he has written about in his book *Pilot,* published by Harper & Row. It is recommended to the reader as a singular document with no equal, covering a broad horizon of flying and flight to capture the imagination of anyone who has ever turned his eyes to the sky.

(I will take the liberty of recommending to the reader another book, this one a work of fiction, which will provide an astonishing in-depth portrayal of the Lightning as a ground-attack fighter in Europe. Alfred Coppel, writing of flights and combat missions in the P-38F fighter-bomber, with more truth than fiction in his words, has prepared an excellent novel titled *Order of Battle,* and published by Harcourt Brace Jovanovich. The historian will find more in these pages on P-38 fighter-bomber operations in Europe than he will in any nonfiction work ever written on this subject.)

Finally, something about a remarkable man without whom this book, and what I hope will be an in-depth and sensitive portrayal of the P-38, could never have been written. During World War II there was a P-38 jock who was "rather intimately associated with the P-38 from 1942 until they were phased out in 1946. I had a 'touch' of North Africa and a 'couple of interesting moments over Rabaul' but nothing like the massive raids of Europe." A P-38 pilot the other jocks called Joe.

Joe Wesley Dickerson, M.D., of Jasper, Texas.

Somebody special; rather extraordinary, really. If this book is what we hope it will be, then thanks to Joe Wesley Dickerson. If the book fails, the failure is mine alone.

When the word passed around that I was researching the book on the P-38, Dr. Dickerson contacted me immediately and offered, in homage to the men who had flown the P-38 in combat, and of the machine itself, his not inconsiderable resources for assistance. Dr. Dickerson, whose name immediately brings up furious activity on the part of other people, performed a miracle in supplying the names and the ready assistance and the cooperation of dozens of men who had flown the P-38 from the first days of its acceptance into military colors, and it is to a very large extent, essentially, their story you will read in these pages.

There is only one way to thank Joe Dickerson. It is this book itself.

An honest, at times a troubled story, but the true story of the P-38.

Some years back I read a book on the Hawker Hurricane fighter flown by the Royal Air Force in World War II. Now, the Hurricane was quite a bird, what could be properly considered a "sterling aircraft." She was sturdy and trustworthy and her pilots said she flew like a dream. But the Hurricane, by the same token, was no fair match for either the Messerschmitt Me-109 or the Mitsubishi Zero, two of its chief adversaries, and despite its vital role in the Battle of Britain, it never achieved status, by virtue of its fighter-vs-fighter performance, as a superior fighter airplane. However, one would never have known from reading the gushing praise of the Hurricane in that book, that the airplane ever yielded an ounce of performance in speed, altitude, firepower, or range to any opposing aircraft. The book so sickeningly overstated its case it did a great airplane a disservice.

You won't find that problem in these pages. In fact, in order to strive for objectivity, those who loyally support the P-38 may find the writer at times a bit too harsh for their liking.

But the P-38 was a tough bird, and it will bear this writer, as it has its not inconsiderable difficulties before me.

2. A New Kind of Cat

A combat airplane is born from a philosophy of need and the P-38 fits neatly into its own category. We know the P-38 as a fighter airplane, but in fact it was never intended to combat other fighters, nor was it created from the purist's viewpoint as a fighter. Clearly and simply the P-38 came into being as an interceptor against bombers; it was a platform to carry heavy firepower to a point in airspace and time in order to intercept and destroy enemy bombers. No one anticipated the P-38 engaging in fighter-*vs.*-fighter combat. No one considered or really much gave a damn about the maneuverability of the P-38 *in fighter terms*. The airplane was intended from the outset simply as a flying anti-aircraft weapon.

The design of new airplanes always conforms to the doctrine prevalent at any one time in the military community. During the period of the 1930's the Army Air Corps preached the ascendancy of the long-range bomber over all other types of military aircraft. Thus the design of the P-39 and the P-40 in the period 1936–1937 dictated primary performance in the ground attack role and condemned from the outset (aided by other factors, of course) the ability of these two airplanes to contest enemy fighters, which had been designed from *their* outset for superiority in air-to-air combat. Which may help to explain the official policy of the Air Corps that by late 1941, only eighteen months after they first went into combat, both the P-39 and the P-40 were already obsolescent, and sorely in need of replacement by superior machinery.

In January of 1937 leading aircraft manufacturers in the United States began to receive a specification from the Air Corps for a new pursuit aircraft that marked a radical departure from existing fighters or, as official terminology then went, as pursuits. The Air Corps stated the mission of the new pursuit was for the "interception and attack of hostile aircraft at high altitude." The specification called for a maximum level speed of 360 mph at 20,000 feet and a maximum level speed at sea level of 290 mph. Further, the airplane must be able to sustain full power for at least one hour at its critical altitude of 20,000 feet. The rate of climb required for the new interceptor raised eyebrows—the Air Corps demanded the airplane reach a height of 20,000 feet within six minutes of starting its takeoff roll. (The P-38 handily met its climb requirements and, in fact, right to the end of World War II, remained one of the fastest-climbing fighters of any combatant.) Another stringent demand was made for what clearly would be a large and heavy airplane—the new interceptor must be able to take off and land within a distance of 2,200 feet while clearing a 50-foot obstacle at runway's end.

Among the companies that went full-tilt into the new competition was Lockheed. This was no small step for the California firm for they had never built a military airplane and plunging into the competition for the high-performance interceptor was regarded by many as Lockheed overstepping its capabilities. The opinion wasn't shared by Robert E. Gross, Lockheed president, who gave the signal to get busy to the design team of H. L. Hibbard and Clarence L. Johnson. "Kelly" Johnson indulged in a series of doodles of a twin-engine design. From the outset he realized that what the Air Corps wanted could never be realized with a single-engine airplane. There wasn't an engine in the world that could meet all the requirements of speed, range, climb, firepower, sustained performance and other specifications. It would take two engines. Kelly Johnson took a hard look at a new Allison engine; the V-1710-cubic-inch-capacity engine had just completed bench tests by running at 1,000 horsepower for 150 hours. This had to be the engine—as a pair. Kelly Johnson narrowed down his designs to six final layouts. The design team considered every possibility, including one interceptor that appeared about as conventional as one might expect, but concealed both engines in the fuselage, each driving its own propeller through a complex system of shafts and gearing from the fuselage through the wing. *Too* complex, decided the engineers. They studied a comparable design with the fuselage-buried engines driving pusher engines and the tail using twin fins and rudders; this, too, went by the wayside. One Johnson sketch bore an amazing resemblance to an interceptor that would show up years later—McDonnell's XP-67 Bat. It was abandoned by Lockheed, however. Of the remaining three possibilities, all mounted twin-boom layouts. One of these mounted the engines in a push-pull arrangement; the fuselage had an engine before and aft of the cockpit. Again, this basic design was to emerge later; sans the forward engine, Kelly Johnson's sketch bore a close resemblance to what would become the Vultee XP-54 Swoose Goose experimental fighter. The fifth design to be considered and discarded mounted an engine at the front part of the long fuselage boom, with the pilot seated in a cockpit in the left boom aft of the engine. Want a better description? Just study a photograph of the North American F-82 Twin Mustang with only the left cockpit and you have the early sketch by Kelly Johnson.

The sixth layout under study became Lockheed's Model 22 design—what emerged was the airplane so familiar to us as the P-38. But not quite yet, early in 1937. There would be obstacles to overcome. The two engines, fuel and other design elements meant a heavy airplane, and that meant wing loadings characteristic of Lockheed, but far in excess of what was considered acceptable elsewhere for fighter designs. This was the Lockheed gamble —they weren't building a fighter demanding turn-on-a-dime performance. They were building an *interceptor* and that made innovations the design order of the day. Lockheed opted for the tricycle-gear arrangement. It further increased weight but improved ground handling and safety. The ability to fly and fight at altitude couldn't be met with standard engines, so Lockheed went to turbo-superchargers for their Model 22. More and more the arrangement of twin booms made better sense. The turbo-superchargers could be mounted in the fuselage booms aft of the engines. There would be plenty of room for the main gear in the booms. The design promised ease in locating air intakes, radiator baths and other accessories. Of course the Model 22 was turning out to be a *big* airplane with a wingspan exceeding fifty feet in the original studies. At the same time, the design layout of a tail with twin fins and rudders increased the total effective lift of the airplane, and Kelly Johnson made risky predictions that they were going to build one of the most stable machines ever put together—a prediction that proved to be one of the most accurate ever made.

There was another quantum jump to be made with the Lockheed interceptor taking shape under the hands of the Hibbard design team. The powerful engines and the central fuselage design promised extraordinary firepower, especially considering standard armament for U.S. fighters at the time, which came to one .30 and one .50 caliber machine gun with some 300 rounds per gun. The P-39 and the P-40 as fighters would be more heavily armed but they had yet to see their first flight. Like most fighter or interceptor designs (and the interceptor role as a distinct mission for the P-38 would be extremely short-lived) the new Lockheed would go through a great variety of armament changes. However, the basic arrangement of four heavy machine guns and one cannon would prevail. For the Model 22 fighter, Kelly Johnson proposed an armament of one 23-mm Madsen cannon with fifty rounds of explosive shells, and four .50 caliber Colt MG-53 machine guns with a thousand rounds per gun; this provided a total of some 4,000 rounds of machine-gun ammunition as well as fifty explosive shells compared to contemporary armament of one light and one heavy machine gun with a total of 600 rounds. But the Lockheed promised even more devastating use of its fire-power since, with all weapons located in the center of the airplane and beyond the propellers' arcs, there was no need for propeller synchronization and the guns fired with maximum speed. The guns and cannon would also fire directly ahead for their full range of a thousand yards, rather than having to be aimed at a point of convergence well ahead of the airplane. All told, the electrically heated guns and cannon of the Model 22 had a combined firing rate of 3,200 rounds per minute.

Bob Gross, Lockheed's boss, grabbed the blueprints and specifications for the Model 22 and flew to Wright Field in Ohio to officially submit Lockheed's bid for the new development contract. The Army, despite the seeming urgency of the program, took its time in evaluating different designs and it wasn't until June of 1937 that the high brass made their decision. It was Lockheed, and the Model 22 gained its new designation—the Lockheed XP-38. It wasn't *that* much of a contract, since Lockheed was being funded only to the extent of one airplane, the sole XP-38. But if flight tests proved out the revolutionary design then Lockheed could look forward to a final order for fifty airplanes. That's *fifty*—the maximum number of the new interceptor that anyone ever expected Lockheed to build. And that conviction itself proved to be first of the many stumbling blocks that would show up to keep the P-38 as a fighter ready for combat on its way to battle areas. Because the airplane that was designed for maximum production of fifty units was, essentially, a handmade machine, and, as far as the factory was concerned, it bore distressingly little internal resemblance to an airplane designed for mass production where getting out the greatest number of machines in the shortest time possible was of paramount interest.

By June 1938, after extensive design work, Lockheed was almost ready. A month later Lockheed engineers were "cutting metal." Despite the radical innovations of the XP-38, which included the extensive use of stainless steel, and the first American aircraft of any type to use butt-jointed flush-riveted external surfaces, assembly of the

XP-38 prototype went quickly. By late December the airplane was considered to be complete and ready for flight test. But not from the field used by Lockheed for its civil operations. Preparations were made to transfer the XP-38 to March Field for its initial flight tests. Engineers stripped the airplane under armed guard within a hangar and loaded the assemblies aboard three trucks, each concealing its cargo with canvas. Starting on New Year's Eve to round out 1938, the convoy of trucks and police took a circuitous route to March Field, near Riverside, California, where the airplane was to be readied for its initial test flights.

Reassembled and ready to take to the air the XP-38 was a gleaming tribute to Lockheed design. A huge machine compared to other fighters it was astonishingly clean to the eye. This attention to clean aerodynamic design was often invisible to the eye; an example of the meticulous detail was to be found in the installation of the turbosuperchargers. Kelly Johnson designed the intercooler to form part of the leading edge of the outer wing, combining aerodynamic sleekness with mechanical efficiency.

There was yet another innovation (and one which is just now, in the period from 1970 on, being returned to aircraft design) in the XP-38 that would endear the airplane to future pilots. All twin-engine airplanes have a critical engine—and Kelly Johnson was determined to avoid this problem with the XP-38. Normally, as seen from the view of the pilot, both propellers of a twin-engine airplane rotate in a clockwise direction. If an engine quits on takeoff, at a time before the airplane has built up appreciable speed, the airplane yaws, or swings sharply, into the dead engine. But because of factors known as torque and the P factor (propeller factor), the yawing motion is much greater if it is the left engine that quits.

Kelly Johnson decided to eliminate the critical-engine factor in the new XP-38. Instead of having both engines turning the propellers in the same direction he designed the XP-38 to have counter-rotating propellers—both props rotated inwardly. This innovation, of course, complicated engine manufacture and maintenance in that it was necessary to prepare modified parts for the engine that rotated in the "opposite" direction. For the XP-38, twin Allison V-1710-11/15 (C9) engines were used; these produced 960 hp at 12,000 feet and 1,090 hp at 13,200 feet. The Curtis electric propellers rotated inward to reduce the torque and P factor. (In all subsequent models of the P-38 the props rotated in the opposite— i.e., outward—direction.)

Fully loaded, the XP-38 weighed 14,800 pounds, but it is unclear whether this figure related to the *intended* weight of the prototype or was the actual weight. The question rises because the XP-38 as it flew at March Field and subsequently never mounted the machine guns and cannon intended for the service models. At any rate, the XP-38 still grossed more than the estimated maximum weight, but the question of flight performance could be put to the test only in flight.

Lieutenant Ben S. Kelsey was appointed project officer for the XP-38, and it may be imagined that he approached the airplane with a mixture of high anticipation and some misgivings. On its first ground test—the airplane to be taxied at progressively higher speeds—the brakes failed and the shining twin-engined interceptor ended clumsily in a ditch. Engineers were quick to repair the ship and on January 27, 1939, Kelsey took the XP-38 into the air for the first time.

As quickly as it left the ground the prototype was in trouble. Kelsey felt the wheel (changed later to a yoke control) vibrating wildly beneath his right hand. The XP-38 was fitted out with new Fowler flaps for increased lift and a flap linkage had failed either during the take-off roll or during initial climb. Kelsey finished the flight —after immediately retracting the flaps—and landed hot, the flaps still up. There are a number of versions of this episode, most of them having it that the flaps were aerodynamically unsound. The fact of the matter is that a piece of metal failed and that was all. Repairs were made after the first test flight and wringing out the bugs of the new interceptor continued.

Unfortunately, the XP-38 was to have all too brief a lifespan. The time it spent in the air was distressingly short—only sixteen days in which the airplane was off the ground for a total of 11 hours 50 minutes. The last flight put the XP-38 into national headlines and lost the airplane to the Air Corps, although, by the strange alchemy of bleating to the press—and the press trumpeting about what it knows so little—the flight was paraded before the public as an outstanding demonstration of a superior new warplane. Anxious to show off to the world what its new machine could do, the Air Corps sent Kelsey off on an attention-grabbing speed dash from March Field in California to Mitchell Field on Long Island, New York. On February 11, 1939, Kelsey took off from March Field, headed for refueling stops at Amarillo, Texas, and Wright Field, Ohio. His flying time for the 2,400 miles has been reported as anywhere from 7 hours 37 seconds to 7 hours 2 minutes; either way, his average speed during flight time was 340 mph over the ground. Still working their mysterious formula for headlines, press agents ballyhooed the XP-38 as hurtling through the air at times during the flight at 420 mph, and conveniently neglected to mention that the 420 mph was a ground speed figure brought about by some rather healthy tailwinds. Nevertheless, the performance by an experimental new airplane *was* something on the extraordinary side, and public attention was brought to bear on the XP-38.

It should have been, for Kelsey wiped out the airplane on attempting to land at Mitchell Field. The point was, however, that it wasn't the XP-38 that failed, but the pilot. Short and simple, Kelsey came in too low. He undershot the runway. Throttled well back, he went forward on the throttles. One engine choked up, the other went to high power and yawed the airplane sharply. Kelsey couldn't keep up with it. Losing altitude rapidly he tried to cut for open country. No luck. The XP-38 went through the top of a tree, stalled out, and crashed into a golf course. It slid into a rather respectable ditch and when it came to a stop it was expensive junk unfit for any further flying.

Now, most of the histories written on the XP-38 have made light of this total loss of the first experimental airplane, emphasizing the speed dash across the United States as justification for that loss, and "proving" the worth of the machine. It makes good copy. In truth, it was nothing less than an unmitigated disaster. American involvement in World War II wasn't that far away, and the loss of the *only* P-38 at a time when a severe regime of flight tests was necessary crippled the program.

What this meant, in the bluntest terms, was that the P-38 as a fighter airplane could have been ready for combat many months before the airplane finally reached combat areas. The speed dash across the United States was nothing less than an irresponsible stunt that grabbed for headlines.

Tony LeVier, one of the great test pilots of this country, and for years the chief test pilot in the P-38 program, laid it out candidly:

"I have always said, and I suppose many people realize it but forget it, that when you are dealing with experimental airplanes you are dealing with something that can mean an awful lot to the security of our country, especially in time of war. If test pilots and the flight test crew in charge of an important new airplane don't take every precaution to keep it from being damaged it could cause a serious loss to the country. I've seen it happen through the years and it is happening today.

"For example, in World War II, the Army grabbed our first P-38 to set a new transcontinental speed record. It was a grand idea, but the only thing a speed record would give them was some newspaper headlines for a day and that's about all. Instead of waiting a few weeks until we knew more about the airplane, they took it when it had hardly been tested. The engines failed going in for a landing at New York . . . and the airplane fell short of the field and crashed. What did that do? *It set the P-38 back about two years,* because we had to start from scratch and build another prototype airplane and run a whole new test program, and as it was the best fighter airplane we had at that time, *that incident may very well have lengthened the war.*"

And, as Lockheed notes in its company history, "Losing the prototype was a serious blow . . . The company had to start over almost from scratch."

Starting again, even from scratch, was debatable, since the Air Corps had had precious little time during which to test out the values of the XP-38 prototype. Notwithstanding the loss of the new airplane (at its own hands, of course) the Air Corps in April 1939 issued Lockheed a Limited Procurement Order for thirteen YP-38 service-test models. Somewhere in the high halls of the brass the word had passed around. This P-38 was "some new kind of cat" in fighter aviation and its development at high speed was recommended.

Lockheed, nursing the loss of the prototype when it was most urgently needed, went back to work.

3. Gestation Period

By April of 1939 Lockheed had received its order for the thirteen YP-38 airplanes to be delivered to the Air Corps for limited-service testing. No one at Lockheed was prepared for what followed next. In September, only five months later, the Air Corps negotiated with Lockheed for a further batch of sixty-six airplanes to be produced for operational service. And then, just under a year later, in August 1940, the Air Corps followed through with an order for 607 P-38 fighter airplanes (it was no longer billed exclusively as an interceptor). Lockheed now found itself with orders for 686 P-38 fighters—and it had yet to deliver the *first* of the YP-38 models.

It was at this early juncture in the still brief lifetime of the P-38 that Lockheed ran into the hornet's nest of its structural design with the airplane. At this point Lockheed began to see the need for a drastic structural redesign of the P-38, for their early model had been prepared, if you will recall, with an ultimate goal of perhaps fifty airplanes as a maximum production order. In short, the P-38 was badly suited to mass production, and here was the Air Corps shouting for hundreds of the machines!

During the brief flight time of the XP-38, however, great promise had been made evident. At a maximum takeoff weight of more than seven tons, the airplane climbed rapidly to 20,000 feet, where Kelsey opened her up for maximum speed runs. The tests were enough to wildly excite both Lockheed and the Air Corps. Despite the overweight condition of the prototype it had flown a steady course at 413 mph. And for 1939 that was performance of an extraordinary degree, especially when one considered that this was not a souped-up racing airplane, but military hardware being prepared for operational service. No question about it—in 1939 the P-38 was far and away the fastest fighter airplane design in the world.

While Lockheed went to work on the YP-38 model another drama was being played out in high offices. Military procedure at the time called for—wisely—a "back-up design" for any new Air Corps warplane. The P-39 was the opposite of the P-40, the B-25, the opposite of the B-26, the B-24, of the B-17; there was always a "just-in-case" backup in the event the favored design came unglued. The decision to go with the P-38 design was no exception, but little attention has been focused on the competitive airplane that lost out to the Lockheed product. For the twin-engine interceptor category, the second-runner was the Grumman XP-50. Those unfamiliar with this airplane, which produced 2,400 horsepower against the 2,000 horsepower of the XP-38, and could outclimb even the swift Lockheed model, we refer the reader to the Grumman XF5F-1 Skyrocket. This was a Navy design for a carrier-based interceptor, startling in its use of two engines, and even more startling in its performance. The Skyrocket—the Grumman design standing between the F4F Wildcat and F6F Hellcat—featured an unusual frontal section. The most-forward part of the fuselage ended some distance short of the leading edge of the wing, creating an impression of engines, wing, and double tail with a minimum of fuselage. The XP-50 weighed some three tons less than the XP-38, was smaller with a wingspan of 42 feet and a length of almost 32 feet, and achieved a speed of 427 mph at critical altitude. The XF5F-1 was Grumman designation G-41, and to enter the interceptor competition against the XP-38, the airplane was modified severely by the company. The nose was extended to normal configuration and a tricycle gear was fitted. Armament approximated that planned for the XP-38. But the XP-50 suffered the same fate as the

XP-38—it crashed. Unfortunately the loss of the XP-50 came without the spectacular cross-country demise of the XP-38, and Lockheed received the nod for their twin-boomed interceptor.

From beginning to end Lockheed re-engineered the YP-38 design, a feat demanding of time and effort little evident in terms of physical appearance. It was a decision that would pay off for Lockheed in ease of future production; the P-38 was never an easy airplane to build, and changes that would have been demonstrated by the XP-38 prototype had to wait for the YP-38s to take to the air. There were other modifications of the basic design. The new structural arrangement brought the gross weight down to a more desirable figure of 13,500 pounds. The XP-38 had been designed to take four .50 caliber machine guns and a single 23-mm Madsen cannon. Lockheed redesigned the nose to accomodate one 37-mm cannon, two .50 and two .30 caliber machine guns (it would be changed again). New engines of 1,150 horsepower (Allison V-1710-27/29 F2R and L) were fitted to the YP-38. The job required more than simply installing the new engines. The thrust was greater, the thrust line different, and the results were engine cowling lines redesigned for the new powerplants.

Test flights with the XP-38 had revealed problems demanding solution in the successor model. The first airplane had been plagued with a grossly inadequate cooling system, and engineers designed an entirely new arrangement. New oil and coolant systems were installed, with cores and intakes measurably larger than for the experimental prototype. The Curtis Electric propellers now rotated outwardly, the opposite of the XP-38. Here, again, was the tragedy of losing the XP-38 before it could be flown through a wide regime of flight testing. When the propellers turned inwardly they set up an airflow over the fuselage nacelle that swirled unpredictably over the wide tail to produce a serious flutter.

Other changes not visible to the eye included the installation of required military equipment and modification to the canopy. The latter deserves special attention, because from the outset the P-38 had been designed with a type of bubble canopy that did not appear on other fighter airplanes until years later.

Another production problem for the P-38 was lack of manufacturing space. Lockheed was being deluged with orders for different airplanes and the Burbank factory simply lacked the facilities for the big fighter airplane. To compensate for this problem during the period that new factories might be built, Bob Gross solved the problem in a unique way. Tony LeVier recalls that "more floor space became imperative. It was soon found down the road in a whisky distillery. Over lunch one day Gross bought the plant for $20,000, and early P-38's were built in the former 3-G distillery."

FLIGHT TESTING

At this point in the development of the P-38, events shifted from a single focus to many activities running parallel to the other. Even before the first YP-38 rolled from the factory, the next model was in production, and the successor to *that* model was already taking shape. It is not possible to delineate each forward event as a separate step in time. It would be convenient, and a blessing to the historian, to record each event of the P-38 history as a sequential step. But it just doesn't work out that way. From this point on, then, our review of events at times must overlap, and we will do our best to keep a firm grip on the many facets of the program. Most histories of a particular aircraft have a straightforward approach to the machine. The X model appeared first, then the Y limited-procurement series, then model A, B, C and so on. Convenient for one and all. Not so with the P-38, for the YP-38 model was still undergoing major testing long after production models were already committed to combat zones. Many of the problems of the P-38, which saw "fixes" in the P-38J and subsequent models, were first solved in the early YP-38 and initial production versions. All too glibly, especially in the matter of the P-38, have writers referred to a problem as being solved, when the application of that solution to combat area fighters took months or years to effect. We'll try to avoid that serious error in these pages.

The first YP-38 took to the air on September 16, 1940, with Lockheed's test pilot Marshall Headle at the controls. A great many people held their fingers crossed until a grinning Headle eased back to the runway; the memory of the lost XP-38 was still too fresh in their minds. But the new YP-38 dispelled fears that the airplane might have been too much for its pilot. Headle's first statement was rushed to the press. "In all my experience as a pilot," he said, "it's the easiest plane I have had to fly."

The YP-38 retained the wingspan—52 feet—and length—37 feet 10 inches—of the XP-38, but stood slightly higher, an increase of four inches to a ground height of 9 feet 10 inches. All future P-38 airplanes would retain these dimensions except for the two-seat P-38M, a modified P-38L intended for use as a night fighter, which had a length of 38 feet 10 inches and a height of 10 feet 4 inches.

But the initial savings in weight effected by the YP-38, down to 13,500 pounds for normal gross, vanished quickly as equipment was added onto the airplane. The gross weight of the airplane as fitted out for full service trials came to 14,348 pounds; yet, it was still lighter than the XP-38 at its heaviest. Nothwithstanding this reduction in weight, the YP-38 proved to be slightly slower than its predecessor. Its maximum speed has been listed as 390 to 405 mph, and it has never been established which was the precise figure. No doubt the readings resulted from various configurations during the test flights. To keep this matter clear for succeeding P-38 variants, it should be pointed out that the Army Air Forces lists the P-38 fighter airplane as having a top speed of "390 to 414 miles per hour," the difference being accounted for by differing models.

A note of more than idle interest to the reader on this matter of maximum speed. In truth all fighters had top speeds that were about as firmly established as quicksand. Quite often two production airplanes, in perfect shape, would have a speed difference of from ten to twenty miles per hour. And when it came to service aircraft, the difference could be even greater. Maximum speed depended on many factors such as temperature and altitude, condition of the engines, the type of propellers installed, the condition of the surface of the airplane (an airplane hand-waxed and kept spotless will be measurably faster than another machine without this attention), and last, but by no means least, the skill of the individual pilot. This latter point is nowhere more evident than in free-for-all air races where six airplanes of exactly the same model will have their final speeds determined solely by the man behind the stick.

In the development of the P-38, engine horsepower went up considerably in the later models; the increase was from 1,150 horsepower per engine in the early P-38s, to 1,475 horsepower per engine in the P-38L series. But again there are factors to complicate the issue of power and speed. Certain models of the P-38 had methanol injection for their engines for critical combat conditions, and under such circumstances a P-38L at high altitude could deliver 1,600 horsepower per engine, which resulted in true airspeeds in level flight of over 425 mph.

While the Air Corps was more than pleased with the initial flight performance of the YP-38, and hopeful for the future of the airplane as a fighter mainstay, it was less than satisfied with Lockheed's performance in the matter of mass production. The official history of the AAF in World War II notes:

Production continued to lag: delivery of the 13 planes first ordered was not completed until June 1941; total deliveries reached only 39 by the middle of August; and, while acceptances in November went up sharply to 74 planes, the AAF inventory on the eve of Pearl Harbor showed no more than 69 P-38's. For these delays, the AAF was inclined to blame Lockheed, and suspicion existed that the company preferred to concentrate on its own commercial Lodestar and on British orders for the Hudson. Whatever the fact, the delay was costly.

No one will agree more than Lockheed that the delays existed, or that they were costly, but the claim that P-38 production suffered because of dollar preferences in getting out the Lodestar and Hudson will produce unprintable responses on the part of Lockheed. And it seems difficult to ignore the realities of the moment. While the Air Corps clamored for the P-38, Lockheed still smarted from the loss of the XP-38 because of an Air Corps publicity stunt. More to the point was the fact that Lockheed had to perform such drastic re-engineering of its basic design, the result directly of Air Corps statements to Lockheed not to expect more than a total production order of fifty airplanes.

There had been an order of sixty-six fighters to follow the YP-38 models, and the first thirty of these were given the designation of P-38. These were hardly to be considered combat airplanes, for the basic design was still undergoing serious flight and ground testing. The P-38 itself differed from its YP-38 predecessor in changed armament of one 37-mm cannon and four .50 caliber machine guns. The weight had again increased, this time to 15,340 pounds; at full weight and best altitude, the test flights showed a maximum speed of 395 mph. But problems had cropped up suddenly in the new machine. The turbosuperchargers were giving pilots and mechanics fits in their operation. At high speed the tail fluttered badly and the airplane vibrated so severely the pilot sometimes lost control.

Even while the search was under way to correct these problems, the production line was already changing to another model, the first of thirty-six P-38D fighters. Delivery of these airplanes was completed during August 1941. Among the changes were aerodynamic modifications redistributing the elevator mass balances, installing new fillets where the fuselage and leading edge joined and changing the angle of incidence of the entire tailplane from 1° 15′ to 0° 0′. These changes were carried

out essentially to eliminate severe flutter of the entire
tail which, on several occasions, had caused the loss of
P-38s when the flutter became so violent that diving P-
38s were torn to pieces in the air.

In almost every history of the P-38 the above change
in the junction of wing leading edge and fuselage and the
modifications to the tail have been referred to as solving
the problem of compressibility with the airplane. Actually,
there were two distinct and separate problems. One was
flutter, which was solved as described, and the other was
compressibility, or what was also known as *shock stall*.

The two were entirely unrelated in the P-38. The flutter
problem appeared almost as quickly as the first test models took to the air; compressibility, about which much
less was known at the time, occurred only when pilots
began to dive the P-38 in high-speed tests.

It must be emphasized that flutter was a problem common to almost every new fighter airplane design. Much
has been written about the tail problems unique to the
P-38, and the emphasis on this one airplane to the
exclusion of others is so much blatant nonsense. The
extraordinarily rugged Republic P-47 Thunderbolt for a
time was earning a notorious reputation as a pilot-killer
when tail flutter in early models tore the airplanes apart
in high-speed dives. Perhaps the most successful dive
bomber of the war was the Curtis SB2C-4 Helldiver; in
the original XSB2C-1 models it earned the lethal title of
"widowmaker" because of the pilots killed when the tail
wrenched free in dives. Even the superb North American
P-51 Mustang went through similar agonies. George W.
Gray, author of the outstanding study of the N.A.C.A.
(National Advisory Committee for Aeronautics), *Fron-
tiers of Flight*, published by Alfred A. Knopf, emphasized this point when he wrote:

"Several Mustangs had recently lost their tails . . .
Tail troubles similar to those that plagued the Mustang
cropped up in other military airplanes. There was hardly
a fighter that did not experience tail failure of one kind
or another in the course of its evolution, as its speed

was pushed up to and beyond the 400 miles per hour level."

(Compressibility—more mysterious and of a far greater severity in its solution than flutter—reached proportions so great in the P-38 that it almost crippled the fighter program. But that will be the subject of the next chapter.)

The P-38D was the first model in the series that could accurately be described as a combat airplane. Air Corps tacticians had already spent much time with officials of the Royal Air Force in England, and what they learned led to priority messages back to the States that the fighters being assigned to American first-line units were not equipped to deal with the combat machines of the Germans. Self-sealing fuel tanks were incorporated in the P-38D. A new low-pressure oxygen system replaced the former high-pressure equipment, and the change would remain a standard feature of all future P-38 variants. A new propeller was installed. Heavier armor plating went into the cockpit for better pilot protection. A retractable landing light was installed, provision was made for air-dropped flares, and the thirty-six airplanes all featured the new elevator mass balances and tailplane changes. Much of the interior equipment was given a thorough overhauling. Armament remained at one 37-mm cannon and four .50 caliber machine guns. Some structural changes were made to ease production headaches.

The full complement of thirty-six P-38D airplanes was delivered by the end of August 1941. Reflecting the speed with which combat-inspired modifications (passed on by the British) had been made, the planned P-38A, P-38B and P-38C models were never built. One early P-38 was converted to the XP-38A designation and fitted out with a pressurized cabin. Sent to Wright Field in Ohio, it was redesignated the TXP-38A. The Air Corps decided the problems of mass-producing the fighter with a pressurized cabin didn't warrant the improvement in pilot comfort and safety at high altitude. Whoever made that decision was to be soundly cursed in future years by thousands of P-38 pilots who found their cockpits intolerably cold and uncomfortable—to such an extent that at times pilots who were half-frozen turned back from combat missions for home.

THE CASTRATED LIGHTNINGS

Until the time the P-38D completed its production run the airplane was officially known as the Lockheed Atlanta. If this seems an extraordinary name for a fighter, then the reader shares the same bewilderment most people felt about the name in the first place. The change from *Atlanta* to *Lightning* took place when the British named their export version of the airplane the Lockheed Model 322-61 Lightning I. (The reader may recall that the P-51 was originally named Apache, and that the AAF adopted the name Mustang only after the British applied the latter identification to their export versions of the North American fighter.) After negotiating with the British government for first orders of the Model 322, which would reach a total of some 667 airplanes (of which only a few were actually delivered), Bob Gross of Lockheed suggested seven different names for the airplane to Air Commodore Baker of the British Purchasing Commission in late 1940. The names were Lightning, Liberator, Leeds, Liverpool, Lexington, Lincoln, and Libra. The British opted for Lightning, and the U.S. Army hastily abandoned the name Atlanta.

The British placed their order for the big fighters in March 1940, with deliveries scheduled to begin in December 1941. The Lightning Mark I was to be the export version of the P-38E, and the Mark II the export version of the turbo-supercharged P-38G-13 and P-38G-15. Despite the intention to utilize hundreds of the big fighters in European combat, the program foundered quickly, the Model 322's became known as the "castrated Lightnings," and none of the airplanes ever saw combat with the RAF.

Few export programs—the direct sales contract was transferred to Lend-Lease on June 25, 1941—ever suffered to the extent of the Lightning program for the Royal

Air Force. The Air Corps refused to give up its limited quantity of turbosuperchargers for export, and the Lightning I fighters rolled from the factory with the older V-1710-C15 engines. Fitted out with mechanical superchargers, the Allisons produced 1,090 horsepower at 13,200 feet. As altitude increased the performance of engines and airplane fell sharply and the original purpose of the P-38—a high-altitude fighter—was beyond realization. Another change made in the Model 322, against the advice of Lockheed, was removal of the counter-rotating propeller system. The C15 engines both rotated to the right, and cancelled out the safety margin in event of engine failure shortly after take off or otherwise at low speeds.

Early in 1942 the first few Lightning I fighters arrived in England, and it is accurate to say they failed to set afire the imagination of British pilots. At the time the Army Air Forces (no longer the Air Corps) was imposing a speed restriction of 350 mph on the P-38 (indicated airspeed reading), and the British, somewhat apprehensive of their twin-boomed reluctant dragon, reduced this figure to 300 mph. British pilots who flew the Lightning I reported it was a nice enough airplane to *fly*, but it offered precious little performance advantage over the twin-engined Westland Whirlwind fighter, already in service for some months and enjoying the reputation of being a docile and predictable machine. The Lightnings fell quickly into disfavor.

The first two Lightnings were shipped from the United States on January 30, 1942 and were ready for flight tests in late March. The first airplane, serial number AF105, went through a series of modifications and test flights, all of which seemed to lead exactly nowhere, and on July 1, 1943 this particular machine was handed back to the United States by transfer to the Eighth Air Force in England. Serial number AF106, the second fighter, was fitted with power-boosted controls, and by September 1942 was being put through its paces by RAF test pilots. They weren't impressed. They reported the Lightning Mark I had excellent takeoff characteristics, was a pleasant machine to fly up to its imposed speed limit of 300 mph IAS, and really not all that maneuverable. No guns or cannon were fitted to AF106 and the airplane was tested with a gross weight at takeoff of 13,860 pounds. It handled extremely well in the low-speed regime. In clean configuration, gear and flaps up, it stalled at 94 mph, and with gear and flaps down, landed nicely at 78 mph. And that was that. In July 1943 the British dusted their hands of AF106 and also transferred it to the Eighth Air Force. A third airplane, AF108, didn't last as long as the others, but was transferred to the Eighth Air Force in December 1942. And that was that for the British Lightnings.

Most of the airplanes built under the British order were absorbed by the AAF in this country, and given the designation P-322. The majority of these were shipped to a modification center at Dallas, Texas, where they were altered to perform as trainers and for different test purposes.

Two other trainer variants of early P-38 models found their way into the AAF inventory. A number of early P-38s were in use as trainers, of course, and the transition to the big and heavy fighter was often "hairy" enough to make even veteran instructors blanch. Both Lockheed and the Air Force came up with the idea that it might be possible to move things about in some airplanes and turn them into two-seat trainers. The first group to be so bastardized came from the original production order of British Lightning I's. Between twenty and thirty P-322s had the radio equipment and armor plating aft of the pilot removed. This exposed the main wing spar, where engineers fastened a crude and uncomfortable "piggy-back" seat. The student pilot crawled and wriggled into his distressingly uncomfortable space, where inevitably he bumped his head against the cockpit roof, and prepared to watch the pilot do whatever needed doing. No dual controls meant much apprehension and wringing of hands on the part of the hapless passenger, who could do nothing but study the movements of the pilot and, during the summer months, suffer abominably from the sun within his cramped "greenhouse." The conversion afforded some daring moments for people who were excited about a flight in a P-38, but it was less than a rousing success for pilots wanting the feel of the P-38 in their hands. The AAF converted some twenty P-38F models into two-seat trainers, with the piggyback arrangement, but the idea never caught on that strongly. Other P-38s, especially in the field, were modified to utilize the piggyback space for carrying passengers rather than student pilots.

Of course, if jamming the student into the upper rear half of the cockpit was worthwhile (the only thing that kept pilots from tormenting their passengers with violent maneuvers was the realization that when the passenger vomited, it *had* to be all over the pilot), why not modify the P-38 into a *two-cockpit* airplane? P-38 Serial Number 40-744 was so modified for the purpose of asymmetric flight tests, although no one seems to be quite clear as to what the tests were for. The turbosupercharger mechanism in the left boom was removed and a second P-38 cockpit installed in its place, part of the cockpit extending beyond the trailing edge of the wing. The airplane was redesignated as RP-38, but the R prefix had nothing to do with training or even flight testing; it meant *Restricted*. Because of flight difficulties at high speed in early model Lightnings, all airplanes up through the P-38D were placed in the restricted category as of October 22, 1942.

FINAL GESTATION

Lockheed produced 210 P-38E models, starting delivery in October 1941. It was the last of the Lightnings before the "fully combat-worthy" models—the P-38F—went into production. And the P-38E, despite considerable improvements over the short-lived D version, cannot be considered as a major factor in fighter combat, since so few of the airplanes were available for fighter missions. Of the 210 produced, a number were set aside immediately for testing purposes. Several went to fighter organizations for training. And no less than ninety-nine of the P-38E airplanes available were converted into the F-4-1-LO, an unarmed, high-speed photographic reconnaissance aircraft. A drift sight was installed in the F-4, along with four K-17 aerial cameras. AAF headquarters dictated, and wisely, that the airplane most urgently needed in the combat zone was not the P-38 fighter in limited numbers, but rather an airplane that could fly deep into enemy territory, take its pictures, and use its superior flight performance to escape enemy fighters trying to shoot it down. Another innovation to the F-4 conversion was the use of an automatic pilot, a blessing to the man who flew an airplane loaded to the maximum with fuel for long-range, maximum-endurance missions.

An idea of priorities assigned to the conversion of P-38E to F-4 models is evident in that the F-4 preceded the fighters to the most distant combat areas. In the Pacific the AAF discovered that the need to use medium and heavy bombers for patrol and reconnaissance missions had "cut down substantially the scale of bombing operations," and that special photographic reconnaissance aircraft were needed. Of the approximately 100 P-38s set aside for this new category, a small group was set aside for immediate training and overseas shipment. By April 7, 1942, Flight A of the 8th Photographic Squadron was in Australia. Nine days later the four F-4s—equipped with cameras and two 75-gallon auxiliary tanks—were in operations under the command of Captain Karl Polifka. For this mission the P-38 modification was a superb performer, and was used heavily in this role throughout the war. (In fact, by the summer of 1945, of the 2,000 photo recon types in service throughout the world with the AAF, more than 800 of this number were made up of F-4 and F-5 modifications of different P-38 fighter variants.)

Each new model in the P-38 series produced a fighter clearly superior to its predecessors and the P-38E was no exception. There was little visible difference in the E as against the D version, but the interior changes were considered extraordinary, an attitude justified by the fact that Lockheed performed nearly *two thousand changes* in redesign and modification between the D and E. Many of these were minor items, of course, cleaning up details in the cockpit and the structure. Among the major changes —some of them dictated by requirements for the British version of the Lightning—was a reversion back to a smaller cannon. A 20-mm Hispano-type cannon replaced the former 37-mm Oldsmobile weapon. The smaller cannon had a faster rate of fire, carried more ammunition, and was considered to be more effective in combat than the heavier equipment. The nose section was again redesigned to take 150 rounds of 20-mm ammunition; this was accomplished by moving the nosewheel retracting cylinder behind the nose gear strut. The hydraulic and electrical systems were overhauled and improved for ease of production and better service life and reliability. New radios were installed. During the production run the AAF ordered a change from the hollow steel blades of the Hamilton Standard Hydromatic propellers to Curtis Electric props with dural blades. More important, in terms of the strategic production picture, was a major change in the production line itself. The E model was the first of the P-38 variants to be manufactured on what was considered a planned and effective assembly line and, for the first time, a system was worked out whereby the latest modifications to the airplane could be accomplished while the airplanes were still under the factory roof. Previously the fighters came off the production line and were rushed to modification centers for latest changes and equipment alteration. The modification centers remained in service throughout the war, of course, but incorporating assembly line changes reduced considerably the time between production and overseas shipment.

The first Lightning involved in a shooting fracas with the enemy never tried to defend itself—it couldn't. An F-4 flying in the New Guinea area was attacked by an unknown number of Zero fighters, and in distressingly short order the F-4 pilot found his airplane riddled with holes and one engine dead. To his good fortune the F-4 was light, with most of its fuel burned off. The pilot feathered the crippled engine, went to full power on the other, and to his overwhelming delight—and the chagrin of the Japanese—slowly began to pull away from the pursuing Zeros.

The first Lightning to engage the enemy successfully was a P-38D model assigned to fighter patrol in the Iceland area. Focke-Wulf FW-200K Kurier four-engine bombers of the Luftwaffe had been taking pictures of Allied installations in Iceland, as well as shadowing Allied convoys and reporting their position to U-boats. On the morning of August 14, 1942, Lieutenant Elza Shahan of the 27th Fighter Squadron, 1st Fighter Group was ordered to intercept a Kurier reported in the area. Before Shahan could be vectored to the German bomber, it was already under attack by a Bell P-39 Airacobra flown by Lieutenant Joseph Shaffer of the 33rd Squadron, Iceland Base Command. Shaffer had managed to pump several cannon shells into one of the Kurier's engines and watched flames blossom back from the wing. Out of ammunition, he watched in dismay as the flames diminished and the Kurier turned for home. At this moment Shahan arrived on the scene, above the other aircraft. He rolled into a dive, took his time, and fired a long burst into the midsection of the Focke-Wulf. Moments later the Kurier exploded.

Three days later, halfway around the world, other Lightnings were in combat. Shortly after the Pearl Harbor strike by the Japanese and a string of stunning Japanese victories in Asia and the Pacific, General George Kenney showed up at the Lockheed plant in California, exhorting Lockheed officials to get cracking on "Project Snowman," which was the special fitting of Lightning fighters for service in the Aleutians. Kenney wanted production workers and specialists on the airplanes twenty-four hours a day until the Lightnings were on their way. "Those ships will be fighting within thirty-six hours after they leave the line," Kenney rasped, "so get 'em *out of here*."

On August 4, 1942, P-38s of the 54th Fighter Squadron, flying patrols from Umnak along the Aleutians chain, ran into several Japanese Kawa 97 four-engine flying boats over Atka. The Lightnings raced in against prey too rarely seen during their long and tedious missions, and sent two flying boats flaming into the sea.

The P-38F was considered to be the first truly combat-worthy model of the Lightning series, and began rolling from the production lines in February 1942, although it would not become available for combat operations for some months to come. It was the principal AAF fighter in the invasion and subsequent fighting in North Africa. But it was also an airplane preceded by disturbing reports of being unable to survive high-speed dives. General Carl Spaatz, in Africa, shrugged off the stories. He needed an airplane that could perform as a fighter, escort fighter, reconnaissance plane, ground strafer, fighter-bomber and anything else that might come along in daily combat operations.

"I'd rather have an airplane that goes like hell and has a few things wrong with it," he growled, "than one that won't go like hell and has a few things wrong with it."

But the "few things wrong with it" were enough to bring both alarm and despair to the people responsible for the P-38.

4. The Phantom Hand

They heard it well before it happened. The eerie whine of the turbos—the howling-dervish sound of a P-38 moving *fast*. This one had started high. They could tell that also by the manner in which the sound wavered ever so slightly, the result of interference with its passage from high altitude. The sound brought apprehension with it, for the P-38 in a sustained high-power dive was an airplane unpredictable, dangerous, liable to turn on its pilot with violent and head-snapping fury. And now, as the volume rose, and the dervish became even more shrill in its cry, the fear quickened. The pilots on the ground listening to the banshee wail knew all too well what was happening, and they looked fearfully into the sky. Then came a new, softer and infinitely more terrible sound. A dull, throbbing boom, an explosion, a rubbery crackling of noise. Several moments later a hand pointed, and the others turned until they too saw what they had all feared. A glistening in the sky, a spattered shining of things reflecting sunlight, twisting and tumbling as they fell, motes of reflection.

Pieces of metal.

Pieces of what had been a P-38 in a high-speed dive.

Pieces, that's all. Of a P-38 that had smashed hard into compressibility, into what aerodynamic engineers called the *shock stall*. Other pilots called it different names. "It resembled," said Tony LeVier of the strange wall in the sky, "a giant phantom hand that seized the plane and sometimes shook it out of the pilot's control."

George W. Gray in his history of the N.A.C.A. edged away from straight engineering terms when he described the shock stall in the P-38:

"The behavior was new to pilots, terrifying, baffling. Several men, in putting this two-engine fighter through its diving maneuvers, underwent the experience: a sudden violent buffeting of the tail accompanied by a lunging and threshing about of the plane, as though it were trying to free itself of invisible bonds, and then the maddening immobility of the controls, the refusal of the elevators to respond to the stick.

In the preceding chapter we stressed that the reader must make the clear distinction between tail flutter as it occurred in early P-38 variants, and compressibility, which pursued the P-38 throughout most of its career. In this instance the point is made that flutter was corrected early in the game. Compressibility took longer to identify, took more to correct, and then continued to plague the P-38 as an operational aircraft for months and years after the solution was found. The time span between discovering the fault and effecting its remedy, and modifying fighters operational on different continents, was entirely another matter. This is why the "quickie" histories of the P-38 so often mislead their readers; almost every student of this airplane appears convinced the compressibility problem of the P-38 always showed up in diving Lightnings suffering tail loss and disintegration.

Flutter at a certain point would almost always destroy the tail of a speeding P-38 (or P-47 or P-51, as so often it did), but compressibility would *sometimes* destroy the tail, or tear off a wing, or hammer the fuselage from the rest of the airplane, and sometimes it would just about do all these things at the same time. Lockheed engineers were distressed to find even knowledgeable people associating the tail failures because of flutter or compressibility to an inherent structural weakness in the P-38 when nothing of the sort was true. The P-38 was structurally an outstanding machine and capable of absorbing astonishing punishment under combat. One example should more than suffice to clear up this matter. A Lightning pilot faced the pilot of a Messerschmitt Me-109 in a head-on attack. Both pilots opened fire, both pilots refused to budge an inch from their calamitous approach. They collided, head-on. When the shower of metal and flames whipped away the Me-109 was a shattered wreck, wings gone, and plunging earthward. The P-38 also was a wreck, but it was *flying*—despite a dead engine (the prop was torn away), despite the horizontal tail being *severed*, despite one boom being shredded into junk. By every law of flight known the P-38 could not stay in the air. It did—and its pilot brought it home and got to the ground safely. He flew again—but the airplane never did. It was listed as "unflyable" and cannibalized for spare parts.

But compressibility could rip a diving P-38 into pieces. And *did*. With the same terrifying symptoms—violent tail buffeting (*not* flutter), an uncontrollable shaking with severe yawing motions, and then the controls "freezing" absolutely solid. There were clues to survival but only clues for a while—sometimes the Lightning could be brought out from its dive by full use of the elevator trim, to a full nose-up position, and only at low altitudes.

But there was another heart-stopping danger. Sometimes the P-38, after the controls became immobile, began to tuck under, began to move its nose still further downward and then through the vertical *into an outside loop*. Now, this is guaranteed to turn *any* pilot white with fear, especially at the speeds involved, for the stresses on a high-speed fighter in a dive going into an outside loop are staggering. But in this very maneuver was a crucial hint—several pilots managed to survive the dives by emerging from their screaming plunges *with the airplane on its back*. Which meant, beyond all question, that the structural integrity of the P-38 could be eliminated as a possible cause.

Now, it should be understood that Lockheed engineers were *not* caught by surprise where compressibility was concerned. They were shocked with the *severity* of the problem, but not its sudden onset.

Back in 1937, when they first considered the design

of the Model 22 (XP-38), the engineering team of Johnson and Hibbard first voiced their fears of compressibility. Until this moment their fears were theoretical. Until the YP-38 test program got underway compressibility—shock stall—in high-speed dives was never accepted as a *practical* problem. But the YP-38 was so fast in a dive that the shock stall, and all its tragic consequences, became a fact of everyday life that refused to go away.

Kelly Johnson in 1937 warned the Air Corps in writing that as the diving speeds of new fighters increased "consideration must be given to the effect of compressibility." Hibbard in December 1938 sent a note to Lockheed's Bob Gross that was more specific: "In order to have the minimum possible drag, it is essential that air flow smoothly over any part of an aircraft structure. As the speed is increased, the air tends to be 'splashed' by the leading edge of the wing more or less like the prow of a boat at high speed in the water. As one approaches the compressibility range, the air is thrown so violently up and down by the leading edge that it does not have a chance to flow over the wing in the proper manner." Hibbard added that compressibility effects would be "appreciable" at 425 mph and "very serious" at 500 mph and greater.

Lockheed and the Air Corps (soon to be the Army Air Forces) by now had lost a number of P-38s in diving tests; sometimes they didn't know whether the in-flight destruction of the airplanes was due to flutter or to compressibility. But when the flutter problem was whipped, and airplanes in very fast dives still came apart, then there wasn't any question. Compressibility was the killer.

Lockheed suspected that the tremendous turbulence of the air hurled back from the wing at very high speeds was pounding the tail to destruction. The shock waves streaming back from the wing, they reasoned, could be locking the elevator in a steel vise against which the pilot was helpless. In a joint research effort, the Air Corps and Lockheed modified P-38E (# 42-1986) by "bending" the booms upward, starting immediately behind the coolant radiators, so that the entire tail was now thirty inches higher than the standard P-38.

It didn't work. Lockheed test pilot Ralph Virden took the high-tailed Lightning to altitude, pushed over into a dive, and plunged to his death. Whatever happened to the airplane the shock stall of compressibility had claimed another victim.

In another test effort a wind-tunnel model of the P-38 was fitted out with canard control surfaces—a "tail" mounted forward of the cockpit on the fuselage nacelle. The reasoning was sound but not the practice. Engineers argued that if shock waves streaming back from the wings were immobilizing the elevator, then by moving the horizontal control surfaces forward of the wing they'd be able to retain control at the higher diving speeds. The wind tunnel tests refuted this theory and Lockheed was right back where it started.

Intensive studies were under way in wind tunnels, both at Lockheed and at the N.A.C.A. full-scale wind tunnel at Langley Laboratory, where a study team under direction of John Stack devoted their full energies to the mystifying—and lethal—problem of shock stall. While John Stack led the program at N.A.C.A., Kelly Johnson and Ward Beman spearheaded the Lockheed investigation.

Both groups, as it turned out, moved in the right direction. They studied additional counterweights to the tail, raising the tail thirty inches, use of a canard surface, redesigning the body of the airplane to make the fuselage longer and more slender, modifying the wing between the fuselage and the engines, and other "solutions." Not until the spring of 1942, when wind tunnel experiments both at N.A.C.A. (including the Ames Laboratory) and Lockheed had been intensified, was the solution found. The answer was a small but vital dive-recovery flap.

Understanding what happened to the P-38 in a high-speed dive was the key. Until this time engineers thought they were aware of all the forces involved, but the wind tunnel experiments widened their horizons.

Visualize a P-38 at high altitude starting into a dive. The pilot eases forward on the yoke, bringing the nose below the horizon. Now as the airplane picks up speed he continues his forward pressure, adjusting his trim in pitch, and increases power until he's at full throttle. The heavy P-38 accelerates slowly but with conviction, and in very short order it's racing hell-bent for the earth far below.

Now the P-38 reaches about 36,000 feet. It has dropped nearly a mile from the point of starting the dive. Its speed is measured in Mach numbers (Mach 1 is the speed of sound at any particular altitude), and at Mach 0.675 (which is about 445 mph true airspeed at 36,000 feet), "something" happens to the wing. The air accelerated across the upper surface of the wing is now moving so fast that some of that air has reached Mach 1. The air, in other words, is now moving at the speed of sound or has exceeded the point of Mach 1. Sonic speed means shock waves, and this is exactly what happens on the wing. The supersonic flow *is* a shock wave, and that also means breaking up the normal flow of air. You can say this another way—*loss of lift*. Wherever the supersonic shock waves struck along the wing surface they destroyed the pressure differential between the upper and lower surfaces of the wing—they destroyed the ability of the airplane to continue flying with the lift it had just before the shock waves appeared.

Something else then happens. As the lift decreases the airflow moving back from the wings also changes in its form and its pattern. The normal downwash aft of the wing toward the tail begins to deteriorate. The airflow across the tail shifts from normal to a condition where there is now a greater upload, or lifting force, on the tail itself.

What happens now? With the greater uplifting force applied to the tail *the P-38 wants to nose down even more*. The steeper the dive, the faster it dives, and the faster it dives, the steeper it dives—*vicious circle*. Soon it is diving so steeply it now descends in a vertical line. The speed is still increasing and the airplane begins to tuck under—to start the dreaded high-speed outside loop which all too often spells complete destruction of the machine. Sometimes, a shocked and frightened pilot survived the terrors of the compressibility dive by emerging from his madly threshing descent with the airplane upside down, flying on its back.

But what about the controls? Why can't the pilot simply pull out of the dive? We mentioned before that the controls went through a "maddening immobility." And here's why.

As the dive steepens and speed increases, the pilot makes his move to prevent rushing into the compressibility zone where he knows he may lose control of the P-38. To come out of the dive he pulls back on the yoke. His purpose in doing this is to change the attitude of the airplane as opposed to the relative wind—to increase the angle of attack of his wing. This produces increased lift. Normally the airplane would have responded by the nose coming up, the speed slackening, and the start of recovery from the dive. But not now.

When the angle of attack increases (the angle at which the wing attacks the wind into which the airplane is moving) for the wing, *it also increases for the tail*. What happens now is what mystified pilots and wrested control from their hands. The increased angle of attack of the horizontal tail meant that the lift of the tail also increased and produced an upward force on the tail.

Which meant that the more the pilot pulled back on the yoke the greater the force exerted by the tail to push the airplane into an even steeper dive. It also meant that the forces required to move the yoke were by now so tremendous that the controls seem to have been fixed in cement. Instead of having an airplane responding to his control movements, the pilot found himself in an airplane in which he was simply an unwilling passenger. And if he were strong enough to get the yoke back, or even to roll in some nose-up trim, the uploading on the tail became even greater—and the dive became steeper—and there was no stopping the nose from tucking under and beginning inverted flight.

But this wasn't all. Remember those shock waves hammering the wing? The supersonic waves became shock fronts and decreased lift no matter what the pilot did. They also distorted violently the air tearing back from the wing. Instead of a relatively thin band of turbulent air, the turbulence became a thick wake roaring back from the wing. This *had* to have its effect; it did, and it was, many times, destructive. The shock waves, at their worst, smashed into and pummeled the entire tail section of the airplane. It was more than turbulent airflow. The shock waves on the wing had become a standing force and the air flowed about this force, whipped to frenzy, and then slammed into the tail. Metal can take only so much and, too often, even the rugged structure of the P-38 yielded to this battering, and the tail broke apart.

But some P-38s managed to reach far into the high-speed region of steep dives, and survive. What drove pilots and engineers to the wall was that there seemed no rhyme or reason to these surviving dives. The pilots experienced the worst of compressibility—shock stall of the wing, violent movement, tail buffeting, nonresponsive controls—and yet the airplane managed to ease its way out of the dive. There was a pattern, of course, but it took time to recognize what was happening. If a P-38 went fully into the high-speed zone where compressibility took place with all its effects, then the airplane emerged from its dive *only after it had descended to a low altitude*.

Those that managed to survive, and to pull out safely, did so no matter what the pilot did to the controls. It didn't matter if he used the control yoke, if he rolled in nose-up trim, or what. No matter what he did, or didn't do, the airplane plunged for many thousands of feet. And then, imperceptibly, mysteriously, the nose began to lift from the vertical and the pullout began.

The solution lay in understanding that the speed of sound changes with altitude. At sea level on a standard day (59 degrees Fahrenheit) the speed of sound is about 764 mph. On that same day, at 36,000 feet, for example, the speed of sound may be only 660 mph.

The airplane moving at 540 mph at 36,000 feet is high up into the Mach zone—close to the speed of sound, where the effects of compressibility are at their worst.

The airplane moving at 540 mph at 10,000 feet isn't that close to the Mach zone. The airplane still flies at 540 mph, but the speed of sound—Mach 1—has increased greatly. Therefore, with lower altitude, Mach 1 was much further along the speed scale, *and the shock waves disappeared from the wings*.

The airplane, of course, now below the compressibility range, responded to the control movements of the pilot.

Once Lockhead (and N.A.C.A.) knew what the problem was, there was the next question to be answered: what to do about it? We mentioned the different possible solutions investigated. The one that prevailed was the dive-recovery flap. N.A.C.A. in the high-speed wind tunnel at Ames Laboratory tested a series of small dive flaps, moving them to different positions beneath the wing. Early tests, with the flap positioned aft of the wing trailing edge, showed a definite improvement in control. But the Ames group, not yet satisfied, kept up their tests, and concluded finally that the best position for the small flap would be "thirty per cent of the chord back from the leading edge." The flaps were installed beneath the wing outboard of the booms and just aft of the main structural beam. To operate the flaps the pilot needed only to depress a button on his control yoke, and electric motors moved them downward into the airstream.

The solution appeared to be simplicity itself—*after* engineers had managed to identify all the factors involved. The key to the flap success was that the pilot, without moving his yoke, without moving the elevator controls in any way (and thereby not disturbing the angle of attack of the wing), could lower the dive flaps and increase the lift of the wing. When the flaps went down they dammed the air flowing beneath the wing. At high speeds this amounts to a tremendous force—the damming effect pushes more air down from the wing, and thereby increases the lift of the wing. The wing generates more lift without increasing the lift produced by the horizontal tail assembly—and the airplane is able to pull out from its dive.

An indication of just how severe this problem was—even aside from the P-38s that were lost in dives—was that pilots were afraid to follow German fighters in high-speed dives. For good reason, of course. Shortly after they raced earthward from high altitude in such dives their airplanes were wrested from their control. Then they faced three immediate problems—they could no longer maneuver in pursuit of the enemy, they could not hope to evade an enemy fighter after them, and they knew their own airplane might suddenly "come unglued."

There is a final episode in this phase of P-38 development deserving our attention. It was one thing to discover the solution, as has been mentioned, and quite another to see that solution applied to P-38s in combat zones. Once Lockheed had all the factors in its grasp the company rushed production of dive-flap kits. These were assembled at the plant and readied for shipment to Europe where P-38s were to be modified at once, enhancing tremendously their capabilities against German fighters. Four hundred and twenty-five sets of the flaps and modification kits were loaded aboard a Douglas C-54 four-engine transport for a high-priority flight to England.

The airplane was shot down by a British pilot flying a Spitfire, and the modification kits vanished beneath the surface of the Atlantic.

This was the "plain damn bad luck" of the P-38 to which so many pilots have referred. By the time Lockheed was able to produce the Lightning with the dive-recovery flaps as production-line equipment, they were already up to their P-38J-25-LO model.

Which means that approximately half of all the P-38s built were already off the production line before the critical dive flap could be installed on the airplane.

Once again, one wonders just how much sooner this modification could have been made to the P-38 had the Army Air Corps not lost the first XP-38 prototype in its speed-dash publicity stunt in January 1939.

NIX MACH

One of the most persistent stories to survive the Second World War, continuing to the present, is that the P-38—and perhaps several other high-powered, heavy, fighter aircraft—managed to achieve supersonic flights in full-power dives from very high altitude.

It never happened—despite even *official* claims to this effect. Some pilots believed they had broken the sound barrier and refer to "sonic booms" heard on the ground by witnesses beneath their diving fighters. Others refer to airspeed indicator readings of 700 mph and greater, "proving" that when at fairly high altitude they had gone past the speed of sound. It behooves us in this history of the P-38 to set the record straight.

The first recorded instance of a "supersonic flight" took place with the P-38 in September of 1942. At that time there had been initial deliveries in the European Theater of Operations (ETO) of P-38G and H models. Because of the bad reputation the P-38 had already earned in high-speed dives, Lt. Colonel Cass Hough, an AAF pilot, was assigned to dive test duties on this type aircraft, and subsequently carried out a series of dives in the P-38G.

As the tests were recorded, Hough climbed the fighter to 43,000 feet, cruised straight and level for some fifteen minutes, and then rolled over for a maximum effort dive —full bore and a vertical descent. He continued through the dive for a total descent of 25,000 feet, some five miles straight down, and, during the dive, ran into severe compressibility effects, pulling out (as indicated later by the official report) with more use of trim tab than effective use of the yoke.

The AAF later made the statement officially—and it was the AAF, *not* Hough, as has been unfairly charged —that the airplane when it pulled out of the dive had exceeded the speed of sound, which was given as 780 mph.

The problem in this particular instance is that no one had any means of measuring the airspeed accurately. The airspeed errors under compressibility were wild. The reader should note, as well, that the speed of sound in the official AAF statement was given as 780 mph at the altitude at which Hough pulled out from his dive. But Mach 1 at this altitude—18,000 feet—is considerably less than 780 mph. Yet it must be explained that to the best belief of the officials involved, this was the speed attained by the P-38G and an official claim was made for the figure of 780 mph.

Three weeks later Hough flew a P-47 to 39,000 feet and repeated his vertical plunge in the single-engine fighter. Again, as has been reported insistently through the years, Republic Aviation claimed a diving speed of 780 mph, which certainly would have put the Thunderbolt through the speed of sound. The fact of the matter is that Republic was only quoting the AAF in its statements.

There was tremendous enthusiasm created over these sensational dives, but the enthusiasm was little tempered with accuracy, for the simple fact is that neither the P-38 nor the P-47 (nor the P-51 for that matter) could exceed sonic speed. Well before that point was reached the aircraft was at its terminal velocity, beyond which it was impossible for the machine to fly. All that could happen at this point was that the airplane either managed to stay together until reaching a lower altitude where the Mach number was higher—or it tore apart in the dive from compressibility.

Later, in March 1944, Colonel Ben Kelsey (who had been the test pilot on the XP-38 prototype), took a P-38 down in another all-out dive, and again the AAF reported the airplane had gone through the sound barrier by reaching a speed of 750 mph. But by this time engineers were somewhat more conversant with Mach numbers and compressibility effects, and the AAF was quick to amend its statement by pointing out that compressibility errors for airspeed readings at these speeds were extreme and largely unknown; official claim to exceeding the speed of sound was quickly denied.

It should be pointed out that Tony LeVier and other Lockheed test pilots, who were doing some rather hairy dives of their own, received the reports of supersonic flight with scorn and derision, and made little effort to conceal their feelings. The best and most experienced pilots used words that simply don't belong in these pages.

During the writing of this book, a Colonel Yahne reported in *Aviation Week and Space Technology* that he had barely escaped with his life in a high-speed dive with the P-38; he stated that he had exceeded the speed of sound (and so believed he had), and that the airplane was torn apart in the air. By great fortune he managed to survive the breakup of the P-38, and fell clear of the wreckage to open his parachute. The Colonel's estimates of his speed as supersonic, based on flight angle and power settings, are wholly inaccurate for correct judgment—especially when engineers at the time knew so little about compressibility and flight in the region of Mach 1.

Colonel Yahne commented about eyewitnesses on the ground being subjected to a "sonic boom" subsequent to his aircraft breaking up in the air; he expressed the conviction that this sonic boom constituted a further measure of "proof" of his supersonic flight. But such statements must be examined in light of the fact that no one had ever heard a sonic boom from an aircraft at that time and so could not hope to recognize it as such. But if you have ever experienced an aircraft breaking up at high speed then there should also be a clear recollection that there is a severe explosive reaction in terms of air pressure—and this effect, plus the noise arriving without warning, produces an explosive sound on the ground, but *not* a sonic boom.

Not even the flight test series of the early Messerschmitt Me-163 (Me-163V1), light in weight, with swept wings and rocket power, could exceed or even approach that closely the speed of sound. The fastest speed ever attained for this aircraft was early in its development when it reached a speed estimated by German engineers (making their measurements from the ground) at 621 mph—fairly high in the Mach range for its altitude—

and was then "taken from pilot control by compressibility forces" until it fell back into lower air levels, decelerating as it did so.

The first consistent sonic booms ever heard were those caused by German A4 (V-2) rockets penetrating the lower atmosphere at speeds of approximately 2,400 mph (from a maximum normal burnout velocity of 3,600 mph). These were reported in many instances and were often confused with the rocket impact as an explosion. But the double cracking boom of the sonic wave was clearly heard and identified as wholly separate from the blast of the warhead.

Not until the fall of 1947 was the speed of sound finally achieved, when Colonel Charles Yaeger (at the time a captain), flew the XS-1 beyond Mach 1.

As a final emphasis, the reader is reminded that the successor to the P-38 was the Lockheed P-80 Shooting Star, a sleek and powerful jet fighter much superior to the P-38 in all its flight regimes. And not even this airplane, and other jets at the time, could exceed the speed of sound. Several of these aircraft, when their pilots attempted to do so, flew into their compressibility range and broke up in the air. At times even the P-80s were affected much as had been the P-38—the airplane buffeted wildly, thrashed about madly in the air, suffered violent tail buffeting, and immobility of the controls.

The solution?

The same type of dive flap as had been developed for the P-38. The legacy for the future jets was indeed a gift from the compressibility-beset Lightning.

5. Test Pilot

Tony LeVier, for many years the chief test pilot for Lockheed, had three distinct and separate careers with his "first love," the P-38. Initially, there was his period as a test pilot and then chief test pilot in the P-38 program. The second phase took place with Tony demonstrating the tremendous performance capabilities of the Lightning to pilots flying the airplane in Europe—and both distrustful and frightened of the machine. Finally, Tony flew the P-38 in air racing competition, when things boiled down to a man and his airplane. We will have the opportunity in the pages following to join Tony LeVier in his unique relationship with the P-38 through all three phases. Initially, of course, we are most interested in the wartime testing of the P-38, when Lockheed was baffled and worried about the strange and frightening behavior of the airplane under certain flight regimes. Tony LeVier provides us with a deeply perceptive and human study of this airplane, and through his experiences, the reader will come to know the P-38 as more than a fighter airplane of historical note, and, perhaps, will share Tony LeVier's feeling that we are dealing with one of the truly great aircraft of all time.

". . . my heart was always with the Lightning. This was the kind of plane I had always dreamed of flying. It was the world's first really high-performance, high-altitude tactical airplane, with a top speed over four hundred miles an hour and a service ceiling over forty thousand feet. I dreamed of specializing in this kind of airplane, and unknown to me, that day was close at hand.

"Two tragic accidents about this time badly hurt the Lockheed flying organization and saddened everyone in the company.

"The P-38 was now flying at altitudes where few men had ever been. Pressure and oxygen were the two great problems for human beings six and seven miles above the earth, and although we had an airplane now that could go that high, it was another matter for the pilot to stay there.

"Without a pressurized cabin he was subject to the bends, a vapor lock in the bloodstream that caused excruciating pain and forced him to come down. Moreover, his oxygen equipment was still meager and rudimentary because the need for it had never existed previously. We were trying everything now that gave promise of being helpful, simulating high-altitude conditions in our pressure chamber and testing every device that made sense.

"Marshall Headle was trying out one of these new devices, a breathing vest that was a forerunner of today's pressure suit. It was an effort to aid the pilot's natural breathing mechanism in the thin air of the stratosphere. He had the vest on in the chamber one morning when it got out of cycle with his own body needs and he began to pass out.

"Recognizing he was in difficulty, he reached for the emergency breathing aid, but apparently shut it off instead of turning it on. We found him unconscious in the tank at very high altitude, and the only way to save his life was to release the dump valve and immediately drop him to sea level. The abrupt change in pressure caused a shock to his heart and nervous system from which he never recoverd.

"About the same time Ralph Virden was killed by compressibility in a dive test in a P-38.* This was an Army demonstration, and at the end of his flight he was to come down in front of the hangar and put on a show.

*This was the modification with the tail raised thirty inches higher than the standard P-38 fighter.

Suddenly we heard the terrible sound of an airplane in a steep dive, followed by a dull thud and then silence. We realized that an airplane had crashed, and the only plane it could be was a P-38. Who was flying a P-38? It wasn't long after that we found out Virden had made his last flight. Diving at high speed he apparently got into trouble in his pullout; the tail failed and came off and he was at too low an altitude to bail out and save his life. With him we lost our only experimental P-38, and vital tests had to wait until we could replace it.

". . . on July 1, 1942, I made my first P-38 flight as a Lockheed engineering test pilot, a job I've had ever since.

"This was really test flying, the thing I wanted—flying new planes and planes that had never flown before. I guess Rudy Thoren hired me because he knew I liked acrobatics and speed flying. In addition, he says I have good co-ordination and calm nerves. I was able to handle emergencies. I didn't know anything about engineering, but I was eager to learn, and I kept trying till I got it. Most important, I loved to fly, and speed was only part of it. I liked to get away from the earth, and now I could go higher than ever. . . .

"Upon arriving in the engineering flight test section I found myself immediately thrown into an unremitting test program on the P-38. . . Although it was now in production and in service with the . . . American air forces, it was so advanced and ahead of its time that it encountered situations which had never arisen previously.

"Some of these problems, like high-altitude flight, were anticipated and could readily be overcome with things like cockpit pressurization and engine supercharging, both of which we pioneered on the P-38. But other problems like stability and control of the airplane at high speeds were completely unexpected and much harder to lick.

"The problem of compressibility in particular, which had not been encountered previously because the P-38 was the first airplane capable of approaching the sonic barrier, required nearly two years to solve after our engineers found the source of the trouble. . . . In the case of the P-38 they [shock waves as the plane approached the speed of sound] caused a considerable loss in wing lift in high-speed dives, which resulted in a tendency of the airplane to nose under and sometimes go out of control.

"As a test pilot, I was just the means used to investigate problems like this, but the job was important because the airplane was too. The P-38 was one of the major weapons in the air war against Germany and Japan, and its success or failure had a direct bearing on the prosecution of the worldwide conflict. With a few minor exceptions, I spent the next two years testing this airplane, going on to other planes only when a faster and better fighter—the jet—came along."

Tony LeVier, reviewing the design competition of the new fighter requirement, then noted that the XP-38 "was much faster than anything else flying, and, eager to set a new transcontinental speed record, the Army flew the prototype airplane to New York City before it was dry behind the ears. Coming in for a landing an engine failed and it fell short of the airport and cracked up, *setting the development program back nearly two years*." [Emphasis added.]

"Starting over again, Lockheed began engineering on the second prototype airplane in April, 1939, and it flew in September, 1940. Thirteen of this model were built. In the meantime work began on a third prototype airplane, incorporating structural and design changes learned from earlier models. Engineering began late in 1939. . . .

"Not until after it was rolling off the assembly lines and was in combat did we start running into . . . compressibility. . . . It was like a giant phantom hand that seized the plane and sometimes shook it out of the pilot's control. Men and planes were being lost, and high-speed flight was stopped in its tracks until this problem could be licked.

"Milo Burcham had already spent a lot of time in dive tests to find the answer when I joined him. In addition to going through the rigors of compressibility, we were working out several other problems such as more engine power, boosted controls and pressurized flight. On my first test flight my cockpit canopy came off in pullout from a high-speed dive. This was old stuff to me, and if it was a sample of experimental flying I felt that my new job was going to be quite interesting, which in fact it turned out to be.

"When testing military aircraft it is not uncommon to press the engines continually to their maximum performance. As a matter of fact, practically all of our flying in those days was at maximum engine power. A test usually consisted of a flight at certain altitudes, generally thirty or thirty-five thousand feet in the case of the P-38, and the climb to altitude was always at maximum power. It was common to have an engine flare up at this extremely high power and start to detonate, a form of violent explosion in the cylinders that was extremely detrimental to the pistons, rods, and crankshaft. Often the detonation would occur so quickly and so severely that the engine would actually explode and tear itself apart.

"These engine explosions also occurred in level flight. On a speed run at war emergency power one day at twenty-five thousand feet the engine started to detonate without warning, and before I could reduce power it blew up. After feathering the engine I returned to Burbank and landed. When the mechanics removed the bottom cowling, parts of the engine actually fell to the ground. Flailing connecting rods had cut the crankcase completely in two and the engine was hanging by the cylinder block. When this happened to an engine Jim White called it 'jumping naked.' It was actually just like that; it exploded and flew apart. As I look back it amazes me that in all the years of experimental flying we did on this airplane we never had any serious engine fires.

"The P-38 was highly maneuverable and I quickly took the opportunity to get in a little acrobatic flying between test flights. It was common practice for our P-38 pilots to spend fifteen or twenty minutes in acrobatics or mock combat after the day's testing was completed. We usually had dogfights with each other, but often we engaged military pilots who were in the air and wanted to play. Milo Burcham was a famous acrobatic pilot in his own name and could put on a show with a P-38 you would never forget. I wanted to follow in his footsteps and be like him, and I took every opportunity to improve my own acrobatics.

"One such occasion arose when I was running P-38 gunnery tests at Muroc Dry Lake, later the Air Force test center in the California desert. For nearly a month I flew to Muroc daily to fire my guns, and on the way home I would practice acrobatics, particularly at low altitudes. Over the Mojave Desert in the vicinity of Lancaster and Palmdale I set up a small program of my own to acquaint myself with low-level aileron rolls, single-engine maneuvers and upside-down flying in this airplane.

"I began rolling it upside down at a safe altitude around five hundred feet and flying it inverted until I learned how to hold it in level flight in that position without losing altitude. Then I repeated this maneuver closer to the ground, finally doing it at fifty or seventy-five feet. When I had mastered inverted flying with two engines I turned one off and repeated the maneuver on a single engine. Pretty soon I was able to do my stunts practically on the deck. . . .

". . . Many Army pilots had found the transition to P-38's difficult because it was a big airplane and had two engines, and I wanted to show the graduating class at Polaris Flying School that despite its size and high performance it was extremely easy to fly.

"My demonstration might have ended in a crash had it not been for my good luck and the fact that the P-38 was a fine airplane. It had a reputation among many pilots for being treacherous on one engine, and when the students asked me to demonstrate a stall on one engine I agreed because it was a chance to prove this report was untrue. I had stalled the airplane a number of times on one engine, although I had never noticed how much altitude I lost before I regained flying speed, and if I stalled this time at one thousand feet I assumed that I would have ample altitude to recover. However, I was completely mistaken.

"In order to get into a stall I had to reduce speed to

eighty miles an hour and reduce power on my good engine; as I did this I immediately fell several hundred feet before I could get the nose down again. I then applied power to my good engine but I continued falling. There was only one thing left to do at that point, fly the airplane toward the ground and continue to apply power, and hope to gain sufficient speed to resume level flight. About one hundred feet from the ground I extended my wing flaps, which gave the wings enough lift for me to pull the nose up and level off. This incident taught me to do my stunts at a safe altitude until I knew what would happen. When I landed I told the students frankly that I had made a mistake and stalled too low.

"The P-38 had many fine qualities: unsurpassed altitude, speed and range; but we were constantly plagued by the problem of compressibility. Although our engineers were well aware of this condition, to fix it was another matter. . . .

". . .[The] solution was the compressibility dive brake, known today as a dive flap or speed brake. Used for the first time on a P-38, these brakes were attached to the main wing spar under the wing, where they offset the loss in lift in high-speed dives and enabled the pilot to remain in control of the airplane. Because of the urgency of the problem, Milo and I immediately began a series of daily test flights to prove these flaps were the answer we had been seeking.

"We had been in this test program three or four weeks when we learned through official channels that an Air Corps colonel in England had power-dived a stock airplane 780 miles an hour without dive brakes, and he and the airplane had both landed in one piece. It seemed the Air Corps thought we weren't getting any place in our tests, so they were sending this colonel over to tell us how to dive the airplane.

"Milo and we other test pilots, together with Kelly and Rudy, met with him when he arrived, and we talked with him the better part of an hour. I must admit that at first I was completely taken in by his story. But I was still puzzled by the fact that he could dive the P-38 at such a speed without dive brakes and still keep control of the airplane, and when we went back to the office I asked Milo about that.

"He came around with the most disgusted look on his face and I think at that moment he would have liked to knock my head off. 'Don't let me hear you being taken in by such a story,' he exclaimed, and nothing more was said about it. Why this colonel made such a statement and what his motive was we never learned, but we knew from our own experience it could not be true.

"We continued our tests with the new dive brakes, pushing the speed up a little higher on each dive and watching for the first signs that trouble was near, but the Air Corps still felt we weren't going ahead fast enough. The Army pilot who cracked up the first prototype airplane trying to set a transcontinental speed record was now the P-38 project officer at Wright Field, and he was still eager, so a few days later he took up the only plane we had equipped with dive brakes to run some tests of his own.

"Instead of the airplane returning when he was due back about an hour later, we began receiving telephone calls from various people in the western part of the San Fernando Valley, saying that a P-38 had been seen falling in pieces, and the pilot had parachuted and fallen to the ground. Not long afterward we were notified that he had lost the airplane and bailed out, receiving a broken ankle when he hit the ground.

"Investigation showed that he broke the tail off in a vertical dive, the same as Ralph Virden. When he tried to get out of the dive the tail loads went up so high they exceeded the design limits of the aircraft. He admitted later that his seat cushion got in the way of the dive flap lever, which was beside his seat on the right-hand side, and he failed to use the dive flaps, which undoubtedly would have saved the airplane. The worst part of his accident was the loss of the only plane equipped with dive brakes, and our test program was delayed several months until another plane could be fitted out with this equipment."

Let us pause for a moment of reflection here. It becomes more and more obvious that the P-38 could not be used to its full advantage without dive brakes to avoid compressibility locking the airplane in a high-speed dive. Had the Lockheed test pilots been able to press forward in the program of perfecting these flaps, then the first P-38s in combat might well have been equipped with this vital under-wing flap. Instead, Lockheed lost the XP-38 through a silly publicity stunt and now, at this vital juncture in their test program, they lost the only P-38 equipped with the flap. How long was this delay in terms of considering the delay begun with the XP-38? How much more effective would have been the P-38 as a combat machine had it had these flaps from the outset of combat missions? This is the "just plain bad luck" many pilots have felt hounded the P-38 through this period of early development.

Tony continues: "When it was ready we resumed our dive tests, and in addition we began evaluation tests on a new hydraulic boost for the ailerons, designed to improve the maneuverability of the airplane. The P-38 had always been considered heavy on the controls, especially on the ailerons, and after trying various fixes Kelly decided to incorporate a hydraulic control boost for the first time on a fighter plane. When Milo took the boost up for the first time he outrolled any known airplane. I later conducted many of the evaluations, and after we made necessary changes in the control mechanism to reduce adverse yaw effect, or the tendency of the airplane to turn when it is rolled by the ailerons, we standardized the installation and it was built into production airplanes on the assembly line.

"The new tests on the dive brakes began at thirty thousand feet and consisted of a series of progressively steeper dives to twenty thousand feet, where we started our recovery. In those days we lacked any cockpit instruments to indicate the mach number of our dive, or the speed of the dive in terms of the speed of sound; as a result we were diving pretty much hit or miss until we thought of using a directional gyro as a dive indicator. Turning it ninety degrees in the instrument panel, we caged the gyro and set it at zero in level flight before pushing over.

"By observing our dive angle on the gyro indicator we could hold it until we reached the desired altitude, where we could recover, pulling maximum G's possible up to the design limit of the aircraft, one G being the equivalent of the pull of gravity. By this method we were able to chart the constant increase in the dive angle, which produced a corresponding increase in dive speed, without endangering the airplane unduly. On each flight we photographed our instruments with a special motion picture camera known as an automatic observer and measured the stresses on the airplane with strain gauges.

"We had progressed well into our second dive program when the Air Corps notified Lockheed they desired to increase the airplane weight two thousand pounds for the dive tests and specified we would make all further dives starting at thirty-five thousand feet. The purpose of course was to meet more demanding requirements. However, it made both Milo and me shudder and we went into a huddle to figure out the best approach to our new problem.

"We knew this extra weight would accelerate our speed in a dive, and coupled with the higher altitude would undoubtedly push us to our critical mach number much sooner, or the per cent of the speed of sound which this airplane was capable of sustaining without breaking up. In other words, the hazards were increased. We were agreeable, however, and we increased our weight and began diving at forty-five degrees from thirty thousand feet, repeating this for each thousand feet until we reached thirty-five thousand feet, at which point we would increase the dive angle five degrees on each flight until something developed to stop us.

"Milo and I were swapping flights now, taking turns on the dives; he would make a dive at a certain angle and then I would duplicate it and raise it. We alternated in this fashion every day, as our dives got higher and faster. The system was new to us, but it enabled two pilots to share the daily strain of the dive program, and we both were getting valuable information and experience. It was probably the first time in the history of flight testing that two pilots conducted dive tests together on the same airplane.

"It was on Milo's fifty-five-degree dive from thirty-five thousand feet that we thought we had reached the limits of the airplane to go faster and we were over the hump. As a double check I repeated Milo's dive and then raised the angle five dgrees, and it was this day that I had my first serious trouble in flight testing.

"I had reached thirty-five thousand feet just south of the Muroc Dry Lake and turned north, intending to enter my dive in the vicinity of the new Air Corps test center. My cameras and recording instruments were operating and my two engines were turning at twenty-six hundred revolutions per minute. With my dive brakes extended I pushed forward on the control wheel and headed earthward.

"Our tests had been going well up to now; even the engineers were satisfied. If the results to date meant anything the rest should be a cinch. I reached a sixty-degree dive angle within two thousand feet after pushing over and everything appeared normal. This dive should wrap it up. Then at thirty-one thousand feet I thought I noticed a different feel in the airplane, as if it wanted to get away from me.

"Before I had time to do anything the plane started to nose under abruptly and entered a steeper dive. This was what killed Ralph Virden, but now I had dive brakes, and the plane was still under control. My first instinct was to pull out of the dive, and I fought the control wheel back with all my might. As I did so the nose came up, and I found I could maintain my original dive angle by pulling hard on the wheel. In this fashion I continued downward, the airplane getting rougher every second and the tendency of the nose to tuck under more pronounced.

"As I passed thirty thousand feet I was again tempted to pull out of the dive, but I was still flying the airplane, and I decided to ride it down. There was only a bare increase of three miles an hour on my airspeed indicator over Milo's previous dive, when the P-38 behaved normally, but these extra three miles had transformed it into a mad demon.

"I rode the bucking plane down to twenty thousand feet and started my recovery. Now I pulled back on the wheel nearly all the way and the nose barely responded. I continued down to thirteen thousand feet, pulling out of my dive very slowly, until the plane was again in level flight. My strain gauge instruments were set for 100 per cent of limit load, and they were all over 100 and all the red warning lights were on when I finally got out of the dive.

"Thinking the plane might be overstressed, I flew back to Burbank at extremely low speed and power. An instrument check revealed I had exceeded the limit load of the airplane, but it had successfully withstood the strain and escaped damage. This was final proof to us that the P-38 could dive up to its design limits with dive brakes before going out of control or breaking up. It meant that the dive brakes had licked the problem of compressibility control on the P-38, and brought our tests to a successful conclusion.

"Milo Burcham was a great flyer and a good friend, but he ruled with an iron hand, as I had reason to find out on several occasions. We had another P-38 modified for two seats, with an extended center nacelle which gave it a long nose, and this plane was called *Nosey*. One day on a test flight in *Nosey* I was carried away by the excellent way this airplane behaved in dives. Although I had completed my test on that flight I decided to dive to low altitude at the critical mach number, for no reason except that *Nosey* dove so well.

"This time I really hung one on. I held the plane right at the mach limit at an extremely steep angle, reaching a top speed of 530 miles indicated, which was 100 miles over the maximum allowed for that airplane at low altitude. Then I pulled out of my dive about one thousand feet from the ground and went on home, thinking no more about it until the next morning, when we gathered in the projection room to view the movies of my test.

"A recording camera in the airplane had faithfully photographed the test instrument panel throughout my dive. We watched the altimeter drop at an extremely high rate, with the speed going up and the altitude going down, until it dropped under ten thousand feet and suddenly I realized what I had done. Milo started to take on a queer look and make unpleasant glances at me, and when the film showed I dove to one thousand feet and pulled 7½ G's getting out, he blew his top. It was not pleasant there at all for a while."

Tony moves on to late in 1943 when: "There were large numbers of P-38s in England by this time, starting to go operational against the German Air Force as fighter cover for our bomber sweeps over Europe, and reports of trouble with our airplane, such as range, fuel consumption and engine performance, were coming back to Burbank. Meanwhile many pilots were being transferred to P-38's from slower planes like the Bell P-39 and the Republic P-47, and were encountering compressibility for the first time.

"P-38's in the field had not yet been modified with dive brakes, and the dive problem was getting serious in many fighter groups. . . .

"We were still having our troubles at Burbank. For several years we had been plagued by improper regulation of the engine turbo-supercharger on the P-38. The regulator was a very tricky device, developed from an automatic manifold pressure regulator and adapted to the turbine feature of this airplane, and it was definitely inadequate.

"In theory the turbine was a combination gas turbine and compressor, using energy from the engine exhaust gases to turn a compressor wheel, which compressed or supercharged the engine air at altitude. About the highest you could fly without a supercharger was twenty thousand feet, and we used this device on the P-38 in order to fly higher. However, its operation was very irregular, resulting in surging that caused the engines to act up in a most erratic fashion, and in the final months of 1943 I flew many tests to find a fix for this condition."

But Tony LeVier had another job to do. P-38 pilots in England were raising a stink about their airplanes. It was a strange set of circumstances. Certain groups were fanatical in defense of the airplane. Others, frankly, cursed and condemned the machine. The stories that came back to Lockheed made it all too clear that most of the complaints were coming from pilots who had never been properly trained or checked out in the P-38, and lack of skill because of improper checkout was the real villian. The Army wanted someone to really demonstrate what the P-38 could do.

Tony was soon on his way to England.

6. North Atlantic

To the persistent requests for P-38's arising from the Pacific theater General Arnold replied with praise for the work of the P-40's in Australia, reminding the Navy that if the South Pacific needed P-38's to cover the broad distances between bases, so did the Atlantic. The success of the North African venture *depended upon the presence of every possible P-38,* because of all fighters then available only this one could cross the Atlantic or move from the United Kingdom down to Oran or Casablanca. *If the P-38's were withdrawn, then the African invasion must be abandoned altogether.**

We believe its important to keep that last sentence in mind:

"If the P-38's were withdrawn, then the African invasion must be abandoned altogether."

No single statement could more effectively dramatize the indispensable role of the P-38 in the invasion and subsequent fighting in North Africa during World War II. It behooves us to lay special stress on this matter because this book is attempting to discuss and to lay bare the problems of the P-38 as much as its superior qualities. Too many books prepared on World War II aircraft are a glorified whitewash, and one would think that certain engineers wandered through the pitfalls of aircraft de-

*From *The Army Air Forces In World War II* (The University of Chicago Press), *Volume IV,* page 49 (italics added).

velopment with nary a stumble. That is a shortsighted and regrettably stupid attitude to assume, although, it must be confessed, it makes for stirring journalism.

The reader will permit a momentary side issue. During the early days of the air war, when the stirring (and accurate) exploits of the Spitfire in the Battle of Britain filled the newspapers of the United States, there arose a hue and cry from dedicated but woefully uninformed politicians that the United States should bend every effort toward producing the Spitfire in this country, rather than emphasizing the production of our fighter designs. The sterling qualities of the Spitfire needed little dramatization, for the Battle of Britain had attended to that matter. Those who championed American production of the airplane understood little about the strategic nature of the air war facing the United States, and it is accurate to say that this country could have made no more devastatingly *wrong* decision than to have rushed production of the Spitfire in favor of such machines as the Lockheed P-38 Lightning, Republic P-47 Thunderbolt, North American P-51 Mustang, Grumman F6F Hellcat and the Chance-Vought F4U Corsair. Indeed, had there been a rush to produce Supermarine's Spitfire in lieu of these fighter airplanes, then there seems little doubt but that the war might well have been extended some years beyond the conclusion we know so well.

The Spitfire, in short, was a brilliant *tactical* design. It was a close-in fighter that needs no outside support beyond its record. But the qualities that assured its success as a tactical fighter airplane also resisted its success as a strategic fighter. It lacked range, above all. It was chained to a short radius of action—it could neither carry the air war to the enemy nor could it support bombers on long-range escort missions. The purist may argue, and correctly so, that the P-38, P-47 and P-51 saw their birth not as escort fighters. True; but the airplanes were of such a design that all three ultimately were flying combat missions of more than 2,000 miles in range. It was this very adaptability to long range that so confounded the German Air Force (whose leaders had predicted such range was impossible in an airplane that could also slug it out on even terms with the best of German fighters much lighter in weight), and, to state the matter bluntly, broke the back of Japan's airpower.

Range was the key to success in aerial combat in Africa and associated theaters when that invasion was planned for November 1942. One may argue—and we will examine—the specific nature of success or failure of the P-38 in North Africa, but all such debates are side issues to the main theme. The P-38 was the bedrock of the invasion and subsequent fighting. Without the P-38 we would have had to abandon altogether our hopes for such an invasion and subsequent defeat of the enemy. In this context, then, the P-38 emerges from that era of the war as a smashing success, and no contention may sway us from this main issue.

Before proceeding to the initial overseas deployment of the P-38 as a fighter aircraft, we must first identify the models involved. As we have indicated, the leapfrog nature of modifications and development often confuses the issue. We have spent considerable time investigating the nature of the compressibility shock stall and its solution in the P-38, but it is important to stress that the underwing dive flaps that freed the P-38 from this problem did not appear until the P-38J model was well into its production run—and the first P-38s to see combat in Europe and Africa (and the Pacific and the Aleutians as well) lacked this innovation.

The three P-38 models with which we are concerned are the P-38F, G and H models. We have already studied the details of the P-38E, production of which began in October 1941. A total production run of 210 aircraft was made, and then production shifted rapidly to the P-38F —of which 527 were built. The P-38F is distinctive in that, historically, it is considered the first truly operational model in the Lightning lineage. Production of this model began in February 1942.

The essential difference in this airplane over the P-38E variant was the shift to the Allison F5 engines (V-1710-

49 and -53), replacing the Allison F2 series of the earlier airplane. The new engines gave the P-38F a military takeoff rating of 1,325 hp. A number of F variants were built; some of these were reported to sustain full takeoff power under war emergency conditions at 21,000 feet. Whether or not this actually was achieved is questionable, although it appears as if engine modifications after production did give high power at altitude. There were other alterations to the engine systems. External sockets were provided for ground power sources for starting the engines, and new air cleaners for the cooling system were installed to meet conditions of tropical and desert areas. The P-38F was more than a new Lightning; it involved a whole new series of modifications to expand its role as a combat machine for many duties. New radios (SCR-535 and SCR-522 models for the P-38F-1-LO) were installed. The P-38F was the first production model to be built with racks between the engine nacelles and the fuselage for carrying external fuel tanks or bombs. Each rack had a maximum load of 1,000 pounds, and different P-38F models were tested carrying two 22-inch torpedoes, two 1,000-pound bombs, smoke-laying generators, gas-spraying generators, or similar equipment. The fuel tanks at first were standardized at 75-gallon or 150-gallon sizes. Some models were reported to have flown long-range and combat missions with 165-gallon tanks. One history of the P-38F indicates it carried two tanks of 310 gallons each, but this is difficult to reconcile with the 1,000-pound limit of each underwing shackle, since each tank would carry at least 1,860 pounds of fuel (without the weight of the tank included).

The P-38E had carried a total of 300 gallons of fuel in the form of two 90-gallon main tanks and two 60-gallon wing reserve tanks. By carrying two 150-gallon drop tanks, the total fuel load went up to 600 gallons, and the range at maximum cruise power with this capacity went up to 1,425 miles. By reducing power and using cruise-control settings for the engines, the range increased to something over 1,700 miles.

One of the more unique modifications to the P-38F

was to equip the fighter with special equipment for Arctic flying—including the use of retractable skis. Plans were made to use the modified airplane on fields where the snow might be deeper than one-third of the main wheel diameter. The skis were carefully built up of hickory, birch and spruce and, to aid in directional control during the takeoff and landing runs, the skis were fitted with micarta runners. Lockheed devised field modification kits for all P-38F and subsequent models (although there is no record of the airplane ever being used operationally with this equipment). Four experienced mechanics could remove the main wheels and replace them with the skis in three to five hours. They removed the wheels and fairing doors, attached the skis to the shock struts, bolted fairing strips over parts of the wheel wells to prevent air leaks when the skis were retracted, locked the swiveling nosewheel strut and damper in the fore-aft position, and the airplane was ready to go in its new role.

Different variants of the basic F model appeared during the production run. The P-38F-5-LO went to new A-12 oxygen equipment. To meet requirements for the British versions of the Lightning, the P-38F-13-LO had specially modified instruments (most of the British Lightning II models remained with the AAF).

There is some confusion in the official documents of P-38 development as to when special modifications were made to the Fowler flaps to permit their use in combat. Normally the flaps were restricted to deployment at airspeeds not exceeding 160 mph. One source indicates that the P-38F-15-LO was the first variant on which the flap modifications were made; another source insists the P-38G was the first model, and there is every reason to believe the confusion arises from the fact that modifications may have been made to the F series after the airplanes left the main production line. In either case, the flap changes were a boon to the pilot in combat. The pilot was provided with a special flap control, for use at speeds up to an indicated 250 mph, where he could extend the flaps to a down position of eight degrees. This increased the camber of the wing, thus increasing the lift of the wing and giving the pilot tighter turning maneuverability.

Twenty models of the P-38F were converted to the F-4A photographic reconnaissance model.

There are several categories of weight for the airplane. Its basic weight is listed at 13,600 pounds, its normal loaded weight at 14,850 pounds, its combat weight (normal maximum) at 15,900 pounds, and its maximum allowable at 20,000 pounds. At combat weight the airplane had a listed maximum speed of 395 mph at 25,000 feet, 376 mph at 15,000 feet, and 347 mph at 5,000 feet. Its rate of climb was 2,800 feet per minute at 5,000 feet, 2,450 feet per minute at 15,000 feet, and 2,100 feet per minute at 25,000 feet. Normal landing speed at maximum weight was just under 100 mph.

In terms of climbout under maximum combat weight, the P-38F, starting from the takeoff roll, reached 5,000 feet in 1.8 minutes, 15,000 feet in 6 minutes, and 25,000 feet in 12 minutes. The service ceiling (the altitude at which the airplane is unable to climb at a rate of more than 100 feet per minute) was 39,000 feet.

P-38G

The G model went to new F10 engines (V-1710-51 and -55) that provided the same maximum power as the F5 models, but enabled the airplane to cruise with slightly higher power. At 27,000 feet the maximum power was 1,150 hp per engine, and at 24,000 feet the P-38G could cruise continuously with a steady rating of 1,100 hp per engine. Starting with the P-38G-3-LO model, Lockheed installed new B-13 turbosuperchargers. Another change was made to the G line in the P-38G-5-LO variant, when a modified supercharger was installed. Production models, starting with the P-38G-1-LO, carried new A-9 oxygen equipment and had SCR-247N radio. The changed oxygen gear included a new three-bottle system of the low-pressure demand type, also fitted out with a demand regulator, lamp and meter gauges.

Different models had the wing sections and racks modified to take heavier loads, and the P-38G-10-LO was sent into the field with a capacity of 3,200 pounds of bombs. To increase the maximum range even further, the last 200 airplanes in the G series were equipped to handle 300-gallon drop tanks—or 3,600 pounds of fuel carried externally. This provided a maximum range of some 2,300 miles or an endurance of approximately ten hours.

Still the load-carrying ability rose, and late-model G's were sent into combat with a 2,000-pound bomb under each wing—a bomb load almost as great as the B-17 (4,800 pounds). Special containers in the form of streamlined tanks, with the aft section hinged for opening and a transparent nose installed, were issued to combat units for special operations. These were used for equipment, or, if necessary, for carrying wounded from the field. Most containers took one person, but the larger models could each accomodate two stretcher cases.

The basic weight of the P-38G is listed as 12,200 pounds, loaded weight 14,650 pounds, combat weight 15,800 pounds, and maximum recommended weight 19,800 pounds.

Maximum speed at 25,000 feet was 400 mph, and at 5,000 feet, 345 mph.

The rate of climb was approximately the same as for the P-38F model, and other performance characteristics generally matched that of the P-38F.

A total of 1,082 P-38G models were produced, but the figure is misleading as to the number of fighters sent to combat units, since so many were converted to the photo-reconnaissance role. A total of 181 P-38G fighters were modified as the F-5A variant, after which another 300 were modified as the F-5B—or nearly half of the entire production run.

P-38H

By May 1943 the first P-38H-1-LO fighters were entering operational service. Lockheed turned out 601 P-38H series fighters, of which ninety were converted to the F-5B-1-LO photo-reconnaissance model. Once again, in both versions, power went up appreciably, to 1,425 hp per engine, using F-15 series Allisons (V-1710-89 and -91) with improved supercharger equipment and, for the first time in the P-38 series, fully automatic engine controls. The new turbosuperchargers were the B-33 model, and power at high altitude was increased through the use of automatically operated oil radiator flaps. Until the P-38H model, the Lightning had suffered consistently from engine cooling problems at high power output. The innovation was put on the production line well after the new production run had started, and field modification kits altered early H models. An armament change also was made, with the new AN-M2C replacing the former M1 model cannon; the cannon ammunition load remained at 150 rounds.

The early P-38H models developed 1,425 hp at take-off, a normal 1,100 hp at 25,000 feet, and a restricted output of 1,240 hp at 25,000 feet. Later, when the engines were modified with larger oil cooling radiators and automatic exit flaps, engine output at 25,000 feet was increased to an approximate 1,350 hp.

The maximum combat takeoff weight increased to 20,300 pounds, some 400 pounds heavier than the P-38F and G aircraft. With 900 gallons of fuel the airplane could be flown nearly 2,000 miles at maximum continuous cruise power at 25,000 feet. The basic weight of the aircraft was (on the average) 13,700 pounds, normal combat weight 16,300 pounds, and maximum allowable weight (as stated in operational handbooks, often disregarded under combat conditions) at 21,000 pounds.

The standard bomb load for the P-38H-1-LO through P-38H-5-LO series was 3,200 pounds, although the airplane often flew with 4,000 pounds of bombs.

Maximum speed at 25,000 feet was 402 mph; at 15,000 feet, 372 mph; and at 5,000 feet, 345 mph. The rate of climb at 5,000 feet was 2,800 feet per minute; at 15,000 feet, 2,500 feet per minute; and at 25,000 feet, 1,700 feet per minute. The rate of climb in terms of time-to-altitude approximated that of earlier models.

The ferry range at 10,000 feet, using the most economical power settings, was 2,200 miles.

A few additional words about the F, G and H series aircraft. Specific performance figures are always held somewhat in suspicion by experienced pilots because of the variation that will always exist in machines appearing to be similar. Condition of the engines, the condition of the surface metal, the particular weight of the specific airplane, the skill of the pilot—all these were factors affecting the final performance that any machine might achieve. Also, the number of fighters converted to photo-reconnaissance models must always remain in some doubt, since a number of such airplanes were converted in the field, with scant attention, if any, paid to the requirements of future historians. Also, the F-4 and F-5 variants of the P-38 as camera airplanes are almost always listed as unarmed photographic reconnaissance aircraft. Most such aircraft were unarmed, but many field groups decided that the pilot should have *some* chance with the enemy, and further modified the photo planes to carry either two .50 caliber machine guns or two 20-mm cannons in the nose, atop the camera installation. Some photo models also carried a plexiglas nose. Others were modified to a piggyback configuration to carry a passenger behind the pilot, as had been accomplished for training purposes. Many fighters became two-seat models so that pilots could give mechanics and other ground personnel the flights they seem to long for so eagerly. And there were still further field "bastardizations" of the basic airplane—the F-5A-10, for example, carried cameras, a plexiglas nose, *and* two .50 caliber guns.

In any aircraft history there is a tendency to rigidize the specific performance figures and the exact number of this or that model, when in practice such inflexibility obscures the role of the airplane as a combat weapon. Field modifications, sometimes carried out as major programs, sometimes at the will and energy of individual pilots with their ground crews, produced a variety of models so different in "style" that their final number will never be known to us.

No better example will suffice as to the misleading nature of specific performance figures than the service ceiling of the P-38H, which is listed as 39,000 feet in some sources, and as 40,000 feet in other sources (both official). Yet it was this same airplane, when flown to high altitude in oxygen tests, that set an official American record at 44,940 feet. Could the airplane have flown even higher? Most certainly, if the pilot were willing to use a favored technique of those pursuing records. The pilot would continue climbing until he ran out of fuel—choosing to gain altitude with an airplane at low weight, and gliding deadstick back to base. But there is yet another constraint. At these altitudes, a pilot breathing 100 per cent oxygen under pressure does not receive the oxygen his body demands because his entire body lacks pressurization. It is not enough to force oxygen into the lungs; they are incapable of absorbing the oxygen required, since under such low pressures the lung space is being crowded with carbon dioxide and water vapor, and the pilot after a while will collapse.

OVERSEAS

The first problem in starting the air war against Germany (and as quickly as possible, Italy as well) was to get to the combat zone. The Germans and the British faced each other across areas rather specific in terms of area; the United States faced a logistics enemy almost as formidable as its combat foe. In April 1942 the AAF began the first movements of the huge organizations to Europe that would become the Eighth, Ninth and Twelfth Air Forces, and in this movement the P-38 figured dominantly in terms of fighter strength. Roger A. Freeman in *The Mighty Eighth,* published by Doubleday & Company, Inc. notes that the fighters planned for the England-based air units were to be used primarily as escort and support for heavy bombers, and that in the early months of 1942:

"The best American fighter for such work was deemed to be the twin-engined Lockheed P-38F Lightning, a beautifully streamlined machine of unusual configuration with a performance far superior to any other American production fighter of the day."

The AAF made its decision to separate as much as possible the movement of its two types of forces—ground and air echelons. Support and other ground units would deploy by ship and the aircraft, with skeleton crews, would be flown across the Atlantic to Europe. The plan was easily acceptable for the bombers and the transports, but what about the fighters? The P-38 could be staged across the North Atlantic (we are talking essentially about P-38G and F models) from Newfoundland to Greenland to Iceland and on to England in terms of range, but such flights demand special training for the pilots, installation of navigation equipment, and careful planning. The AAF was already flying worldwide, but to fly fighters such distances—despite the casual nature with which this is done today—was at the time a daring decision not taken lightly. There was also the matter of ground facilities which simply were not adequate to the support needs of mass air movements. And above all there was the grim specter of weather; North Atlantic weather is at its best always questionable, and at its worst, unthinkable.

The author in 1961 flew as copilot on a B-17G, being flown to England for a motion picture, routing from Gander, Newfoundland via the Azores, to Portugal and on to England. Our forecast on departing Gander was for excellent weather; some scattered clouds at 3,000 feet and winds in our favor.

What happened? We flew through violent storms most of the way, often down to the deck trying to hold formation with two other B-17s in our formation. So much for that forecast.

Two years later Greg Board and I tried again along the northern route—Gander to Iceland directly, and over-flying Greenland. We had another excellent forecast. This time, in a B-25 bomber (again for a movie), we overflew Greenland at 14,000 feet in the teeth of a howling snowstorm. In *July!*

The third time I made the flight was aboard an Air Force C-130, and again in the right seat of the flight deck. This route was from South Carolina to Bermuda and then on to Spain and France. The first leg of the flight went smoothly enough. Out of Bermuda, we were delighted to see a forecast of 20-knot tailwinds to help us across the Atlantic. The morning following the word was no joy. Winds—*head*winds—of 100 knots grounded us for three days. And all this in the age of science and modern forecasting.

1942 is a period of ancient systems in comparison with the present, and it is in this light that we must try to appreciate what those pilots faced.

The AAF set up the route they considered best. The aircraft would stage from Presque Isle, Maine, to Goose Bay in Labrador, then either to Bluie West 1 (Narsarssuak) on the southern coast of Greenland or Bluie West 8 (Sondre Stromfjord) on the west coast of Greenland, on to Reykajavik in Iceland, and finally on to Prestwick in Scotland. From Goose Bay to Bluie West 8 the distance was just over 1,000 miles through some of the foulest and most unpredictable weather in the world.

Wisely, because of the navigation involved, and the unreliability of radio systems, a B-17 was assigned as a mother ship to each flight of six P-38 fighters. Special training proceeded, mechanics again and again went over the airplanes, and then the tight schedule fell apart as the Battle of Midway loomed in the Pacific. "The critical hour had come in the Pacific, and all available planes were moving west," notes the official history of the AAF. P-38s were ordered to the California coastline as emergency defense fighters; they would be released from that assignment within a week, but the temporary changes in plans scrambled the careful progress to move the fighters to England.

The first flight of bombers—eighteen B-17s—deepened the worries of the pilots concerned. Three bombers were lost (the crews survived) before they could land in

Greenland when weather and communications difficulties forced them down, and it was obvious that if four-engine bombers with two pilots for each plane, as well as a navigator, were having all sorts of fits in the Atlantic crossing, the lot of the P-38 pilots could hardly be envied.

Between June 23 and July 15, 1942, however, several formations of B-17s and P-38s were making excellent progress toward Europe. Then, on the 15th, the boom fell —"stinking weather" and misleading radio directional broadcasts by the Germans sent a number of planes wandering aimlessly until they were forced down. Six P-38s and two B-17s went down along the eastern coast of Greenland—but again, all crews survived and were rescued, no mean feat in itself.

Only time and sufficient takeoffs—compared with successful landings at the end of the long route to England —would determine whether the AAF gamble would pay off. The AAF expected, and was willing to accept, the loss of ten percent of all the planes dispatched across the North Atlantic. It was felt that a lesser number of personnel might be lost as against one out of every ten aircraft, since rescue facilities were kept alerted in the most dangerous areas.

By the end of August a total of 164 P-38 fighters, 119 B-17 bombers, and 103 C-47 transports flew into England along the North Atlantic route. Most of these were for the Eighth Air Force, but on their heels were aircraft of the Twelfth, and by the end of 1942, a total of 920 machines of all types had left the North American continent. Thirty-eight of these were lost to all causes, but this meant that 882 safely reached their intended landing fields—and the anticipated loss rate of 10 per cent had dropped to an astonishing 5.2 per cent, or just about one out of every twenty aircraft. The figures became even more bearable when they were broken down into twenty-nine planes listed as "wrecked," from which most of the crews were rescued, and only nine aircraft "lost" without any trace of the crews.

And the P-38s? An astonishing performance was turned in by the fighter pilots. One hundred and eighty-six of the twin-boomed Lockheeds left for England. Six were wrecked, as noted, in July because of weather and misleading radio direction signals (the pilots were rescued). *Only one was lost;* a total of 179 (out of 186) of the big fighters arrived in England under their own power during 1942.

During the worst of the winter months the AAF considered the North Atlantic route to be closed, especially to the fighters. Massive weather fronts all but made impossible the opportunity to maintain the "shepherd flights" where a bomber would navigate for the fighters. But in the early months of 1943, with the demand for P-38s "frantic" for the North African and Mediterranean fighting, approximately fifty of the fighters flew to North Africa via the South Atlantic.

So impressed were the AAF leaders with the performance of the P-38 in these crossings that elaborate plans were drawn up to ferry three to four *thousand* fighters, all P-38s, across the Atlantic to their destinations in Europe and Africa. Such plans never came to pass. Ferrying the airplanes was far more costly than water transport, and by the summer of 1943, the Allies had broken the back of the German submarine offensive. "Miracle production" in American shipyards had also made available far more deck space than had been anticipated, and the AAF decided to go the water route. Tankers plying the Atlantic were quickly modified with deck stands to accomodate P-38s, and in the month of December 1942, the AAF in this manner shipped 475 P-38 fighters to England.

But the air route, while it endured, was considered the immediate prelude to air combat over Europe.

7. No Contact

The official histories provide the statistics of the first fighter airplanes ever to cross the North Atlantic. They fail, however, to show the human side of the story. There's another element to those flights—pilots who have flown their fighters through such conditions tend to emerged from their experience with a deep confidence in their equipment. And so it was with the men who took their P-38s across a distance of some three thousand miles.

Of course, there were some unusual human elements to the missions . . .

The first airplane to attempt the route, paving the way for the fighters, was a B-17 that managed an uneventful flight from Canada to Iceland. Its mission was to gather meteorological data for the bombers and fighters waiting to roll; unfortunately, the return trip from Iceland ended in near disaster for the Fortress crew. The weather data collected during the eastward trip led the pilot and navigator to conclude there would be little difficulty in flying back to Goose Bay. The experience of this initial trail-breaking Fortress gave bleak promise for the fighters. Lieutenant Teague, flying the B-17, found out he couldn't trust even his own weather data. Over Greenland, Teague discovered the southern field socked in. No promise for conditions to improve. Teague dropped to 300 feet to stay beneath dark clouds and bored northward over Davis Strait. They reached the entrance to the fjord that led another hundred miles inland and contacted the field by radio.

"Socked in," was the reply to their query of field conditions. Teague and his crew stared bleakly at one another. Flying up the fjord was suicide. Teague turned back over open water. No choice but to fly back down the coast and hope the southern field was open.

It wasn't. Now the possible choice of action was reduced further. Simple, really. The fuel gauges were near the empty mark. Do we land on the sea, or do we turn inland and dump this thing atop the icecap? A ditching meant possible drowning. A crash-landing on the icecap meant a good chance of destroying the bomber on the rugged ice. Teague hammered southward. He flew; the crew crossed fingers, cursed and prayed.

Then it happened. A sight that belongs only to fiction. Teague and his men stared at a miracle. A short strip of beach, sandwiched between rugged cliffs and roaring breakers. The *only* open beach along the entire west coast of Greenland.

Teague dropped gear and flaps and landed the Fortress. The engines quit as they were rolling, the pilot and co-pilot standing on the brakes. They came to a stop—no damage! For the next five days the crew lived on apples and onions, which they had loaded aboard the Fortress for ground crews. A Coast Guard cutter showed up with 800 gallons of fuel and the men hand-loaded the tanks. When there came a break in weather—Teague flew her out, concluding as about an impossible a story for Greenland flying as one might imagine.

The P-38 pilots listened grimly to the report of the "lost-then-saved" Fortress. They watched silently as a group of bombers, under the orders of Washington, bored into the air despite reports of worsening weather conditions. Because if the bombers couldn't make it, what the hell were they supposed to do in their single-seat fighters? The experience of ten Fortresses that took off June 26 didn't improve their spirits. The bombers were en route from Labrador to Greenland when the weather deteriorated so swiftly the Fortresses were ordered to return to their takeoff points.

Six turned back. The other four didn't have the fuel to return. One of those four remained over the cloud-covered field along the southern tip of Greenland, the pilot deciding he was better off ditching when people knew their exact position. Finally low on fuel, he took the bomber beneath the clouds, lined up between an island and the mainland, and dropped her into the water. The crew got into their rafts barely in time; later a Coast Guard cutter picked them up.

The remaining three B-17s had cut up north. One actually found the airfield and through a small break in the clouds, at night, raced for the airstrip and landed. The remaining two bombers crash-landed, one on open ice and the other on a gravel beach.

In Labrador they received the news with stunned expressions. Not merely that three bombers had gone down—but that every man had been rescued.

The night of July 1–2 the weather cleared and the pilots scrambled for immediate takeoff. Twelve Fortresses took to the air, a P-38 flying on each wing of each bomber.

Twelve Fortresses and twenty-three P-38s arrived in Greenland. Missing: one P-38, flown by Lieutenant Peyton Mathis.

Before his friends could properly mourn the lost pilot, Mathis showed up, going hell-bent-for-leather for the runway. The men on the ground stared at the feathered blades of one prop. Mathis was trying to bring in his fighter with his drop tanks still beneath the wings, a nasty trick in the P-38F, which had a habit of rolling over and into a spin on one engine with that extra drag jutting into the airstream.

Mathis had been about two-thirds of the way across the waters of Davis Strait when his right engine quit. Fortunately, he had two things going for him. A second engine, and, altitude. He also had another plus on his side—he knew how to fly the P-38. Immediately he reduced power on his good engine, dropped the nose to pick up airspeed, trimmed the fighter and then brought in power again on the left engine. He watched in dismay as the formations faded from sight before him and, just as the bombers and fighters disappeared, he caught sight of mountains ahead.

Mathis struggled along in his crippled fighter, working his way slowly toward the airfield on his route manual, and saw ahead of him a flash of sunlight off metal—the other planes circling to land. But he didn't have it made —not yet. He went to full power on the left engine to climb high enough to clear a 3,000-foot ridge. He kept circling to the left, into the good engine, for better control. Then he made his decision: it was all the way the first time or that was *it*. He dropped the gear, tramped rudder and held in heavy aileron, and eased back power to an indicated 150 mph. A 10-mph tailwind didn't help, but he gritted his teeth and went for the edge of the steel matting. Brakes squealing, power off, he ground to a halt with the end of the runway only twenty feet before him.

Four sections of four P-38s each left Labrador on July 6, with promise of an 8,000-foot ceiling and visibility of thirty miles. Hell, that was great for the North Atlantic, and the fighter pilots rolled down the runway with enthusiasm. It should have been tempered because the weather went to hell in a handbasket. The first section of four Lightnings, Tomcat Black, halfway to Greenland ran into heavy icing conditions. They tried to cross over the front that loomed before them, but the P-38s, already laden with ice, couldn't make it over 25,000 feet. One pilot suddenly found himself alone; he'd lost sight of the mother Fortress and the other fighters. He gambled, and headed for Greenland, and stumbled around in the murk long enough to find a break in the clouds and land successfully. Not so the others; the B-17 pilot decided, wisely, to head back for Labrador with the remaining P-38s in tow. They landed successfully.

Tomcat White had taken off only ten minutes behind the lead section and they hit the same front. When the pilots queried the Fortress as to its intentions they heard only static. The B-17 had its own share of woes. The power source for the radios ripped into flames and killed all hopes for communication. Then a turbosupercharger went out. The bomber pilot turned back in disgust. So did the P-38s, but the weather worsened so swiftly the P-38s were scattered. One found the B-17 soon afterward and tucked in tight. The others wandered back by radio beam to land at their starting point.

Eight P-38s had gone out and one made it to Greenland, but the others were at least safe. The pilots learned that the two remaining sections were in the air; in fact, by this time Tomcat Yellow and Tomcat Green were over Davis Strait, the pilots fighting the same rotten weather. They went through a radio blackout and were unable to contact the Greenland field. They tried to break over the front and climbed to 20,000 feet, only to be dismayed with the sight of clouds another two miles above them. Tomcat Yellow saw a hole at 10,000 feet and ran for the deck, the Green section right behind. It was a sucker hole; they dropped to wavetop level and saw a wall of clouds ahead of them. *Then* they began to ice up and the pilots knew real fear. Green bored upwards as fast as the planes could climb and at 4,000 feet breathed a bit easier between cloud layers—above and below, but at least they were out of icing.

"Let's pack it in," one of the P-38 pilots called, and they turned back for Labrador. They made it—eight hours after taking off. The pilots were so cold and exhausted they were physically unable to climb from their cockpits. Ground crews—literally—had to lift the men from their airplanes.

Tomcat Yellow, weaving through cloud layers, finally entered thick clouds and kept climbing until they were staggering at 25,000 feet. By now the men were steeling themselves for bailing out when their tanks ran dry. Fifteen miles from the Greenland coast one fighter pilot yelled in disbelief—the way was open before them. They pulled the plug and ran for the field far below.

Pity the pilots of Green Flight. They tried it again on July 10, and whatever bad luck they'd encountered before stayed with them. Two more P-38s joined the section of four, and a B-17 led the six Lightnings off on another derring-do. They made Greenland and as soon as the weather cleared struck for Iceland. No joy this time. A scant 200 miles out the weather closed in and they decided to return—Iceland was closed down completely. But by the time they worked their way back over the great ice sheets of Greenland their home field was also shut down. The bomber and six fighters turned south, pursuing reports of better weather.

"We better get where we're going *fast*," one pilot told the others. They knew it—they'd been in the air eight and a half hours and their tanks were sloshing the last gallons of fuel. They had less than thirty minutes to make it to the next field. "We'll never make it," one pilot warned.

His flight leader agreed. Lieutenant McManus dropped his gear and dragged the icecap. There was always the chance of finding a level area. McManus didn't find it. He stared at deep crevices and gaps in the ice. They were closer than he thought—both engines quit at the same time. McManus smashed into the ice, snapped off his gear, and spun flat across the ice field. He ended up with nothing worse than a badly sprained shoulder. Halfway out of his cockpit he was treated to the incredible sight of five P-38s, gear up, belly-landing on the ice cap, hurling back huge plumes of frozen spray. Then *they* stood back and watched the Flying Fortress follow them down— and without a casualty!

Nine days later the rescue party, spearheaded by a dog sled, and guided by a Catalina flying boat, reached the fighter pilots and bomber crew. Not a man was lost.

The pilots sweating out weather at Greenland never knew when the call would come through to get to their planes. Waiting in the primitive facilities brought more than a few of them to the edge of being stir-happy. There was only so much poker and gin rummy—and nothing else. Except being a tourist. A few pilots decided to climb the mountains nearby, returning exhausted to their huts, to be greeted with urgent cries to get to their planes at once. Fifteen minutes later, at 2:30 in the morning, they were in the air.

One pilot—Lieutenant McCord—almost didn't make it. The lack of sleep, droning and vibration of the engines, monotony of flight, all took its toll. The other pilots watched McCord's Lightning drifting away—with McCord sound asleep in the cockpit.

"Mac! Wake up! For Christ's sake, wake up!"

The chorus of agitated fighter pilots had its effect in McCord's earphones. Somewhat shaken to realize he was drifting to almost certain death he returned to the formation and slid back into position.

Another pilot faced the same problem—he too couldn't stay awake. He sang and shouted and yelled, slapped himself in the face. No good. He tried something more drastic. He eased out of formation and, notwithstanding his heavy fuel load and external tanks, started great soaring rolls with his P-38. He later told other pilots he was so scared in his heavy plane the adrenalin shooting through his system kept him awake.

One pilot at the controls of his P-38 had no difficulty in staying alert. He was scared silly just to be in the airplane because he'd never before flown one. Colonel John W. Weltman, USAF (Ret.), in 1942 was a major commanding one of the P-38 squadrons fighting its way to Europe. Weltman was no stranger to the Lightning. He picked up the ninth YP-38 to come off the production line and spent almost his entire Word War II career as a fighter pilot in Lightnings over Africa and Europe.

"We were just about to take off from Goose Bay," Colonel Weltman related to me, "when one of my pilots came down ill. He was really under the table; he could hardly walk, let alone fly. I looked at that P-38 sitting on the field and took a long shot. I went into operations where I spotted a ferry pilot. He'd never flown anything hotter than a C-47, but there wasn't any harm in trying. I asked him if he would like to fly a P-38.

" 'Across the ocean?' That was his first question. Sure, I told him.

" 'How would you like to go climb a rope?' That was his second question.

"I told him there wasn't anything to it. We gave him a ten-minute cockpit check. That's all. Thirty minutes after that he was taking off, and he flew that ship like a veteran. By the time we got to England he was so elated we gave him another P-38 to fly."

Earlier in these pages we reviewed the first combat air kill of a German airplane in World War II, shot down by Lieutenant Elza Shahan in a P-38F. Colonel John Weltman filled me in with some more details of that air battle of August 15, 1942, out of Iceland.

Weltman was in the operations shack when the word came in that the Focke-Wulf Kurier was in the area. He took off immediately and was told by radio that another Lightning, as well as a Bell P-39 Airacobra, were already airborne. But Weltman was the first to see the Kurier. He went to full power and charged his guns; as he closed in he started firing short bursts at the four-engined bomber. The German gunners were good and Weltman didn't stay too long in the fight—the Kurier knocked out his guns and cannon and shot out one engine. Weltman banked away, feathered one prop, and watched the rest. The Airacobra and Shahan in the Lightning each made a pass, and then Shahan went in for the kill to less than a hundred yards away. That did it—the Kurier exploded.

A few days later both Lightning pilots were on their way to England. And, strange to relate, their air combat over Iceland was just about the only combat the P-38s were to see in the next few months.

The Eighth Air Force in England was under urgent orders from AAF Headquarters in Washington to "introduce the P-38 to combat." The North African invasion hinged on the ability of the P-38F to meet German fighters on both defensive and offensive missions and to at least hold its own, and the AAF fretted over the lack of positive proof that only air combat could supply. Yet, despite all such efforts, the Official History of the AAF in World War II notes that on the eve of invading North

Africa, in November 1942, "except for tests against a captured FW-190, there was no indication of how the P-38 would stand up to the Luftwaffe."

Upon arrival in England, the P-38s thirsting for first combat with the German Air Force found themselves virtually grounded. First they had to learn the areas in which they were to fly. Their HF radios were to be replaced with the superior British VHF systems. They had to coordinate with British defense systems, to avoid heavy anti-aircraft and balloon defenses. There was the matter of aircraft recognition. They had to fit into the systems of air traffic control. And there was modification after modification to the P-38F to better its chances against the Luftwaffe. By the end of July all they knew about the P-38F against a German fighter were the results of a mock combat with an FW-190A flown by a British pilot. The results were mixed. The Focke-Wulf apparently had better acceleration and a superior rate of climb. But to everyone's surprise the P-38F at lower altitudes could turn slightly better than the FW-190A and more than held its own in acrobatic maneuvers.

By late August the AAF was ready to commit the P-38F against the best of the German pilots flying from Europe. On September 1 a force of thirty-two Lightnings struck across the European coast on a heavy sweep intended to bring enemy opposition from its fields. Not a German fighter showed.

Nor did the Lightnings manage to engage in a single encounter with the enemy during a series of escort missions during the two months following. The German pilots were avoiding all escort fighters, including the P-38s, and going after the bombers. By the end of October the P-38s were withdrawn from European operations to prepare for their role in North Africa.

Combat evaluation would have to wait.

8. Desert War

North Africa was where the P-38 earned its name—
Der gabelschwanz teufel.

The fork-tailed devil.

It took a while, though.

Because for a long time after starting combat the P-38
pilots in North Africa were still gaining experience. They
were green to the finer points of air war, and their op-
ponents, some of the best German fighter pilots, and the
best the Italians had to offer, had been around a long
time. There were some other problems. There weren't
enough Lightings to go around. Operational demands were
stretching their numbers thin. The enemy outnumbered
them on most occasions. They were often restricted on
escort missions to sticking with the bombers instead of
being turned loose to turn some of the odds in their
favor. Maintenance at its best left a screaming demand for
improvement. Replacements of both men and planes were
slow coming in. And then the theater commanders decided that since the demands on the P-38s were already
nigh unto impossible they couldn't make matters too much
worse. So they assigned the P-38s to bombing missions as
well.

There were other problems. The first Lightnings were
the P-38F models and, as we've seen earlier in this book,
the G model was considerably superior to the F, and the
H was a much better airplane than the G. But it took
time to get the later models in (and the best of the
Lightnings, and J and L models, were a long ways down

the pike). The P-38F had more than its share of teething troubles—but it was *the* airplane for North Africa, and that was it.

The men might have done even better in the air if things hadn't been so rough for so long on the ground. John Weltman remembers it clearly—it's hard to forget. Water was more precious than gold; there was never enough of it. Living facilities were a testimony to GI ingenuity. For some time the men didn't even have tents, and they slept in blankets and sleeping bags on the open desert or using mud for a pillow; they didn't have much choice, really. And sometimes the temperature went down to 20 or 30 degrees at night. Which is a hell of a way to spend your sleep before a mission. You could tell the temperature by watching the constant change of clothes. At night the men wore everything they could get their hands on. Then, during the day, as the sun came up, the garments were shed steadily. At midday they walked around in shorts and no shirts. Then it started to cool and the clothes went on again until everyone was swaddled up like a freezing Eskimo. Great fun.

Two meals a day—not three—was standard. It made missions of four to seven hours pretty rough.

At least the ground crews and the pilots dispensed with the nonsense of military formality. No one stood formations. No one was either in or out of uniform. You shaved when you had the chance—if you felt like it. The whole operations manual was written around a single thought: keep the fighters in the air and everything else would be ignored.

The P-38s found themselves in the wildest mixed bag of missions the pilots could imagine. They escorted attack, light, medium and heavy bombers, as well as transports and reconnaissance planes. They found weather and lack of navigation and communications facilities to be about as tough an enemy as the German Air Force. On November 21, 1942, a force of P-38s moved into Youks. On their first day they flew two murderous strafing missions against a German armored column, but escaped without loss. That night, with the Lightnings milling around over a field wrapped in darkness, six of the P-38s crashed and were destroyed. No one dared to put on the lights for fear of German attack. The pilots were bitter about that.

Many of the combat problems faced by the P-38s were beyond control of the fighter pilots. Early in the North African campaign fierce German and Italian attacks forced the B-17s to retreat from their bases in the Algiers region. The P-38s had been effective in escorting B-17s, but were helpless at night to stop enemy raids launched from Sardinia, as neither the P-38s nor any other Allied fighters were equipped to make night interceptions.

Weather proved to be a serious obstacle to striking at enemy targets—the problem lay in the fact that much of the weather conditions were encountered over enemy territory and it was impossible to prepare accurate forecasts. Again the range and speed of the P-38 came into the fore—the fighters (not photo planes) were sent into the heart of enemy country to report on weather conditions for the bombers.

The enemy found the range of the P-38s particularly disconcerting when it suffered disastrous losses in German and Italian transport aircraft. The Germans and Italians had enjoyed comparative freedom in mass overwater flights of their transports—until the arrival of the Lightnings, which flew well beyond the reach of the other Allied fighters. The long legs of the P-38s wiped out that advantage, and dozens of transports began falling in a deadly rain from the skies. The fighters, as the AAF history notes the events, "had a field day" against such air transport, but all too quickly the P-38s were thrown into full protection of Allied ground forces, restricting their freedom to come to grips with the enemy in the air. And that was the gist of it—the P-38 had come to Africa as a fighter and had quickly been thrown into every possible role of the air war.

Again a note from the AAF History:

The P-38's at Youks found the range more convenient, but there were not enough of them for the job.

Over the Allied fighters, which had to escort paratroops and bombers and to cover the coastal shipping, the Me-109's and FW-190's were consistently enjoying numerical superiority. On sweeps over the battle area the Spits and P-38's frequently were hard put to defend themselves, let alone scatter the enemy bombers.

A typical mission of December 2, 1942 showed the P-38s making two powerful sweeps in the heart of the battle area, where they "broke up a Ju-88 bombing formation in the teeth of its Me-109 escort, and shot up the Stuka landing ground at Sidi Tabet."

On December 9, the P-38s were escorting B-17s over Bizerte harbor and were under strict orders to "stay close to the bombers." Tied down, frustrated, the Lightnings were sitting ducks when a force of Me-109s swept in from higher altitude. The P-38 pilots fought valiantly and shot down three Me-109s with the loss of three P-38s. But two more Lightnings failed to return from the mission. Yet headquarters was more than satisfied— the bombers *were* getting through.

Still, no matter how one looked at it, the odds were brutal. Pilots flying and fighting almost every day, tied to bomber formations, were being swarmed over by German fighters enjoying odds of two to one and as high as five to one. Again, and the repetition here is deliberate, the P-38s were making the difference between success and failure in the air campaign.

Referring to December 1942, the AAF History notes that

[the] B-17's discovered new and formidable yellow-nosed FW-190's at Bizerte . . . The twelfth's B-17's attacked Tunis and Bizerte day after day, going in with forces which seemed pitifully small in comparison with the armadas of 1944 and 1945. That their losses remained low must be attributed to the fact that they usually had P-38's escorting, not many P-38's but enough to divide the opposition's attention.

Bad enough in the opening phases of the North African air war, but worse when it came to replacements, until the shortage of P-38s, "which because of their versatility and endurance were used in a variety of roles," had become critical. Official documents note that the demand for the P-38s was so great, and the number reduced so steadily, that "at times the bomber command could not find a dozen P-38's for escort, and . . . pleas for fighters became progressively more desperate during January."

With good reason. There were less than a hundred P-38 fighters still flyable. At this time the AAF went to total commitment with the P-38 in Africa—every airplane was to be shipped immediately, by air and by sea, from England and the United States.

Ernie Pyle lived for a while with a P-38 outfit in what was then French North Africa. Excerpts from the report he filed with the *Los Angeles Times* tell some of the human side of the story.

. . . I wish somebody would sing a song, and a glorious one, for our fighter pilots. They are the forgotten men of our aerial war.

Not until I came up close to the African front did I realize what our fighter pilots have been through and what they are doing . . . they are the sponge that is absorbing the fury of the Luftwaffe over here. They are taking it and taking it and taking it. And everlasting credit should be theirs. . . . There have been exaggerations in the claims that the Fortresses can take care of themselves without fighter escort. Almost any bomber pilot will tell you that he is deeply grateful for the fighter cover he has in Africa, and that if he had to go without it he would feel like a very naked man on his way to work.

Our heavy bombers now are always escorted by Lightnings. It is their job to keep off German fighters . . . It means longer trips than fighters ever made before. Sometimes they have to carry extra gas tanks, which they drop when the fight starts. They mix it with the enemy when they are already tired from long flying at high altitudes. And then if they get crippled they have to navigate alone all the way home.

The P-38 is a marvelous airplane and every pilot who flies it loves it. But the very thing that makes the Lightning capable of these long trips—its size—unfits it for the type of combat it faces when it gets there.

If two Lightnings and two Messerschmitt 109s get in a fight the Americans are almost bound to come out the little end of the horn, because the Lightnings are heavier and less maneuverable.

The ideal work of the P-38 is as an interceptor, ground strafer, or light hit and run bomber. It would be a perfect weapon in the hands of the Germans to knock down our daylight bombers. Thank goodness, they haven't got it. . . . Although our fighters in North Africa have accounted for many more German planes than we have lost, still our fighter losses are high. I have been chumming with a roomful of five fighter pilots for the past week. Tonight two of those five are gone.

Of course, there was the other viewpoint, this time provided by Hans Pichler, a German fighter ace who finished his World War II career with seventy-five confirmed victories. Pichler was transferred in October 1942 to North Africa, and remarked later in notes that the fighting in the air became heavier and more dangerous as the months went by. From his diary (*Air Combat,* Vol. III, No. 5) Pichler noted:

Over Tunisia, my flight encountered four P-38s and we slipped behind them, virtually unnoticed. Although our Gustavs [Me-109Gs] gave all they could, the distance between us and the Lightnings hardly diminished. At a distance of about 500 meters, I fired all my guns, but my shells exploded behind one of the P-38s. After several more ineffective bursts, the U.S. pilots obviously sensed danger. Applying full war-emergency power, they disappeared, leaving us with our mouths wide open. The five-minute chase caused my engine to seize. One of the connecting rods pushed itself right through the cowling. . . .

The interrupted development of the P-38, from its earliest days of flight testing (loss of the XP-38, Lockheed's only prototype, by Ben Kelsey) now returned with a vengeance, as we can see from another excerpt from

Pichler's notes. It might be said that the "ghost of compressibility"—which by this time had been solved, but without the fix yet applied to models in combat theaters—had come to haunt the Lightning. Pichler remarks:

In my estimation, the P-38 was more maneuverable and faster than our Bf-109G-6, especially since the latter was equipped with the two cm (20-mm) underwing gondola weapons. I had never been keen on dogfights with the P-38, but I did manage to shoot down three of them plus four or five Mitchells. An excellent method of breaking combat was to go into a power dive from high altitude. The P-38 pilots rarely followed us. At first this was unexplainable to us but the mystery cleared up a few months later when a captured P-38 pilot told us that their ships became too fast to be pulled out of a dive efficiently.

By early 1943 the AAF felt sufficient experience had been gained to offer a clear evaluation of the P-38, noting that the AAF fighters "habitually went into a region where the German Air Force held superiority," and that the P-38s "inevitably took some losses protecting their charges, but their pilots discovered with satisfaction that the P-38 stacked up well with the current Me-109 and FW-190, being able under certain conditions to outrun and outturn both types."

Several missions in February showed that the P-38F was becoming a weapon well honed in the hands of the more experienced pilots. On February 8, 1943, fourteen P-38s escorted a mixed force of fifteen B-26 Marauder and eighteen B-25 Mitchell bombers. The Germans met them in force and hit particularly hard at the Mitchells. For a cost of four Me-109s the Germans shot down four bombers and crippled two others. The B-26s were having their own nasty party with about two dozen Messerschmitts when the P-38s came in like a pack of hornets. In the ensuing melee one Lightning went down, but the P-38 pilots confirmed eight Me-109s.

But more and more attention was being paid to developing the P-38 as a bomber. Special minimum altitude techniques, including skip-bombing, had been worked out in the States, and the combat leaders in Africa were anxious to have a go at these new methods with the Lightnings. But it took time to get new bombsights and delayed-fuse bombs, and while the pilots trained for their new missions they were kept busy escorting bombers going against enemy shipping on the deck.

They also had plenty of practice in ground-support missions, which was considered a guaranteed way to get clobbered from above. On January 21, 1943, two squadrons of P-38s scourged enemy convoys with devastating effect. They destroyed sixty-five vehicles and killed several hundred ground troops in their merciless strafing. The manner of flying is exemplified in the case of one P-38 that was flown into a telephone pole. The wing sliced the pole in two—which in turn smashed in much of the leading edge—and the Lightning careened wildly upward. The pilot got it back under control and all P-38s returned safely.

Not so the next day. The Lightnings were back to wreak hellish destruction in the long convoys. Ten German fighters dove without warning against eight P-38s and in the brief battle shot down two Lightnings. No Germans were claimed. On January 23, with the P-38s again down on the deck, they were bounced by German fighters—two Lightnings were shot down and by day's end another four failed to return to base for "reasons unknown." Six out of sixteen Lightnings lost during the day was a bitter pill for the pilots to swallow, especially when they'd been forced into a situation where they were sitting ducks.

By late the next month, however, the P-38s found themselves in an extraordinary position to return the German favors. Even as the Lightnings concentrated on ground strafing and bombing, attacking ships, flying defensive patrols, escorting bombers, the shape of the war was itself changing. The Germans were more and more hard-pressed for supplies, and they put increasing reliance into their air transport supply system. By the middle of March 1943 the daily transport flights were exceeding a hundred planes each way. A total force of some 500 air transports, made up of Junkers Ju-52, Savoia-Marchetti SM-82, and huge six-engined Messerschmitt Me-323 transports. They flew in the morning and through the afternoon, usually with a top cover of at least a dozen fighters.

"This traffic," notes the AAF History, "had long been greedily eyed by the Allied air [forces]. . . ." And so it was. The basic plan evolved to cut into enemy air supply was to carry out P-38 sweeps over the Sicilian strait, timed carefully with a shipping sweep also escorted by P-38s, while other bombers and P-38s hammered at the airfields used by the enemy.

The reader will recall the name of John Weltman, who had cut his teeth on the Lightning going back to the YP-38, and who made the first firing pass against that Focke-Wulf Kurier over Iceland. Weltman's P-38 outfit drew the brass ring for having the sweeps against the airborne transports.

On April 5 they were full swing on the merry-go-round. Early on that date a force of twenty-six P-38s caught a massive enemy formation made up of some seventy Ju-52 transports, twenty Me-109s, six Ju-87 Stukas, four FW-190s and a single FW-187. The Lightnings ripped into their targets, and before the fight ended the Germans had lost eleven Ju-52s, two Me-109s, two Ju-87s and the lone FW-187 for the cost of but two Lightnings.

At about the same time medium bombers were tearing up an enemy convoy, while escorting fighters knocked down another fifteen enemy interceptors.

By day's end more than 200 enemy planes had been destroyed in the air and on the ground.

Five days later the P-38s had another field day—they went out for blood with two formations, one on the deck and the top cover at only 1,000 feet, and ran smack into the shuttle racing to reach Tunis. The low flight wiped out twenty transports and the high flight confirmed eight Me-109 and Mc-200 fighters shot down. Later that same morning a heavily escorted B-25 force shot down twenty-five more planes, all but four of them transports.

And the next day the Lightnings were at it again, now the most feared airplane of all the Allies, because the

German and Italian pilots never knew when it would show up next—or *where*. The day after the slaughter of April 10th, two P-38 sweeps littered the seas with the wreckage of another twenty-six Ju-52 transports and five more of their escorting fighters—without loss to the Lightnings.

Another element was entering the picture. P-38 strength had been cut to the bare bone by the extraordinary demands placed on the airplanes, often forcing the fighter pilots into compromising situations where the odds were heavily against them. Now, with a free hand to roam in the sweeps the pilots desired so fervently, they were being cut loose, and the results were the staggering losses suffered by the enemy. To the grim displeasure of German and Italian fighter pilots, the men flying the P-38s, released of their burdens in escort and ground attack during these sweeps, had turned into aggressive and bloodthirsty killers rushing in against anything in the air that was enemy, and such encounters had no respect for the odds.

Still another factor began to bear its muscle. Long months of foul weather, shortages of spare parts and a lack of replacements began to change. New planes—including the latest models with improved performance—began to show up in increasing number. "The escort fighters," notes the AAF History, "viewed high and low . . . as the bombers' best friends, were now relatively abundant . . . and the rejuvenated 14th (P-38s) was back from rest and refitting."

The men had cut their teeth in early bombing raids and they started gaining skill with a vengeance. In April, John Weltman, now a lieutenant colonel, set something of a highwater mark for other pilots to beat. Four P-38s, led by Weltman, flew a special mission to Porto Torres in Sardinia, and found two enemy cargo ships waiting for them. Weltman told the other pilots to provide top cover at a thousand feet while he took his Lightning to within a few feet of the water—low enough to leave a trail of spray behind his twin Allisons. There was water of another sort—the harbor was filled with destroyers and a cruiser and a few hundred guns opened up on the speeding fighter. Weltman stayed low and then released a thousand pounder from beneath his wing. No one expected what happened next. The bomb shot ahead of the P-38 as if it were an artillery projectile, smashed into the first vessel high and amidships, tore through the superstructure and then whistled into the *second* ship. Apparently, as Weltman recalled later, the second ship must have been carrying fuel or ammunition because it disappeared in a terrifying blast that shook the P-38 madly. It also destroyed and sank the ship, inflicted severe damage to the first vessel, and resulted in "the total destruction of the surrounding cargo-laden docks."

By June 1943 no one questioned the "killing power" of John Weltman's P-38 group; the record the men had carved against the enemy in the worst days of North African air fighting spoke well enough for itself. Now, with new planes and better equipment, they found themselves dishing out punishment instead of staving it off. The group counted eleven aces among its pilots and they had come to know the P-38 so well it was a weapon much more effective in their hands that it could have been with fledgling pilots. On June 18, 1943, they flew an escort mission to Aranci, Sardinia, and an estimated forty to fifty enemy fighters swarmed up against the B-25 bombers. The P-38s hit them quickly and shot sixteen fighters out of the air, as well as marking off two probables and eight damaged.

Weltman and his pilots had come a long, hard road.

Several pilots flying the P-38 North Africa had the rare distinction of becoming "aces in a day"—shooting down five or more enemy aircraft either on one or several missions between sunrise and sunset. In October 1943 the 14th Fighter Group was based at Ste. Marie-du-Zit, Tunisia, flying missions in bomber escort and fighter sweeps to the north to support the growing war against the Italian mainland. On October 9, Lt. Colonel William L. Leverette was leading a force of seven P-38s over an Allied convoy. Someone radioed that they had company —twenty-five Ju-87 Stukas escorted by an unnumbered force of twin-engined Ju-88s. The combat-wise Leverette ordered three Lightnings to remain above them as high cover, and led a force of four P-38s into the enemy, by now starting their dives against the convoy. The Lightnings hit them fast from behind, breaking up the dives and scattering the enemy dive bombers. In a brief but fierce mixup, Leverette shot down seven Stukas. A young lieutenant, Harry T. Hanna, confirmed another five shot down.

The worst part of the fight was that the other P-38s couldn't leave the convoy to finish off the stragglers. The Lightnings rejoined and continued their weaving patrol. But it wasn't a bad afternoon.

Captain William J. Hoelle, who commanded the 49th Fighter Squadron of the 14th Fighter Group in North Africa, was generous enough to write me in some detail of his P-38 experience in Africa, along with some requested evaluations of the models they were flying at the time. Hoelle wrote:

"No plane has taken more criticism than the P-38, and to my mind no plane has more thoroughly demonstrated how unfair and uncalled for that criticism has been. The Lightning proved of inestimable value in the fighting in North Africa, and without any doubt it came out as one of our most effective all-round fighter planes. In three months I flew forty-seven missions with the 49th Fighter Squadron and I've seen what the P-38 can do under any and all circumstances.

"When we first arrived in North Africa, we thought the P-38 wouldn't work out well as a ground support airplane, but after seeing the results of concentrated firepower against trucks, columns and tanks, we knew we really had something. The ease and accuracy with which firepower can be controlled in a P-38 is important. The fighter pilot is able to put a bead right on the target and the firepower, centered in the nose, doesn't have to converge toward a point but remains intact throughout the pattern.

"Another criticism of the P-38 has been directed against its alleged inability to perform on a single engine.

Nothing could be further from the truth. Such tales of single-engine operation caused apprehension among new pilots. When the engine quit on either side, the tendency is for the good engine to pull the plane over and into a spin. But this could readily be offset.

"In the 49th Squadron and its sister squadron, the 48th, commanded by Major Wade C. Walles, there were numerous experiences where one engine was shot up, yet the pilot always managed to return to his base. This proved to us that one-engine operation could be performed successfully even under combat conditions. The procedure followed when an engine quit was to cut back both throttles and then gradually feed the good throttle forward, using rudder to offset engine thrust. Ability to relax and think clearly, which comes automatically after experience, allows a pilot to cope with any emergencies that arise when one engine quits. In the event both engines cut out at the same time, it was wise for the pilot to turn the selector switch to the tank containing the reserve gas supply.

"This may sound like we were offering needless advice, but we actually had a couple of instances where pilots ran out of gas and crash-landed, only to discover to their chagrin that their reserve tanks still carried plenty of gas. They simply had forgotten all about them.

"I can readily cite a number of examples where P-38s came through combat on one engine, and did a good job of fighting the enemy at one time. On one occasion, Lieutenants Robert Carlton, Virgil Lusk and James Butler were strafing the airport at Gabes. Carlton's plane took a flak hit and disabled the right engine. The flight decided to head for home. On the return, some thirty miles north of Gabes, the three ships ran across nine Italian troop transports. The trio of P-38s, with Carlton on one engine, proceeded to shoot down *all* nine transports, and all heavily loaded with troops. Lusk got five, Butler three, and Carlton in his crippled P-38 knocked off one for himself.

"In flying over to inspect the blazing ships on the ground, Lusk's left engine was knocked out by an Italian soldier on the ground firing a tommy gun at him. Both Lusk and Carlton had to limp home with Butler watching out for them and navigating at the same time. But the boys got back without any further trouble.

"Another example of single-engine performance by the P-38 occurred when Captain W. P. Moore shot down a giant flying boat over the Mediterranean. Moore was on a fighter-escorted bomber sweep looking for enemy shipping when he caught sight of this monster—a Blohm & Voss Bv-222 with six engines. He went after the huge ship to about fifty feet over the water; the flying boat caught fire and exploded almost immediately. But at almost the same moment enemy fighters bounced Moore and shot out his left engine as well as destroying his hydraulic system. Moore somehow managed to escape and rejoined the bombers, staying with them on one engine all the way back to his base. He used the manual hand pump to lower his gear. This is a job that required about 400 strokes—and every stroke was comparable to the stroke used in rowing a boat. Moore couldn't hold up his arm when finally he got down.

"Still another single-engine experience was chalked up by Captain Charlie Earnhart when he was on a strafing mission to Gabes. He destroyed two planes on the ground and was chewing up ground installations and flak batteries when flak got to him. A cannon shell exploded in the cockpit, cutting Earnhart's left leg and imbedding shrapnel deeply in the leg. At the same time his left engine quit. Earnhart started home, trimming the P-38 for single-engine flight and also administering to his wounds. He even went so far as to apply a tourniquet, and any good first-aider knows this is no simple job under normal conditions, let alone while flying a P-38 on one engine.

"Then there's the criticism that the P-38 was a death trap because the pilot couldn't bail out. This is so much nonsense. We found that in combat every pilot who had to hit the silk did so without any trouble whatsoever. Bailing out could be accomplished by the pilot either rolling the plane over on its back and falling out, or, by pulling the ship up into a stall and jumping out between the booms and elevators just as the plane started to spin.

"Bob Carlton discovered still another way of getting out—one of the most unique methods I've ever heard of. We were in England when Carlton was ordered up to intercept a Junkers Ju-86P high-altitude photographic ship. Carlton's plane iced up in a solid overcast and fell off into a steep dive. The indicated airspeed was 600 mph. Carlton decided to leave the thing at 25,000 feet. He tripped the canopy release, unfastened his safety belt and the next thing he knew he was floating through space. Apparently a vacuum sucked him right out of the plane and with no more injury than being shaken up a bit.

"In North Africa, another member of our squadron was escorting bombers over Sfax when he was hit by flak and his P-38 caught fire. He simply rolled the ship over on its back and bailed out from 1,500 feet.

"I also had occasion to bail out one day. Six of us were strafing tanks when we were attacked from above by sixteen German fighters. The first I knew about the attack was when the fellow flying on my left was shot down. Immediately I pulled the ship up into an Immelmann, which brought me out above the fighters tailing me, and headed in the opposite direction. It was useless for the enemy to follow me because the radius of their turn in a loop or an Immelmann would have brought them out well below me. When I rolled the plane over and out of the Immelmann, I found myself in the midst of another enemy flight. There was a Messerschmitt in my sights and I shot it down with one long burst, but immediately I discovered enemy planes on my tail.

"I put the maneuvering flaps down in an effort to turn away, only to have a cannon shell hit the flaps and make them jam in that position. When this happened, the best speed I could get wasn't sufficient to let me outdistance them and by this time I was separated from my flight.

"I tried to maneuver out of range but couldn't do so because of reduced speed. Finally they succeeded in hitting the left engine and it burst into flames. At this point I was only fifty feet above the ground. I pulled the plane up into a stall because I knew I had to get out. To crashland at this particular point over the terrain would have been fatal. As the ship stalled at about 500 feet, I jumped out through the booms and elevators just as the plane fell into a spin.

"Fortunately, I landed behind our lines and, with the help of the Arabs and French, I managed to make my way back to base. I wish I had pulled the ripcord a little sooner. Flying pieces of metal from the plane entered my body, but did no serious damage.

"The P-38 was designed, as you know, as an interceptor and high-altitude ship. But we soon discovered that if we were to get into combat in North Africa, we had to fly at altitudes below 12,000 feet. There was far greater action at lower levels and certainly there were more ships to attack. This put us on the offensive and was far more advantageous than entering combat by first warding off an enemy attack from above.

"We had a motto in the 49th Squadron: "The sooner you start shooting, the better." We always tried to remember that the other fellow has much the same thought in mind, and since we were his idea of a target this motto wasn't to be forgotten.

"We were constantly looking for something to pick off, such as the Junkers Ju-87 and Ju-88. These were more plentiful at lower levels and were seldom to be found above 15,000 feet. Therefore, despite the design of the P-38 for high altitude fighting, we had to come down to lower levels to find a target. Our low-level work included the strafing of trucks, tanks and columns, or anything else we could find. One day I wound up in a rather ticklish position, but once again the P-38 proved its worth and came through in grand style.

"We were strafing trucks and tanks at low altitude, when the commanding officer of the 49th Fighter Squadron was shot down. A pillbox gun got him, and as I looked back to identify the crashed plane, the tail of my ship hit a telephone pole. I immediately kicked full top rudder and full left aileron, and this rolled me back into a right bank position. The ship trembled all over and sort of bounced crazily along through space. By holding full left aileron I retained this position and kept the plane flying about fifty feet above the ground. I thought for a while I was a goner for sure.

"Finally I put the flaps down and this proved just what was needed to gain control of the plane, pick up altitude and return home. The flying speed had been greatly reduced by the accident and I had to hang on to the wheel for dear life, the plane vibrated so badly.

"Other ships in the squadron saw I was in trouble and I succeeded in telling them over the radio what had happened. As I headed for home, the rest of the squadron circled over me constantly to ward off any enemy attack. It was 360 miles back, or a two-hour trip at my reduced speed. When I landed, the pressure I had been forced to exert on the wheel had caused large blisters to break out on my hands. I was also dripping wet from sweat. But I owe plenty of thanks to that P-38 . . . I don't mind saying I was scared to death when the plane hit the pole which, incidentally, was knocked to smithereens.

"I've been asked many times how the P-38 stacked up with the Focke-Wulf FW-190 and the Messerschmitt Me-109. My answer is that due to the P-38's greater speed, we capitalized on that speed to come in and make a quick attack, then climbed to regain position for another attack. In doing this, we achieved far better results than would have been possible in attempting to turn and dog-fight with single-engined planes.

"Nearly any single-engined ship can turn inside a twin-engined one if given the opportunity; consequently our tactics were based upon the fact that we had greater speed than the German planes. We always flew in units with teamwork between flights of four to afford us protection against attacks and place us in position to go on the offensive.

"The smallest flying unit was a two-unit element. We found it better for personal safety never to attack individually but always fly with at least a unit of two ships. With this as a base, we devised our tactics accordingly.

"In most cases our flights (a flight of two two-ship elements) would fly almost abreast, each looking back across the tail of the other flights. This afforded complete protection from the rear in that we could see and turn towards any attack from that direction.

"When attacking enemy planes, especially fighters, we enjoyed our greatest success in chasing them down to ground level. Using our overtaking speed to good advantage, we nearly always were able to either shoot down the enemy or leave him in bad shape. One thing we had to adhere to when attacking in this fashion was to have some of our planes as top cover to protect us against rear attacks while concentrating on our own offensive.

"This top cover wasn't always available, however, and at such times we had to remember 'to look out the back way before going down the front way.' The Germans often sent decoys down to draw some of us in pursuit, and then sent in others to take on the remaining planes in combat. Usually they planned this so that we were greatly outnumbered.

"Whenever we started combat at a disadvantage, our first action was to ward off the enemy with a quick turn into the direction of the attack. Immediately after this maneuver we attempted to climb for altitude to deliver a return attack. If the situation was such that this wasn't possible, our flights would maneuver into abreast positions, which proved to be our best defensive order of flight. In this way we could continue safely until we were able to maneuver in such a way that the advantage of the next combat would favor us.

"Too much stress cannot be placed on having "the advantage of the moment" in combat. Every fighter pilot must be ready to ward off attacks when at a disadvantage and always take immediate offensive action when certain of his advantage. The uppermost thought in a pilot's mind should always be to complete his mission successfully whether it be bomber escort, fighter sweeps or reconnaissance. Upon completion of the job, he must concentrate entirely on getting back to his base. Stooging around, especially in enemy territory, without any definite purpose in view, has always brought unhappy results.

"The P-38 proved its worth as an all-round fighter by performing effectively on long-range missions, either providing fighter protection for bombers or putting on a surprise attack on ground forces well behind enemy lines. The only disadvantage, if it can be called that, was the discomfort forced on the pilot by being strapped to his seat for five or six hours at a time.

"I said it a long time ago: I'll take fighter duty and the P-38 every time. I meant it then and I wouldn't change a thing today."

The North African air war—
Case closed.

9. Across the Channel

From this point on we must break up the combat lineage of the P-38. The Lightnings operating from North Africa were now striking out to the north to encompass all the Mediterranean, Sardinia and Corsica, most of Italy, and were swinging beyond into the Balkans. Finally, mainly in the form of strategic missions of the Fifteenth Air Force, they would join the heavy bombers in pounding targets in Germany itself. This phase of the air war, especially where the P-38 is concerned, forms a separate chapter by itself, to which we will return after a study of operations from England. The Pacific waits beyond that as a P-38 story strangely removed from Europe, as though the two air wars had only the most tenuous of relationships.

In England it had become a matter of waiting for the return of the P-38s after their urgent shipment to North Africa. The emphasis on the P-38 had long abandoned its original role as an interceptor, and few Lockheed engineers would have recognized that the long-range escort fighter about which the AAF was so anxious was its original XP-38 design. The AAF, for its part, had come to admit its single most drastic error in aircraft philosophy of the war—that it had not, in fact, planned for long-range escort fighters. It had been blinded by its own doctrinal faith in the ability of the big bomber to slug it out with the best of German fighters over the continent, and the eyes of the AAF were being rudely opened by the shocking effectiveness of the enemy fighters. In fact, it was during the period that the P-38s were being blooded in North Africa, notes the AAF History, that "now under pressure of necessity engineers in the ETO and the United States combined to improve and enlarge auxiliary tanks which gave seven-league boots to conventional fighters—the P-38, P-47 and especially the P-51. To Goering's discomfiture these fighters eventually went to Berlin and beyond and mixed it with German interceptors on better than even terms, but it was months before there were enough of them to provide adequate protection."

The first of the new fighter groups with the new P-38H models arrived in England during the summer of 1943, and the 55th Group, after a succession of moves only to be described as stumbling, bumbling and frustrating, was declared operational on October 15. It pleased less people than one might have expected, since on the day before, October 14, or Black Thursday, German fighters, aided to some extent by flak, had shot down sixty B-17 bombers out of a force numbering barely more than 220 airplanes, and had so damaged another sixteen they never flew again. Had the P-38s been available one day before they might have reduced measurably the staggering loss suffered by the heavies. But the P-38s weren't available, and although the history books show the 55th Group as operational on October 15, that is stretching a point to its utmost. There exists a tremendous gap between a stated ability to operate and that level where an outfit has been blooded and functions as a gung-ho combat force.

When the 55th Fighter Group went operational (at least on the books) it joined seven P-47 fighter groups already operational with the VIII Fighter Command. The heavy Jugs, unfortunately, were sorely limited in range, and everyone longed for the Lightnings which, with two 75-gallon drop tanks, could escort bombers a distance of 520 miles from home plate.

Excerpts from the official history, *The Army Air Forces in World War II,* Vol. III, provide a concise review of the situation at the time:

On the Wilhelmshaven mission of 3 November the superior endurance now possessed by this group [55th] proved especially valuable during the farthest leg of the journey and made the escort virtually continuous throughout the bomber route. In the process the P-38's, already favored among fighters in the Mediterranean and the Pacific, saw their first real combat in the ETO and enjoyed their first victory, claiming three of the enemy without losing a single one of their number. They could probably have destroyed more but remained, according to the strict orders then governing their tactics, in close support of the bombers, warding off attacks and refusing to be drawn off in independent combat.

The AAF history then notes the great promise of the P-38H on November 13, during a pathfinder mission to Bremen when the Lightnings:

. . . demonstrated their ability to go the distance (the longest to date for fighter escort), tangle on more than equal terms with the enemy, and provide invaluable support for the bombers over the target area. The enemy fought tenaciously . . . Rocket fire had by this time become the most deadly of the tactics used by the Germans against the bomber formations, and it was consequently a matter of the keenest concern to both sides to see how effective the new long-range fighter escort would be in foiling these attacks as well as the more routine passes attempted by the single-engine Me-109's and FW-190's. Left alone after the P-47's had reached the limit of their endurance the relatively small force of forty-seven P-38's found themselves outnumbered, possibly as much as five to one. As a result they were badly mauled. Although only two of their number were known to have been shot down, five others failed to return. . . . Despite the losses and damage suffered, and despite the fact that the number of enemy aircraft shot down was not impressive, the P-38's were responsible again for holding bomber losses in the target area to a supportable level; and it could reasonably be hoped that a larger force could do the job still more effectively and with relatively less cost to the escort itself.

The P-38 was clearly a most effective fighter, and the

Germans honored it with an increasing share of attention . . .

These initial missions, with their preliminary successes, tended to obscure the wicked difficulties the fighter organizations were already encountering with the Lightnings sent to fight under the specific conditions of European skies —winter skies, especially. Starting on October 15, the P-38Hs of the 55th had begun their series of sweeps into coastal Europe to build operating experience, acquaint the pilots with combat procedures, and generally shake the bugs from their systems. One Lightning was lost on the early sweeps, but the loss was due to mechanical failure and not to enemy guns. The mission of November 3 comes a bit more alive with this excerpt from the Group's records:

As someone yelled "bombs away" I looked over and saw thousands of bombs falling on a flare marker dropped by the lead bomber. About that time flak hit one B-17 in the third box and he rolled over and spun earthward. Some of the boys say he exploded shortly after being hit. A second later, I saw two FW-190s attacking the rear of this box. I took my flight in and closed on one Hun, firing all guns. He burst into flames and spun earthward. I claimed him as destroyed. I started home "driving" along the boxes. Towards the front I noticed another box being attacked by two Me-109s. I closed in on one, fired two long bursts and he burst into flames, rolled over and bailed out. We joined up and came home without further incident. All our lads returned safely. We claimed 6 destroyed (only 3 allowed) and several damaged. Morale is sky high and the mechanics are going wild.

Good start, to say the least. Two days later the planes of the 55th Group, accompanied by more P-38s of the 20th Group, fought through rotten weather to meet Liberators high over Munster. Engine trouble forced a number of Lightnings to quit and run for home. Only one squadron, the 38th, met with the bombers over target just as German fighters and rocket-carrying bombers were going after the Liberators. Major Milton Joel, leading the Lightnings, realized at once his sixteen planes were outnumbered by about three to one. Just as quickly he led the P-38s into a fierce attack against the enemy fighters, driving them away from the Liberators, and then sticking with the bombers instead of pursuing the enemy when they were at their most vulnerable. All sixteen P-38s that engaged the enemy returned home without loss, and claimed five kills and three probables. They also held bomber losses to three planes, news that greatly satisfied bomber headquarters.

Two days later the odds changed. Focke-Wulfs bounced the P-38s while escorting Marauders. One Lightning staggered back to the Channel where the pilot bailed out. Another failed to make it home for "unknown reasons." The Germans got away without loss.

November in mid-month was a bitch when it came to flying weather; the 55th's problems were aggravated sorely by a rash of mechanical failures that sorely tried the tempers of the pilots. Of forty-eight Lightnings taking off on an escort mission, one aborted almost at once. Two more quit to go home shortly after crossing into Europe. The fighters climbed to 26,000 feet and the pilots soon were cursing bitterly. The weather was horrible, the cockpits were savagely cold, and one after the other pilots were reporting engine problems. However, the forty-five Lightnings went all the way to target with pilots stiff and numb from the cold, where they were hit with many times their number of German fighters.

Seven Lightnings went down. Five were seen to have been shot down, two more "vanished." But what brought the pilots to anger was that some of their losses resulted from engine failure in battle, leaving the planes wide open for swift German attack. One P-38H came home on one engine, riddled with over a hundred bullet holes and five big tears from cannon shell strikes. Another fifteen were heavily damaged.

On November 29 a force of Me-109s hit the Lightnings out of the sun at 31,000 feet just as they were crossing the Dutch coast. Once again, seven P-38s went down. They made claims of only three Me-109s confirmed destroyed.

Morale began to sink in the P-38 operations rooms and barracks.

Again, much of this discomfiture came from the operational headaches with the airplanes. Mechanical problems that never appeared in the North African fighting sprouted alarmingly in the airplanes operating during an English winter, and one after the other engines were failing. Worst of all to the pilots on a personal basis was the problem of bitterly cold cockpits which at times brought real physical agony in the form of frost-bitten hands and feet. Pilots swaddled themselves in heavy clothes until they walked like bears to their airplanes; anything to fight the brutal subzero temperatures in their cockpits.

Once again there arose the paradox that the airplane intended to be a high-altitude interceptor failed to perform properly at altitude, and was turning out to be a superb fighter at lower heights. Below 18,000 feet the P-38H was more than a match for the Me-109G, and could handle itself admirably against the FW-190A. Which really didn't impress the Lightning pilots too much because they were required to fight between 26,000 and 33,000 feet, and up there the engines simply couldn't hack the demands made on them. At high altitudes the rate of roll suffered, the acceleration was poorer than the opposition and the danger of compressibility restricted high-speed dives.

Before his tour of duty in the European Theater of Operations came to a close, Brigadier General Edward B. Giller, USAF, (then a major) shot down a variety of German fighters, including such types as the Me-109, Me-410, and the Me-262 jet fighter; Giller flew both P-38s and P-51s during this period. But the General's greatest value to us in this history of the P-38 is that he flew P-38s in groups first receiving the airplane and went through some of the more difficult teething periods to bring the Lightning up to snuff as an operational fighter.

In our first exchange of letters for this book, General Giller answered a list of questions I had sent him. One of those was the matter of bailing out of the P-38. Before we move on to the General's remarks, I would like to take special pains to stress to the reader that this man lacked the enthusiasm for the P-38 that came out of Africa, and was something less than exuberant about the airplane, which was certainly the attitude of the pilots who flew it in the Pacific, where it mauled Japanese fighters with terrible effectiveness. What is most important in this across-the-board evaluation of the P-38 is that Ed Giller was an extraordinary pilot, first, and also an extraordinary P-38 pilot as well. General Giller wrote:

Bailing out of the airplane was always the subject of considerable debate. However, the consensus was that you should bail out at very high speed or at very low speed just above stalling. It was intended that you would crawl out of the cockpit and slide from the wing and go out under the boom. At high speed, greater than 350 miles per hour, one would remove the canopy, roll full forward trim, then suddenly turn loose of the wheel and give yourself a kick upwards and thereby go out over the tail boom. Unfortunately, a considerable percentage of people ended up hitting the tail boom and probably accounted for a number of unsuccessful bailouts. Our group [55th Fighter Group] had little interest in rolling the aircraft on its back and trying to go out.

Going to the question of losing one engine on takeoff, I have heard many times the story of Tony LeVier taking off from the dry lake bed at Edwards Air Force Base on a single engine in a P-38 by going in ever increasing circles at higher speeds until such time as he had enough rudder control to keep the aircraft straight. Of course, Tony could fly anything. Our problem was with more of our younger inexperienced pilots with a fully loaded aircraft losing power on one engine just after liftoff, and trying to stay airborne with full power on the opposite engine with not enough rudder to maintain stability. The good engine simply pulled the aircraft over into a roll. Of course, we practiced this maneuver at altitudes and it meant reducing power somewhat on the good engine as well as rolling in opposite trim to compensate for the very high rudder pressure. It was the one thing we feared most on pilot checkout as we were almost certain to lose a pilot if this happened. Of course, the safest thing to do was to pull power off the good engine and simply land straight ahead. I remember this happening in a little village in England once where the P-38 left an engine on each side of an alley and the cockpit slid quite safely down the alley with no injury to the pilot. We often said "just land straight ahead and go between two big trees."

The question of putting Merlin engines in the P-38 was always an interesting idea to us. We often heckled the Allison technical representative with this suggestion. There were, of course, stories that Wright Field had actually done this and that the airplane had performed beautifully. However, the industrial armament firms concerned had too much power to permit the Air Corps to do this on a grand scale. How much of this is fact and how much is fiction, I am sure I don't know. However, I am sure the airplane would have been easier to maintain with a lower abort rate and perhaps even one might have been made with a good cockpit heater, but I do not believe it would have made any fundamental difference in the net outcome.

As you will recall from my previous letter, the P-38 at high altitude in England had two serious drawbacks. One, its recognition enabled the Germans to commit to attack at greater distances than we could even see them—a very real disadvantage. Two, the roll rate and dive limitations at high altitude enabled the Germans to escape by using a split-S any time they wanted to.

I seem to have trouble recalling any exciting combat incidents involving the P-38 in which I was directly involved. The group normally flew with three squadrons of sixteen each in flights of four and elements of two. Practically every mission used long-range fuel tanks which we dropped when contact was imminent. At this point, the action usually broke up the group all over the sky to the point where only a series of individual engagements between elements took place. Therefore, no one had a very clear picture of what was going on except right where he was.

There are obviously numerous incidents of excited radio conversation, people losing an engine and wanting escort home, and people shooting somebody else down. One incident perhaps of interest resulted where one squadron of sixteen was jumped by fifty Me-109s and in order to defend themselves went into a "double Lufbery" with one half of the squadron circling to the right and the other half turning to the left. This enabled us to keep from losing most of the squadron and for some reason the Germans did not stay very long or they would have run us out of gas. This was obviously a defensive maneuver and one not becoming to fighter pilots. The P-38 was just not a good aircraft at high altitudes.

Subsequent to these letters, two documents arrived from General Giller. One of these was prepared by the General with the title of "The 55th Fighter Group," and is an outstanding look inside the history of this organization and its experience with the P-38. The second document, by Kenneth J. Sorace, was a diary kept throughout his tenure with the 343rd Squadron, 55th Fighter Group.

We shall read first General Giller's study, and then Ken Sorace's diary.

10. Edward B. Giller

The 55th Fighter Group

"The 55th Fighter Group was formed in the Pacific northwest area in 1942 and as I recall, the initial cadre came from the 20th Fighter Group stationed in the San Francisco area. Approximately one hundred second lieutenants from the class of 42-D, first class from Lubbock, Texas, having trained in AT-6s and AT-9s, were sent to Paine Field, Everett, Washington, as the bulk of this new fighter group.

"When we arrived there in the middle of May 1942, things were a little confused, to say the least. There were a few old P-43s and two or three Lockheed 322s on the field. The 322 was the initial P-38 without turbosuperchargers and with aluminum gas tanks. This aircraft had fantastic performance up to about 15,000 feet and then ran out of power. What with one hundred new second lieutenants on his hands, the squadron commander had quite a job to do. There were approximately five or six first lieutenants who were our flight leaders and whose job it was to start us training on the P-38s which were beginning to be delivered about this time.

"A very sad accident occurred during the first week —four second lieutenants and a flight instructor in a C-45 made a hard landing, caught the prop tips, took off again, climbed 1,000 feet in the air, rolled over, and dove straight into Puget Sound with most of their remaining classmates watching. This was the beginning of a great number of training accidents for the 55th.

"After being at Paine Field for three weeks, two other

125

second lieutenants and myself were sent to Wright Field for one month to assist in accelerated service tests of P-38 fighters. Checkout in those days was casual, to say the least. After reading the technical order files for two hours, one climbed into this aircraft, had a civilian mechanic explain the various switches and off you went. It turned out we did not get very much P-38 time. We worked on P-40s, P-39s, and B-25s with only a few hours in P-38s. Maintenance had a miserable time keeping this aircraft in commission.

"In July, the three of us returned to our group which consisted of the 37th, 38th, and 39th squadrons which had gone to Portland for the initial checkout in the P-38. Shortly thereafter, the 38th Squadron to which I was assigned, returned to Paine Field, and, as I recall, the other two squadrons went to other bases in the general area. About this time, the 39th squadron was transferred to either Alaska or North Africa and the 37th went to the other of these two places. At that time, the 343rd and 338th squadrons were formed and I was transferred to the 343rd.

"Between the summers of 1942 and 1943, the 55th headquarters stayed primarily at McCord and the 343rd moved to Pendleton, Oregon; Olympia, Washington; and then back to McCord. The other two squadrons similarly moved around the Pacific northwest.

"During this year we spent our time in flight training of various kinds, including aerial gunnery and dive bombing, with special emphasis on weather dodging. The only radio we had was a battery-powered, low-frequency one which never seemed to work and which we didn't trust anyway. Our new UHF voice radio was also unreliable. Our lack of instrument training in flight school plus our indoctrination in the cloudy northwest increased our desire to stay out of instrument weather.

"It is during this period that we suffered many fatal accidents due to several things:

1. Engine failure on takeoff caused the aircraft to half roll and dive in. Recovery from this was very difficult and

the subject of much simulation. I will never forget one Lt. Colonel Keating who used to stand on a chair in operations and graphically attempt to demonstrate how you recovered from this.

2. Probably the greatest killer was weather. People would get caught above it and would let down into a mountain.

3. We also lost several pilots due to buzzing. At that time, it was considered great fun to fly as low as possible since there was a minimum of restrictions. Three such instances come to mind:

(a) During a horse race in Seattle, complete with Commanding General in the audience, two pilots buzzed the race to the point where they broke it up. This resulted in quite a furor.

(b) Buzzing sailboats on Puget Sound and trying to blow them over was considered fun. This resulted in killing at least two pilots by hitting the water with their props.

(c) One day somebody buzzed a large freighter which turned out to be loaded with ammunition. While it did not blow up, it sure raised a rumpus through military channels.

(d) When the squadron was stationed at Pendleton, it was considered a challenge to take off from group headquarters at McCord, fly south along the valleys to the Columbia River at Portland and then up the Columbia River gorge to just opposite the Pendleton airport so that the altimeter up to this point never read higher than the airport at Pendleton. At this point, one pulled up out of the gorge, put the wheels down and landed. You could not turn around in the gorge if the weather became bad and I dare say we lost more than one pilot to this maneuver.

(e) A final incident was getting a flight of four P-38s down inside the crater at Crater Lake, Oregon. It sure must have been noisy in there.

"I personally was involved in two deals which might be of interest. One was when I had my first command of a Flight Gunnery Camp at Burns, Oregon. We had a single 5,000-foot strip with a modest collection of tents with four airplanes plus sufficient mechanics and we rotated the pilots from our squadron at Pendleton. We lived in an old CCC camp and wore our winter flying clothes day and night. The local population was extremely friendly, throwing dances for us all the time . . . . This is where I almost ended my career by slow rolling at 100 feet over my girl friend's house and almost not making it. Often on the way from the airfield to the gunnery range, it was standard practice to fly twenty-five feet above the highway, thereby forcing all the citizens off in the ditch. How they put up with us, I will never know. Relaxation consisted of shooting rabbits with submachine guns and pheasant hunting with our skeet ammunition. We shot 100 pheasants one afternoon and fed the entire camp for three days.

"The other incident of command was when the Japanese submarines were scaring the northwest by letting out a single-engine plane from their deck with a few fire bombs. We stationed a flight of four aircraft and mechanics on Moon Island located at Hoquiam, Washington. At high tide, this strip was a mile long and 300 feet wide. We were continually being scrambled and chasing mythical targets that we never did see. We got into trouble here by shooting up the seals on the beaches.

"During this year of training we did a considerable amount of ground gunnery and dive bombing with practice targets, and a lot of acrobatics between 10,000 and 15,000 feet, never going much higher. The aircraft was a delight to fly in acrobatics in that it was completely stable and no maneuver was forbidden with the exception of extremely high speed dives, which resulted in compressibility with a complete reversal of stick forces. We lost several pilots to this characteristic. At high speed the dive fillets would blow off followed by the canopy popping off and then complete disintegration. The airplane was extremely stable on one or two engines and was very forgiving.

There was a control center at Seattle which directed us against unknown aerial targets in the local area.

"We always had a flight on alert which meant sleeping at the end of the runway in a tent in your flying clothes and ready to leap off on a few minutes' notice. Occasionally, when things were dull we would take off in the middle of the night and fly up over Seattle to give the searchlight crews practice as well as wake up personnel in the control center. Several clear nights the fellows attempted some aerobatics and in one case, an attempted loop resulted in a pilot going straight in.

"This was our first exposure to night flying in the P-38 and we learned how really red those superchargers were and when you cut back the throttle, fire gushed forth in great amounts, so much so that all new pilots immediately thought they were on fire until some calmer voice assured them this was SOP.

"Life for those who survived was a ball. We enjoyed flying very much and, of course, our social life. We also thought the P-38 was a very fine aircraft and were eager to take it into combat. Those that survived became quite proficient in the aircraft and fairly accomplished in ground gunnery and dive bombing but not so good in aerial target practice. It was very difficult to get enough of this due to the shortage of tow planes. One incident here might be of interest.

"The squadron was assigned a B-34 which was a Lockheed Ventura built originally for the British. We used this as a tow plane. Remember this was a middle-sized twin-engine bomber. At 7,000 feet one day, Lieutenant (now Colonel) R. C. Franklin had the following experience: When the gunnery was completed, the target was released by letting a ring slide out the cable to the end, thereby tripping the tow target. There was a weight at the end of the cable which gyrated wildly while the cable was being reeled in. There was an enlisted man who operated the electric reel in the rear of the plane and in this particular instance, as the end of the cable approached the tail of the aircraft, the weight became lodged in the crack next to the trim tab in the horizontal stabilizer (elevator). The cable reel was running at full speed and immediately pulled the whole elevator full down, resulting, of course, in the stick flying upward to the instrument panel and putting the airplane in a full nosedown maneuver. This threw the reel operator to the ceiling away from his reel. The pilot in a last desperate attempt, heading straight for the ground, put both feet on the instrument panel and, being a large man and assisted by considerable adrenalin, pulled the stick back, actually bending the trim tab such that the weight came out of the slot. Recovery was affected at 300 feet. Needless to say, that whole crew had a week off.

"The group was alerted for overseas deployment in August and departed by troop train to Camp Kilmer on the 22nd. The mood was . . . one of reckless abandonment as far as any concern was felt. As we sat in the back of the observation car, which was promptly made into a bar, we amused ourselves by shooting insulators off telegraph wires at 60 miles per hour. The train stopped twice a day for exercise. At one small town in Illinois we marched the whole squadron through a saloon where everybody drank a bottle of beer on the way through. Also, the saloonkeeper delivered forty cases of mixed alcoholic beverages to the train just before we pulled out of the station. Two of us bummed a ride in the locomotive cabin for a couple of hundred miles and decided that was a lot more dangerous than flying airplanes.

"We arrived at Camp Kilmer 27 August, then spent one week preparing for embarkation. On 4 September we embarked on His Majesty's transport *Orion,* 300 officers and 6,200 enlisted men on a boat whose normal load was 1,500. Things were a bit crowded. There were 150 lieutenants in one room stacked seven deep. Enlisted men in the holes were truly worse off. The British cooks were less than satisfactory and there is nothing like a combination in one large dishpan of two gallons of stewed tomatoes, one gallon of oatmeal, and a gallon of scrambled eggs all generously mixed together.

"We arrived in Scotland on 15 December and disembarked for our airfield known as Nuthampstead. This place was promptly named Mudhapstead due to the tremendous amount of mud always present. The complete story by K. J. Sorace [which will be our next chapter] contains information you will find useful at this point.

"Our first P-38s showed up on 21 September. We spent the next few weeks getting our aircraft ready and learning the English countryside.

"On 15 October the 55th went operational with a short penetration over Holland. In this case, the group was headed by a colonel from another operational outfit who came along for our first show. The 20th Group with P-38s also was in England and went operational shortly after the 55th.

"The Sorace document gives more detail of our activities for the rest of the year. It is during this time that we began to learn some of the more important shortcomings of the P-38 in European combat. The first few weeks were spent in short-range escort duty of B-26s in France and eventually one day we picked up long-range escort of the B-17s after the P-47s had gone home. This left the 55th alone with the entire German fighter force and the bombers. We discovered several major items during this period:

1. We were forced to go to very high altitude, 30,000 to 35,000 feet. Even so, the Germans went way above us.

2. The Germans would escape by a split-S maneuver from these altitudes and the P-38 could not follow due to compressibility.

3. The twin tails provided positive recognition for the Germans at distances greater than we could see them. Therefore our initial engagements were always at a disadvantage.

4. This was the world's coldest airplane and we tried every combination of suit, glove and heater imaginable, including some that would short out and give you a hot

foot. We were so cold sometimes we did not even want to fight.

5. Flying around 30,000 feet resulted in extreme fouling of the plugs in the Allison engine as well as a great number of thrown rods and swallowed valves. Needless to say, a P-38 on a single engine was in an unenviable condition. Our record during this period was very poor, about 1.5 Germans shot down to each American lost to all causes.

6. Returning to England with considerable undercast always presented a severe problem of location. We had only four channels of VHF which were always crowded. Once over England we could only let down straight ahead until you could see the ground. Needless to say, several people let down into the ground. The other P-38 groups were operating with the same problem as the 55th. But one thing we liked about the P-38 was its instrument flying stability.

"This period also dampened somewhat the normal frighter pilot's aggressiveness and we became perhaps a little defensive-minded. This was never really cured until the group was equipped with P-51s at which time the kill ratio jumped to about seven to one.

"During the spring of 1944, the long-range P-51s became more numerous which improved the escort safety of the B-17. As D-Day approached, we took to ground strafing of mostly locomotives and other rolling stock. During this time another feature of the P-38 showed up: having two engines doubled the chances of being hit. However, instead of being able to come home on the other engine, the damaged engine caught fire, thereby forcing you to bail out. They never did put fire extinguishers on that aircraft. The gun camera was located with the guns and the resulting vibration practically guaranteed we would get little gun camera film. We finally mounted the camera in the wing and obtained some reasonable pictures in late spring. The P-38 was used during the invasion as local beach cover because of its recognizable form. Nevertheless, it was discouraging to see the local U.S. gunners shooting at us whenever we flew over their ships. There were so many American airplanes over the beaches that flight collision was the greatest hazard. The controller would give a grid location of a bogie and at least 200 airplanes would converge on that spot.

"I shall now relate a few incidents:

"On leaving our new base at Wormingsford, which was near Colchester, in support of the D+2 Day operations, *my squadron passed in the soup through a full group of B-26s going in the opposite direction.* This is, to say the least, a hair-raising experience. Fortunately, there were no midair collisions.

"In the spring of 1944, a technical expert with some drums of 150-octane gasoline showed up at our airbase. This they claimed would give us 10 percent more power on our engines. The stuff was so corrosive everybody had to wear rubber gloves when fueling an aircraft. After one or two ships tried it out, we loaded the whole group and took off on a mission. After 90 minutes out on low cruise, many engines began to run rough followed shortly thereafter by many engines throwing a rod. The whole mission was aborted and we staggered back to England. On landing, examination of the plugs showed every one to be so fully leaded that they looked like a solid chunk of the metal. Every plug in that squadron had to be changed plus over half of the engines. Needless to say, that expert and his gasoline were drummed out of England. The test unit in the United States never tested the gasoline under our conditions.

"The maintenance on the P-38 was something to behold. It was an extremely closely cowled engine with much piping and no space. The mechanics did a magnificent job with extremely long hours of tediously trying to fix coolant leaks, rough engines, etc. It was truly a crew chief's nightmare. The plane employed oleo shocks on all three landing gear struts. These had a habit of leaking as soon as it got cold and required considerable maintenance to reinflate. The turbosupercharger regulator had a delightful habit of freezing at high altitude, resulting in only two throttle settings available, 10 inches of mercury, which would not sustain flight, or 80 inches, which would blow up a supercharger. I recall one very cold day over the Ruhr Valley where both the pilots and the regulators were so frozen that, in spite of the heavy flak in that vicinity, we let down to 3,000 feet to warm up both us and the airplane.

"Some time during the spring of 1944, the American heavy bombers started going to Berlin. There is some argument as to who was the first fighter group there. However, I think the 55th was. This occurred on a day in which we were scheduled to escort the B-17s over a target in Berlin. However, the bombers were recalled about 200 miles short of target. The 55th didn't get the word and we went the whole route over Berlin, although there were clouds up to 30,000 feet. We didn't see anything but a little flak.

"We didn't usually worry about individual flak and fighters; however, the barrage flak which occurred over the cities we tended to avoid. On our first few missions over Bremen, we flew into the flak with the bombers along with the German fighters. Shortly thereafter, we adopted the tactic of leaving the bombers when they entered the heavy flak and joining them when they came out. The Germans did likewise. However, there were single flak batteries located on the Dutch coast. I recall one day our Commander, Major Webb, and three others, in box formation, received a single burst dead center in the box from one of these very efficient batteries. This resulted in three of them making the rest of the trip on a single engine. After that when everybody crossed the coast, they used the evasive pattern of making unscheduled turns of 30 degrees every 30 seconds and changing altitude every two minutes.

"The 55th was much more efficient at ground strafing, leaving aside the vulnerability question, and we tended to shoot up much railroad rolling stock, including an enormous number of locomotives. The aircraft was more than a match for the German fighters at this altitude but they very seldom engaged.

"Prior to the Normandy invasion, the 55th took to bombing with a Droop Snoot. This was a P-38 with the guns removed from the nose section, a bombardier position and bomb sight installed. There was no way for this fellow to get out in the air. The whole squadron or group would be loaded with either 1,000-pound bombs or anti-personnel bombs and then go over the targets in very tight formation; everybody would drop on the bombardier's countdown. I don't think our bombing was extremely effective. I remember dive bombing a French bridge which resulted in one 1,000-pound bomb going into an enormous greenhouse and it probably set back the brussel sprout production for a whole year. Another 1,000-pounder went into a huge haystack and as a result, there was hay in the air at 2,000 feet. I am not sure anybody hit the bridge.

"Some time during May or June 1944, we received our last model of the P-38 which had both hydraulic-boosted ailerons and dive flaps on the underside of the wing. This was to enable us to have a faster roll rate and to dive from high altitude with the German fighters. It accomplished this to a certain degree.

"In summary, I think the consensus of the 55th and of all P-38 groups in England would be that the P-38 was not really suited for the European continent combat, for reasons which I described above, but I will list them again:

1. Recognition.

2. Pilot comfort.

3. Engine problems at high altitude.

4. Roll rate.

5. Dive limitations.

6. Fire vulnerability.

When all the groups converted to P-51s in the summer of 1944, their kill rate and morale zoomed. This story, of course, is not the same for the Pacific."

EDWARD B. GILLER

11. The Sorace Diary

The diary that makes up this chapter was written by Kenneth J. Sorace, a P-38 pilot with the 343rd Squadron, 55th Fighter Group. It covers the period of August 11, 1943 through June 12, 1944. I have taken the liberty of editing this diary only to the extent of deleting personal material.

"This story starts with a parachute jump. It really can't start with the jump because one needs to reason for a parachute jump. So, I'll start it with a mid-air collision of two P-38s. The author had his airplane's tail cut off in a simulated dogfight over Olympia, Washington on **August 11, 1943.** The jump was successful but I suffered a sprained ankle. After eight days of hospitalization I was released to join my group leaving for overseas.

"**September 20, 1943.** In the past four days since our arrival at Station 131 (England) several things have happened. The arrival day was quiet and everyone was glad to get some sleep that night. We live in small hutments made of corrugated steel and wood. Our sole heating unit is a potbellied stove, very small indeed! Friday, the 17th, we walked around the post doing very little. We had a lecture on security and were told what we could write in the way of letters and were told of our general conduct in the ETO.

"**September 21, 1943.** Today marked the arrival of three P-38s for the group. We were assigned one but the shakedown inspection and general looking over took up most of the day so no one got a chance to fly it.

"**September 22, 1943.**   The group bigwigs, Colonel James, Colonel Jenkins and Major Crowell took our ships on a flight and did a poor job of buzzing the field. In the afternoon I took a thirty-minute ride in our ship and found that the forty-day layoff hadn't bothered much. We still have no ammo for our guns so our ships are nose light.

"**September 27, 1943.**   More airplanes came in today. Lectures on recognition and air-sea rescue take up our time. Rollo more or less started operations today with a meeting and an assignment to flights. I have May, Fluty, Dripps, Porter, Birtoiel and a Captain Guthrie from the group.

"**September 28, 1943.**   The arrival of some typical English weather—rain, drizzle, and showers all day. The beautiful countryside turned into a sea of mud and bicycle travel became a tough proposition. Time spent on the line seemed to be wasted. Organization is definitely lacking.

"**October 4, 1943.**   Monday. Things have been dragging along rather quietly. We have had a few geography lessons and the squadron pilots went up to visit a Norwegian Spitfire squadron last Friday. Other than that, nothing startling has occurred. Our stock of airplanes has reached ten but lack of tools prevents us from flying them. There is an air of restlessness among the group and tempers are getting a real test. If only we could start doing something I'm sure everything would smooth out.

"**October 11, 1943.**   It has been a long week. The tension of inactivity is telling on most of us. On the 9th I took my flight on a cross-country. It was about a two-hour ride around and the biggest thing I learned was that the visibility over here is really bad. We made out O.K. but I was plenty glad when I got my six ships safely around. Sunday, the 10th, was a rather quiet day and the thick fog that arrived then is still here. There is no flying to speak of but two more ships were ferried in. Operations are running pretty smoothly now. I had a talk with Jimmy May and find that my qualms about my short temper, his actions and mine were well-founded. As he described it, ever since my accident my actions have been cold toward almost everyone. All my boys resented them and I feel that I am very much to blame. It will take considerable effort on my part to restore their faith in me and for us all to get in the groove together both on the ground and in the air.

"**Tuesday, the 12th.** A very quiet day. The main activity was centered around the parachute room where Sgt. Hicks was fitting dinghies to our chutes and working on our flying clothes. About 25 war correspondents arrived around noon and looked over our airplanes and talked with our pilots. Their purpose in being here was apparently to give out advance information and ballyhoo about P-38s in this theater.

"**Wednesday the 13th.** A poor day but the squadron did get fourteen ships in the air and we all logged another hour's time.

"**Thursday the 14th.** We were scheduled for a mission today but it was scrubbed. The weather was really poor all day so little was actually accomplished. Carey passed out Landmark Folders and scheduled me for a lecture tomorrow on the geography of the Dutch Coast.

"**Friday, October 15, 1943.** Today was a gala day for the 55th Fighter Group. In the morning I gave my geography lecture as planned and we did a bit of code work with lights. At noon word was passed around that we were to be briefed at 1300. We assembled in Group HQ and were told of a fighter sweep to be accomplished at 1400. Everyone came through in fine shape considering the advance notice on the mission. Thirty-six ships cleared the ground in eight minutes and completed a two-hour sweep over the Dutch Coast going in at Schowen Island at 25,000 feet, circling inland and coming out near Ostend. All ships performed O.K. The only enemy activity noted was a flak burst of about 20 shells near Ostend. Flights consisted of Major Webb, Barnett, Ryan, Stevenson, Captain Malmstedt, May, Giller, Buttke, Captain Franklin, Hooper. Sorace and Fluty. We are operational AT LAST!

"Saturday the 16th. D-Flight wasn't scheduled to fly today so we missed out on two missions. Carey and Kelly awakened the pilots at 0630 and at 0900 they took off on a bomber escort mission as a diversionary raid. The afternoon brought forth another sweep with the whole group out again. Things are getting in the groove again.

"Sunday the 17th. The day dawned gray and dark but by noon showed promise of clearing. All missions had been cancelled so we started to relax. Around 1500 a sweep was called with Colonel Jenkins leading. Due to inadequate preparation it turned out to be a farce as we barely touched the French coast at Boulogne.

"Monday the 18th. We were scheduled for a bomber escort deal but as we left our coast we were informed that the bombers had aborted. We continued on and swept the area of the Dutch Islands anyhow. There were 50-plus enemy fighters in our vicinity but we never found them and didn't get into any scrap.

"Tuesday the 19th. D-Flight finally flew its own flight! Sorace, Birtoiel, May and Fluty. It was a cold mission and a nice long sweep over the French coast. We entered at St. Valerie and went out around Calais. We saw no enemy fighters and are as yet "virgin" fighters.

"Wednesday the 20th. D-Flight didn't fly but the group flew withdrawal support for some B-17s. There were enemy fighters in the vicinity but no action for our boys.

"**Thursday the 21st.** Kelley and Carey got us up at 0430 to be briefed for a mission at 0700. As it turned out, rain caused the mission to be scrubbed; we all retired to bed until noon. In the afternoon the group flew a show bomber escort mission for the newsreels. Giller, Hooper and I matched coins for the squadron leader honors and I won, or lost, as the case may be. The mission was completed successfully but we all found out some of the limitations of belly tanks as we lost about ten in the group. They appear to be dropping off because of faulty mechanical release that we put on the ships over here.

"**Friday the 22nd.** Today we had a mission. It was planned for us to escort seventy-two B-26s over Cambrai, France. The Field Order came late and the entire briefing and takeoff was rushed. To further complicate matters, Colonel James' brakes locked and prevented his takeoff. One Colonel and two Majors from the 20th Group arrived to fly with us and to top it off the weather was really poor. We carried belly tanks which we were to drop at the French coast. Only the 343rd arrived at the rendezvous on time and escorted the bombers. Rollo lost the rest of the squadron a short way inland and so we started home in a four-ship flight. The ceiling was below 10,000 feet and as we were under it, we encountered considerable light flak as we came over the coast. Some tracer and HE were shot up but no hits noted. Rollo had no radio or compass so finally back over England I took the flight and brought them home. Had to pump my wheels down. We had one scare over France when Smith popped out of the overcast and joined our flight. We thought at first that he was a Jerry. The mission could not be called successful as only one squadron went over and really bad weather prevented decent escort. Major Webb claims to have seen three Me-109s over in France.

"**Saturday, October 23, 1943.** Today, the 343rd got its first taste of combat! We were briefed at 0900 for an escort mission at 1130. With Rollo leading and I flying

Colonel Jenkins' second element (No. 2 Flight) we met seventy-two B-26s at mid-Channel at 12,000 feet and took them about sixty miles into France. Near the target, when our section of eight ships was about three miles from the bombers,, we were bounced from above by two FW-190s and two Me-109s. Rollo broke into them and Colonel Jenkins got a short burst at one FW-190. For a few minutes they gave us a lot to look out for. Fluty was in the last flight and had to do a lot of turning to shake an Me-109 off his tail. We were the only ones to have any fights and the other squadrons were a bit jealous. On a sortie basis I now have eight missions but actually have made only six trips. After lunch I tested my new ship again with a new prop on the right engine. That was the trouble and "Ole 66" is now O.K.

"Monday, October 25. We slept late again due to bad weather. It was a much needed rest for all of us and as the weather continued bad we were released until tomorrow morning.

"Thursday. Still foggy! Tempers are getting shorter and the bad weather is getting longer. Squabbles between the group bigwigs and squadron C.O.'s are getting worse. To be frank, this damned weather and inactivity is raising hell with everyone. The sooner we start flying again the better.

"Friday. Oh joy! Oh bliss! Dinghy drill! We took a trip over to Saffron Waldes and tried out our dinghies in a swimming pool. Sure felt nice to go swimming again. The rest of the day with the fog was the same as yesterday. Damn it! Why doesn't the weather clear up so we can fly?

"Saturday, October 30. As if someone had heard our plea, the dawn broke with pretty fair weather and with a mission scheduled. Briefing at 0945, takeoff set for 1115 —a B-24 escort down into the Ruhr Valley. The weather kept getting worse but we took off anyhow as planned. We climbed through a low overcast in very poor formation and everyone immediately got lost. Major Webb, leading three flights, attempted to bring his formation home but Ryan took his element above the stuff and both Giller's and my flight followed him. We wandered around over the overcast until finally I left his formation and started to bring my four ships through the stuff directly over the field. Fluty got split off then and even with perfect vectors home got lost and landed, with disastrous results, at an R.A.F. base about six miles from home. He completely wrecked his ship when he overshot. Ships are on the ground all over England. Malmstedt and flight will not be home tonight. It has been a sad day for the 343rd. Can't understand Fluty's mistake but we are all thankful that all pilots are safe!

"Tuesday, November 2, 1943. A late rising again and little of interest. Bad weather 'til noon. In the afternoon Hooper and I tried out some camera gunnery with only a 1,500-foot ceiling and poor visibility. We also had quite a time with some P-47s. The last remaining members of the squadron, ten in number, finally went to dinghy drill.

"Wednesday, November 3. A big show scheduled and off we went to escort some B-17s to Wilhelmshaven. We carried two belly tanks and had quite a time of it. Our squadron did most of the work. Major Webb had to go home so I ended up leading my own flight. Saw my first ship shot down when a B-17 gunner set an FW-190 on fire. Got a shot at an FW-190 myself and my wingman, Porter, also shot at him, possibly crippling him. We saw him spin out after we fired and May says he spun into the overcast. Kelly talked us into claiming a probable. The squadron claimed three destroyed, five probable, and one damaged. Colonel Jenkins got one for sure and Buttke got two. We all learned a lot from the mission and only Bauer ended up with holes in his ship. And so to bed—early!

"**Thursday, November 4.** Bad weather all day. The pictures Hooper and I took were no good due to poor weather conditions.

"**Friday, November 5.** Another big mission scheduled for Munster. A B-24 escort in and out of the target. Only the 38th succeeded in rendezvousing with the B-24s but we spent three and one half hours cruising around Germany with our belly tanks on. We were practically to Berlin but were not bothered by fighters. We saw plenty of heavy flak over the Dutch Islands and Amsterdam and saw a lot of enemy territory. The 38th destroyed five enemy fighters.

"**Sunday, November 7, 1943.** Our S-2's made general nuisances of themselves at a very early hour today by announcing a briefing at 0730 and dragging us out of bed around 0545. The mission turned out to be a B-26 escort to an aerodrome near Paris. The eight ships of the 20th Group were bottom cover for the box and when eight or ten Germans came through head-on, Herb Cummings was hit. After feathering one engine and trying to come home, he bailed out over the channel and hasn't been seen or heard of since. Their executive officer, a Major, took off after the mission and just disappeared into thin air. Two planes and pilots lost and no victories for our side! The bombing was not completed due to an overcast over the target but the escort was highly successful and instructive. The afternoon mission was a sweep over Lille. We didn't scare up anything exciting. We all went to bed plenty tired. One thing we did prove in the afternoon was that the 343rd can really fly a good formation. We had a beautiful sixteen-ship flight with Malmstedt, Giller, Franklin and Sorace leading the four-ship elements.

"**Monday.** The S-2 section was awake bright and early again and got us up in our cold barracks. The weather was none too sharp and the mission was scrubbed before briefing.

"**Tuesday.** Not up too early and not scheduled to fly. Around noon there was a briefing for a sweep over France at 12,000 feet but at takeoff it was scrubbed. The 338th got off the ground but came back right away.

"**Wednesday.** Not up very early as the day was a bit wet. By noon it had cleared and so the group was briefed for a B-26 raid near Paris. No bombs were dropped and there was no action. Reihmer picked up a few flak holes while flying too close to the bombers. No hits, no runs, no errors! Yours truly was Flight Control Officer but everyone came back O.K. and so landings were uneventful. Only highlight was DeYoung trying to burn up his tires and brakes.

"We had five aborts out of eighteen ships which was rather poor. Major Webb is getting discouraged. He has had about four aborts in a row now.

"**Thursday, November 11—Armistice Day.** Tried to have a big mission of Forts to Munster and the Ruhr but everything got screwed up. Never did get to the Dutch Coast and spent two and a half hours flying over the North Sea. Either our entire group aborted or the Forts did; the facts are not straight as yet. Jimmy May and I had a big talk together about the squadron and feel firmly convinced there is much internal friction and a definite clique running things to suit their personal whims. Oh, well; we are just cogs in the wheels so can't complain. It does seem, however, that some of the "cogs" are a bit noisy and in need of some "repair."

"**Sunday.** (After spending two days in London) caught an early train back and reading the papers found we had missed a big raid to Bremen. Arriving home we found six pilots had been lost and nine other planes too beat up to be flyable!

"**Monday.** The whole group is licking its wounds from Saturday's raid. Started to get busy again on painting of the ships but had little success due to the cold weather.

"Thursday.   A lovely morning but no combat missions scheduled. Hooper and I took off around 1430 for camera gunnery and landed at Wittering after chasing around the area for a half hour hunting for it. We were even attacked by an FW-190 over our own country. It was, of course, a captured one. We came back about 1730. I was leading back and Hooper insisted on flying close formation even in the dimming light. Well, that's all, brother; he got a little too close and cut off my right rudder with his left wing. My plane was a bit unmanageable so I dropped my belly tanks and landed with only a little difficulty. I was really angry, both at Hooper and also because my ship was damaged. I spent four hours in the hangar, from 8 P.M. to midnight, helping my crew put on a new rudder. After we got "Pitter Pat" back in shape I took all the boys working there to the Pilots' Room for coffee and sandwiches.

"Friday.   A warning order came through for a mission and briefing was scheduled for 0900. The weather was bad but everyone expected to go anyhow. Colonel Jenkins decided not to go and although all the 343rd was parked on the runway for a half hour we didn't take off. As it turned out the bombers needed no escort as no fighters came up. Lt. Proctor and I took the Cub for a weather hop in the afternoon and shortly afterwards Lts. Suiter and Bailey from the tower ran into a truck with it and wrecked it. All the "Docs" are really sorry to see it cracked up because that's the only way they get their flying time.

"Saturday, November 20.   A welcome addition to the squadron arrived tonight when Goudelock showed up. D-Flight is now all back together!

"Sunday, November 21.   Started teaching Goudelock all I know about combat and the squadron, group, wing, and 8th Fighter. With so few pilots in commission we can use him. Jimmy May with his "game" arm is doing most of the work getting the new boys ready for their first missions.

"**Friday, December 3.** In the hospital with the flu! To take up the story where I left off on the 20th of November. There was little activity until I went on a 48-hour leave on the 24th. The next day the squadron went on a sweep, at 12,000 feet to St. Omer covering a P-47 dive bombing attack. Our first casualty occurred that day when Aldecoa was seen to bail out after his plane was shot up. Everyone figures he stands a good chance of coming back O.K.

"The following day, **Friday the 26th,** the group escorted B-17s to Bremen again without loss of fighters.

"The two days activity netted Rollo a destroyed and a probable and the Major a destroyed. Giller's previous claim of a destroyed Ju-88 was confirmed so R.C. must now shave off his moustache.

"**Sunday** night a warning order came through for a mission. Sorace was all eager to go but Doc confined me to bed.

"**Monday's** mission was a sad one, to Bremen again, and the group turned up seven men missing. Among them Major Joe, C.O. of the 38th and his flight, and Gilbride from our squadron. Franklin and Gil had gone back alone to help some boys in trouble and Gil turned up "missing in action" trying to help R.C. We have lost a really good pilot.

"**Tuesday's** mission lost one from the 20th in the Channel but he is reported safe now.

"**Wednesday** the 38th lost a man over the Ruhr and Turner crashed in England; Penn landed out of gas in a peach orchard and washed out his ship. George had one engine shot up and came all the way out of Germany at 2,000 feet on that one engine over flak areas and an FW-190 aerodrome but still got home safely—some job!

"**Thursday** should be outlined in black—one of the most tragic accidents during our time here occurred on this 2nd of December. On the takeoff of a test flight in his own ship, Rollo lost his left engine. He tried desperately to save the ship, doing a complete barrel roll at 1,000 feet in an attempt to level the ship and belly-land it, but it mushed in with the left wing very low and completely disintegrated. Rollo was a good pilot and a bold one, his is a great loss, but to turn an old proverb: "There are no old, bold pilots.""

"**Monday, December 13.**   The happenings of the past ten days have included several Bremen missions with no loss of planes or pilots. Seven new pilots arrived and R.C., as the new operations officer, rearranged the flights, taking Fluty from me and adding Lloyd on the end. May is still grounded with his fractured arm so Fluty will still fly with us for a while.

"D-Flight started working again with a scheduled escort for yesterday and a mission of escort to Kiel today. Around the target area Goudelock lost his left engine and Dripps, George (338th) and I escorted him back from Germany. On reaching England Jim headed for the nearest field and tried desperately to save his ship by making a single-engine landing. On his last turn into the field his right engine failed due to lack of gas and he crashed in the village of Ludham. Through a miracle he lived through it although the plane was completely demolished and burned immediately. We landed and made certain that he was taken care of and sent to a hospital. Things are running along in pretty good shape now and morale has improved noticeably. We are getting more ships from the 20th Group and have a P-38J-5—sounds like a good deal!

"**Wednesday, December 29, 1943.**   It looks as though your narrator has been lazy and I'm afraid that is the most correct explanation. Our boy Goudelock has returned to the fold but still cannot fly due to a nasty gash on his head that is not completely healed. May returned to flying for one day and then was hospitalized for a week with a bad cold. Dripps also had a session in the hospital so D-Flight hit another new low in flyable pilots. We have had several raids since Kiel and I had to abort twice when my airplane failed to operate properly at altitude. It seems to be fixed now but I'm keeping my fingers crossed. These airplanes have around a hundred hours and are starting to have more things go wrong more often. . . . My new boy Lloyd seems to be shaping up O.K. and I think he will become a welcome addition. Frankly, Porter has me a bit worried. Something is lacking in him but I can't find out what. Perhaps it's just he talks a much better flight than he realizes he flies. Fluty has been putting out a rather sad performance lately, too. His main trouble seems to be a slight lack of ability, a tremendous lack of confidence, and a lack of desire to accept responsibility. Although D-Flight is low on time and missions, I'm sure the boys can and will produce if Doc and I can manage to keep them flying. R.C. has really been swell about giving my boys a chance to fly to get them caught up. Operations has started the ball rolling to get rid of some of our deadwood men among the new boys and will undoubtedly transfer Chelohowski, Vieck, and Marshall. It is too bad these things have to happen but it is for the good of all of us.

"**January 14, 1944.** We have to add Barnett, Larson and Kenning to our "missing" list. Larson went down in France, New Year's Eve. Barney and Kenning were lost over Kiel. A recent raid over Ludwigshafen netted me a damaged Me-109. With Birtoiel and Major Cromwell behind me, I chased two Me-109s away from a P-38 but couldn't get on their tail before they split-essed and went down.

"**February 9, 1944.** Almost a full month has passed since my last entries due primarily to my own laziness but a contributing factor was a bit of heavy flying. The end of January was rather quiet but February has kept us on our toes with nine missions in ten days. All of them were good long ones but our P-38Js have been doing rather well with their wing tanks and all of us have been coming back with plenty of gas. One rather rough mission took its toll of the 38th when Love, Steiner, and several other of the boys turned up missing. We netted seven destroyed for six of our boys missing. A show below Paris several days ago gave Tommy Beaird a destroyed Me-109 when he chased after one on the deck. The following day another show in the same area resulted in a loss of Lieutenants Ashton and Sumpter. Ashton was shot down by an FW-190 and Sumpter spun into the Channel after a mid-air collision with another P-38. We have not been able to determine if Sumpter ever got out or not. Such losses are a bit hard to take and with Hiner and Stephenson away at an O.T.U. training new pilots, we are in pretty bad shape trying to keep the squadron "in the blue." A bunch of boys from Italy came up the end of last month and took all our P-38Hs down with them. We have also got in a new bunch of Js including some silver ones.

"**February 27, 1944.** Life has been pretty hectic recently with a bunch of long-range escort missions to places like Leipzig, Gotha, Regensburg, and close to Berlin itself. There have been no big kills but Hooper shot down a 210 and Giller got his second one, an Me-410, on the latest Regensburg raid. The last one on the 25th was perhaps the most successful trip I have been on. The weather from the French coast in was CAVU, flak was light, the bomber rendezvous was good, and the bombing results were excellent. Our effectiveness was slightly hampered by the appearance of several P-51s in our area just as we were about to chase some 410s. Tibbetts failed to return from a mission to Gotha, reason unknown. There was one other combat loss in the group since last writing and one of our Js crashed around the 14th. Other squadron news includes the transfer of Major Franklin to the 20th Group and the promotion of Buttke to Flight Leader of A-Flight. Changing of flights now leaves me with May, Dripps, Goudelock, Lloyd, Coggeshell, and a new boy, Weisel. Giller has operations and should be really doing O.K. Buttke is close to becoming an ace since he got two more twin-engine ships around Brunswick and had a rough ride home on one engine.

"May 21, 1944. It is over two months since the last entry was made in here. Losses in the squadron include Fluty, who spun in and was killed; Penners, MIA, and Captain Guthrie, MIA. Lloyd caught on fire and was not heard of. Gourley, a new boy, went the same way. Tony Piscitelli bought it over an aerodrome near Paris when he was hit and exploded. Other group losses have been light. Victories . . . add one for Ryan, two more for Buttke (six now), one for Porter and a probable for DeYoung. It all sounds pretty good but there have been some rough times. Our group was alerted to move to Wormingford near Colchester; we moved the middle of April. Giller took over the squadron and I was sent to Milfield near Edinburg for Flight Leaders School.

"June 5, 1944. Nancy and I were married May 26, 1944, first by a registrar in Colchester . . . a cold cere- mony entirely without fanfare or feeling and then at a gay affair by Chaplain Bill in the chapel on the base. At a crucial moment, eight P-38s buzzed us nearly taking the roof off. We had four days together in London but were back on the 1st of June to go to work. We have been alterted for D-Day. The ground crews are painting stripes on the ships, on the wings and tails. Its going to be a big show!

"June 12, 1944. We have patrolled until we can't move any more. We fly twelve-ship squadrons and have been patrolling sections across the channel. Flights leave an hour and a half before daylight. Patrols are two to three hours long. The last patrol gets home an hour and a half after dark. Ryan forgot his wheels the other night and washed out his ship. We were forced to land our patrol on the South Coast several nights ago because Jerry was over. It's a rough fight but Jerry hasn't been up in daylight yet."

KENNETH J. SORACE

That was the last entry. It is believed Sorace went down in France soon afterward, survived, and spent a hectic period evading the enemy.

12. LeVier in Europe

Early in 1944 Tony LeVier received orders to get to Europe—fast. He was to visit P-38 bases and demonstrate the Lightning to pilots who held less than polite opinions of the airplane, and whose effectiveness in combat, because of their gun-shy attitude, was being reduced dangerously. As Tony noted: "Although this plane had done a remarkable job in the North African campaign and was now being used successfully in Italy, new problems arose when it went operational out of England.

"To begin with, very little testing had been done at higher altitudes in cold weather, and air temperatures were much colder in that part of the world compared with southern California. What had caught up with us, as well as others, was the fact that the P-38 was primarily designed as a short-range fighter-interceptor and not as a long-range escort fighter. Like other fighters, it had great capabilities, but it would take time to develop them.

"Ward found the morale of the pilots was the biggest problem. There were a lot of sharp boys but they were spread too thin through the ranks, and even many of them had much to learn about the P-38. Some of the problems confronting us in England were a sudden increase in engine failures, malfunctioning of the turbosuperchargers, and most dreaded of all, the compressibility dive that was almost sure to cause a crash and often kill the pilot. If an engine quits that's bad; a troublesome supercharger is almost as bad; and if the poor pilot freezes because of a poorly-heated cockpit you are defeated before you

153

start. It was these and many other things that troubled us."

Upon arriving in England: ". . . After drawing my flight equipment I was immediately driven to Nuthampstead, headquarters of the 55th Fighter Group, which was the first P-38 group in England to go operational the preceding October. Ward Beman and Phil Nelson were waiting for me, together with Glenn Fulkerson, one of our most experienced P-38 crew chiefs, who was on loan from Lockheed Overseas Corporation at Langford Lodge in northern Ireland. The airplane assigned to Major Webb, a squadron commander, was waiting for me, and within an hour after arriving at this base I made my first test flight in England.

"Ward had already outlined the test to be made. It required a cruise climb to thirty thousand feet, drawing fuel from 165-gallon drop tanks, and upon reaching altitude continue to cruise at best power setting for maximum range.

"After a certain period of time the engines were to be run at war-emergency power for five minutes, then reduced to military power for fifteen minutes, and finished off at a low-power cruise condition, returning to base with fifty gallons of fuel remaining. The purpose of the test was to find out how long I could fly and how many air miles I could go under these conditions.

"During the test I had to record certain data at each five thousand feet in my climb and each fifteen minutes during my cruise—engine rpm's, manifold pressure, oil pressure and temperature, and carburetor and coolant temperatures. With this information, Ward would be able to estimate how much the performance of the airplane had already been improved, and what still needed to be done.

"At twenty-nine thousand feet the right engine blew up and fell apart. As I had already had ten Allison engines blow up on me in the last two years, this was nothing new; usually I could feel it coming, but this time it just went wham and that was it. I switched from my drop tanks to regular wing tanks. My drop tanks were not yet empty so I kept them with me, although I was pretty heavy and on one engine it was sort of cutting it close. However, we had done this quite often in California and I didn't figure I would be in any sweat.

"I had been flying due north toward Scotland, figuring this would keep me over land. Being on top of a heavy overcast, I did not know my position, so when I turned south toward my base I asked for a radio fix. They immediately came back with my exact position and distance from home so fast I thought this was going to be wonderful; you couldn't get lost over here with this kind of service. I flew the heading they gave me and figured out I should be there in about fifteen minutes.

"About ten minutes passed when they came back on the air with landing instructions; if I was west of the perimeter I should turn hard left and land on runway 29, into the wind which was blowing about thirty miles an hour. At once I looked down and there was the field right below me. I thought to myself this was peculiar, as I hadn't figured on being there yet, but everything was just like I left it and the tower had a green light on me. I swung around left but as I looked at runway 29 the wind was across it, so I called the tower and asked them again what runway to use.

"Getting no answer this time, I picked an alternate runway with a headwind, which was the logical thing to do under the circumstances. I turned left into my good engine and with my landing gear down I entered the base leg for runway 24. I was still extremely busy with drop tanks on, and as I turned the airplane started to buffet. I had partial flaps down at the time, but even so I realized I was making too tight a base leg. I opened the throttle and pulled the gear and flaps up and made a wide circle to the right, and this time I came in and landed with room to spare.

"Again I called the tower on the radio, requesting taxi instructions, and again there was only a deep silence. Then I looked around to see if anyone was waving at me, and for the first time I realized this was not the field I had taken off from. I could see now it was a B-26 bomber base, laid out identically to the fighter base I had just left. There was nothing to do now but roll to a stop off the side of the runway and get out of the airplane. A jeep came out on the field to get me and I was driven to base operations, where I identified myself. The boys said they sure were sweating me out. They saw me with a dead engine, and the idea was general in the Air Corps over there at that time that a pilot with one engine out on a P-38 was a sad sack.

" . . . I probably saved Major Webb a ride home on one engine, because he was going out on a fighter sweep in that airplane the next morning."

After being in bed with the flu for a week:

" . . . Phil Nelson and Glenn Fulkerson picked me up and we drove to the 364th Fighter Group at Honington, another P-38 outfit.

"This was a base where we could really do some good, because they had all just arrived from the States and there were plenty of green pilots. Few had ever flown above twenty thousand feet. Ward Beman arrived a few days later and we prepared a series of lectures covering the best operating procedures for the P-38, and dealing in particular with high-speed flight, with emphasis on the evil of compressibility.

"It was here that I was first challenged as to whether the P-38 could be dived safely. Hadn't a colonel made a vertical dive from forty-one thousand feet and recovered okay? Other pilots had made similar claims—what about it? In every crowd there are always a few skeptics, and this gang was no exception.

"I tried to be completely honest with them, saying that they were going into combat very soon, and not to get any wild ideas about chasing the Jerries when the German pilots peeled off at altitude, because if they tried to follow suit their goose was cooked. At low altitudes and on the deck they could take on anything, as there was no match for the P-38 down low.

"I explained, however, if they ever did get into dive trouble there was only one way to save themselves, so far as I knew. The first thing to do was to pull the power off the engines, put the props in low pitch to create lots of drag, take a firm grip on the wheel and pull back carefully. If the elevator load became too heavy, use the trim tab a very small amount but don't over do it, because when you get down to lower levels where the air is dense and powerful, the trim tab becomes very effective and can overstress the airplane. Just ride the thing and try to keep the dive angle from getting any steeper; if you pull too hard you increase the loads on the tail and it might come off. An airplane can only stand so much.

"From Honington we continued to Bovingdon, the headquarters of the Eighth Fighter Command, for a series of engine tests and dives. Here I demonstrated how well the P-38 could fly on one engine. I wasn't in England to sit in a corner, and I stuck my neck out farther than I ever had before, just to get the work done. On altitude flights to collect test data here and at the 20th Fighter Group at Kingscliff, I went up daily in heavy weather, flying as high as thirty-five thousand feet without seeing the sun, to get information on engine performance. One week I pumped the landing gear down by hand three times because of poor maintenance on the airplane. Everyone was doing his best. But there was a war going on and they were shy of everything.

"While at Bovingdon the P-38 pilots told us of their trouble doing a split S. This was a tactical maneuver required at high altitude, and it was from this maneuver that many of them crashed. It was simply a half roll to your back and pulling through like a half loop, but it was often done when they were attacking an enemy plane, and if he did it you would have to follow. When we left Bovingdon, Ward, Glenn and I went to Langford Lodge, the Lockheed modification center near Belfast, to pick up a special P-38 equipped with dive brakes, and I set out to see for myself if I could do a split S in this airplane.

"To do this maneuver you have to commit yourself to it, which meant getting into a dive, and committing myself in a marginal airplane was what worried me. I didn't commit myself until I knew it was safe, and this is how I did it:

"Starting at twenty thousand feet, I pushed the control column forward until I was in a vertical attitude, headed straight down, and then pulled out immediately and recorded my altitude. Then I went up to twenty-one thousand feet and repeated the same maneuver, and continued to do this in increments of one thousand feet until I was able to do it from thirty thousand feet, at which point I knew the airplane would take it. I was getting up to mach numbers around .71 and the true speed of the plane was up around 550 miles an hour.

"The new dive flaps on this airplane made it possible for the P-38 to do a split S in perfect safety. They changed the characteristics of the wing in compressibility toward a normal subsonic condition, and also increased drag which permitted the plane to take on steeper dive angles without accelerating too rapidly. Later on I was able to prove to the Air Corps that the P-38 would do a split S; I actually had mock combat with several other planes and did it very well."

The author brought up this point a number of times with wartime P-38 pilots, many of whom have their say in these pages, and the comment was virtually identical each time. In essence: Everything Tony says is absolutely true, of course. He's one of the true masters in flying. The point we want to make, especially where the P-38 was concerned in Europe, is that Tony made those tests in a ship modified with dive brakes. The ones we were flying did *not* have those dive brakes yet, and well ...

A tough one to answer.

Tony LeVier continues: "When the airplane was ready, I flew back to England to take the new dive flaps on a demonstration tour. Bovingdon was weathered in, so without waiting to start my tour at command headquarters I began my rounds, visiting all the P-38 bases in England as weather permitted. It was April now and winter was over, and the flying conditions improved steadily. The Ninth Air Force was now operational from England, flying medium bombers in raids on the Continent and building up a tactical air force to furnish ground support for the coming invasion. In addition to Eighth Air Force P-38 bases, the Ninth Fighter Command had three P-38 groups, with squadrons dispersed at several air fields in southern England. I visited them all during April and May, demonstrating the good features of the airplane, and emphasizing its vastly improved safety and performance with compressibility dive brakes.

"I paid a return visit to Nuthampstead, the first base I had visited when I came to England. From there I went to Kingscliff again and gave them a lecture on the P-38. When I was finished they didn't seem too impressed and I wasn't getting the interest I had hoped for, so after supper I went out to the field while it was still light and took off. I climbed to twenty thousand feet and then came down in a vertical dive straight over the officers' club. When they heard me coming they all rushed outside, expecting to see me auger in, and now that I had their attention I came down on the deck and did some slow rolls across the field on one engine, and after landing I had plenty of fellows to talk with.

"They were all interested in what I had on my airplane, and the next day I let the squadron leaders fly it and find out for themselves what they could do with dive brakes. I told them to go up to thirty thousand feet and dive it at a sixty-degree angle and see what a tremendous improvement we had made, and they all came down bug-eyed at what they could do with this airplane.

"I was next sent to Goxhill, a transition base, where a most deplorable situation had arisen over the past week or ten days. They were losing an enormous number of pilots in transition training that was going on up there— more than was even conceivable; even if you didn't know what you were doing you shouldn't lose them like that. I went up there immediately and the things I found out amazed me.

"To begin with, the base commander didn't like P-38s. He admitted at the bar that night that he was strictly a P-40 man, and we thought to ourselves it was a fine state of affairs to have the instructors against the airplane they were teaching people to fly. As a result, he had the most misinformed group of pilots I have ever come in contact with, and their feelings toward the P-38 weren't fit to print. In view of this situation, when I gave them my demonstration the next day I really poured it on.

"It included things I normally don't do. I went all-out to prove that any young man with average intelligence and courage could fly the P-38 just as well as myself. These kids were young, twenty or twenty-one years old on the average, and all they needed was good leaders.

"Before I went up I told them the maneuvers they were going to see would prove to them that their mistakes were uncalled for, and their buddies were killed because they were not trained properly. When I came down I had never seen such enthusiasm; it was just like they had been saved from hell. After that I think they were all convinced that the airplane had real possibilities, even the base commander, and was far from being the killer it was tagged for.

"My next stop was a P-38 base at Andover, which was headquarters of the Ninth Fighter Command under General Pete Quesada, who later became a Lockheed vice president and manager of our missiles systems division. The Andover pilots came from a P-47 outfit in the States and had just gone operational. The change from a single-engine to a multi-engine airplane was more far reaching than most of them realized, and what with one thing and another their morale was pretty low.

"I came in over the base at twenty thousand feet and gave them the old razzle-dazzle to wake up the countryside, starting with a nice vertical dive, and when I came down across the base I got real eager. The air was clear and nobody was flying, so I decided to give them the works. I really beat up the joint. I flew upside down on one engine in front of the hangar and then got into some accelerated stalls circling the base with my dead engine hanging down, which usually had them jumping. When I landed almost the whole base turned out to greet me, and I have never seen such a bunch of eager pilots in my life.

"Engine failures were always a big problem on the P-38 because of the jobs assigned to it, and I devoted a lot of time on my tour explaining and demonstrating single-engine performance. The P-38 engines . . . would frequently blow up and tear themselves apart. During the four months I spent in England the Air Corps made almost two thousand engine changes on the P-38s based there; in other words, practically every P-38 in England at that time had at least one complete engine change. That was the seriousness of the engine trouble. It was partly due to the various problems we had with the engine that General James Doolittle finally made his decision to transfer the P-38 out of the Eighth Air Force.

"Knowledge of P-38 single-engine performance was extremely helpful in getting home, and it was the pilots who were not familiar with it who often ran into trouble. Despite the many problems confronting them they did a good job, however, and when things got tough they learned fast. They were all operational within a month after I reached England, and they would often fly missions in weather that shouldn't happen to your worst enemy.

"One day I flew into Kingscliff under a very low ceiling about two hundred feet, with low scattered scud around one hundred feet, and as I approached the base I could see P-38s all over returning from a cross-channel sweep. They were coming back all over England at that very moment in that kind of weather, and landing with very few accidents. I had to circle fifteen minutes before I could squeeze into the traffic pattern and land too. I ran across them quite often over there, coming back or going out, and to this day they can't be praised enough for the way they flew.

"They had victories at high altitude, but they really shone down low. Often after these fighter sweeps they would drop down on the deck on the way home and beat up enemy installations. The P-38 could make very tight maneuvers at low altitude, and when the pilots found the Germans on their tail all they had to do was turn hard right or left and get behind the enemy plane. They used to pull hard turns to the left, for instance, which often caused the German Me-109 to stall out and snap-roll into the ground.

"After completing my P-38 demonstration tour I flew back to Langford Lodge to await the first bulk shipment of dive brakes for installation on combat planes in the European theater. While I had been in England demonstrating this modification, the Lockheed factory back home was building several hundred special kits on highest priority, with new planes coming out of the factory getting them installed right on the production line.

"Early in May about four hundred sets of dive brakes were loaded on an Army C-54 cargo plane and dispatched to Langford Lodge for field installation in Europe. We were looking for them, as we knew that would lick the dive problem for Army pilots and save lives and airplanes. Joe Johnson, Lockheed's P-38 project engineer, came over on another plane to set up the modification line.

"The days passed and no kits. Joe moved heaven and earth trying to find them, only to learn the worst—*the C-54 was shot down by mistake by a British pilot over the North Atlantic* and its precious cargo of dive brakes for combat airplanes was lost at sea. Through lack of time and press of other matters, they were never replaced." (Italics added.)

TONY LeVIER

13. J, L, and M

The casual observer would be hard-pressed to distinguish between the first operational models of the Lightning, from the P-38E through the H. Despite the major changes to the airplane, most of the modifications were internal and rarely apparent at a glance. Not so with the "new series" of the Lightning, starting with the P-38J and continuing through the L. Despite their late appearance, the J and L models made up by far the bulk of P-38 production. Of the 9,923 P-38s produced of all types and models, the J and L (including 113 L models built by Convair) amounted to nearly 7,000 airplanes.

The P-38J/L series could be distinguished immediately by the deep intakes beneath the propeller spinners. The "chin" or "beard" intakes gave the J/L series something of a pugnacious look, and some purists feel (and rightly so, agrees the writer) that something in the beautiful lines of the earlier P-38s was lost forever.

But what it might have given away in looks, the P-38J more than made up in terms of improved performance and safety for the pilot. In the earlier model Lightnings the turbosuperchargers passed compressed air from the turbos through the leading edge of the wing; the air traveled a laborious path from the boom all the way to the wingtip and back, in order to provide cooling, before it went into the carburetor. It was a complicated process that drove maintenance crews to distraction. It led to problems in controlling the turbosuperchargers, which were manifested in the form of explosive backfires of the engines and, to the great unhappiness of the pilot, engine fires. The backfires blasting through the system were sometimes so severe they warped the leading edge of the wing. The P-38J was the first model in which Lockheed could dump the whole system and go to a new arrangement. The AAF was just as eager for the change since, in addition to calming the man behind the controls, it would eliminate a system vulnerable to being knocked out by enemy fire.

It was this change in cooling systems that modified the appearance of the J from the preceding H model, although the two airplanes used the same engine. The old intercooler was eliminated, and replaced with a core-radiator beneath the engine, creating the so-called chin or beard look. Now the cooling air went through a central duct immediately behind the propeller, and was eliminated through an exit flap, the size of which was controllable instead of being fixed. Now the pilot had the cooling system on his side instead of wondering when the engine might chew itself up in this one particular area; what the J gave him was control of the temperature of the air as it moved into the carburetor.

Lockheed was after killing several birds with one stone in transitioning to the J model; changing the cooling system made it possible to eliminate the ducting within the wings, and produce a new internal wing section. In the early J models (P-38J-5-LO through P-38J-10-LO) alternate variants came off the production line. The airplane might have a wing of normal structure (with just the ducting removed), or it was built with additional self-sealing fuel tanks making up the leading edge. Once production started on the P-38J-15-LO the variety was eliminated; all J-15 and subsequent models (including the L) were produced with the internal leading edge tanks. With maximum external fuel loads, this brought the fuel capacity of the P-38J and L series to something over 1,000 gallons—or a remarkable 6,000 pounds of fuel for a single-seat fighter.

The alterations to the basic wing sound easy enough but they brought with them a host of engineering and structural aggravations. In order to prevent buckling and deforming of the leading edge, Lockheed found it necessary to add heavy chordwise strips within the wing structure outboard of the engine nacelles. (All P-38L models came off the production line with the modifications.) Special attention was also paid to the movement of boundary layer air to improve its flow through the new intake ducts, and, at the same time, to reduce aerodynamic drag.

As mentioned, the J model had the same engines as the earlier H, but the changes to the powerplant system permitted the J to utilize the engines more efficiently and actually show a power increase. The J series under emergency conditions could produce the planned 1,425 horsepower at 26,500 feet, and most of the J series (in the P-38J-5-LO through J-15-LO blocks) underwent engine modifications to provide a war emergency boost rating, at altitude, of 1,600 horsepower. Depending upon the many variables affecting performance, a stock P-38J-5 or J-10, without the additional weight of the leading edge tanks, could turn in a top speed of 425 to 430 mph at 30,000 feet, and a respectable 406 mph at 20,000 feet. Most pilots, however, were willing to sacrifice some speed at altitude for the increased fuel weight, since the new leading edge tanks provided an additional 110 gallons internal fuel, which often meant the difference in making it back to home base or going down somewhere short of that field.

As the P-38J moved through its production run (2,970 were built) a series of modifications was passed on to the airplane to sustain the latest changes for improved performance and serviceability. The first 220 J airplanes carried the same curved windshield as earlier models, but starting with the 221st P-38J (a J-10) to be built, the curving windshield was replaced with one of flat bulletproof glass. This improved forward visibility, reduced reflections and provided better protection for the pilot. All subsequent J and L models had this feature.

In August 1943 the first P-38J-1-LO rolled from the factory. Ten of these aircraft were built and then production shifted to the J-5 variant. The last of this series built, before the P-38L, was the P-38J-25-LO.

Among the modifications to the airplane was an item for which pilots had been screaming loudly—improved heating arrangements in the cockpit. A foot warmer was provided for the pilot (if you will recall, the P-38H models at extreme altitude had resulted in *frostbite* of the extremities), and a hot air defroster was added, which the pilot could now direct along any part of the canopy interior, helping to both maintain visibility under icing conditions and keep hands warm.

In the cockpit the pilot now had more room through the simple expedient of modifying the control wheel by cutting out a major lower part of the wheel, resulting in more lap room. Mechanics dreaded working on the radio gear of the P-38 since in all pre-J models it was necessary to remove a major section of the armor plate in order to reach the radios. The J model provided fast-removal Dzus buttons to the radios.

No longer did the pilot have to work a manual gun charger-selector; the guns were charged on the ground prior to flight. At times the P-38 had given the pilot nightmares with electrical problems. The J eliminated most fuses and replaced these with circuit breakers, which the pilot could reach in flight for resetting if necessary.

After most of the J-series fighters had rolled from the factory, Lockheed initiated production of the P-38J-25-LO, of which 210 were built before the P-38L series went into production. The J-25 must be considered as the first of the "all-up" combat Lightnings, since this was the first production model to have the electrically-operated dive brakes (to offset compressibility) installed as a production item. The J-25 also featured the aileron-boost system, which was made up of a hydraulically actuated bell-crank and push-pull rod. With the boost system the pilot needed only 17 per cent of the previous force applied to the control yoke, greatly increasing the rate of roll of the fighter at any weight or altitude.

One P-38J-1-LO was flown with the retractable skis first tested on the P-38F.

A total of 951 photographic reconnaissance models were built from the production run of the P-38J and L series.

There were many changes to the basic P-38J series, some of which, after being carried out in the field as "retrofits," became production items for the L series.

Rockets were first tested on the P-38G-15-LO in the United States, and then kits for rocket projectiles were rushed overseas for field installation on the P-38J models. The first of these was a twin-pack. Each pack was a three-tube launcher mounted close to the fuselage nacelle for a total of six tubes. These fired a 4.5-inch spin-stabilized rocket from each tube. Nearly a thousand of these paired launchers were sent to the field, but evoked something less than enthusiasm on the part of the pilots using them because of severe interruption with the airflow and the general unreliability of the rockets.

One P-38G-15-LO model was also tested carrying four of these launching-tube packages, for a total of twelve rockets (including six tubes beneath the wings, outboard of the engines), as well as two inboard external fuel tanks.

Different types of rocket-launch systems were included. The major type finally adopted for the J series in field modification was a zero-length system, in which ten rockets, of the 5-inch finned type, were carried beneath the wings. In the P-38L this would be increased to fourteen rockets on the zero-length launcher, although this was quickly dropped because of the major changes necessitated to the wing structure. The final production item for rocket launching, which became standard on the L as a factory item, and as a retrofit for many J aircraft, was the so-called Christmas Tree launcher, which mounted five rockets in a stepped-down cluster beneath each wing.

Earlier in the book, as related by General Edward B. Giller, we had mention of the Droop Snoot Lightnings. This airplane, as first flown, was a P-38J-15 modified by Lockheed at Langford Lodge. The nose section of the fighter was cut away and replaced with a bomber nose, actually a combination bombardier-navigator facility for a second crewman (General Giller pointed out there was no way for this man to bail out in the air in the event of fire or destruction). The front of the Droop Snoot was a conventional transparent nose with an optically-flat aiming window. In effect, it was a smaller version of a B-17F nose with full bombing equipment, including the Norden bombsight. One Droop Snoot would act as navigator-bomber-leader for a tight formation of P-38s carrying up to 4,000 pounds of bombs per airplane.

Most Droop Snoot modifications were carried out by field units in many combat theaters throughout the world, including all areas of the Pacific and Asia. The bastardizations by field units sometimes considered the pilot and his passenger as well as the mission to be flown, and retained at least two .50 caliber machine guns for "insurance."

Another major change to the P-38J-15—which was, in fact, to replace the Droop Snoot as a bomber leader—was the Pathfinder, developed by Lockheed at its modification plant in Dallas, Texas. Once again the nose section was removed and a new installation added, this time a thick and elongated nose containing elaborate ground-mapping radar. Using the radar—known as "Mickey"—the Master Bomber Pathfinder could lead his tight formation against enemy targets no matter what the weather, and since weather was so often a crucial factor, the Droop Snoots were replaced as quickly as possible with the radar models. (Which provided a number of surplus Lightnings with the bombardier nose; enterprising mechanics converted the nose sections into plush accomodations for a VIP passenger, a VIP being anyone friendly with the pilot.)

The P-38J-5 and P-38J-15 series are listed as having a basic weight of 13,700 pounds, a combat weight of 17,500 pounds, and a maximum recommended weight of 22,000 pounds, although the latter was often exceeded in the field for combat missions.

The maximum bombload of the airplane is given as 4,000 pounds. The writer has never seen an officially stated higher figure when carrying bombs, but experience teaches that official documents often contain less than the full story. When I was the historian for the Fifth Air

Force during the Japanese occupation it was my job to sort through whatever combat files and photographs had been retained during the war. And within those files were photographs—and the operational records—of P-38J and P-38L airplanes, each carrying not 4,000, but 5,200 pounds of bombs. Beneath the inner wing, between the engine nacelles and the fuselage, were two 2,000-pound bombs. Beneath the wings, outboard of the engines, were four more bombs of 300 pounds each for the total of 5,200 pounds. A careful study of the records at the time indicated that the airplanes flew on short-range combat missions carrying these staggering loads, which must leave the P-38 without question as the champion load carrier for single-seat fighters in World War II.

Maximum speeds for the P-38J-5/15 at combat weight are listed as 360 mph at 5,000 feet; 390 mph at 15,000; 421 mph at 25,000; and 426 mph at 30,000 feet.

The rate of climb improved sharply over earlier models. Again, at standard combat weight, the airplane had a rate of climb of 3,900 feet per minute at 5,000 feet; 3,600 feet per minute at 15,000; and, 3,100 feet per minute at 25,000 feet. Interesting; the J model had a better rate of climb at 25,000 feet than any earlier model had at *any* altitude. The J series reached 5,000 feet from a standing take off in 1.4 minutes; 15,000 feet in 4.3 minutes; and 25,000 feet in 7.8 minutes.

Fully fueled with 1,010 gallons internal and external the airplane had a maximum range of some 2,260 miles, and an endurance, at best economy, of some twelve hours. Once again, the official statistics are open to serious question, since both the P-38J and also the L model, when flown with cruise-control procedures worked out in the field, flew missions (in the Pacific) in excess of 2,300 miles. This meant takeoff, formation assembly, climbout and cruise to target, allowance for combat maneuvers, the return home and emergency fuel allowance after scheduled landing. (While the P-38L had a listed maximum range of 2,600 miles under ideal conditions, the writer points out that actual combat missions flown with the P-38J exceeded by several hundred miles the maximum "official" range. It would appear that the only single-seat fighter to match the seven-league boots of the P-38J and L airplanes was the P-47N, designed from the outset for missions of over 2,000 miles.)

Service ceiling of the P-38J series was 43,800 feet, although the airplanes rarely, if ever, reached such heights in combat.

THE BIG L

This was the big one—a single production order, when finished, of 3,924 P-38L models from the P-38L-1-LO through the P-38L-5-LO, and including 113 P-38L-5-VN aircraft. The VN refers to Vultee-Nashville, a division of consolidated Vultee (now Convair). After the 113 aircraft were built and delivered, the AAF, on VE Day, cancelled a further Vultee order of 1,887 airplanes. An undisclosed number of Lockheed L models was also cancelled, both because of VE Day and Lockheed tooling for the P-80 Shooting Star jet fighter.

There had been a star aborning between the J and L series—the one P-38K-1-LO to fly. The K was actually a modified P-38E (Serial Number 41-1983) which, in production, would have superseded the P-38J-25-LO. The K flew with modified Allison engines—V-1710-75 and -77—intended to overcome the high-altitude deficiencies of the P-38 in European combat. The airplane was fitted out with propellers 12 feet 6 inches in diameter, but with unusually thick blades—the so-called paddle-blade propeller. The airplane promised good performance at high altitude, but there was a serious question as to Allison's ability to deliver the engines in quantity. The AAF decided, finally, to abandon production of the K for the L model, and to include in the latter the design improvements of the K. These included more efficient turbosuperchargers and a revised fuel system.

There were 1,291 P-38L-1-LO fighters produced. The L went into production with the new Allison V-1710-111 and -113 (F30R and L) engines, which produced a full

1,600 hp at takeoff and at altitude. The new engines turned out a normal rating of 1,100 hp at 30,000 feet (compared to this power rating at 27,000 feet for the J series). Going to war emergency rating the engines also produced their 1,600 hp at 30,000 feet. The pilot enjoyed extensive changes in controlling his power from earlier models with the use of automatically controlled systems. The manifold pressure, mixture, and propeller rpm were selected by the pilot with his cockpit controls and then, up to critical altitude, these settings were maintained automatically, with no further pilot changes, by the auto systems of the engines.

The single feature that most easily distinguished the P-38L from the J series was the installation of a flush-mounted landing light in the leading edge of the left wing, replacing the retractable light of earlier models.

The P-38L-5-LO was much the same as the L-1 model, except that the droppable fuel tanks of the L-5 were pressurized, and the airplane had tank-mounted fuel booster pumps contained in small fairings along the bottom surface of the wing. Internal fuel tankage of the L series increased slightly over the J, with a total internal load of 424 gallons, providing a maximum load (with two 300-gallon drop tanks) of 1,024 gallons.

The four machine guns normally carried 300 rounds per gun, or could accomodate 500 rounds per gun. The cannon had 150 rounds. Due to earlier complaints of gun camera vibration when this equipment was mounted in the nose with the armament, the AN-N-6 gun camera was mounted in the bomb shackle fairing to the left of the fuselage.

One of the more unusual additions (and a welcome one to the pilot) to the P-38L was the installation of tail-warning radar. A AN/APS-13 radar system was fitted within the aft part of the left tail boom. The transmitter-receiver system picked up the presence of an aircraft in a cone behind the P-38L, and immediately warned the pilot of this approaching machine by ringing a warning bell and flashing a warning red light alongside the gun-sight.

Basic weight of the airplane is given as 13,700 pounds; empty combat weight (with permanent equipment) as 14,100 pounds; combat weight, between 17,200 and 17,600 pounds; and maximum recommended weight, 22,000 pounds.

Maximum speed—at war emergency power at 17,500 pounds at 25,000 feet—was 414 mph. The airplane could reach 20,000 feet in 7 minutes with a takeoff weight of 17,500 pounds, and had a service ceiling of 44,000 feet. With a weight of 21,600 pounds, carrying 1,024 gallons fuel, the P-38L had a normal maximum range of 2,600 miles at just under 200 mph at 10,000 feet. Carrying a bombload of 3,200 pounds it would normally operate to a range of 450 miles at 290 mph at 10,000 feet.

NIGHT FIGHTER

There were seventy-five of them—all a deep glossy black—and known as the P-38M. These were P-38L models converted to two-seat night fighters, of which an undisclosed number were rushed to the far Pacific in the closing months of the war. The airplane was modified with a second "jump" seat behind the pilot; however, the radar operator who wedged his way into this seat was far more comfortable than former piggyback passengers, thanks to a bulbous canopy providing some decent head-and-shoulders room. The A.S.H.-type radar scanner was mounted in a streamlined housing and placed on a bomb release shackle directly under the nose ahead of the nose landing gear. Flash nozzles to reduce flareback when firing the guns were fitted to the standard armament. Some experiments were conducted to shield the flaming exhaust of the turbosuperchargers, but the shields soon glowed as brightly as the turbos, and the attempt was shelved.

An undisclosed number of P-38M fighters saw combat against Japanese night intruders—no further details have been made available.

It would be impossible, as the writer has emphasized earlier, to list all the many variants and modifications to the different P-38 models throughout the war. Some of the official records have been lost to us forever, others simply were never filled out when airplanes at combat fields were modified to suit local needs or as expressions of individual ingenuity.

One of the rarer breeds in the P-38 family carried a different designation—the XP-49, which was powered with Continental XIV-1430-13 and -15 engines of 1,350 horsepower each. The airplane, built up from an early-model P-38 airframe structure, was intended to test out new oxygen and cabin pressurization systems. It suffered countless delays and, although having started in 1939, the experimental fighter never made it into the air until November 11, 1942. It was longer—at 40 feet 1 inch—than the standard P-38, and was flown with a combat weight of 18,830 pounds. Armament differed from the standard P-38 with four .50 caliber machine guns and two 20-mm cannon, each cannon containing 90 rounds. Maximum speed was listed as 406 mph at 15,000 feet, and a blistering 458 mph at best altitude. Only the one airplane was built.

The AAF tested two interesting armament modifications to the P-38L, one of which mounted three .60 caliber machine guns (13 mm) with extremely long barrels protruding far ahead of the nose. The test went down in the record books as a failure; the guns were never developed properly and often failed in flight during firing, and the shell links themselves failed whenever the airplane was subjected to either positive or negative acceleration.

What was unquestionably the most heavily armed of all the Lightnings was a specially modified P-38L-1-LO, which the AAF intended to be an unusually lethal ground-attack fighter. The nose was modified to hold eight .50 caliber guns, and beneath each wing went a special pod holding another four guns, or a total of *twelve* .50 caliber machine guns for one airplane. The project was not completed when it became clear that the standard armament, along with bombs, napalm, incendiaries or rockets, could do the ground attack job just as successfully.

There exists no clear record of the different organizations and countries that flew the P-38 fighter or photo plane during World War II. An unspecified number of photo reconnaissance models were transferred to the U.S. Navy during the North African fighting. Other photo variants in the F-4 and F-5 series flew with the Australians and the French. P-38 fighters were flown by U.S. Marine Corps pilots during the war, and a number of P-38J aircraft were built specifically for the Chinese in late 1944 and early 1945.

The other service records of the P-38 during the war have, unfortunately, vanished with the years.

One final word on the airplane that almost made it into another war—this time in Korea. In 1949, more than 150 P-38L-5-LO Lightnings were stationed with the Fifth Air Force in Korea. At that time, for reasons mainly of economy (since the P-38s were almost all "low time" aircraft), the Fifth was ordered to convert to the North American P-51D Mustang as its standard fighter.

What to do with the Lightnings? Those people on the scene expected to turn them over to the South Korean Air Force. Washington, however, with the State Department breathing down its neck, refused the transfer on the grounds that the South Koreans, with these fighters in their hands, might "unnecessarily provoke the North Koreans."

The Lightnings were destroyed by having them chopped up with hand axes and bulldozers.

Washington officially denies this ever happened.

Little matter. The writer, and several hundred other men of the Fifth Air Force, *saw it happen*.

And one is led to wonder what the presence of these airplanes might have meant in the opening days of the Korean War, when we had a handful of P-82 fighters and all-too-few P-51s and P-80's.

However, that's another war and a big, unanswerable *if*.

Back to the Lightning in the final phase of the air war in the European Theater of Operations.

14.   Finish in the ETO

QUESTION: Where does the man doing the history draw the line? Because there are too many statements that simply don't stack up.

The most objective evaluations of the P-38—by the men who flew them, and this includes those who were ardent enthusiasts and thought the 38 was the greatest thing ever to come down the pike, as well as those who wanted the hell out and into anything else with wings—have run a strikingly similar theme. At the higher altitudes of European combat, say, from 20,000 feet and up, engine problems plagued the P-38 to such an extent that the aircraft's performance was compromised in *maneuvering combat* with German fighters. There were a few other goodies that puckered up the P-38 jocks, too. Until the advent of the P-38J-25-LO the airplane couldn't be rammed into a high-speed dive without compressibility taking control away from the pilot. And because of the slower rate of roll (again until the J-25 appeared with boosted ailerons), the Me-109 or FW-190 could flick onto its back and split-S out of harm's way. One other item. Being a heavy airplane, the Lightning took just a bit longer to accelerate and a Jerry could be out of gun range too fast for comfort.

Okay. Even the enthusiasts are quick to admit all this. The enthusiasts who flew the P-38L fighters draw the line right there. The veterans stand up on a chair and shake their fists and insist that the L was a whole new breed of Lightning, and there wasn't a German piston-engined fighter they wouldn't take on at *any* altitude. Full power all the way upstairs, aileron boost, new heating systems, dive flaps; it made *all* the difference.

Again, okay. But we'll stop short of the 38L, or even the J-25 series, and stick to the earlier variants. There's a reason here.

All the enthusiasts, and the most disgruntled detractors, are unanimous in that below 20,000 feet, and especially below 15,000 feet, the Germans didn't have an airplane that could hack the P-38. Even those hammering their way out of the P-38 cockpits for other airplanes draw up short, nod wisely, and insist this was true. Heavy airplane or no heavy airplane, the Lightning at these heights, all the way down to the deck, was *the* airplane in which to fight the 109 or the 190. It could turn inside the German jobbies without any sweat. It was extremely stable, dove and climbed well, could hang on a stall, could snap through turns left or right, and—well, more than one 38 jock has sighed and wondered how wonderful it would have been had they fought all their battles below three miles. "We'd have beaten their heads into the ground . . ." and that sort of thing.

Well, the facts are that the battles over Europe were fought from the deck all the way up to 35,000 feet. The upper half of that airspace gave the Germans the edge; the lower half saw the P-38s clobbering everything around them. That was one of the lessons learned in North Africa. Even the older P-38s at these heights held the advantage. The use of the Fowler flap snapping back to eight degrees position as a maneuvering flap let the 38 jocks tighten up their turns even more. And as we saw from the comments of a German pilot (with seventy-five victories) who had often tangled with the P-38, and shot down a few of them, he felt the Lightning was faster and more maneuverable, and he wasn't too happy about ever tangling with them in a mix-it-up dogfight.

So comes the question. In "general" books by German pilots or experts there runs the same refrain throughout— that the P-38 was generally the easiest of the American fighters, in the African or European fighting, to take on and defeat. Now, this is a bit strange, because such general-izations are dangerous—and misleading. In North Africa it patently wasn't true. The P-38 held a slight ratio over enemy fighters shot down as against P-38s lost, *but this includes P-38s lost from all reasons*. And that means en-gine failure, collision, lost in weather, cracking up in land-ing; in short, the works. And since the P-38 was on the deck much of the time attacking ground forces, armor, shipping and what-have-you, it becomes more and more clear that most P-38 losses in Africa were due to causes other than German fighters. Which changes the victory/loss ratio considerably in favor of the P-38.

Now let's get back to the European situation. If the reader will recall the remarks of General Giller, at one point he made it clear that the victory/loss ratio wasn't something to brag about. He said they were shooting down, statistically, 1.5 German fighters for every P-38 lost. Now once again we run in a strange porridge of statistics, be-cause the General unwittingly set up a most interesting comparison.

We have 1.5 German fighters, the *best* German fighters, battling it out on their home grounds, on short-duration flights, well-experienced, being shot down for every P-38. Three Jerries shot down (confirmed) for every two P-38s lost.

But this includes P-38 losses from all causes.

And General Giller, like so many other veterans of that area, makes a special point of emphasizing that the Allison engines in the P-38, at high altitudes over Europe, were the worst enemy of the airplane. Its own engines and *not* the German fighters. In the early months of P-38 combat in the ETO, starting in the fall of 1943, it's believed that about half of all the P-38s lost over Europe were the victims of their own engines.

Now that changes the ratio of victories and losses, doesn't it? It jumps the ratio to perhaps three or four German fighters shot down for every P-38 *shot down*. Even the P-38's worst detractors, remember, will run back to the cockpit if the fighting is to be below 15,000 feet, and as the war went on, and the 38s went down to the deck, most of their fighting in the ETO took place at these lower regions.

Which makes that victory/loss ratio even more interesting.

Now, one thing must be made very clear. This is a matter of *if* and juggling statistics. No one knows for certain, beyond any doubts, how many hapless guys went down because their Allisons blew up or quit or froze or what. But there were a hell of a lot of them. General Giller lumped all P-38 losses in a single pile—weather, training, general accidents and collisions, people screwing around with airplanes, *and* the enemy. Giller has a fighter pilot's straight-ahead look in this subject; a no-nonsense look. He doesn't care *why* the number of German fighters shot down by P-38s wasn't better, in the ratio column, to all P-38s lost from all reasons. He wanted to get out there and clobber the enemy without statistical crutches of *any* kind. It's about the healthiest attitude of a pilot. It makes him a winner.

The gist of all this is that I find it extraordinarily difficult to accept this blanket categorization on the part of the German aces—and their legion of authors—that the P-38 was always such an easy mark. Of course, the man who has engaged in a few hundred air battles and shot down a hundred airplanes considers *any* other fighter below his par, but that's even more the man than the airplane.

There's the old saw that if you have two pilots of equal caliber and put them into two different type airplanes, the airplane with better performance will win. It makes nice conversation for hangar sessions but its not necessarily true, especially if one pilot always takes advantage of certain superior qualities of his airplane. For example, the Zero could outmaneuver the Grumman F4F Wildcat. No two ways about it. The Zero was faster, climbed faster, dove faster, turned in a shorter distance, and in the early days of the war, the Japanese pilots were some of the best around; no green kids there. But look at the record of Zero-*vs.*-Wildcat and you end up shaking your head and wondering what happened.

The German ace who shot down a dozen P-38s is convinced he'll whip the 38 every time, because he's done it.

The American ace who shot down a dozen Me-109s or FW-190s is convinced he'll whip the German every time, because he's done it.

The German pilot who flies an Me-109G, and knows his next ten fights will be against a P-38 at 34,000 feet, has a tremendous edge on the P-38 pilot. He knows that at that height neither airplane climbs too quickly. The Me-109G has a faster rate of roll, all to its advantage. He knows that the P-38's heavy wing loading, especially at altitude, gives him an even chance in that maneuver. And he knows that any time he gets in real trouble, he can flick through a half-roll onto his back, split-S and get the hell out, and come back for more later.

Now get down to around four or five thousand feet. What happens? Suddenly the German pilot is flying an airplane slower than the P-38. Without combat flaps the P-38 can easily turn inside the Me-109G; with use of these flaps the odds get even better for the Lightning jock. The P-38 can outclimb the enemy. He has far better slow-speed characteristics and can really reef it in tight, inside the other fighter. He can get right down to the edge of a stall where the Me-109G, despite those beautiful slots, can't hang in there with him. What about high-speed turns left or right? With contra-rotating props the 38 can go either way without giving an inch; not so the 109G with engine torque and P factor to mess him up.

And the 109G *can't* just split-S out of trouble. Down here the 38 doesn't have the compressibility problem, and there's too little room to plunge for the deck. The 38 is quite a bit faster, so he makes up that way for the faster initial acceleration of the 109G.

Pretty soon it becomes a matter of former intangibles turning into vital issues—and the odds flicker and change faster than the eye can see.

One of the conclusions of the ETO war in the air hasn't received much attention, and it concerns the use of the P-38, P-47 and the P-51. No one questions that the

Mustang was an absolutely beautiful creation in the air, one of the greatest fighters ever built. No one questions that the heavy Jug, the P-47, wasn't a mix-it-up fighter. Yet the official evaluation was that the P-38 first hit the Germans in the vitals, the P-51 delivered the *coup de grace,* but it was the P-47 that broke the German back in the air. Interesting . . .

We've read a great deal, of course, about the problem the P-38 experienced with compressibility. Well, the P-47 was a big and heavy fighter, but we didn't read too much about its problem with compressibility. Let's see what happens in a Jug when the same sort of situation arises.

The following is an excerpt from *Thunderbolt!,* which I wrote with Robert S. Johnson, who performed the dandy feat of shooting down twenty-eight German *fighters* in eleven months—from the ranks of some of Germany's greatest fighter pilots. The period was the fall of 1942:

. . . My first meeting with compressibility was a frightening experience. I rolled the fighter on her back and dropped the nose in a vertical plunge earthward. The engine howled with power and the Thunderbolt ran wild. In seconds I was in compressibility range—and absolutely helpless.

No man was strong enough to pull the fighter out of a compressibility dive. I've gripped the control stick in both hands, jammed my feet against the instrument panel for leverage, and hauled back with all the strength I had. The stick might have been imbedded in concrete for all the good the frantic pulling did me. All I could do was to hang on to that stick, straining with all my might, and wait until the fighter screamed her way into the denser air at lower altitudes. Between 12,000 and 8,000 feet the air was sufficiently dense to allow the controls to grab. Then came the brutal and crushing g-forces of the pullout, when my blood rushed downward and drained from my head, and the world turned grey and then black—and finally the blackout caused by a brain deprived of blood. I'd come to, groggy and shaken up, as the Thunderbolt hung on her propeller, rushing upward in a tremendous zoom climb.

Now for one other item, to which we have referred before. The "if" situation. What about the Thunderbolt in a fight with that magnificent British fighter, the Spitfire IXB? A dogfight, no less.

And what if the Thunderbolt were an early model—which means it still didn't have the paddle-blade propeller and water-injection for the engine, which virtually doubled its rate of climb and increased its speed? Let's set up that "if" dogfight with one of the early model Thunderbolts against the Spitfire IXB, and see what happens.

It did. Bob Johnson had the chance to slug it out in a mock dogfight, with both types of the above-mentioned aircraft involved. The reader is going to be surprised, and a great lesson in flying will be provided. It might even spice some of those hangar flying sessions. Again, from *Thunderbolt!*:

Aloft to familiarize myself with the local terrain, I spotted a Spitfire 9B flying nearby. This was my first look at the new Spitfire with which the Royal Air Force hoped to regain qualitative air superiority from the Focke-Wulf FW-190. We flew together in formation, and then I decided to see just what this airplane had to its credit.

I opened the throttle full and the Thunderbolt forged ahead. A moment later exhaust smoke poured from the Spit as the pilot came after me. He couldn't make it; the big Jug had a definite speed advantage. I grinned happily; I'd heard so much about this airplane that I really wanted to show the Thunderbolt to her pilot. The Jug kept pulling away from the Spitfire; suddenly I hauled back on the stick and lifted the nose. The Thunderbolt zoomed upward, soaring into the cloud-flecked sky. I looked out and back; the Spit was straining to match me, and barely able to hold his position.

But my advantage was only the zoom—once in steady climb, he had me. I gaped as smoke poured from the exhausts and the Spitfire shot past me as if I were standing still. Could that plane *climb!* He tore upward in a climb I couldn't match with the Jug. Now it was his turn;

the broad elliptical wings rolled, swung around, and the Spit screamed in, hell-bent on chewing me up.

This was going to be fun. I knew he could turn inside the heavy Thunderbolt; if I attempted to hold a tight turn the Spitfire would slip right inside me. I knew, also, that he could easily outclimb my fighter. I stayed out of those sucker traps. First rule in this kind of fight: don't fight the way your opponent fights best. No sharp turns; don't climb; keep him at your own level.

We were at 5,000 feet, the Spitfire skidding around hard and coming in on my tail. No use turning; he'd whip right inside me as if I were a truck loaded with cement, and snap out in firing position. Well, I had a few tricks, too. The P-47 was faster, and I threw the ship into a roll. Right here I had him. The Jug could out-roll any plane in the air, bar none. With my speed, roll was my only advantage, and I made full use of the manner in which the Thunderbolt could roll. I kicked the Jug into a wicked left roll, horizon spinning crazily, once, twice, into a third. As he turned to the left to follow, I tramped down on the right rudder, banged the stick over to the right. Around and around we went, left, right, left, right. I could whip through better than two rolls before the Spitfire even completed his first. And this killed his ability to turn inside me. I just refused to turn. Every time he tried to follow me in a roll, I flashed away to the opposite side, opening the gap between our two planes.

Then I played the trump. The Spitfire was clawing wildly through the air, trying to follow me in a roll, when I dropped the nose. The Thunderbolt howled and ran for earth. Barely had the Spitfire started to follow—and I was a long way ahead of him by now—when I jerked back on the stick and threw the Jug into a zoom climb. In a straight or climbing turn, the British ship had the advantage. But coming out of a dive, there's not a British or a German fighter that can come close to a Thunderbolt rushing upward in a zoom. Before the Spit pilot knew what had happened, I was high above him, the Thunderbolt hammering around. And that was it—for in the next few moments the Spitfire flier was amazed to see a less-maneuverable, slower-climbing Thunderbolt rushing straight at him, eight guns pointing ominously at his cockpit.

The next morning . . . I took the opportunity to fly both the Spitfire Mark 5 and the newer Mark 9B. The flights were a revelation. Two fighter planes couldn't have been further apart than my big Thunderbolt and the agile little Spitfire. The Mark 5 fairly leaped into the air after a short run. With several thousand feet below the wings I hauled back on the stick. She just wouldn't stall! I pulled the stick back against my belt, and the little fighter went around and around, hanging on her nose.

When I rolled her over, I nearly passed out. Without warning the engine coughed, and quit! Quickly I snapped over to level flight and dropped the nose—and the engine started again. It was the carburetor, and it seemed like a primitive arrangement to me. Imagine mixing it up with a couple of Focke-Wulfs and, just as you need power, the engine quits because a lousy carburetor isn't designed for inverted flight!

Whatever the Spitfire 5 lacked, the Mark 9B more than made up for it. She was a sweet, agile machine, incredibly responsive in turns and climbs. But she just couldn't roll, and she couldn't dive worth a nickel. . . .

One final item on the Thunderbolt, because it demonstrates so effectively how truly important is a major change, a technical change, as it were, to the performance of an airplane. During his combat tour, Johnson had his P-47 modified with a new propeller, about which

. . . our engineering officers were making a terrific fuss. They insisted that the fat paddle blades of the new propellers would bring a tremendous boost in performance, that the increased blade area would permit the props to make the greatest use of the Thunderbolt's 2,000 horsepower. We listened to their enthusiastic ramblings with more than a grain of salt—and never were we more mistaken. What a difference these blades made. At 8,000 feet I pulled the Thunderbolt into a steep climb. Normally she'd zoom quickly and then slow down, rapidly approaching a stall. But now—the Jug soared up like she'd gone crazy. Another Thunderbolt was in the air, and I pulled alongside, signalling for a climb. I'm not an engineering officer, and I don't know the exact feet per minute that we climbed. But I left that other fighter behind as if he were standing still. The Jug stood on her tail and howled her way into the sky.

Never again did a Focke-Wulf FW-190 or a Messerschmitt Me-109 outclimb me in the Thunderbolt. The new prop was worth 1,000 horsepower more, and then some. Later I had the opportunity to mix it up with a Spitfire 9B, the same model fighter that had flashed past me in a climb. This time the tables were reversed; I was astonished as we both poured the coal to our fighters, and the Thunderbolt just ran away from the Spit.

Of course, you'll find plenty of people who argue that the Thunderbolt, in an old-fashioned dogfight, couldn't survive against the FW-190, or the Me-109, or the Spitfire.

One bit of advice to the "experts." Don't tell it to Bob Johnson.

Okay. Back to the Lightning. Back to the inescapable fact that Jimmy Doolittle finally had reports of Allison engines blowing up, coming out of his ears. Those damned engines! To begin with there were two to every P-38, and almost all of them had to be changed. The abort rate was staggering. Once the 38s got into combat with the Germans, things were fine. The record showed *that*. The bomber losses were going down, and that was the final judgement. Then the overall picture changed. Production was running away back in the States. The Thunderbolt had eliminated its bugs. The first long-range Mustangs, which initially gave their pilots fits because of systems freezing up at altitude, guns jamming, little goodies like that, were coming through in fine shape. Okay, make a decision. Do we try to wrestle our way through with those damned Allisons, or do we go with the Mustangs for the really long-range missions?

Well, you always go with what gives you the least static. Doolittle's decision was to phase the P-38 out of the Eighth Air Force as a high-altitude escort fighter. Never mind what we're hearing about the J-25 and the

L and the rest of it. We *know* what we have in the Mustang. What to do with the P-38s? Well, Ninth Air Force is screaming for them for low-altitude work. Well, Fifteenth down in Italy is yelling for every P-38 they can get. Well, there's the Pacific, where the P-38 is chewing the Japanese into little pieces. They *all* want the P-38 . . .

So the decision was implemented. The front-line fighter of the VIII Fighter Command would be the Mustang. Most P-38s and P-47s would go to tactical air. But not overnight, of course. In the meantime there was that air war to be fought.

In January 1944 the 20th Fighter Group made everyone sit up and blink. The P-38s of the 20th mixed it up with a big mess of German fighters and shot down ten of the enemy. Ten? How many 38s were lost? Only *two?*

Can't happen again. On February 8 the 20th Fighter Group was on another long-range mission when a P-38 in the 77th Squadron developed engine trouble. The flight containing this airplane was given permission to drop down to 12,000 feet and go on home. The pilots were unhappy about it. For a while, anyway. One pilot, Lieutenant James M. Morris, liked the way his airplane behaved way down there at 12,000 feet. Sneaking for home he spotted a German fighter at low altitude. He peeled off and dove with everything he had—no worry about compressibility down here. He clobbered the other plane and climbed back up to his flight. Then he saw another Jerry, and repeated the performance. He blinked when a third target presented itself—and got his third kill of the day. Near Saarburg, now well separated from his flight, he blew up a locomotive. He turned for home, saw another fighter ahead of him, and creamed number four. The fact that this was, at the time, a record for the number of kills on a single mission for all American pilots in Europe, understandably brought some new attention to the P-38.

But it was the "If only those damned Allisons . . ." kind of thing. Because only a few days before, nearly half of all the P-38s sent out by the 20th and 55th Fighter Groups had to abort with engine trouble.

That's the way it went. Everywhere else in the world

the Lightning was *the* fighter. But operating at high altitude in Europe . . . There was April 8, 1944. A P-38 escort mission for B-17s to Oldenburg was scrubbed. Lt. Colonel Harold Rau chafed at the bit. So the B-17s couldn't go. So what? He was there to fight. Rau called Wing and asked permission, almost begged for it, to take the 20th Fighter Group out on an independent fighter sweep. A balls-out mission, the P-38s free of bomber escort, down low, just spoiling for trouble. Wing thought Colonel Rau was out of his mind, but gave the approval for the mission. The Lightnings stormed from their fields and headed for Germany.

Where?

Eighty miles from Berlin.

Where?

Where the Luftwaffe lived. *Right into their home airfields.*

Forty-eight Lightnings went out. Not too many when you think about it. Forty-eight fighter airplanes that were not supposed to be in the same air with German fighters. One hundred and twelve minutes after takeoff they were diving against a field near Salzwedel. They made four strafing passes and set thirteen airplanes aflame, most of them bombers. Then they found an army barracks and chewed hell out of *that* target. They found a train and exploded the locomotive.

This sort of thing couldn't go on forever. Lightnings were all over the place. Seven Me-109s came down from the sun, fast and hard, to bounce the P-38s. One Lightning was shot down in this first pass. Rau came around in a climbing turn to take a Messerschmitt off the tail of a P-38. The Me-109 tore apart, and then crashed into the P-38 it was pursuing. Both went down. Moments later two more Messerschmitts were burning and had crashed and exploded. The remaining Me-109 pilots took off as fast as they could fly. They weren't used to this sort of nonsense with P-38s.

The 77th Squadron chewed up an airfield, destroying eight planes and damaging another twenty-one on the ground, and in the process of that little job shot down two

German fighters. The 55th Squadron couldn't find a handy airfield, so the pilots went on a devastating strafing spree at any likely military target. When they got home the P-38s toted up the score. Only one Lightning had been shot down by a German fighter. A second was lost in the aerial collision. Two more P-38s went down to heavy ground fire.

Three Me-109s had been shot down. The Lightnings had destroyed twenty-one on the ground and damaged another two dozen. They shot up eighteen locomotives, fifty rail wagons, sixteen flak towers, factory buildings, barracks, hangars and a few oil storage dumps.

During this period of working out the bugs of the P-38, prior to the J models, engineers in England tried every manner of emergency fix to improve the reliability of the airplanes at high altitude—and it must be stressed that it was only at extreme heights with extreme cold that the Lightnings were running into their difficulties. More than one mechanic soundly cursed Allison for low oil temperature operation, which had to be fixed, temporary as it was, by blocking off oil cooling radiators in order to raise the temperature of the engine oil and improve lubrication when it was most desperately needed. Turbo-superchargers had been hindering operations at altitude by producing a thick contrail that marked location of the Lightnings to an inordinate degree. Mechanics produced a water trap (this was the 55th Group) and enlarged duct scoops; to answer directly the most intense complaints of the pilots, the savage cold in the cockpit, they routed warm air directly to the cockpit from the engines, easing pilot problems and helping to more effectively defrost the inside of the canopy.

One month after the Normandy invasion the P-38s were starting to get up steam, and on July 7, 1944, in a massive fighter movement through Germany, P-38s scored about one-third of all the kills garnered by P-38, P-47 and P-51 fighters. But the showing meant more than that, for minimum P-38 losses were involved.

The 20th Fighter Group sailed into a huge German fighter force tearing at B-24s, and in the ensuing melee shot down seven German fighters for the loss of one P-38. Captain Orville Goodman of the 55th Fighter Group led a squadron into a swarm of FW-190s and Me-109s, and when that fracas ended eight FW-190s and three Me-109s had been shot down without loss to the P-38s. The 38th Squadron, also of the 55th Group, led by Major John D. Landers, shot down three Me-410s.

When the day ended, twenty-one German fighters had been confirmed as destroyed for the loss of one P-38.

On August 25, 1944, Captain L. E. "Scrappy" Blumer of the Ninth Air Force's 367th Fighter Group had just completed, along with other P-38s, a dive-bombing strike near Saint Quentin. Another P-38 force was sending out a frantic distress call as they were attacked by some fifty FW-190s.

Blumer led his pack of P-38s to the attack, rolling in after a Focke-Wulf hammering a Lightning. Blumer went in close, fired a short burst, and the FW-190 disappeared in flames, with the pilot bailing out. A second FW-190 took a hammering burst and snapped into the ground. Blumer zoomed up from a dive, rolled over and dove again after a third FW-190 that literally exploded into pieces. A fourth victim went down when Blumer's concentrated fire smashed into a Focke-Wulf cockpit. Then there was number five; the pilot half-rolled and bailed out of his crippled FW-190, and that made it five in a single fight for that particular P-38 pilot.

By now eyebrows were raising everywhere. Had they underestimated the Lightning, after all? Its initial showing had been, on the face of mechanical reliability, something less than anticipated. But then, after screaming delays, engine blowups, and similar problems, the people in the P-38 cockpits seemed to be getting a second wind. It was difficult to ignore the results of twenty-one Germans for one P-38 on the July 7th mission, and now, here was a Ninth Air Force pilot clawing his way to being an ace in a single fight—in which his P-38 maneuvered inside and outflew the best of the German fighters.

The P-38 was being phased out rapidly in the VIII Fighter Command in favor of Mustangs. The 55th

Fighter Group in the period of September 3–13 brought more questions to the fore—they were turning in tremendous performance, with the late-model, much improved P-38J and L fighters right around the corner, which would increase the P-38's qualities even further.

During this ten-day period—as stated in the official award of the Distinguished Unit Citation—the 55th Group:

> Compiled one of the outstanding records of enemy aircraft destroyed or damaged by one group in any similar period of air combat over Europe during eight heavy bomber escort missions flown in 11 days. In the tremendous task of wresting superiority from the German Air Force, the Group made a material and noteworthy contribution by destroying 106 planes and damaging 51 in the air and on the ground, while losing but nine aircraft. This ratio of nearly 12 to one was achieved both at high altitude during the escort phase and in medium and low level combat after the bombers had been brought safely through the target area.

Major Herbert E. Johnson, Jr., 77th Fighter Squadron, 20th Fighter Group, told his new pilots—and emphatically—that at high altitude: "We can definitely turn inside any German aircraft. This particular advantage is especially valuable when escorting bombers on deep penetrations when we are actually in a defensive position."

And at low altitude: "I do not recommend hitting the deck if altitude can be maintained, unless you become separated completely and then be damn sure of your approximate whereabouts. If jumped on the deck the best evasive maneuver is a tight level turn. Due to the beautiful stall characteristics of the 38 you can turn much tighter without the danger of spinning than any German craft."

Keep one thing in mind. When losses of P-38s are added up against German planes shot down, *all causes of P-38 losses are included*. And what did some of that flying include? From a history of the 20th Fighter Group:

Spark-plugged by Lt. Colonel Wilson, the 20th literally scourged everything that moved along the rails and roads of Germany and German-occupied Europe, and set the pace for Eighth Air Force Fighter Groups in the destruction of ground targets. The campaign was intensified as D-Day approached and the smashing up of everything German that moved near and behind the battle lines became "Priority One" until the end of August. The effect of these attacks was enormous. They not only helped to paralyze the enemy communications system, which many German war leaders such as Field Marshal Von Runstedt and Reich Marshal Goering have declared the single most important factor in the defeat of Germany, but also threw terror and despair into the hearts of German troops and civilians.

Ground attack missions were always dangerous, the most dangerous that fighters could engage in, but our pilots pressed them home with daring and skill, as the records shows. Between April 8 and July 24 . . . the 20th destroyed or damaged 315 locomotives, 100 ammunition cars, 87 oil tank cars, 1,000 freight cars, and 370 motor vehicles, including armored vehicles. Barges, boats, radio stations, railway stations, military barracks, radar installations, high tension towers, small factories and hangars had also been attacked. . . . Our pilots machine-gunned, dive-bombed, skip-bombed and even high-level bombed enemy targets.

From some of the more determined criticism of the P-38, and much of it in high-altitude operation certainly was warranted, certain numbers emerged. Considering all the problems one would be led to believe that P-38s were shot down by the hundreds, and with only a fraction of that cost to the Germans.

That's what one might believe. But he would be wrong. The 20th Fighter Group, before it converted to P-51s, shot down eighty-nine German aircraft and destroyed another thirty-one on the ground. Total P-38 losses— from *all* causes (being shot down, engine failures, collisions, becoming lost, being lost due to weather, etc.) —came to eighty-seven P-38s.

The 55th and 364th Fighter Groups, by the time they

phased out of the Lightning, found their losses—again from *all* causes—barely higher than their confirmed claims of German fighters shot down in air combat.

And just at that time when the Lightnings were "getting up steam"—such as the July 7th, 1944 mission, when they shot down twenty-one German fighters for the loss of one P-38—the story ended.

The P-38s were assigned to ground attack missions, chewing up the enemy on the ground. Perhaps, considering their terrible effect in these strikes, they did more to break the back of the German military than they might have done in the air.

Perhaps.

15. Tough Underbelly

There's something of a problem in relating the P-38 story in that period following the end of fighting in North Africa. The Lightnings went on to Sardinia and Italy and lower France, and stormed up beyond Italy into central Europe and Germany, and fanned out to the nations on the far side of Italy, and even flew shuttle-bombing escort missions to and from Russia.

The problem? Well, for one thing, the P-38 wasn't a controversial airplaine here. No one questioned what it could do. They saw that in the weekly combat reports and evaluations. No one questioned the worth of the airplane; everyone wanted it, and desperately. They wanted 38s in the Ninth, the Twelfth, and the Fifteenth Air Forces. They wanted them for convoy cover, for long-range patrol, ground attack, against enemy fighters and bombers, for anti-shipping strikes, night fighting, bomber escort—in short, there was a constant din for more and more P-38s. Production was turning them out in ever-greater numbers back in the States, but everyone, it seemed (with the exception of VIII Fighter Command, which was still puzzled by the extraordinary showing of the Lightning in its final months of combat), beat the table for P-38s.

The description of ground attack—loco busting missions—of the 20th and 55th Fighter Groups over Germany and France was almost a duplication of ground-attack missions of the P-38s stampeding out of North Africa against Sardinia, Sicily and Italy. There the mission was stated simply enough. Destroy the enemy in the air and then chew him up on the ground. Stop him where he stood—wreck his rail communications, turn his highways into deathtraps, his seas into bloodied waters, his airfields into carnage: in short, to the maximum extent possible destroy his mobility and set him up for the Allied ground forces.

The effectiveness of airpower in a campaign often defies statistical evaluation, simply because a covering screen of fighters, if they do not shoot down a single airplane, can be 100 per cent effective simply by their presence—which keeps enemy aircraft away from the ground forces. In the Sicily invasion (and the entire island was taken in thirty-eight days) Lightnings were assigned all-out strafing missions over the western and southeastern parts of the island. Every available fighter of every type was thrown into the campaign, and another example of little-publicized success was in the mission of fighters assigned to Coastal duties, which managed either to shoot down every reconnaissance plane of the Germans or Italians, or else drive them off, so that the enemy remained completely in the dark about details of the invasion. The surprise was of course tactical rather than strategic, but its effect was enormous on the outcome of the invasion and subsequent drives inland. But even the full strength of available tactical airpower wasn't considered enough. As noted in the official AAF History:

. . . The air forces undertook a special effort toward interdiction of the enemy's movements from the interior toward the assault areas. They met the new commitment by temporarily transferring two groups of U.S. P-38 fighter-bombers from Strategic Air Force to reinforce the two U.S. A-36 groups of Tactical . . . with orders to attack all movement. Formations dispatched every thirty minutes throughout D-Day destroyed many enemy transports. Especially effective were attacks delivered along the eastern coastal road and the roads radiating from the Axis concentration area around Enna in central Sicily . . . Almost 1,000 sorties flown by Twelfth Air Force day fighters and fighter-bombers . . . left the roads

of Sicily blocked with burned trucks, seriously hampered
the enemy's road movements, and helped the Allied
ground forces to strengthen and enlarge their beach-
heads.

But the most pressing demand for the P-38s was back
in the higher air, as long-range escort to the medium and
heavy bombers. Major strikes against Italian targets included the bombing of such cities as Naples and Rome. It
is not our intent in these pages to review a step-by-step
procedure of the missions flown, since that would be in
the nature of an entirely different story; instead, selected
missions representative of P-38 activity are more our interest. An idea of the growing size of the raids is found in
the numbers of airplanes employed. On July 17 a massive force of medium and heavy bombers struck at
Naples. The next day, in an afternoon raid, 97 Fortresses
and 179 Marauders of the Twelfth Air Force, with 164
P-38 fighters as escort, went after the city again. The
immensity of the strikes is found in the number of escort
fighters—more than was to be found in ETO operations
months later.

Another raid representative of the growing force of
such strikes was the mission of August 13th, 1943 against
Littorio and Lorenzo. A first wave of 106 B-17s was
escorted by 45 P-38s, and a second attack of 102 B-26
Marauders and 66 B-25 Mitchells was made with 90
Lightnings flying escort.

A see-saw of demands for P-38s went back and forth
between such strategic requirements, and the tactical demands of ground forces. Throughout the period of August
8–17, P-38s and P-40s teamed up for massive fighter
sweeps of Sardinia and lower Italy, and the P-38s came
from three Groups—the 1st, 4th and 82nd. Once again
the missions flown were repeats of the mauling given to
enemy ground forces and facilities, in this instance, however, with special emphasis on evacuation routes. The German Army, and the Italians as well, were trying to ex-
tricate themselves from Allied advances by withdrawing
with most of their forces intact. The P-38s and P-40s

were turned loose with the job of preventing such movement. They met little or no opposition on most strikes. Loaded with 500-pound and 1,000-pound bombs they tore up roads, canals and railways, wreaking particular havoc amidst transport and rail equipment already backed up and jammed by earlier bombings.

Every now and then the rare event happened—the enemy arose in number to stem the furious onslaught from the air. For some reason the German command ordered unusually fierce defense of Sardinia, more so than for Sicily and Italy, and on July 30, 1943 a fierce battle raged over the island. One P-40 was shot down for the confirmed destruction of twenty-one enemy fighters. The unusual ratio was due to several factors, not the least of which was the fact that by now the American pilots were veterans at the game, and aggressive as well. This was compounded by the reverse among the enemy which was noted by the AAF History:

> The poor tactics and coordination displayed by the enemy pilots indicated that they were inexperienced and had little knowledge of the capabilities and limitations of their own Me-109's or of the Allies' P-40's.

The effectiveness of the fighter sweeps against the enemy could hardly have been more dramatized than in the air requirements for the invasion of Italy proper. The AAF found itself in an unexpected situation, in which it was unnecessary to mount "a blitz on enemy airfields such as had preceded the Sicilian campaign . . . for the back of the Axis air forces already had been broken." Instead of mass sweeps, the fighters, sometimes with bombers, went after particular airfields and complexes. On August 25, no less than 140 P-38s came in against the Foggia complex of fields, flying on the deck, strafing planes, hangars, trucks and rail transport. Soon after, with the enemy reeling, afraid to show any movement on the airfields because of the rampaging Lightnings, a force of 136 B-17s, with heavy P-38 escort, showed up to finish the job. The main purpose was to wreck the fields to deny their use to the enemy; in the process the P-38s and the bombs from the Fortresses destroyed at least forty-seven planes and heavily damaged another thirteen. How successful were these attacks?

There was little air opposition to the invasions that followed and, as important to the AAF, "thereafter there was a sharp decline in the number of Allied bombers lost to enemy fighters."

Not until some time after the invasion forces were ashore on Italy did the enemy manage to rush additional planes down from the north. On the 10th and 11th of September, some 100 enemy fighters and bombers attacked invasion targets. By now Allied fighter pilots were exhausted from flying long missions day after day. Land fighters flew 1,250 sorties and Seafires operating from British carriers flew another 400 sorties. In this two-day period they broke up some forty attacks and shot down some twenty enemy planes, losing only seven of their own number. But the greatest enemy—to the fighter pilots— was fatigue, and more planes were being lost in landing accidents than in fighting enemy aircraft. As advance fields were taken and engineers moved in, the Allied fighters themselves advanced closer to the front lines, and the problem was considered solved.

The P-38s were called on to use their seven-league boots as the air assault moved into the Balkans, and the Lightnings operated as escort fighters, sweep fighters and fighter-bombers across Greece and Yugoslavia, then began to branch out still further. They escorted B-17s and other bombers far to the north against major industrial targets such as Turin (ball bearings) in Italy, ranged into France, and started hitting major targets throughout central Europe as well. Under the restrictions of escorting —and staying close to—the bombers, the Lightnings sustained their record of shooting down approximately five enemy fighters for every P-38 lost.

FRANTIC

FRANTIC was the code name for using airbases in the Soviet Union as a terminal point for shuttle bombing —bombers and fighters would operate from England, Africa and Italy against enemy targets on one-way missions terminating at the opposite ends of the FRANTIC mission lines. It began in 1943, it dragged on for month after month while the Russians procrastinated. Finally, with the intervention of Stalin himself, the plans were rushed forward. If all went well, figured the AAF, the problems of range would be reduced, the Germans would soon be hit from all sides, and beyond that lay the use of Siberian bases by the AAF for strikes directly against Japan.

More immediately, however, lay the means to strike at targets that otherwise could not be reached with B-17s and B-24s from current bases. And that meant major work; the Russians finally provided fields at Poltava, Mirgorod, and Piryatin, fairly close to Kiev. The Russian fields needed massive rebuilding—longer runways, control towers, supplies of fuel, bombs, ammunition, spare parts, hangars were just some of the items. In essence it represented a tremendous logistical effort, with supplies sent to the USSR through Murmansk and Persia. The story of preparing the bases, and of selecting the targets finally to be bombed, is one of monumental and mysterious frustrations on the part of the Russians, who were secretive, unpredictable, often uncommunicative, unfriendly, and sometimes uncooperative and even hostile. That was the official attitude. The Russian civilians were friendly, open, hospitable and altogether open-armed about welcoming the Yankees.

In June, 1944, the first shuttle missions were flown from Italy to bomb targets and then on to Russia. Later the strike force, Fortresses and Mustangs, went back to Italy. On June 21, 1944, the Eighth Air Force got into the act with 114 B-17s and 70 Mustangs striking at Ruhland, near Berlin, in perfect weather, and then heading for Poltava. But unknown to the American strike force they were being trailed by a Heinkel He-177, and that night, with perfect timing and astonishing accuracy (and a complete disregard for Russian night defenses) the Luftwaffe struck. First they split open the night with flares and then, with something on the order of 110 tons of bombs, they demolished the Poltava field. When they were through dropping bombs they came down on the deck strafing and scattering dozens of small but murderous antipersonnel bombs.

The Germans didn't lose a single plane in what the AAF was later to admit was a "brilliantly successful" strike. Small wonder. With absolutely no loss of life the Germans destroyed *forty-three* B-17s and damaged another twenty-six. They wiped out fifteen Mustangs plus a large number of Russian planes, detonated several ammunition dumps, destroyed 450,000 gallons of aviation gasoline brought in at tremendous cost and effort, and wrecked facilities everywhere. The same Russians who had proven so deplorable in their conduct with the Americans now refused to let the Americans endanger themselves in fighting the fires and manning flak guns. Only one American was killed as the Russians ordered them away from the blazing explosions and went in themselves; twenty-five Russians died that night.

A month passed and the AAF decided to do its best to keep FRANTIC alive in several missions that for some reason have remained obscure and known by relatively few people. It was the time Lightnings went to Russia.

On July 22, 1944, a task force of seventy-six P-38s and fifty-eight P-51s of the Fifteenth Air Force set out for Rumania. As they neared their targets another force of B-17s was hammering Ploesti oil fields. The Lightnings and Mustangs, freed of restrictive escort duty, ran wild against German installations and airfields in a mission officially described as "devastating." The P-38s and P-51s destroyed fifty-six German fighters and bombers and continued on to their Russian base. Three days later the mixed force of Lightnings and Mustangs hit other

Rumanian targets, crippled a major airfield, and chalked up seven more planes destroyed. The next day, on the 26th, they started back for Italy, and on their way slammed into several more airfields to destroy another twenty planes.

A week later another huge fighter task force, this time made up only of P-38s, operated for several days in direct support of the Russians in shuttle missions between Italy and Russia, sweeping low against airfields and railroad lines. But after three days of heavy strikes, the P-38 pilots reported they were running out of targets, and the Fifteenth decided future fighter-bomber attacks using Russian airfields simply weren't worth the hassle. Future missions of this sort were dropped. (The Eighth Air Force flew its last mission in shuttle bombing in August; by then the front lines had changed so greatly the value of the FRANTIC bases had dissolved.)

BUILDING MUSCLE

An idea of how the fortunes of the fighters changed in a period of only a few months is seen in the buildup of fighters for the Fifteenth Air Force. When it came into being as a strategic air arm, the Fifteenth started off 1944 with hand-me-down equipment and organizations. It had four fighter groups, all at half-strength, and not until May 1944 did it receive its full seven groups. The next month it was exchanging its old P-38s for the new J models, had given up short-range Spitfires for Mustangs, and was accepting P-47s to replace its P-40s. From then on, as the Germans learned, it was an all-new ball game.

An idea of what this kind of equipment means was given a masterful demonstration in a one-two punch against German airfields in Austria, which the AAF History unabashedly claims was "one of the cleverer tricks of the air war."

A heavy force of B-17s and B-24s from five bomber groups, with very heavy escort by P-38s from three fighter groups, set out for German fighter fields in the

Udine area of Austria. The controllers made certain that the P-38s and their bombers flew at normal altitude. This assured that the Germans would be plotting their position and their approach, and it also meant heavy fighter interception.

Which is just what the Fifteenth Air Force *wanted*.

Because, unknown to the Germans, P-47s of the 325th Fighter Group had taken off well after the bombers were gone from their home fields. The Thunderbolts went out over the Adriatic on the deck and finally caught up to the P-38-escorted Fortresses and Liberators. At this point the P-47s climbed as fast as they could get to altitude and raced ahead of the big formations. They hit the German fields just as the enemy planes were in the process of taking off, climbing slowly and positioning themselves for formation assembly.

Few pilots have ever been greeted by so glorious a sight and the Thunderbolts came in with all the surprise attributed to their name. They destroyed at least thirty-six German planes, including fourteen Me-109s, and probably destroyed another eight. Then came the bombers with 29,000 fragmentation bombs. By day's end, at a cost of six bombers and three fighters, the Fifteenth wrote off another 140 German aircraft.

SOME NOTES

During the North African air fighting, the Twelfth Air Force, despite its concentration on ground attack and bombing missions, and stay-close-to-the-bombers escort missions, managed enough air fighting to produce its top ace for that part of the war—Lieutenant W. J. Sloan with twelve confirmed air kills.

One Fifteenth Air Force P-38 pilot who worked his way to ace status in a single fight likely wishes he could have avoided that day. On June 10, 1944, a mixed force of Lightnings—P-38 fighters flying top cover for P-38 fighter-bombers—went after oil refinery targets in the Ploesti area. The planes went in at low level and, according to plan, the fighters moved ahead near the target to go in fast and hard to mix it up with German and Rumanian interceptors, and generally clear the way so the P-38s could go after their targets with a 1,000-pound bomb from each plane. P-38s of the 71st Squadron dropped their auxiliary tanks, spotted six bombers below them, and sent eight P-38s on their way. All six bombers went down almost at once. Immediately the P-38s climbed for altitude to reform. At least they tried to. They didn't have the chance. Scattered, slow, spread out, they were caught in a vicious bounce by German fighters all too eager for the rare opportunity. The P-38 pilots all heard it at the same time, an unknown voice yelling: *"Break left! Break left!"* Lieutenant Herbert B. Hatch looked up at a gaggle of Focke-Wulfs coming down like winged raindrops. Hatch and his wingman hesitated a moment too long, and the other P-38s broke sharply to the left. Hatch looked to his right, and there came another large force of FW-190s, all with the advantage of speed and superior numbers. They were in deep trouble up to their earlobes and they knew it; Hatch had no choice but to break right, straight into the oncoming Focke-Wulfs. No time to fire. He sailed through the enemy fighters and then clawed around in a steep turn to his left, his wingman glued to him.

As they cut their turn tight a Focke-Wulf flashed before Hatch, and he had just enough time for a burst that went from nose to tail, literally tearing the airplane in two. Hatch broke fast, this time to the right. He went after an FW-190 just as it poured cannon shells into a diving P-38. The Focke-Wulf exploded almost at the same moment its victim tore apart.

Hatch was now scraping the treetops and, coming out of a turn, faced an FW-190 racing in with a head-on attack. It was a perfect position for the P-38, and the concentrated stream of four guns and one cannon ripped the big engine away from the enemy fighter. It was closer than Hatch wanted; the disintegrating Focke-Wulf, as it flashed overhead, sprayed his P-38 with oil and sliced several inches from his left rudder.

Hatch hugged the trees at full power to build up speed, saw another FW-190 after a Lightning, reefed it in tight for a deflection shot and exploded the fourth airplane. He didn't like it this low; he had no maneuvering room except for level turns or a sudden climb (which could have been suicide). He eased into a high-speed climb and stared from his side window—at a Focke-Wulf flying formation with him! Hatch chopped power and kicked rudder and slid quickly behind the startled German pilot; before he could react Hatch had him with a long burst into the cockpit. The 190 hit the trees and exploded.

That made five for Hatch—in his first combat.

P-38s were going down in all directions; the German bounce had been devastating. Hatch, somewhere in the melee, had lost his wingman. Looking for him, Hatch saw a P-38 flying with one prop feathered, two FW-190s chewing up the crippled fighter. Hatch pumped two short bursts into one Focke-Wulf, forced the other to break off. Then, silence. Hatch was out of ammunition.

Several P-38s in sight of each other assembled quickly, looked for stragglers, and started home. They were *all* out of ammunition. Over Yugoslavia the worst happened. Another group of German fighters came diving after them in a bounce. The P-38s turned and drove into the teeth of the enemy planes. One P-38 went down—but not that single-engine cripple they were escorting. That was the last of the fight, however, and they went the rest of the way uneventfully.

P-38s were reported down everywhere. Many had survived the fight only to run short of fuel on the way home. Others were landing at any nearby base, still others were going down in fields. It was some compensation that some of his friends might be included among that number, for Hatch's P-38 was the only fighter of the 71st Squadron to return home that night.

In November, 1944, Captain John J. Voll of the Fifteenth Air Force slid wearily to the ground from his P-38. This was the 16th of the month and Voll was tired. He had just flown his fifty-seventh and last combat mission. The past five months were eventful ones. Johnny Voll had shot down seventeen planes. Not bad. Today, on his last mission, he had shot down another four to give him a grand total of twenty-one confirmed air kills.

He almost didn't live long enough to get back to base. Sometimes the last one is the roughest. It was for Voll.

He was on his way home from a bomber shepherd mission over Germany. A lot ventured, and little gained except to have had his radio shot out—and to lose himself from the rest of the Lightning force. So Voll scooted for home, and he would have made it without too much fuss except for catching sight (while still over north Italy) of a Junkers Ju-88. The Ju-88 saw *him* and dove for safety at full throttle, Voll right behind and gaining. Smart German—almost. He took Voll into a hornet's nest, right over a German field with the air filled with fighters. Voll saw seven FW-190s coming at him from behind while five Me-109s, racing in from another direction, started to knock out the lone Lightning first.

Voll, by now rather unhappy about it all, facing what was certainly to be a brief fight at the hands of a dozen single-engine fighters, decided he might as well take care of unfinished business. That was the Ju-88, and Voll gave it a burst that brought forth a tornado of fire. Then, before the twelve fighters after him really knew what to make of the "crazy" Lightning, Voll wracked the P-38 around as tight as it would move—and the P-38, in the hands of a good pilot, turned a lot tighter than most Germans would admit.

It cost them this day. Voll shot down two FW-190s, broke through that pack, flamed an Me-109, and then in a brief but hysterical scramble, hit two more fighters so hard they dropped out of the fight, and damaged another two. Five fighters were left to argue the point, but Voll got his opening and slammed the throttles to war emergency power. Whoever said the FW-190 and the Me-109 were faster than the P-38 weren't around that day— Johnny Voll outdistanced his pursuers and was home free.

Quite a last mission.

Then there are *other* missions ...

Let the pilot, 2nd Lieutenant Jack Lenox, Jr.—fighter ace, P-38 driver, Fifteenth Air Force—tell *this* one himself. Lenox had just shot down a German fighter and had another one cornered, with the German pilot trying desperately to get out. Lenox quit shooting and kept his gun camera working. He should have looked behind him because an Me-109 saw the P-38 holding a straight course and:

"The next thing I knew, my canopy was shattered on the left, my engine was burning and I was in a tight spin. My first reaction was to recover from the spin and my P-38 responded beautifully. Acting almost automatically I went right into my fire-feather procedures on the burning engine. My spinal column must have been doing all my thinking for me, for the next thing I realized was that the fire was out and the ship seemed to be doing all right, so I took off for home.

"After I had gotten settled down on course I began to take inventory of the cockpit and myself. The canopy was shattered and the metal behind the throttle quadrant was twisted. My left sleeve had been torn and to my horror I saw blood oozing out. I checked my arm feeling for broken bones and wiggling my fingers. So far I had felt no pain. But as I tried to raise my arm I suddenly realized I was paralyzed—my arm would not move. Figuring that I was in shock and suddenly scared that I might lose my left arm, I broke open the first-aid kit strapped to my chest and took out the morphine hypodermic. Giving myself the needle was the hardest thing I ever did; but I realized that when I came out of shock my shattered arm would be in extreme pain, and I still had to land my crippled Lightning.

"I was nearing the field and figuring my procedures for making a one-armed landing when to my relief, surprise and embarrassment I discovered that all this time I had had my jacket sleeve caught on the throttle lock.

"I waved my arm around the cockpit in joy ..."

Now, *really*.

16. Mediterranean Personals

Two more items to close out the P-38 air war in the European/African side of the world.

One that reads more like fiction than fact, but checked out thoroughly—and was substantiated.

The other from a man named Val Phillips, P-38 driver who was there, and provides us with one of those invaluable inside studies of the P-38 that can come from no other source except being in the cockpit in the right place at the right time.

First, Africa and the Mediterranean . . .

HAROLD FISHER

It began on June 4, 1943 when a formation of B-17s was returning from a "hammer" mission against the island of Pantelleria. Well behind the bunched four-engine bombers, visible only as a small dot in the sky, a last Fortress dragged its way home to Africa. The B-17 was crippled with both engines on the left wing dead and feathered. The pilot, 1st Lieutenant Harold Fisher, fought the controls of his battered airplane. This was his twentieth mission and he had the skill and experience to handle the machine. But he questioned how much longer he could maintain full control. Fisher thought seriously of ditching while the airplane responded to his movements, because if the Fort ever "got away" from him, his crew would have to bail out, and *fast,* and some of them might not make

205

it from a gyrating bomber. Yet, Fisher didn't like the idea of his men parachuting into the sea. That was always a tricky proposition. He was a veteran; they weren't. For the nine other men aboard the Fortress this was their first mission.

Fisher committed himself to staying with the B-17 as long as she would fly. He ordered the crew to dump excess weight—machine guns, ammo belts, flak suits—everything that would come loose. A few pounds would make a difference of a gnat's hair, but with two engines gone even that was enough. He didn't want to think about German fighters. Jeez, not now. The Fortress, *Bonnie Sue,* was already wobbling through the air. A single lazy pass by a Messerschmitt or a Focke-Wulf could ruin what was left of the day.

Then the dreaded call. "Fighter one o'clock high," shouted the right waist gunner. "Closing fast."

There wasn't that much time for panic. The crewmen were at their chutes immediately, hooking up, checking last items. Then, almost immediately, they relaxed. No mistaking *that* baby. No one could mistake the twin-boomed signature of the P-38. One of the "Little Friends." By God, they were glad to see *him*. The Lightning eased in so close that Fisher grinned at the sight of the pilot waving to him. Fisher went to VHF radio, asked the 38 driver for escort back to his base. The pilot agreed and eased back to take up a weaving escort position above and behind the Fortress. Harold Fisher looked down at the Mediterranean four thousand feet below. It didn't look so bad now. That P-38 was good news.

Until a moment later. A locomotive seemed to crash directly against the Flying Fortress. A sudden, savage blow heeled the B-17 over sharply. They heard a roaring, continuous crash as a stream of heavy machine gun slugs and exploding cannon shells tore apart the airplane. Fisher barely had the time to see the P-38 closing in fast, the long nose ablaze with the five weapons. Just enough time to see the P-38 chopping the Fortress into slashed ribbons; just enough time to hear the cold laughter in his earphones. Then the bomber dropped in a screaming dive toward the sea, banking into a spiral that kept tightening. Fisher fought the controls with all his strength. Just before they hit the water he righted the airplane, brought up the nose. They plowed into the Mediterranean with all the force of smashing into a stone wall. The nose gave way and at more than a hundred miles an hour the sea burst through the airplane, killing men, trapping the others. Fisher remembers crawling through a shattered windshield. He struggled to the surface, grabbed at a raft floating alongside him.

He was the only survivor. That night a British rescue team fished him from the water.

The next day Fisher found himself the target of unchecked fury on the part of P-38 group and squadron commanders. They'd listened to his story and they reacted unpleasantly to his details of being shot down by a Lightning. They didn't like it, they didn't believe him, and they read off the equally incensed bomber pilot. The Intelligence officer, Major Walter B. Higgins, soothed the ruffled feathers of those at the interrogation. What he had to say put a new light on the matter. It didn't matter much at first, but it turned out to be everything.

Several weeks previously a P-38 pilot, low on fuel and lost over the Mediterranean, sighted land and ran for it, bringing his Lightning smoothly to earth at Elmas Airdrome, just outside the main port city of Cagliari, Sardinia. Before the pilot could set his fighter aflame with a few well-placed shots from his .45, Italian troops hauled open the canopy and dragged him unceremoniously from the big airplane. That's where it began. The Italians tested their new toy until they'd soaked up whatever technical information there was to be had. Lieutenant Guido Rossi, one of their better pilots (and also one of their more imaginative and colorful fighter jocks), looked long and hard at the Lightning and beamed with a sudden inspiration. He presented his idea to his superiors, who in turn bucked it up to Rome, who in turn took it into the *Duce,* until Mussolini himself personally approved Rossi's suggestions.

Rossi had himself his own personal Lightning. His plan

was simple. He would leave the airplane unchanged; not a marking would be altered. Then he would wait for progress reports on American air strikes. After the Americans made their bombing raids Rossi would take off and follow the formations, looking for stragglers. Who would suspect a P-38? Indeed, any bomber crew in trouble would be delighted to see the fighter to gain the protection of its speed and heavy firepower.

The system worked beautifully and Italian headquarters was delighted. Guido Rossi, taking his time, always waiting for the right opportunity, shot down several B-17s. No crewmen survived his unexpected attacks to report the ruse to the Allied camp. Not until the British netted Harold Fisher from the sea and came home with his startling tale of the renegade P-38 did we get wind of what was happening.

Bomber crews were alerted to be on the watch for a strange P-38 that might suddenly attack their aircraft. Most crews thought headquarters had fractured its collective skull. How were they to tell what was happening until it was too late? Rossi, despite the warnings, maintained his unnerving manhunt for crippled or straggling bombers. Finally he caught his quarry trailing a formation swinging away from Naples and shot another Fortress from the sky.

Fisher went to Colonel Bill Hall, his group commander, with a suggestion to try to set up Rossi. Since he was so fond of stragglers, why not set up a decoy? Not a standard B-17, but one of the experimental YB-40 gunships then being tested out of England. Engineers had modified a standard B-17F into a flying gun platform. They installed a power "chin" turret beneath the nose with twin fifties to overcome weak forward armament against head-on attacks. Where the radio operator had fired a single ball socket-mounted fifty amidships, they placed another power turret with two heavy guns. Instead of the single fifties in each waist position there were now two guns per position. Into the bomb bays went ammunition boxes to keep the YB-40 firing long after the normal B-17 ammo supply would have been exhausted. The concept of the YB-40 was to provide self-escort to the bomber formations

in cases where fighters were not available for escort, or
targets lay beyond fighter range. Each YB-40 had sixteen
heavy machine guns, a major ammunition supply and extra armor for the crew. While the concept was not being
sustained where mass fighter attacks were involved, and
the YB-40, with its heavy weight could not keep up with
the bomber formations once they were free of their bomb
loads, chances were that a P-38, its pilot unsuspecting of
the heavy firepower, would be a fair target for the YB-40.
Especially if they could sucker in the Italian in precisely
the same manner he used to trap the crippled Fortresses
into setting themselves up for the kill. Bill Hall gave his
approval, and the request for a single YB-40 was bucked
up to England. The gunship arrived in Africa early in
August and, as he had hoped, Harold Fisher received his
assignment to fly the gun-bristling decoy.

For the next two weeks Fisher and a picked crew did
their best to flush out the marauding P-38. Returning
from missions against Salerno, Foggia, Naples and Rome
he dragged back of the main formations, an "obvious
cripple" trailing the safety of the formations and a sitting
duck for fighters. But Lieutenant Rossi came nowhere near
the YB-40, and instead went after the real thing. On
August 19 the Italian flamed a straggler south of Bene-
vento. A week later Rossi chopped down another Fortress. As Intelligence pieced together the fragments of information, Rossi then flew formation with a strafing P-38
and at the right moment was reported to have shot down
the unsuspecting American pilot.

Fisher kept badgering Intelligence for details of his
elusive quarry. The break came when he learned that
Rossi's wife lived in Constantine, *occupied by the Allies.*
That night Fisher visited Gina Rossi and her child—
never seen by its father—and as soon as he returned to
base he dragged an artist from his workbench. When the
artist finished his job, the YB-40 carried on its fuselage a
painting of a beautiful dark-haired woman. In large letters
beneath the painting was the name *Gina.*

On August 31 Fortresses struck targets in Pisa, with
Fisher's gunship holding trail position. They didn't see

Rossi during the bomb strike but might have preferred sight of the Italian, instead of the German fighters slashing at the B-17s. They stayed with the Fortresses through the bomb drops and then, as they swung away from the bomb run, Fisher planned to ease back to the position of a straggler. But his copilot, Lieutenant John Yates, blanched at what was going on about them. Not even the extra guns and firepower of the YB-40 were going to do *that* much good against formations of fighters.

Then the Germans took all decisions out of their hands. Two Me-109s shot out the number four engine. Overloaded from the heavy weight of guns, ammunition and armor plating the YB-40 swung into a wide, helpless roll. Before Fisher and Yates could bring the bomber-gunship around the YB-40 rolled onto its back, picking up speed and dropping swiftly. Fisher had no help from Yates; the copilot had been hit and was unconscious.

It took 10,000 feet to pull out of the rolling plunge. Fisher came back on the power, rolled in nose-up trim and hauled back on the yoke with all his strength. The YB-40 threatened to leave its wings behind as Fisher pulled out at 5,000 feet. Somehow the metal stayed glued together and the airplane groaned its nose upward—and blacked out Fisher from the g-forces. He came to with the airplane still descending. Fisher went to full power on one and two and feathered four. Then he discovered number three was also out and he had to feather *that* one. It was only a temporary reprieve. With all that weight aboard the YB-40 would never make it home on two engines. Responding quickly to the pilot's orders the gunners started dumping everying except the ammunition in their guns. Yates came to slowly. His first move was to stare through his window and then bang Fisher on the arm.

"Hey! There's a P-38 out there . . . He's got one feathered."

The P-38, one engine showing its propeller blades knife-edged into the wind, slid beneath the wing and eased alongside the YB-40 on its left side. The P-38 pilot waved at Fisher. Could it be Rossi? There was no way of telling. Yates went on the intercom and told the gunners to stay alert for anything from the P-38. Fisher switched radios to the assigned fighter frequency. The voice he heard spoke perfect English. The pilot told Fisher he'd like to ride home with the bomber. Fisher agreed, then turned his attention back to more pressing matters. They were down to 2,000 feet and still descending. But with that P-38 along they could dump even more weight. Fisher told his gunners to get everything overboard. The order was to jettison the ammunition and every machine gun they could release from its mounts.

Then he sat bolt upright in his seat. The P-38 pilot was talking to him.

" . . . pretty name, Gina. She's from Constantine?"

Fisher snapped back to reality with warnings pounding in his ears. He switched to intercom and shouted for his men to keep their guns. The left waist gunner and radioman had already heaved theirs over the side. Fisher went back to fighter frequency. During the next several minutes he baited Rossi, wanting to be absolutely certain of who might be in that P-38. So he told the pilot details of what it was like to shack up with the girl named Gina.

Rossi blew his stack. Even as the P-38 eased away from the YB-40 Rossi—for it was him, all right—started the dead engine and with a string of oaths pulled ahead of the Fortress. His maneuver was clear to Fisher. Rossi would bring the P-38 around in a long, head-on run to pour his concentrated firepower straight into the YB-40 cockpit. Rossi took his time. He had a cripple and cripples were easy. He bored in carefully.

At the last possible moment Fished roared: *"Now!"* Every gun that could fire forward opened up. Two turrets blazed away, the gunners dead on their target. The P-38 seemed to stagger in mid-air, then slid off to the side with a heavy smoke trail behind. A gunner called out on the intercom that the left aileron of the P-38 seemed to be shot away. Rossi was now the man in trouble. Flames erupted from the smoking engine and streamed back almost to the tail.

But the Italian wouldn't quit. Cursing Fisher, he brought the Lightning in without wavering. Fisher was afraid Rossi would ram. The four heavy guns and cannon of the P-38 chopped into the Fortress, slamming the big airplane to the side. Closer and closer came Rossi, finger jammed on the firing tit, apparently determined to take the Fortress and its crew with him.

He almost made it. The P-38 was coming apart in the air from the furious battering of the YB-40's multiple guns. The flames lengthened, the canopy twisted wildly through the air, and pieces of airplane were shedding steadily. Rossi couldn't hold her up. The P-38 dropped its nose and they watched the fighter head for the water in a long, flat glide. She hit in level flight and threw up a huge plume of spray. When the water settled they saw Rossi standing on the wing, shaking his fist at them. The crew wanted to go down and shoot "the son of a bitch while we got him." Fisher ordered his men not to fire. He notified Air-Sea Rescue of the position of the Italian pilot.

The Twelfth Air Force awarded Lieutenant Harold Fisher the Distinguished Flying Cross, and each crewman the Air Medal, for their roles in the bizarre aerial duel.

Harold Fisher and Guido Rossi both survived the war. Fisher's luck ran out several years later when he flew a transport on the Berlin airlift. There was a crash, and Fisher was dead.

One of the men who mourned his passing was Guido Rossi.

VAL PHILLIPS

You need to get the word from the cockpit, as we have said several times in these pages. Now we turn to F. Val Phillips who was a P-38 driver in the Mediterranean and lower European areas, and who brings us with him into the cockpit of the fighters he flew. Val Phillips exchanged a series of letters with me, each communication providing more and more detail, until it became crystal clear that this was the man with whom we can best close out this chapter of the P-38 story.

Val wrote me not merely the big picture but the bits and pieces that make up the reality of men and the machines in which they fly. He recalled, for example, "an escort mission in which our squadron leader passed out, apparently from lack of oxygen. Only one thing saved his life—the inherent stability of the P-38. We watched helplessly as he went into a slowly descending orbit. Finally, at a lower altitude where there was more oxygen, he regained consciousness and then returned home. Could you trim a single-engine plane, a *fighter,* to perform such a maneuver? Highly unlikely."

Turning to a personal incident, Val Phillips described "a hectic day over Bucharest when my flight became separated from the rest of the Group, and we had a miserable time trying to defend ourselves. Two of us returned, separately, and two were lost. I had fits with my airplane for a while. I lost most of the power from one engine when the throttle linkage separated, and then lost all of my oxygen when the regulator malfunctioned. I ended up this mission by escorting a crippled B-17 across the Adriatic and eventually landing on one engine well after the group had returned.

"A point to make about single-engine operation in the P-38. So much has been said about how difficult it is, and everyone seems to forget how many pilots time and time again came home on that one engine. My tentmate, Larry Mars, was returning from a mission on one engine along with a damaged B-17. Two cripples dragging their way home and *then* they were jumped by two Me-109s. Remember, Larry was flying with one feathered. It didn't stop him. Larry shot down one of the German fighters— a victory that was confirmed by a *very* happy bomber crew."

Earlier in these pages we described the mission in which two P-38 pilots shot down twelve Ju-87 Stuka dive bombers between them in a single air fight. Val Phillips, in a special note marked "sometime in mid-1943," with the

14th Fighter Group, 37th Fighter Squadron, added details to that particular mission:

"What happened that day attested to the value of the concentrated firepower of the 38. Those four fifties and one 20-mm cannon concentrated in the nose were pretty lethal.

"Major Leverette, leading the squadron, and Lieutenant Hanna, leading the second section, both became aces on this same mission. The 37th Squadron was patrolling an area south of Greece to provide air cover for a convoy en route to Egypt. In this convoy was the *Queen Mary* loaded with troops. While the Allies had control of the Mediterranean Sea such control did not always include the air. German forces still controlled the Balkans, thereby sustaining a threat to the safety of any shipping.

"Whoever dreamed up this mission deserved the Medal of Honor and the Victoria Cross in one. Leverette and troops intercepted a flock of Ju-87s, led by a single Ju-88, en route towards the convoy. The Ju-88 recognized immediately that the situation was not as briefed. He did a quick one-eighty and headed for home as fast as he could go, but not alone. Several P-38 escorts had a hard time catching up but they finally did and soon disposed of him. Major Leverette and the others drew up behind the Ju-87s and firing in short bursts, started thinning down their ranks. Those Germans were much more dedicated than their former leader. They were pressing on, come hell or high water, apparently relying on their rear gunners to keep the 38s off long enough to permit a few Ju-87s to dive on the troop convoy.

"Their dedication was commendable. It cost them every last Ju-87 in the group. Major Leverette personally accounted for seven dive bombers, Hanna shot down five, and others contributed to the complete destruction of this unit."

I requested of Val some personal observations:

"My personal experience with the P-38 in training, combat and pleasure flying convinced me that it was the greatest. No torque, a good gun platform, good visibility, long range, easily identified—well, it's a long list. There were certain weaknesses, such as compressibility dives, which were restrictive and prevented an enemy going through a split-S from being pursued at very high speed down to the deck. However, in a battle at comparable altitudes the 38, properly handled, could cope with the best. It became our policy to stay with the bombers and do all our fighting at or close to their altitude. They, the bombers, loved it and while we were somewhat less successful in achieving kills than some of the single-engine types, we still did quite well and suffered fewer losses to the enemy.

"Although the P-38 was extremely heavy for a fighter, by World War II standards, the secret to maneuverability was contained in a little control lever on the right side of the cockpit. By slapping this lever to a stop, maneuver flaps would extend. This was merely a slight extension of the Fowler flaps with eight degrees of deflection. A much better turning radius could be achieved with very little loss in speed. Either offensively or defensively it was extremely valuable and I used it frequently.

"On one occasion (December 16, 1943) we were on what was supposed to be a milk run to northern Italy. Due to the short distances involved, P-47s were to rendezvous with us in the target area. Such a rendezvous was sure to cause a high pucker factor. Making sure that they were P-47s—and not FW-190s—was extremely difficult, particularly under high stress conditions. We were caught this time. Thinking they were 'friendlies' we were jumped by a flock of FW-190s while we still had partially full belly tanks and, in most instances, 'cold guns.'

"I can remember jettisoning tanks at about the same time somebody called, 'Break right!' The urgency of the situation was evident in the tone of the voice, so I complied right then. The guy behind me said I had a belly tank hung up. That extra weight and drag accounted for the stall I was getting into as I tried to stay on my leader's wing. I slapped down the maneuver flaps—fast! It was just in time, too, for when I looked back there was Jerry.

An FW-190, with flashing guns, was right behind me with his nose pointed into my cockpit. I was momentarily transfixed by this sight and grimly held the yoke hard back, burbling on the verge of a stall. He couldn't quite pull enough lead and moments later must have pulled just a little too many g's because he snapped. Without those maneuver flaps that would have been my last mission. Upon return to base the tank shackles were examined and proved to be working. The hangup was attributed to frozen moisture from the water on our strip at takeoff.

"Another incident (April 6, 1944,) which again raised my adrenalin took place in the vicinity of Zagreb, and also involved belly tanks. You could, at least in my old Number 76 you could, overswitch the fuel control valves when going from belly to internal selection, resulting in fuel starvation a few seconds later. On this occasion, as the bogies appeared above us, I overswitched the left engine selector as we dropped our tanks. At exactly the same moment a right break was called, my left engine quit, throwing me into a left bank. Rather than taking a chance on rolling back to the right I broke left while resetting the fuel selector and imploring the leader to make it a three-sixty. I sure didn't want to end up as a solo in that melee. Sure enough after completing the 360-degree turn I was able to rejoin the outfit and complete the mission with the rest of the troops."

Then there was a mission dated January 16, 1944:

"As I recall this mission, Lieutenant Smith was leading Green Flight as part of the Second Section on a bomber escort flight. The target was the Messerschmitt plant at Klagenfurt and we were told to expect heavy fighter opposition. I had the element in the flight opposite that of Smith, but no wingman. That made me Tail End Charlie. Our job was to provide top cover for our 'Big Friends' while they were in the target area.

"Just prior to reaching our rendezvous point, before we formed a weave over the bombers, bogies were called out and the order was given to drop tanks. Cleaning up our planes was also the automatic signal to activate our guns and increase power, rpms, and the rate of head rotation. The slightest specks on the canopy, previously ignored, immediately became enemy planes and the adrenalin flowed at a rapid rate.

"There was considerable conversation at this point but above all you could piece together the impending crash:

" 'Bogies at one o'clock!'

" 'He's coming in head-on!'

" 'You got 'em! You got 'em!'

" 'Look out!'

" 'Holy Christ!'

"About this time what was left of an Me-109, spewing fuel and shedding hunks of metal, passed by just to my right. Only a wing stub remained on one side and the aircraft appeared to be cartwheeling during the instant I saw it.

"Apparently Smitty had actually killed the pilot but was unable to maneuver away from the uncontrolled '109. The inevitable happened. The 109, still in a vertical bank to port, hit the P-38 somewhere between the right engine and fuselage, and his fuselage passed just under the wing root of the P-38. If the Me-109 had been only a few inches higher both planes would have disintegrated and in all probability several other following P-38s.

"The damage to Smitty's plane was extensive. The right engine froze with the prop blades at a high rpm setting, nice and flat, a severe drag even with a complete aircraft. *The Me-109 prop, still turning, tore chunks out of the tail boom at about four-foot intervals and finally some portion of the Messerschmitt passed completely through the horizontal stablilizer right at the junction of the tail boom.* Not only was the right prop causing tremendous drag, but damage to the right boom and severance of the stabilizer left the right rudder useless.

"Smitty almost immediately dropped below and behind the rest of us. He made his decision. 'I'm bailing out!' There were numerous parachutes in the vicinity, but which was Smitty's? Nobody had a chance to figure it out —too busy. LaRue disappeared without a word and Stahl went down in flames during the next few minutes.

"We were sure sorry to report him a probable prisoner

but what other choice? We'd heard him say he was bailing out, chutes were seen, and he was nowhere around when we started home.

"Well after the debriefing, as we tried to relax from a pretty rough one, and while Smitty's, Stahl's and LaRue's belongings were already being divided up, Big Fence—our 'homer'—called and wanted to know if we still had a bird in the air because one had just called in.

" 'He *what?*'

" 'Coming home on one engine?'

" '*Good God!*'

"The tents of the 37th Fighter Squadron emptied in a simultaneous explosion and the whole squadron, from cooks and bakers to the C.O., stood around in complete amazement as a plane soon appeared from the northeast. *Smitty had made it.* As he passed slowly over our area you could see the dead prop but most obvious was the severed stabilizer. It was hanging from the left boom and must have dropped two to three feet below the right boom.

"You could just feel each of the pilots starting to sweat. How Smitty could possibly land that wreck was the question on everyone's mind. Well, Smitty was thinking about it also, but he really had to sweat—the gear wouldn't come down!

"We talked to him, silently, in our own ways, and I'm sure all of us said: 'Don't try it, Smitty—bail out!' He didn't. Instead he lined up for a long straight-in from the south. He'd have to clear the dike just short of the end of the runway and belly it in.

"Several of us joined 'Doc' Curtiss in his ambulance and tore off to the strip, waiting there, along with the fire crew, for the inevitable crash landing.

"As we got into position, Smitty started down, but for some reason which I can't recall, he thought he wasn't going to clear the dike. Landing short was his only choice, but now he was in a real lousy position, too high, with no chance of going around. He actually dove towards the wheat field and we all panicked. Could that crippled elevator take the pullout? To bring that wreck back this far and then get killed just didn't seem fair.

"Well, Smitty had a better feel for his problems than we did. He made it. He bellied it in about a half-mile short of the dike and slid up just short of it.

"We could see Smitty get out of the cockpit, slide off the wing onto the ground, and collapse. The ambulance and the fire truck couldn't cross the dike but had to take a three-mile trip to reach poor Smitty. It didn't take us long. When we arrived moments later we were damned happy to find him in one piece. He was extremely tired, cold, and in a mild state of shock. As I recall, the only physical damage to Smitty was a lump on his noggin. He hit the gunsight in the belly landing.

"The beginning and end of this episode had been only a small part of Smitty's ordeal. As we learned later, the hours between his cry that he was bailing out and his arrival over our base were also hair-raising.

"When Smitty had decided to bail out he jettisoned his canopy and prepared to slide off the wing, the preferred means of exiting the 38. But as soon as he released the controls the plane rolled violently to the right. All that damage turned the usually stable P-38 into an uncontrollable monster. He decided right then that a bailout would have to wait. Control of the aircraft became his first concern and he managed this by placing both feet on the left rudder pedal, reducing power in his good engine, and exerting full thrust on that good rudder.

"Having leveled off the bird, he decided maybe he had a chance. The next problem, then, was to take a heading for home. Not too difficult as long as you could make a right turn. Just release some back pressure on the left rudder and she'd start off toward the right. The real problem then was to maintain enough altitude to get back across those rugged mountains. It wasn't simply a matter of adding power and climbing. It had to be a balance between engine power and Smitty's leg power. Enough engine to gain a little altitude would be too much of a strain on his legs. Smitty soon discovered that to hold a straight course the power wouldn't permit him to hold his altitude. To solve this he periodically added enough power to gain a few feet per second but had to orbit slowly to the right each time he did this. So his course home consisted of a series of 360-degree turns to the right interspersed with periods of approximate headings towards home. I say approximate because when Smitty jettisoned the canopy that four-button VHF radio soon responded to the minus fifty degrees Centigrade temperature.

"The frequency for Big Fence, the local homer, was frozen out. It wasn't until Smitty was somewhere over the Adriatic, safely beyond enemy territory and the rugged mountains, that he was able to drop down to a lower and warmer altitude. Only then was he able to switch from the tactical channel and finally get an accurate fix and steer for home. In the meantime poor Smitty had one other very trying moment. He flew over, inadvertently, due to his uncertain position, the city of Trieste. His first indication that things weren't quite right was when he heard the 88-mm flak guns going off. Without his canopy the sound came through loud and clear, and it was enough to scare a man out of his wits.

"Smitty left for home shortly after this mission. In the close-to-fifty missions flown he had absorbed all he could. This last mission had brought to a harrowing end what was almost an ill-fated tour. He had been missing in action for several days once before, late in 1943, and been pretty well shot up on another occasion.

"When we were stationed in North Africa, Smitty had started home from Southern France on a single engine. Somewhere off the west coat of Corsica the second engine failed and he had a choice of bailing out or riding it down into the Mediterranean. He chose the latter. The landing was successful, but in a matter of seconds he was floating along on the surface in his Mae West. For some reason his dinghy wouldn't inflate, leaving him with no choice but to swim ashore.

"Portions of Western Corsica drop precipitously into the Mediterranean. This is where Smitty made landfall. It took him some time to find a piece of cliff that he could scale. Carefully and slowly he climbed to the top only to be confronted by hostile natives bearing pitchforks and clubs.

"Apparently he had been spotted while still in the water and these Corsicans, not too friendly a bunch under the best conditions, weren't sure whether he was friend or foe. Some hasty and serious negotiations took place before the group was convinced that he was a Yankee and in trouble. It was around three or four days later that word filtered back from that rather remote island that Smitty was in good shape and would be returned shortly. His belongings were gathered up and put back in his tent before he was welcomed home.

"A third rather eventful incident also befell this 'jinxed' officer. P-38s had a flat piece of armor plate directly behind the seat which protected the head and torso, but only from the rear. There were no extensions, sort of wrap-arounds, which would protect protruding arms or the body itself from angled shots. Smitty's solution to this problem was to scrounge some old armor plate and have 'wings' welded to the installed plate. Having installed it, his next job was to test it. He managed that one or two missions later. Somebody had dead aim on Smitty and that armor plate stopped a Hun slug and saved his life.

"As you can see, Smitty had rather an eventful tour. I would venture to say there were times, such as during his Corsica vacation, that he had some doubts about the P-38. After his last mission, however, I'm certain that Smitty, and the rest of us associated with him, were damn sure that the P-38 was the most rugged fighter ever built.

"No other fighter could have survived a head-on mid-air collision with an Me-109 and managed to make it home."

Wow!

17. The Other War

The first combat action of World War II with the P-38 took place in the cold and unfriendly skies over Iceland, a mission in which two P-38s and one P-39 attacked and finally shot down a Focke-Wulf FW-200 Kurier. That was, however, an isolated and even a singular instance. It happened by circumstance, so to speak. The P-38 went into combat, in terms of an air campaign, in skies similarly cold and unfriendly, but on the other side of the world—in the North Pacific.

NORTH PACIFIC

Six months after they wrecked Pearl Harbor the Japanese quickly overran Attu and Kiska in the Aleutians. As the AAF and other services saw the move, it was the beginning of heavy operations against the rest of the Aleutian chain, and then movement against Alaska and Canada. No one knew the full strength of the Japanese commitment to their North Pacific venture, but we did know that American defenses were so weak that they might be considered pitiful. And certainly they were unable to stand up against any Japanese onslaught. Among the military aircraft rushed to the theater was the P-38, and some measure of the critical nature of the North Pacific campaign is to be found in that movement because, as we have seen, the P-38 was in "screaming demand" from every theater in the world, and only the highest priority could be assured of a hope of receiving these airplanes.

One thing was certain—both the Japanese and the Americans were to learn that the Aleutians had a "northern climate and terrain too retarding, too confining, too costly for satisfactory offensive operations dependent largely upon air power."* It was also a theater where, after initial brutal operations where the weather was more an enemy than the Japanese, the Eleventh Air Force finally settled down to two frustrating years of holding operations. It was not the nicest place to spend a few years, as Vern Haugland reported:

"The Aleutians—120 bleak, volcanic islands extending from the tip of the Alaskan Peninsula to within 90 miles of Russia's Kamchatka Peninsula—in terms of air power could represent a succession of dromes across the shortest part of the Pacific. They were virtually timberless, and the swampy lowlands were blanketed with tundra or muskeg as much as three feet thick. Under this spongy carpet was a fine volcanic ash, water soaked to the consistency of slime. The weather was as uncomfortable as could be found anywhere—constant rain, wind and fog with highly localized violent storms and hardly two weeks of clear weather in a year."

Airplanes were rushed in May 1942, to the Eleventh Air Force to build up some sort of barrier to the Japanese. By early June the 54th Fighter Squadron with P-38s showed up at Elmendorf to supplant the P-39 and P-40 fighters also rushed to the area. On June 6, 1942, eight of those P-38s staged on to Cold Bay, and on the next day, for the first time in the war, P-38s went into combat. It was hardly the most auspicious of combat initiations. The P-38 pilots were confused by a red flag they saw flying from a ship, and seven fighters shot up a *Russian* freighter off Umnak Island.

On August 4, six P-38s flying with a B-17 found three Kawanishi four-engine flying boats in the air, promptly shot down two and damaged the third.

*Vern Haugland, *The AAF Against Japan* (New York: Harper and Row, 1948).

On September 3, P-38s flew an astonishing mission for that time—1,100 miles, all over water, non-stop round-trip. This was an escort mission to Kiska; out of six P-38s taking off, four turned back because of weather and two went on to target. They got a Kawanishi 97 on the water, shot up troop barracks, and came home on little more than fumes in their tanks. The operation of the P-38s then became much the same as other fighters—weather mauled them and their opportunities for meaningful combat remained low key. The datelines indicate the manner of operation:

September 10, 1942: A new airfield was completed on Adak. The next day fourteen P-38s arrived on the strip along with three B-17s, three cargo transports, and one Lodestar troop transport. The day following (September 12) another P-38 flew in, as well as fifteen B-24s, sixteen P-39s and one B-17. This same day two P-38s covered a B-17 on a reconnaissance mission; over Kiska they shot down one Japanese interceptor.

September 14, 1942: Fourteen P-38s and fourteen P-39s flying ahead of B-24s divided up Kiska Harbor as their target. The P-38s took the north side, the Airacobras the south. The 'Cobras shot down two float fighters, chewed up a Kawanishi bomber on the water, damaged three submarines, and strafed forty gun emplacements. The P-38s destroyed two float-type Zero fighters, one bi-plane, and hammered flak gun emplacements. The B-24s found little opposition to their low-level strikes. No American planes were shot down, but two P-38s racing after the same Zero fighter collided and were destroyed.

November 24, 1942: The first P-38s landed on the new runway on Atka Island, just east of Adak.

November 9, 1942 (fifteen days earlier): Four P-38s made the first fighter attack against Attu. It was a round-trip mission of nearly 900 miles. They destroyed eight floatplane fighters.

Also, late in November two P-38s were destroyed on the ground when a B-24, out of control in a belly landing, smashed the parked Lightnings.

December 25, 1942: A P-38 lost both engines on takeoff. The careening Lightning sliced a B-24 in half and exploded. No one was killed.

December 30, 1942: On an escort mission to Kiska, P-38s were bounced by a dozen Zero floatplane fighters that hit them without warning from overhead clouds. Two P-38s were shot down immediately, the others were shot up badly but returned to base. The P-38s shot down one of the enemy.

December 31, 1942: Nine P-38s escorted six B-24s in a strike against Kiska.

January, 1943: The weather was rotten and action for a while was limited to patrols without enemy contact by the fighters. On the 18th, P-38s escorted twelve bombers out of Adak, but all planes had to return because of weather. The fighters and medium bombers ran for safety and barely made it. As an indication of the weather problem, two B-24s disappeared in the fog and were never heard from again. A third crash-landed and the crew barely escaped from their wrecked bomber. A fourth reached Umnak and ground crews fired flares to help light the runway. The B-24 overshot and smashed into two P-38s, destroying both. Score: no contact with the enemy, six planes lost, two bomber crews lost.

Again, the weather. On January 21 two Fortresses collided in flight; one crashed with the loss of the crew, the other staggered back to base. Later that day a P-40 crashed into Kuluk Bay. Two days later two B-25s crashed together in the fog and went down.

Local patrols continued whenever the weather permitted. On the 8th and 10th of February, heavy and medium bombers took advantage of weather breaks, and with P-38s as escort, pounded Japanese positions at Kiska.

On March 12, 1943, operating from new advanced fields, P-38s and P-40s teamed up to hit Kiska with fighter-bomber strikes.

The next month, April, the weather permitted a sudden buildup of strike operations. From the 8th through the 21st, the Eleventh Air Force managed to average some sixty fighters and bombers over Japanese targets on Kiska—every day of that period. April 15th provided astonishingly clear weather and 112 planes showed up during a period of twelve hours to blast the island with 92 tons of bombs. Amchitka, now being used by American fighters and bombers, was barely 85 miles from Kiska, and this sort of range spelled trouble for the Japanese. As many as eight fighter missions could be flown, if the weather permitted, during a single day. The P-38s loaded up with two 500-pound bombs per plane, and P-40s went along with a single 500-pounder and another six smaller bombs under their wings. Sometimes the loads varied, and 300-pound or 1,000-pound bombs would be presented to the enemy. Glide-bomb attacks, rather than dive bombing, was the strike method preferred. Once the bombs were away the fighters went right down to the deck to strafe everything that even looked like a target. In April, the P-38 and P-40 fighter-bombers flew 685 sorties and dropped 216 tons of bombs—almost half the weight dropped by *all* the medium and heavy bombers.

And the conditions? Not a single Japanese fighter rose to do battle. One P-40 and one B-24 went down to flak guns, but nine fighters were wiped out by operational losses.

During the ensuing months the P-38s went out with bomb loads including small parafrags and heavy 1,000-pounders. It settled down to a war of attrition, flying whenever weather permitted. On May 21 the P-38 pilots got a rare break when a Navy PBY caught sight of sixteen twin-engined Mitsubishi bombers (Bettys). Five P-38s on patrol headed for the Japanese planes and hit them in a diving attack. The P-38s shot down five of the enemy force and claimed another seven as probably destroyed. One P-38 ditched in a bay and the pilot was rescued. Another pilot in a damaged P-38 started out for home base, but disappeared and was never heard from again.

For the remainder of the war, action slowed down. There were months when not a single contact with the enemy was made, although fighters were scrambled to intercept bogies that never appeared. In the fall of 1944 there was a flurry of action, and then the weather swept in and covered the northern part of the world again. It was a smothering blanket of inaction that would persist for the remainder of the war.

SOUTH PACIFIC

It gets difficult to tell the players without a scorecard here. The P-38 went into action in the Pacific in November of 1942—they entered what was officially the South Pacific as emergency reinforcements flown to Guadalcanal, but their first combat was in the Southwest Pacific where they scored their first kills against Japanese fighters. Then the P-38s were moving on to other areas, and the historical narrative becomes a chore of chasing back and forth from one theater to another, and with different air forces, because once the supply line opened up, the 38s started arriving in greater numbers.

In the South Pacific—which included Guadalcanal, mainly a huge Marine scrap with the Japanese, with support by the Navy and the Army—the P-38 introduction to combat was slow, delayed, intermittent and almost wholly inconclusive. On Guadalcanal, under the most primitive of conditions, the Marines were slugging it out in fierce melees with the enemy. They were supported by an Army force of Bell P-400 fighters (the P-400 was the British export model of the P-39, numbers of which were diverted to U.S. control after the start of war) which produced more ulcers and frustrations among their pilots than they did numbers of Japanese planes shot down. The P-400, in the blunt terms of the AAF History, "was no match either for the Zero or for the enemy bombers now striking Henderson [Field] from altitudes above 20,000 feet." The P-400s, however, finally were turned loose in low-level strafing and bombing attacks against the Japanese. Where the airplane had been an unmitigated disaster in air operations against enemy planes, it turned out to be a superb weapon for ground strikes—

for which it had been designed in the first place (as everyone seemed to forget).

But until the P-38s showed up at Guadalcanal, *all* fighting at high altitude was the province of the Marines' Grumman F4F Wildcat fighters. However, there's a break needed in here. When the first P-38s arrived at Guadalcanal—this was in the period of November 14–22, 1942—things were so fouled up, conditions so primitive, coordination so lacking that the P-38s contributed more by their presence than they did by their effectiveness in combat. The AAF History indicated that on November 12, 1942, Major Dale D. Brannon made it into Guadalcanal with eight P-38s of the new 339th Fighter Squadron. The next day another eight P-38s, this time from the 39th Fighter squadron, flew direct from Milne Bay in New Guinea to Henderson Field on Guadalcanal where they remained until November 22.

The P-38s of the 39th Fighter Squadron concern us for the moment. One of the pilots reaching Henderson Field was Charles W. King, then a young lieutenant. Today a colonel, Charles King spent months piecing together his combat record from his logbooks and diaries to bring us a personal story of the brief initial tenure of the Lightnings—or at least those of the 39th Fighter Squadron—in those dark days on Guadalcanal.

The following is the personal story of then-Lieutenant Charles W. King:

"The first use of the long-range capability of the P-38 finally came about in mid-November of 1942. Lightnings had arrived in Australia in August, and a month later were showing up in New Guinea. Only one squadron in the entire Fifth Air Force was as yet equipped with the P-38, and they were having fits trying to get their airplanes ready for combat. Meanwhile, as the weeks rolled by, the Japanese on Guadalcanal were giving the Marines an exceptionally brutal time of it as we fought to take that island. The Marines with their F4F fighters and the Army with P-39s (and some P-400s) were having a particularly hard time of it with the Japanese fighters. The little Grummans handled themselves well enough but the P-39—which had already proven deficient in New Guinea —was a lumbering sick cow of an airplane. In fact, its record was so poor in air fights that the decision was finally made at Guadalcanal that unless an absolute full-blown emergency was involved, the P-39s were no longer to be committed to the same air with the Zero fighter. It was *that* bad.

"A few P-38s had also arrived in the Thirteenth Air Force, and the word 'few' is used carefully. They expected, by mid-November, to receive no more than eight of the P-38s and, in fact, sent these on under control of Major Brannon, who was an old P-39 pilot, to help out the Marines on the 'Canal.

"Intelligence made it clear to Allied headquarters that the Japanese were planning a massive seaborne reinforcement of Guadalcanal. Everyone was asked to help, and a message went to MacArthur's headquarters for twelve P-38 fighters and crews. General Kenney from the Fifth Air Force, however, couldn't meet the request. The mechanical problems with P-38 engines at the time were horrendous, and Kenney told MacArthur that he could spare only eight Lightnings.

"We got the word when volunteers were requested to take the 38s on up to Guadalcanal. Before this occasion, it was the habit of Bob Faurot, my flight leader, to volunteer for everything and to speak for his whole flight. I don't know why he suddenly changed the procedure. Perhaps it was because of Major Prentice, our relatively new commander. But rather, I think, there was so much involved here that was unknown, that someone made the decision that each individual really should have the chance to decide his own fate. Eight volunteers stepped forward and sounded off pretty loud that they *were* volunteering. I wasn't one of them. For fifteen months I had followed Faurot on a lot of crappy missions and I guess I was beginning to get the idea that in the Army it might not be the wisest thing to volunteer. Even second lieutenants get smart eventually.

"So Bob and seven others leaped off from Port Moresby to Milne Bay as a starting place for the long flight to Guadalcanal. They came back the next day with word that the mission was cancelled. Actually, it was merely postponed and was to be rescheduled in a few days. Again volunteers were called for and again I kept quiet.

"I discovered meanwhile that Bob Faurot was being very cool toward me. This bothered me because we had been through a lot together and I didn't see how he had any right to question my contribution. When we flew broken-down P-39s I had flown as much as, or more, than anyone else in the outfit and I'd also done my share with the P-38. But Bob made it obvious he was disappointed in my not going along as his next senior man.

"In the interim one of the volunteers, Dick Suehr [who had experienced a couple of bad accidents], got word that he would be receiving orders in a short period of time to return to the States. Despite this he still planned to go on the Guadalcanal trip. I worked on him so I could take his place on the mission. After a while I convinced him he should stay on in New Guinea. I still had a little problem with Faurot. He had agreed Suehr should be relieved, so he couldn't very well object to someone taking his place. But he was still walking around with a bad case of the peeves, and he let me know in no uncertain terms that I wouldn't be the deputy leader—a threat he kept up only for another day or two. So I soon had the dubious honor of leading the early morning patrols.

"The briefing we had for the Guadalcanal mission is a prostitution of the word. As far as the flight was concerned, we were told a B-17 would lead us there, and we must maintain strict radio silence all the way. People held high hopes that the B-17 would be able to receive weather reports en route to indicate whether or not we could proceed safely into the Guadalcanal area. The B-17 pilots, and those of us in the P-38s, had maps of that portion of the South Pacific. Not very elaborate. An X marked the spot of an unnamed reef, which was computed as the point at which we could still return to Milne Bay on the extreme eastern tip of New Guinea. Beyond that

X . . . well, if we went beyond that point we were advised we had better press on regardless.

"Let me make something clear—we had no long-range or endurance training. We just didn't know that much, or even anything at all, about the subject. Most of our experience had been in the Bell P-39 Airacobra in which an hour and forty-five minutes was an extremely long mission. We had flown our P-38s on missions normally two hours long, and never beyond three hours. So the four hours fifteen minutes we flew was quite a butt-buster. But with the adrenalin we had flowing the time element mattered little.

"We were told that the Japanese held almost all of Guadalcanal and specifically they held the west side of the island—the direction from which we would approach. No one stated for sure whether the Japs had any airfields but we were given two rather poor aerial photographs (which I'm studying even as I write this) of the area held by our forces. Its only annotations were some AA positions and a *proposed* runway location. It did show our beachhead and we were told the only positive information anyone had was that the Marines were hanging on to a perimeter of 4,000 yards.

"The trip proved to be uneventful. The weather was quite good. Eight started and eight got there. The B-17 carried eight of our ground crew (six mechanics, one armorer and one radioman). Each of us carried what could be put into a musette bag and could be stuffed into the extremely small baggage compartment in the boom of the P-38. My musette bag held one change of underwear and my shaving kit. The others probably had more because I had to get something else into my boom. It was one of the two air mattresses in the whole squadron. I had been lucky enough to find this prize back in June while selecting a bedroll from a number left us by the departing 35th Squadron. At first I wasn't envied too much because there were a number of regular stateside mattresses available. But as we moved back and forth between Australia and New Guinea they became very scarce. So an air mattress meant I could get a good night's sleep which for many of the pilots was impossible on a bare canvas cot.

"Ed Hess, our armament officer, bunked in the same tent with me at Port Moresby. We were close friends because even after he ran out of funny stories to tell he thought up new things to amuse us. Such things as the weird and sometimes obscene plans he had prepared to make money after the war. It meant a lot in a steamy tent in the middle of the jungle with the Japs over the next hill.

"Early in the game Ed informed me and everyone else in the tent that he deserved an air mattress and if anything happened to me he was the rightful heir to mine. Until the trip to Guadalcanal the inference never bothered me. While I was packing he asked—pointedly—why I was deflating my air mattress. I told him I planned to take it with me. First he tried to convince me that it wouldn't fit into the plane. When I assured him it would, he berated me with 'You may not come back, you know. And if anything happens to you that mattress belongs to me. How the hell can I get it at Guadalcanal? Some stranger will get the thing!'

"All of a sudden Ed just didn't seem funny anymore. I told him I was damn well going to take the mattress and that if I was going to die, well, the night before it happened I was going to sleep comfortably on that mattress. I told him that if he wanted it that bad he could damn well get on the B-17 in place of the same airman he was sending along as an armorer. I don't recall his reaction (if any). But my prize went along with me and, of course, I brought it back. I used it long after Ed left the outfit and until enough air mattresses arrived so all the officers had one.

"As we approached the 'Canal we saw a number of planes approaching from the north. They weren't Army. We wondered if they might be Japanese. But they were too low and too scattered for that. A closer look showed us they were U.S. Navy dive bombers, torpedo bombers and fighters. Quite a bunch of them.

"At the 'Canal we found two operational airfields. There

was a pierced steel plank (PSP) runway on Henderson Field and it contained various types of Army, Navy and Marine bombers. All the fighters were on a relatively wide dirt strip quite properly, and simply, known as 'Fighter Strip.' We landed there without incident. Along one edge there was a line of lights with a portable generator at one end. The Army fighters sat on one end of the strip. The Marines sat on the other end, on alert. Normally there weren't any Navy fighters, but when we arrived we were surprised to see quite a few of them around. The aircraft we had observed on our approach had been launched from one of our carriers. They had flown north, past Guadalcanal as far as they could fly safely, searching for a Japanese task force. They didn't find it. However, after they turned south they found what they were looking for. Working with Marine pilots operating from Guadalcanal they apparently did a good job of mauling that task force. But they couldn't make it home that easily. Their carrier was operating with considerable damage, and wasn't considered capable of defending itself against further enemy attacks. It was ordered well to the south beyond the range of Japanese planes, and the Navy aircraft, low on fuel, came into Guadalcanal.

"After we landed we were signalled to park along one side of the strip. Being kind of stiff from the long ride I took my time getting out of my bird. Then, all of a sudden, I realized no one was in sight. I saw that everyone had made for the slit trenches beneath the trees. I didn't waste any more time joining the crowd. Right away I discovered why the trenches were suddenly so popular. The Japanese were directing shell fire at the strip. That meant the Japs were either closer than 4,000 yards or they had some pretty big guns that could range more than this distance.

"That night we camped with the Army pilots who were assigned to Guadalcanal, sharing their tents with them. They had dugouts instead of slit trenches. In the middle of the night we found out why. The place was hit with the damndest barrage of 14-inch naval shells as a fight raged offshore. Our Navy did all right, but we were told (later) that a huge, dazzling green flash we saw was an American destroyer which had been hit and completely blew up just off the Jap landing beach.

"Early the next morning the Army P-39s and Marine bombers were on the job. Before we even had breakfast they had set three Jap transports blazing; they'd been hit but not sunk the day before. The Japanese deliberately beached the transports so their troops could get ashore and the supplies could be salvaged, but after the Marines and 'Cobras got through there wasn't that much left to salvage.

"Because of such events our contribution to the fighting done by the Marines was relatively small. However, it proved to be a most valuable experience for us. We got together with other pilots to compare experiences, and you always learn a lot this way. I doubt if any Fighter Symposium was ever conducted under more realistic circumstances. During daylight hours everyone on the Marine end of the strip who had his airplane in commission sat on alert status, ready to go at a moment's notice. A few P-39 pilots and some people from the Army driving P-38s (Brannon's outfit from the Thirteenth Air Force) came down to our end of the strip, and the Marines related their battles, and explained their tactics on using their F4F to fight the Japs over Guadalcanal. The Navy pilots awaiting orders to move to their carrier or 'anywhere else' told us of their engagements. We found that our own experiences in P-39s in New Guinea was very similar to the tribulations of pilots flying Airacobras there at Guadalcanal.

"Every now and then the Japanese broke up our conversations with shell fire. Some of the troops ducked; others just didn't bother. The Navy pilots seemed to be the most jumpy. They explained it as conditioning. One pilot told me he really didn't mind the shelling on land, but aboard ship, that was another matter. It was a case of the 'cooped up and can't hide' feeling that they found almost unbearable.

"None of us felt any desire to trade places with the Navy pilots despite their other advantages. We had been on Aussie rations at Port Moresby. To us the U.S. cannon rations were sheer heaven. Hotcakes, sausages, canned vegetables, canned fruit and things like that made meals something to look forward to instead of dreading the next meal. It was difficult for us to understand the Navy types griping about 'lousy' food. The Marines, who had originally come into the island by carrier, explained to us how well the Navy ate aboard their ships, but it was *still* hard for us to understand their gripes.

"After several days the Navy pilots left. I guess their carrier came back within range; no one bothered to tell us. The Navy stayed close-mouthed about ship movements. Maybe it paid off. Our Navy was able to give the Japs a run for their money because we had cracked their code and were able to 'read their mail.'

"I found out more about this Navy passion for security one morning on dawn patrol. I spotted a large warship headed south. It appeared to be one of ours and I guess a P-38 was easy enough to identify so they didn't shoot at me. But when I saw the guns tracking me I broke off.

"When I told Marine Intelligence I'd spotted an American battleship quite close to Guadalcanal at that time of the morning I stirred up a hornet's nest. Frankly, they gave me the third degree. How could I, an Army pilot, know it was a battleship? What did Army pilots know, anyway? A Marine officer told me flatly we didn't have any battleships in the area. On and on it went. I didn't like it and I told him that what I saw was a battleship and I didn't care if he believed me or not. Later, half-apologetic (but not too much), he called me back and admitted it *was* a battleship, it *was* one of ours, and it had been very late getting out of a secret position near the shoreline where, well concealed, it lay in wait each night for Jap shipping. Apparently some of our Navy types preferred to keep grimly silent about their ships. They changed that one day when we were called on to provide cover for some of our shipping. A fast call; Japanese dive bombers and Zero fighters showed up going for the ships. It wasn't a good mission for us. The Marines got into the Japs pretty good but they turned back before we could get to them with the P-38s. Radio problems screwed us up.

"We had one escort mission during our stay. The P-38s of the Guadalcanal squadron were assigned to cover the B-17s, while our outfit went out to cover the B-26 Marauders on a raid to Bougainville.

"The B-17 leader, Colonel Saunders, briefed the mission. The bombers would take off from Henderson Field and when we caught sight of them in the air we were to take off and catch up with them. That's simply not the way to operate. It worked out fine with the Fortresses but our people never did catch those B-26s. We flew all over the Solomon Islands and landed three and a quarter hours later without seeing a thing. It really teed us off when we found out the B-26s ran into sixteen Jap biplane floatplanes and shot one down. We decided we had misread our inadequate maps (all too easy to do) and we did most of our flying around Choiseul instead of Bougainville. The 339th Squadron of eight planes got separated from their B-17s in a fight and Colonel Saunders' plane was shot down. They rescued the crew the next day. At the time I was so disgusted with the way things were being run I felt little sorrow about his situation.

"On November 22 it was felt that the immediate threat to Guadalcanal had been repulsed by Navy and Marine fighters and bombers, and we were ordered to return to New Guinea. Again we were lucky and the weather favored us. We arrived over Milne Bay with plenty of fuel so we proceeded westward to Port Moresby, landing after five hours of flying. This wasn't a combat flight, but it should have alerted us to the long missions which were to come later. We still hadn't fired a shot at a Zero with a P-38. All we cared about at the moment was that we were tired and glad to be 'back home.' All of us were thinking about the same thing. We knew the Nips would come back over Moresby, and we were anxious to see what we could do in the P-38 against them. What we couldn't tell, of course, was that real use of the long-range capability of the P-38 was still about a year in the future. My own thoughts soon left more combat with the Japanese. I came down with a severe case of malaria and spent the next month in hospitals, on a sea trip to Australia, and in rest camps."

CHARLES W. KING

It must have worked. Charles King went back into combat and shot down five enemy aircraft in his P-38, putting himself up in "ace country."

By the end of December, some five weeks after King and his fellow pilots of the Fifth Air Force returned to New Guinea, conditions at Guadalcanal, especially where the air situation was concerned, had undergone a vast improvement. He was impressed with the spirit and aggressiveness of the Army fighter pilots, and the question of effectiveness of the P-38 appeared to have been answered by combat performance. He expected the worst, but found that the P-38s were being flown with a minimum of maintenance, which had not been the case when they were first introduced to the theater. The reports flowing back from Guadalcanal, in fact, singled out the P-38 for special praise, and the number of Lightnings began to increase slowly. They were proving worth their weight in platinum as bomber escorts, reconnaissance planes, and as a high-load-carrying bomber.

But no one felt there was even a minimum number of P-38s needed. Bomber escort was the rough assignment and there weren't enough fighters to go around. Only the P-38 could go the full route, for example, with the B-26 Marauders, but the pilots were forced to stay down low where, according to the AAF History, they "operated at a most serious disadvantage when forced into combat at the B-26 altitude, or even lower."

It was a strange reversal of the situation in Africa and Europe.

18. Charles W. King, P-38 Driver

In October 1942 General George Kenney of the Fifth Air Force sent a warning to Hap Arnold in Washington: "The Jap is two days from the factory to the combat zone, and he may swarm all over me." Kenney reported to Arnold that he was making good use of the P-40 fighters the Fifth had, to a lesser extent he was getting good service from the P-39, but above all they were desperately in need of the P-38. The Japanese bombers enjoyed good escort from their Zeros, and bomber escort was something the Fifth needed in spades. But without the big twin-engined Lockheed it just wasn't possible.

"If we take out his fighters, his bombers won't go," Kenney wrote Arnold of the Japanese. "If his fighters don't go, his troops and boats don't go either." The P-38 meant that the Fifth could engage "the Zero coverage up topside while the P-39s and P-40s take on the bombers."

It took a while to get P-38s all the way down to New Guinea, and when they arrived it was into a nightmare of maintenance. Pilots operated from primitive fields that mangled landing gear units. They flew through tropical storms so violent they were considered worse than Japanese fighters, and often overstressed the airplanes. There was another dandy item in the New Guinea atmosphere—so much humidity that electrical equipment didn't just become balky, it grew a weird corroding fungus that made mechanics and radiomen (and their pilots) want to weep in frustration. Any metal surface was an open invitation to wicked corrosion almost as soon as it was exposed to the air. Fighter aircraft in the icy cold in Europe had headaches with oil that became sluggish and refused to lubricate. Here, in steaming temperatures and so much moisture, the lubricating problem was one of oil running off like slippery slime, or just evaporating altogether.

The mechanics in New Guinea laughed humorlessly when they heard of maintenance problems elsewhere in the world. As General Kenney wrote of their maintenance: "We are salvaging even the skin for large patchwork from twenty-millimeter explosive fire; to patch up smaller holes we are flattening out tin cans and using them. Every good rib and bulkhead of a used airplane is religiously saved to replace shot up memebers of other airplanes."

The Allison engines for the P-38, the P-39 and the P-40 drove men to pounding their heads against trees. Not simply the fault of the engines. The mechanics were desperately short of bearings for the Allisons, so short that dozens of fighters had to be grounded while Theater Command screamed for the necessary parts. Not until October did the replacement bearings arrive, and by that time, as Kenney said grimly, the main bearings in five out of every six engines of the airplanes they had needed to be changed. The AAF History notes:

Perhaps most discouraging of all was the difficulty experienced in getting the P-38s ready for combat. By October approximately sixty of these fighters had reached the theater, but none of them had seen combat. First, the fuel tanks began to leak, requiring repair or replacement, and then superchargers, water coolers, invertors and armament all required major adjustment or repair. As a consequence, it was not until late in December that the P-38s flew a major combat mission over New Guinea.

The official records show the first interception by the P-38s of Japanese planes to have taken place on December 27, 1942. Twelve Lightnings split up into three flights of four planes each, and then dove against a Japanese formation of more than twenty fighters and seven bombers. In the wild scrap that took place one P-38 was forced down, but by then the P-38s had slashed their way through the enemy, shooting down nine fighters and two dive bombers. Eleven to one was an impressive beginning, and when the P-38s repeated their performance four days later, General Ennis C. Whitehead in unrestrained jubilation wrote "we have the Jap air force whipped." He was referring, of course, to the qualitative role of the Lightning. Early in 1943, the Fifth Air Force had 330 fighters. Only eighty of these were P-38s, but they were still considered to be the main force. Their value lay in more than their accomplishments as fighters flying alone. Teamed up with fighters like the P-40, they flew top cover, took the Zeros off the other planes, and made up a walloping one-two punch against the enemy.

On January 6, 1943, several formations of P-40s and P-38s tore into heavy Japanese cover of a troopship and warship convoy. Veteran 49th Fighter Group P-40 pilots shot down twenty-eight Japanese planes, and a smaller number of P-38s of the same group bagged thirteen more (three went to Dick Bong, who would become the top American ace of the war with forty confirmed air kills). Before the day ended the P-40s and P-38s were claiming more than fifty Japanese planes against a loss of ten Allied aircraft of all types.

This was the beginning of the great "P-38 sweep" of every Pacific theater in which the big twin-boomed fighters were to operate, a record that would show more Japanese planes shot down by Lightnings than by any other American fighter of any service.

But it was a long road. Once again, the author brings into our story the personal records and experiences of those pilots who were there. In the last chapter we were introduced to Colonel Charles W. King. Now we have a rare opportunity to turn back the calendar with Colonel King, to the beginning of his experience with the P-38 and with other fighters, and carry us into full-fledged fighting in the Lightning. First, the colonel and I exchanged a series of letters in which we worked out the periods of interest. Then, at my request, Colonel King was extraordinarily helpful in putting down many thousands of words going over specific points and areas. We shall join them with these shortly. First, the colonel's letter that started us off:

A friend of mine, Lt. Colonel Val Phillips, told me you were writing about the P-38 and had asked for assistance through the *Historical Review* from pilots with service in this airplane.

Having fought in the Pacific with both time in the P-39 (25 combat missions) and the P-38 (176 combat missions), I was very interested in some of the books you have written, especially *Zero!* and *Samurai!* In appreciation of what you have done, I write this letter. Perhaps my recollections will be of some use to you.

I was assigned to the 31st Pursuit Group when I graduated from flying school in May 1941. At Selfridge Field I was further assigned to the 39th Pursuit Squadron, which was the first unit to be equipped with the Bell P-39 Airacobra. In late January 1942, the three squadrons of the group were sent to Australia with a full complement of new P-39s and P-400s (British P-39 variant). In Australia we became the 35th Fighter Group.

We had our first combat in New Guinea in June and July of 1942. The Zeros and Oscars badly outclassed the P-39s. As I recall the events, the 40th Squadron in this period lost sixteen aircraft and eight pilots. We in the 39th lost eight aircraft while getting about an equal number of the enemy. The 41st Squadron came to New Guinea when we were relieved together with the 80th Squadron of the 8th Fighter Group. I do not recall their losses. I mention the P-39s because having fought in them, I believe I had a better idea of the value of the P-38, in which I had five confirmed victories.

As we pulled out of Port Moresby, General George Kenney was arriving, and he managed to have enough P-38s sent to Australia to equip one U.S. Squadron. By the flip of a coin, the 39th Squadron was picked over the 40th Squadron to get these airplanes. The only P-38s in the Southwest Pacific Area before this time were some F-4 and F-5 photo reconaissance ships of the 8th Photo Squadron which operated with us out of 14-Mile Airstrip at Port Moresby (also called Laloki and, later,

Schwimmer). One or two of our pilots had had a ride or two in old P-38s in the States, but most of us flew the airplane for the first time in Townesville, Australia. Two or three flights and that was it, and we headed back up to Port Moresby.

The 39th had gone to Australia with only ten pilots, all second lieutenants, including Frank Royal who took over the squadron from Marvin McNickle (now Lt. General McNickle). Before we went north in P-39s, Major Jack Berry, who had been personal pilot to Lt. General Brett in the Orient, took over the squadron. However, in late July he was killed in a practice skip-bombing accident and Royal, now a first lieutenant, again assumed command. When we got the P-38s, however, General Kenney insisted on a new commander. A major from the 49th Fighter Group (which was flying P-40s at Darwin) got the job. It was Major George Prentice. He was later promoted and organized the 475th Fighter Group which was formed entirely within the Theater, and was also the first group to be fully equipped with P-38s. (Later, Prentice turned over the Group to Charley MacDonald.)

After my squadron received P-38s, next in line for the new fighters was the 9th Squadron of the 49th Group, and, after them, the 80th Squadron of the 8th Group. The 475th was still a bit down the line.

All these squadrons were very successful with the P-38. However, my squadron, the 39th, was the first squadron to achieve 100 confirmed air victories.

The Japanese fighters could of course turn inside every aircraft we had. The Aussies who fought first at Port Moresby in P-40s, as early as March or April of 1942, learned this lesson quickly and told us the details. Some of these Aussies in the first days of fighting had fought the Japs in Whirraways, an Australian version of the old BC-1 and BT-14 trainer, but with a bigger engine. It didn't give them the best of odds against the Japanese.

The P-39 had a definite speed advantage against the Zero *if* we were down real low, and this is what kept a number of us alive. The biggest advantage the Jap had over the P-39 was altitude. The P-39, without a two-stage blower or a turbosupercharger, was completely outclassed at the maximum altitudes we used, which sometimes went as high as 24,000 feet. In our battles over and around Port Moresby, we were always attacked from above.

We found out, however, that with the P-38 *we* had every advantage there was over the Zero and Oscar except in turning ability. A few exceptional pilots like Bong, Lynch and Frank Adkins, by engine jockeying and other tricks, even managed to outmaneuver the Japs, but most of us stuck to conventional speed and climb advantage to win victories and stay out of trouble.

With the P-38s, as before, we were almost always outnumbered. We soon learned, however, that with a squadron of sixteen P-38s, we could take on many more Zeros and be very successful. It was an extraordinary thing to go into battle against a greatly numerical superior force and still know you were going to come out on top.

Through July 1942, the Japanese struck at Port Moresby with regular raids. They were then slowed down in some pretty fierce fighting, but came back with one very heavy raid in August. When we went back to Port Moresby in P-38s, the air war was beginning to change. The P-38 was a big surprise to the Japs. The Zero's armament of two 20-mm cannon and two small caliber machine guns wasn't very effective against our fighters. The same was true of the P-39s we flew, which had four .30 caliber, two .50 caliber machine guns and one 37-mm cannon, which seldom worked. The P-400 export version had a 20-mm cannon and it worked fine. But the P-38, with four fifties and that one 20-mm cannon concentrated in the nose was extremely deadly. In the initial encounters, the Jap losses were very high and they soon found out it paid to avoid Port Moresby and the surrounding area. After these initial encounters, we were unhappy because we ran into a period of limited contact with the enemy.

It was also after these initial encounters that we ran into some serious airplane problems. Fortunately, General Kenney had a Major Jake Schuster come out from air materiel headquarters at Wright Field to help us. The major problem was with our superchargers; the things were blowing up on us. The trouble was caused by leaks in the intercoolers. On the early P-38 the intercooler was ducting back and forth through the leading edge of the wing. As the aircraft aged, air leaks developed and to get the necessary amount of air, the throttle position that was called for brought the turbos to overspeed. Major Schuster showed us how to detect the leaks, repair some of them, and replace the leading edges that were beyond field repair. He also helped us in adjusting the turbo cut-in range and other engineering problems. He was an excellent pilot and helped us to get maximum performance out of the P-38.

Major Schuster was a friend of Kelso, a pilot who had done much of the test work on the P-38. We never worried about engine failure on takeoff—no matter what you may have heard about this problem. We found that by reducing good engine power, trimming the aircraft and feathering the prop, and then increasing power on the good engine, even a failure at 100 feet wouldn't result in an accident. I've seen it happen and seen the pilot climb out safely.

As I mentioned earlier, I requested of Colonel King comments on various aspects of the P-38 as he was involved with this airplane. Each of these comments is presented now, and the headings are those of Colonel King. I think that this material constitutes one of the finest and most incisive contributions to the history not only of the P-38, but also of the air combat aspects of World War II itself. Colonel Charles W. King, USAF comments:

"COMPRESSIBILITY AND THE P-38 BEFORE WORLD WAR II

"When I arrived at Selfridge Field in June of 1941 the First Pursuit Group was being equipped with the Lockheed P-38 Lightning and the Republic P-43 Lancer. The two squadrons first equipped with the P-38s had a wide assortment of models, including even the YP-38. These aircraft had various armament configurations, one of which included two cannon, and there didn't seem to be any with the final configuration we used later. Most of the airplanes didn't even have weapons; it appeared to be a hodgepodge of test arrangements. The squadrons were beset with many maintenance problems. The Allison engine in the P-39 was a headache, and the two Allisons in the P-38 simply compounded the problems.

"The Curtis electric propeller for a long time was universally mistrusted by all the pilots. It had a bad habit of "running away" to where it could tear apart an engine. Actually, the prop wasn't the only culprit. Experience showed quickly that the new electrical systems in our new series of aircraft caused many of the propeller problems.

"The 1st Group was committed to the big maneuvers in the fall of 1941. I found myself at Nachitoches, Louisiana, and remember vividly a silver P-38 that landed at our field one day. The whole bottom of the airplane was stained green, and the color had a grim story behind it. The stain was the result of a landing and takeoff from a farm field. The P-38 pilot had observed his buddy bail out of another crippled Lightning. When the pilot who had bailed out, and whose chute had opened, reached the ground but did not move afterwards, his friend landed nearby, in the same field. He found his buddy dead. He had never pulled the ripcord. When he went out of the P-38 he struck the horizontal stabilizer. It severed both his legs at the hips and killed the man instantly, and the blow also opened the chute. (It was one of the first incidents, macabre as it was, to create the belief that bailing from the P-38 was suicide.)

"Two squadrons of the 1st Fighter Group moved to Savannah, Georgia, during maneuvers to develop interception procedures. One of these squadrons had P-38s and the other flew the P-43 Lancer. They operated mostly at night, and for seven days in a row—or seven nights in a row—they suffered a major accident. One of their major problems was a lack of oxygen. One P-43 pilot reported he came awake over the ocean and was headed due east—over more ocean. He did a one-eighty and after flying west for an hour he sighted an airfield and lost no time getting safely on the ground.

"The early 38s had a stability problem, which was corrected later to a great extent by changing the angle of incidence of the horizontal stabilizer. Aircraft already in the Air Corps inventory were modified as soon as the fix was made known to the units. Later, we got a couple of these older planes in Australia, already modified, and we used them strictly for training. They weren't fit for combat.

"Even with the change to the tail the P-38s we flew (and also the P-47s that were coming into service) had a pretty severe problem we later identified as compressibility, and I'm sure you will have covered this in your development of the airplane. I knew of no specific accidents due to compressibility in the Lightning during our combat tour in New Guinea. But at a later date Ken Sparks, who was an ace early in the operations of the 39th Fighter Squadron, killed himself and his element leader as well. They were on a training mission in Southern California, and Ken started a steep dive-bombing attack from high altitude. They really wound up those airplanes. Both of them came apart—literally—when the shock waves of the compressibility forces pounded the tails to destruction. They were in pieces before they hit the water.

"Many of us encountered this problem. Remember that we were in the field with the P-38. We didn't have the benefit of wind tunnels or the latest theories from the engineers back home. Not for quite a while, anyway. But without knowing too much about the theory of the problem, experience taught us to reduce power in a dive and then hang on until we reached denser air at about 12,000 to 15,000 feet. At that point we eased—and I mean *eased*—the aircraft out of its dive.

"For a long time I was able, fortunately, to avoid the problem. It caught up with me in combat over the big Japanese base at Wewak. That day I was leading two squadrons of P-38s. At first we had only some minor enemy activity, nothing to write home about. The cloud cover was heavy between seven to fifteen thousand feet. Through a break in the clouds I spotted two Jap fighters far below us, well below the heavy bombers we were escorting, in fact. I advised my squadrons to remain at high cover and dove my flight of four planes after the Japanese fighters. The one I selected as my personal target saw me coming. Immediately he pushed over into a dive at full power to get away. In my eagerness to clobber him I steepened my own dive and quickly, almost before I knew what was happening, I overshot the other plane. At just about the time I passed the Zero I realized I no longer had control of my aircraft—not the nicest feeling in combat. I didn't hit that guy, although I passed close enough to see the expression on his face—one of surprise.

"When I tried to pull back on the yoke I inadvertently fired my guns. I was pretty angry at myself for such inefficiency. I also scared hell out of myself because I thought at the moment the gunfire I heard was the Jap shooting at me. I went right on down to between seven and ten thousand feet, and when I moved into the denser air the controls responded properly. There was one other little problem. I was in and out of those clouds, *fast,* right over that big enemy base of Wewak. I knew my own people had seen my plunge into the clouds, but they could be thinking anything. *I* might be the one to get shot down. I called them rather hastily, told them I wouldn't rejoin over the home field of the enemy, but would pick them up somewhere on the way back to our base.

"THE P-38 VS. JAPANESE FIGHTERS

"The first Japanese fighters to be shot down by the P-38 were knocked out of the air on December 27, 1942. Some of the official records have the events a bit mixed up. Twelve P-38s led by Tommy Lynch scrambled from 14-Mile Field at Port Moresby and over Dobodura 125 miles away they intercepted a mixture of enemy fighters and dive bombers. The pilots estimated the number of enemy planes, bombers and Zeros, at twenty-five. But they were a lot more certain about what they did— they shot down fifteen of those planes.

"Prior to June 1942 everything we ran into, in the way

of fighters, was the original Zero, which we code-named Zeke. In late June, over New Guinea, we ran into a newer Zero that seemed to have a bigger engine and some more zap to it. Later we encountered the Oscar, and soon after this the Zero with a bigger engine and squared wing-tips, which got the code name of Hamp. It had better performance and sure could dive better than the earlier models.

"All during 1942 and during the first part of 1943 the Japanese based their aerial combat tactics upon aero-batics. They used Immelmanns, half-rolls, tight climbing turns, and even loops. Against the P-39 and the P-40 these tactics (especially with a pilot foolish enough to fight their way) gave the Japanese a distinct advantage. It was a difficult thing to determine, because of all the wild activity going on at the moment, but it didn't seem to us that the Japanese made any special effort to remain to-gether once a fight began. They couldn't dive as fast as either the P-39 or the P-40, but on the deck they were slightly faster than the P-40 and, as I've mentioned be-fore, slightly slower than the P-39. But with any altitude beneath them they had a marked advantage over both these American fighters. To us, who flew out of Moresby, it appeared that they preferred altitude in a fight, and they certainly had all the advantages on their side at alti-tude. When we moved heavy reinforcements into the area the Japanese increased further their operating altitudes—which was a measure of survival for their bombers and fighter escorts. It must have worked, because we seemed always to be attacked from above. We were always get-ting bounced. We staggered as high as 24,000 feet, but it is extremely questionable if we should have even tried to operate any higher than 15,000 feet. I started a saying that we sometimes survived by using coordination.

" 'Stick and throttle forward together.' Actually, just about all the time, where altitude was concerned, we al-ready had the throttle full forward.

"Everything changed with the P-38. With this airplane it didn't take long to realize that now we held every ad-vantage in the book except sharp turning radius and steep climb. But we were ahead of the game. We had earned our earlier experience flying against a superior fighter and in superior numbers. That's a pretty good classroom. So we developed highly successful defensive maneuvers. The Japanese were a long time in copying our tactics, and it was partly this lack of change on their part that enabled us in the P-38 to enjoy such a great kill ratio over the enemy.

"A highly disciplined squadron, such as our 39th, even when fighting repeatedly against superior numbers, enjoyed a success ratio on the order of twenty to one. Those numbers aren't from any press release. They're from those of us who were there flying the P-38.

"In addition to stressing mutual element and flight support we emphasized the value of maintaining a minimum high speed in combat of 250 mph, and absolutely avoiding steep climbs or tight turns. We developed an up-and-down *yo-yo* maneuver which kept the Jap most of the time from getting a decent shot at us.

"Our armament of four fifties and one 20-mm cannon was at least two to four times as effective against enemy fighters as was the Japanese armament against us. The concentration of firepower in the nose, with a concentrated mass, was far more effective than we realized at the time. Also, in 1943, we were confused by the fact that not many of the Japanese aircraft exploded or burned violently as the Navy was always reporting—and mystifying us. (It wasn't until Korea, with really high-altitude combat between the MiG-15 and the F-86 that I realized the difference between Navy kills burning so easily, and ours not burning or exploding, was due to the height of the combat in which we found ourselves in our large strikes against Rabaul and Wewak.)

"P-38 'NIGHT MISSION'

"After the Japanese landed at Buna and Gona and made the attempt to attack Port Moresby by crossing the Owen Stanley Mountain Range, the first real ground warfare in New Guinea got under way. And one day a strange mission was planned, as the direct result of an intelligence report that several enemy destroyers were en route to Buna to resupply the Japanese beachhead there.

"Up until this time we had never used bombs on the P-38 fighters in the 39th Squadron—and at the moment we had the *only* P-38s in the theater. Late in November, 1942, eight 500-pound bombs were delivered to the squadron. We were given orders to load one bomb on each plane, retaining an external fuel tank on the opposite wing shackle. Then eight pilots were selected to fly the aircraft to 7-Mile Drome which had runway lights. At the briefing held shortly before dark, we learned why we were there, along with eight P-40s with bombs and their pilots from the 49th Fighter Group.

"Lt. Colonel "Fighter" Hutchinson conducted the briefing. Colonel Paul "Squeeze" Wurtsmith, commander of the Fifth Fighter Command, was also present. He had almost nothing to say and had, in fact, scheduled himself to fly as a wingman in the P-40 formation. We were given the latest reports on the Japanese destroyers. They were on their way. We had a heavy bomber shadowing the warships and as the enemy vessels approached Buna we would be dispatched to fly across the mountains. There was one other hitch. Intelligence anticipated the destroyers would arrive during the night, and a bomber mission was laid on to be in the area to drop flares so we would have some light to dive-bomb in our fighters.

"The whole thing came close to being insane. As one of the pilots selected for the mission I can say all of us had serious doubts not only about its success, but also about its survival factor, and what kind of desperate situation would force this kind of a mission to be ordered. We had good reasons for doubts and some of them were:

1. The *only* bombing any of us had ever done was in the P-39 Airacobra and that was skip bombing. None of us had *ever* done any dive bombing.

2. The only lights we were likely to see were the runway lights on takeoff.

3. There were *no* radio aids. It would be flying in the middle of a black bottle. All navigation would be by magnetic compass and in those P-38s, errors up to 30 degrees were very common.

4. We would have only the barest of weather information. That meant bad trouble. Thunderstorms over the Owen Stanley Range towered to up to 60,000 feet and were prevalent at least 50 per cent of the time.

5. *None* of the pilots had any recent night flying experience. *None* of the pilots had any flying time of any kind at night in the P-38. In my own case, I had a grand total of four and a half hours at night, and all in training planes in the United States. We were about as unqualified as one could possibly imagine.

"We sat around the grass operations shack until midnight and then stretched out, fully clothed, on some bare canvas cots. It wasn't a restful night. We expected at any moment to be scrambled on a mission from which I, for one, questioned whether any pilots would ever return. We considered something else—if we ever did get to the target area our results wouldn't be worth a damn.

"Dawn came—no order to scramble. About 7 A.M. we were told the mission was cancelled. We were damn glad.

"Later I learned just how narrow was our escape. The Japanese destroyers had successfully resupplied Buna, and were out of range before an incredible error was discovered. The reconnaissance reports from the bomber shadowing the destroyers was sending its information in GMT—Zulu—Time, and someone in headquarters was reading those reports based on *local* time!

"FAUROT'S BOMB KILL

"Lieutenant Robert Faurot, one of our flight leaders in the 39th, was credited with a bizarre kill of a Zero fighter at Lae Airdrome in New Guinea. As far as we know it turned out to be the first Zero kill made by the P-38; and my logs and diaries indicate the date was November 26, 1942. Faurot was trying to dump a 500-pound bomb on installations at the Japanese base, which was a prickly thorn in our side. Faurot overshot the runway in his attack and his bomb exploded in the water just off the runway's end. A huge geyser plumed high into the air. At the same time a Zero was just scrambling into the air to intercept the five P-38s making the attack, and just as the blast wave and geyser erupted from the water the Zero flew overhead. It was as if the Zero flew into a brick wall; it went right into the sea. The other pilots saw the whole thing and because the Zero was airborne Faurot recieved full credit for the kill.

"The bombing raid was the aftermath of that abortive attempt to dive bomb Japanese destroyers at night off Buna. When that mission was cancelled—and I've explained why earlier—headquarters felt it would be better to make a bombing strike against Lae rather than to download the bombs. But we had problems with the bombs and only five of the P-38s made it into the air with their loads. And not only was this the first P-38 bombing strike in the Southwest Pacific—it was the last to take place for more than a year to come.

"DICK CELLA

"Official histories rarely give full credit where it's due. You can say all you want about how many planes we or somebody else shot down, but behind every scoreboard there's usually an individual or a small group who made the real difference between success and failure. We had one of those individuals; the 39th Squadron got a tremendous break when Dick Cella showed up to join our ranks. Dick was an aeronautical engineer who had worked for several of the top airplane companies in the States. But more than anything else he wanted to be a pilot. When a friend told him he could join the Air Corps and get his wings and then receive assignment to the engineering center at

Wright Field Dick dropped his civilian status and signed up. He was in flying school when the war started, and on graduation he went to P-38 school on the west coast. He was in the first group of stateside pilots we received after we got our Lightnings. Most of these kids had more time in the P-38 than we had, but we had something called *combat* time, and we ended up teaching each other a great deal.

"But it was Dick Cella who proved to be our fortune. He went to work on us with a vengeance. He refined our single-engine procédures. A lot of people in the States were getting killed because of engine failures on takeoff in the P-38, because they were being taught to fly by twin-engine pilot-instructors. That's no paradox, either. With the P-38 on one engine at full power, especially at low speed, you simply could not control the airplane. She'd go over on a wing and that was that. Dick taught us the opposite of all standard training—he taught us to *reduce* power on the good engine, crank in some trim, *then* advance the good engine and feather the prop on the dead engine. Between combat and the unpredictability of the Allison engine we had a lot of single-engine landings —but not a single serious accident that I can recall. We always felt safer with a tricky engine shut down and feathered rather than messing with an engine producing intermittent power and all sorts of unexpected thrust when we least anticipated it. So we shut down the engines quite often.

"During the period of a year, I would judge that each of the forty or more pilots who passed through the outfit in this time, had at least one single-engine landing. I had two of them. One occurred when the engine was shot out in combat, and the other when the electric prop went to low pitch and couldn't be controlled anymore.

"Dick was doing so many things for the squadron, trying to improve our maintenance (and succeeding) that at first he seldom had his chance to fly. When I took over the squadron I changed all that—for his benefit.

"The first gun cameras on our airplanes were mounted in the nose. Since the guns were also there we got a beautiful camera *angle* but mighty poor pictures. Film was often the only evidence a pilot had of a kill (especially over so much water) so it was very disappointing after waiting several days or a week for your film, to find out that all you could see was a blur caused by the gun vibration. Dick knew that we had electrical wiring to the tank shackles under the wings, so he bolted the cameras to the side of a shackle. To cover them he merely removed the access plate on that side and built a new access plate with a bulge in it to house the extra width of the camera. *Then* we got good pictures. Later, when we complained of dust and moisture on the lenses, Dick came up with a lens cover which could be removed in the air. A wire from the lens cover was fastened to the belly tank under the shackle, and since we always dropped our tanks prior to combat we soon had the best fighting film in the whole southwest Pacific.

"IN THE COCKPIT

"The early P-38s had cockpits in dire need of redesign, and it would be kind to say only that they had some undesirable switch locations. The one to which we objected the most was the system for the belly tanks. These were dropped by working toggle switches on the left side of the cockpit. When you were bounced, or got into combat with minimum time to figure out things, those switches were anything but easy to reach in a hurry, and there were too many times when you went through a mental debate on whether to use the time left to jettison your tanks or to bend the throttles forward. Remember, it was more than just banging the switch. You also had to switch each engine to a new tank (internal) to prevent the engine from quitting.

"Another unpleasant feature was a gun button on the right front of the control yoke, and the cannon button on the pilot's side of the right yoke. The third item was the microphone button on the center of the yoke, very similar to the horn button of an automobile.

"There were quite a few ideas tossed around on how to rewire these switches, but we were smart enough to realize that we had better standardize what we were doing. Since there were six squadrons in four different groups, all pretty well scattered, and most things were done informally, well, not everyone was satisfied with the results. Lt. Colonel Prentice had three of the six squadrons; his ideas got the nod. Not because of his rank, but merely because we were pretty well democratic about the whole thing, and he had the most votes behind him from the pilots.

"Just about everyone agreed it was a good idea to put the firing switch for all the guns and the cannon on the old gun switch. A lot of us wanted the tank switch on the old cannon switch. We didn't mind the inconvenience of the mike switch on the yoke. Radios weren't used very often in those days. But Prentice wanted a three-way change and he got it. The mike switch went to the cannon button, and the yoke center (horn) became the belly tank release.

"There were a lot of unhappy and embarrassed pilots in the days following. Numerous "old timers" were "talking through their drop tanks" and every time they wanted only to talk through the radio to someone else they were dumping belly tanks on runways and everywhere else. It took a while to get everyone squared away.

"TRACER AMMO

"Tommy Lynch supervised the writing of a tactics manual for the squadron when we didn't even know what a tactics manual looked like, was supposed to be, or what it did. As a result of several of our flight leaders having been in Britain as observers with the British, right after graduating from flying school in December 1940, those of us flying in the States were using Royal Air Force tactics. For example, we flew a string formation instead of a tight V. That always left something to be desired because most of the time we had only four aircraft in the air, and this forced us back to two elements of two each.

"In P-38s we soon learned that this must be a rather loose flight of four, and when flights worked together we had to be both loose and yet mutually supporting. Tommy didn't stop just with tactics. He also decided we would all do better in combat if we removed the tracer ammo from our guns. We had been told a number of times about the fallacy of tracer ammunition. First, that it had a slightly different trajectory from other rounds, and, second, that when you saw the streak of the bullet it was already dropping below or behind the apparent visual path. No one had really bought these arguments. We all felt we could compensate for these problems as all gunners had been taught to do.

"But Tommy had different ideas and he was adamant about them. He ordered the tracer ammo removed. As his operations officer and self-appointed squadron gunnery officer I made some strong objections to the whole thing. I was convinced the lack of tracer would take many new pilots that many more combat missions to learn proper lead in gunnery (for sights we had merely a lighted circle and to learn "by guess and by God" and by watching the tracers and our hits).

"Fortunately my arguments didn't convince Tommy of a thing. I don't remember what *his* arguments were, but I'll never forget the spectacular results we got. Our kill rate went up from 50 to 100 per cent. Our analysis worked out this way: The Jap knew he could outmaneuver the P-38. He preferred to turn rather than to dive away, which he did if he thought he was in extreme danger. So now we often got two chances at him in a single pass. If our opening burst of fire missed him, and he didn't see us, he maintained his direction. If he did see us firing, but saw no tracer near him, he merely turned. Often his turn was still within our capabilities to adjust our fire and still get him. At any rate, we were faced with much less violent evasive action which was the result of his seeing tracer going by. This decision by Tommy Lynch was one of the main factors in our 39th Squadron being the first outfit to reach 100 confirmed victories in the air.

"BATTLE OF THE BISMARCK SEA

"The Battle of the Bismarck Sea was one of the great and classic events of military history. As the only Allied fighters involved in the attacks on a Japanese convoy, the P-38 played a major part in this brilliant victory. It was made possible, to a great extent, by our ability to "read the Japanese mail." But that applied only to the high brass. Those of us who were doing the actual fighting had no knowledge that our government had broken Japan's secret code. To us we were going out to fight, and codes had little use when you and the other guy were trying to kill each other. So early in the game, when we were getting ready for the big battle and we ran a skeleton-force rehearsal (February 28, 1943) some of us wondered what kind of foolishness was afflicting Bomber Command and Fighter Command.

"Late on 1 March, in the preliminaries to the big fighting, the enemy convoy took their first attack from nine B-17s. At that time the convoy was north of the eastern part of New Britain Island and beyond the range of our fighters; but the next day we had our parts cut out for us. Twenty-four heavy bombers with sixteen P-38s for escort struck at the convoy despite poor weather in the area. The fighters got no further than over the south coast of New Britain. We were sore about this but fate plays its strange games. While we were trying to find a way through the clouds eight of our pilots caught sight of three Zeros attempting to trail the heavies, and hit them without warning.

"Two of the three were shot down—and one of these was my first confirmed kill.

"On 3 March we went all out. We put up a maximum effort of 109 aircraft from bases in the Port Moresby area. We formed up over Cape Ward Hunt on the north coast of New Guinea, with our 39th Squadron with eighteen fighters serving as top cover. The 9th Squadron, then only partially equipped with the P-38, flew ten airplanes for close cover. The attack force consisted of a group of B-25 bombers, eighteen heavy bombers, twelve B-25s acting as strafers, thirteen Australian Beaufighters, and twenty A-20 attack bombers. The weather was near to perfect with only scattered clouds over the water. It was quite a sight for pilots who were accustomed to only small operations and who were almost constantly outnumbered in the air. One big circle and we all headed for a point in the Huon Gulf fifty miles southeast of Finschhafen. It wasn't long before we saw the convoy, and at 10 A.M. things started happening.

"Major Prentice, leading his squadron, had decided the best thing we could do would be to find the largest bunch of enemy fighters and just tear right into them. Just as easily done as said. Some ten miles before we reached the convoy we ran into a loose formation of at least twenty-five enemy fighters. Most of them were about 3,000 feet higher than our position. Both the Japanese and our fighters started a large climbing turn to the left. In less than one full turn the fight started. Bob Faurot dove his flight after three or four Zeros below the main bunch. All but a few of the Zeros came down and before long the main scrap was going on at about 5,000 feet. The fight was a relatively long one for this sort of business. It took place less than 200 miles from Moresby but the mission lasted three and a half hours. The 39th Squadron scored nine confirmed victories. We suffered our *only* multiple loss during the entire time we were flying the P-38. In addition to losing Bob Faurot we lost two pilots in this flight, when neither Eason nor Shifflet returned. The only loss suffered all day from the strike force was a single B-17.

"We were turned around in short order at Port Moresby for another crack at the convoy. By now the size of the strike force and the fighter groups were reduced considerably. Our squadron, this time assigned to close cover, had only ten airplanes. The 9th was able to get only three P-38s to Cape Ward to act as top cover. We were lucky to get there. The afternoon cloud buildups over the mountains were large and vicious. But Tommy Lynch was leading and as always he got us through. When we arrived over the convoy—now pretty well crippled—we saw many lifeboats and much floating debris. We also encountered several bunches of single-engine fighters. The first group of eight was about 4,000 feet higher than we were and they headed north without wasting any time. We couldn't go after them without breaking our cover for the attack force so we watched them move out of range. We then spotted five enemy fighters at different heights extending from the water up to 5,000 feet. Immediately there was a lively flight but no one could score a confirmed victory (the RAAF Beaufighters managed to get one kill).

"We also got into two other flights of Zeros and these were flown by *extremely* skilled pilots. The only good shot I had in the whole mess was at a Zero just behind one P-38, and just in front of another. Later, I found out that Lynch was flying the second P-38—but neither of us got the Zero.

"There was one particular Jap that set some sort of a record. Almost every one of us got at least one shot at this fellow. We put plenty of holes in his airplane but when last seen he was flying north. We later heard a rumor that a real hot outfit—so-called Cherry Blossom Squadron—had been in the fight with us. Regardless of who they were or what they were called they were among the best we ever encountered in many, many engagements.

"Our 39th Squadron ended up the day with ten confirmed victories and three losses. Again, this was the only time we ever lost more than a single P-38 in a particular fight. By the time the mixup ended we had no chance to get back across the mountains to Port Moresby. We did the same thing many other pilots found necessary—we landed at Dobodura Airstrip which was still under construction. Even though we landed on the north side of the island, some distance from our home field, we still logged three hours for the mission. We were all extremely tired. Some of us couldn't help but believe that we may have lost Bob Faurot because he had been flying too much.

"Another mission was planned for early morning. But

the number of ground personnel available was simply too low to service so many planes. They filled our fuel tanks but couldn't reload our guns. It didn't matter too much. The Japanese convoy had been almost completely destroyed and we were ordered back to Moresby.

"THOSE FIRST 100 KILLS

"Give the credit to the P-38—the first squadron of our air force anywhere in the world to reach 100 air kills. As mentioned before, we were the first squadron in the States to get the P-38, and the first to receive the fighters (finally) in New Guinea. Before this we flew the P-39 and the P-400. In the initial combat period with these airplanes we shot down two enemy planes at a cost of one of our pilots shot down and seriously injured. During June and July we lost eight fighters in combat—but saved all the pilots—and scored eight kills to bring the score up to ten.

"We did some weeding out of the pilots who were to get the P-38. Some of the older types were sent home because of their age and their harrowing battles in the early months of the war in the Philippines and Java. If any of the younger or newer pilots had been involved in more than one crash, or shot down more than once, we sent them home also.

"Each of the other pilots was given about three flights in the P-38 and then sent back to New Guinea; we were together as a squadron by mid-September, 1942.

"We didn't go roaring into battle. Maintenance problems drove us up the wall and kept us out of combat for a while. The next factor was the Japanese. We had stopped their advance from Buna, and both sides were sparring for the initiative. Despite our continued flying out of Port Moresby, and trying to commit to battle, our contacts with the Japanese were few and unfruitful. Until 27 December, when twelve P-38s shot down fifteen enemy planes. Then the fights built up with increasing frequency. Nine scalps were added on 31 December. By 7

January Tommy Lynch had run his total to six, Dick Bong had five and Sparks was up to four. Bong wasn't assigned to our squadron but flew his first missions with us while the 9th Squadron was awaiting the arrival of enough aircraft to get into business on their own with P-38s.

"By the end of March our kills had climbed to eighty-one. The 9th Squadron was up to fifty-six victories at this time, even though they had a head start on us while stationed at Darwin, Australia.

"The next month we posted Number 100.

"THOMAS J. LYNCH

"Tommy Lynch led the first mission during which P-38s scored their first big kill of the war, when the Lightnings destroyed fifteen Zero fighters and Val dive bombers over New Guinea. On that day, 27 December 1942, Tommy Lynch got two kills, Dick Bong got two and Ken Sparks scored his two. (Bong wasn't assigned to the 39th Squadron but had ferried an aircraft to us, and he remained with us until the 9th Squadron of the 49th Fighter Group was brought back up to New Guinea.) Lynch already had some victories in the P-39, which was no small accomplishment. When he flew the 'Cobra, Tommy got shot up once and in another scrap was shot down.

"The early race for victories (all *air* kills) involved Lynch, Bong and Sparks. They were quite different individuals. In my opinion Lynch was the only leader among the three; at any rate he was the best fighter leader in New Guinea. Sparks got a lot of victories but he wasn't even a good flight leader and, in fact, was sent home early. Bong never became a squadron commander. Lynch took command of the 39th when Lt. Colonel Prentice left us to form the 475th Group.

"Tommy Lynch was a great leader. He got his outfit to the target, he got them into a fight, he shot at twice as many aircraft as anyone else, and then he led his outfit home. I handled all of the squadron film. When reviewing it I was amazed at how many more aircraft Tommy shot at than anyone else. He made no extra claims. There is no doubt that Tommy got more victories than those with which he was credited.

"On 8 May 1943, we ran into Zero fighters over the water near Madang—and Tommy's belly tanks hung up on him. He called me to take over the squadron and turned away to try to jettison his tanks. Somehow, most of the squadron followed him instead of me. When he saw this he immediately turned back into the Zeros. With one tank still hanging on he got one Zero, while the rest of the squadron also did well. It was Tommy's tenth victory. After that, especially on the big missions (when he sometimes led as many as six squadrons), the deputy squadron leader flew as an element leader in the first flight. This proved to be a very wise improvement in our procedures.

"By 10 September 1943, Bong had sixteen kills, Lynch fifteen, and Sparks eleven.

"On 19 September Lynch left on temporary duty (TDY) to the States, and I then became the squadron commander. When Lynch returned he was assigned to Fighter Command, and then ran his score up to twenty air kills. Then he was shot down by *ground fire* while he and Bong were on a two-man fighter sweep.

"Had it not been for this incredible freak of circumstance, Tommy Lynch would have been right there on top of the heap. Of the early leading aces, in my opinion it was a matter of but two men who were real, even great, combat leaders. These two were Tommy Lynch and Gerald Johnson (commander of the 9th Squadron and, later, commander of the 49th Group; like myself, Johnson took over the squadron while still a captain) and Tommy was unquestionably the best.

"Lynch had been a very good boxer while at the University of Pittsburgh. I'd heard that he was never defeated during his period as an intercollegiate boxer; I can't vouch for a perfect record, but I do know he had many offers to turn pro. Tommy discussed this with me a number of times. He said he had seen too many punchy fighters to even consider his taking up the sport professionally. He was in the class of 41A; he had an engineering background and had a habit of subjecting every problem he found to his own painstaking personal analysis. When several pilots got into a heavy argument on the capabilities of their own or other aircraft, Tommy would sit back and take it all in, not saying a word. But if he were asked for an opinion then he would be ready with just not that opinion, but a statement based on demonstrated performance.

"Let's say the question referred to the altitude needed to split-S a P-38. If Tommy answered with a definite statement then everyone *knew* that Tommy would already have tried this maneuver time and time again over a cloud deck until he knew absolutely what particular speed would produce what specific results.

"Tommy went overseas the first time as a second lieutenant, and the junior of three flight leaders. He was the first to get into combat; he was one of the five pilots who were picked to augment the 35th Squadron when they were taking high losses from the enemy. The move was also made to provide us in the 39th Squadron with some combat experience.

"As expected, Tommy studied everything about him, learned what the other people did that was right, what they did that was wrong, and, bless him, brought us all through it.

"THE TONY APPEARS

"Until 21 July 1943, our combat in New Guinea was mainly against Navy Zero fighters (Zekes and Oscars). As far as we knew we were fighting Japanese Navy pilots. I knew of no Intelligence at the time to indicate that the Japanese Army had an in-line engine fighter about to make the scene.

"But on that day, 21 July, during a mission covering B-25s to the Bodajim Road, the 39th Squadron got into a huge fight with the Japanese.

"I fired at four Oscars, and hit one so hard the pilot almost immediately bailed out. When I got back my film

I was extremely pleased to discover I had fired at him from a three-quarter inverted position and close to 90-degree deflection. Hot damn! Maybe I was really learning to shoot, after all.

"During the debriefing, several of the pilots reported they had seen in-line engine fighters. Our first reaction was that we were now up against the Messerschmitt we had all heard so much about (this was supposed to be the Japanese version of the Me-109). Although at first I didn't recall seeing any of the Type III fighters, a mental reverse rerun of the mission brought back some impressions. Our reports brought some Technical Intelligence people rushing out to our squadron. We each described what we saw, and since it would be several days at the least before our gun camera film would come back, an artist drew a picture of the mysterious Japanese fighter from our descriptions.

"There was a big discussion about the exact location of the underside airscoops. I would have never trusted my own memory except that this was something that came back to me vividly. They accepted my description, and it was completely different from the scoops on either the Spitfire or the Messerschmitt. When the films finally were developed they were so close to the artist's drawing, the Intelligence people sent our squadron a couple of cases of (very hard to get) Aussie beer.

"The P-38 pilots all liked the Tony. It may have been a bit faster than the current Jap fighters we were fighting, but we had plenty of speed to spare, and the Tony was a lot less maneuverable than either the Zero or the Oscar, so it was an easy victory when encountered. It also appeared, to our delight, that the pilots who flew them were not of the highest skill.

"THE P-38 AT WEWAK AND RABAUL

"After the Japanese had been repulsed at Buna in New Guinea, and at Guadalcanal in the Solomon Islands, the key to Allied movement was to eliminate the large enemy air strength buildup which could be used to resist and perhaps even stop new Allied advances. As events finally shaped up, it turned out the complexes to be neutralized were Rabaul on New Britain, then a long-established and powerful base, and, the airdromes on New Guinea centered around Wewak (Wewak, But, Borum, and Dagua).

"For a long time Allied bombers had been hitting Rabaul. We weren't getting the results everyone hoped for. The distance from Allied bases, and the size of the Japanese forces at the targets, limited the scope of the raids and confined them mostly to night attacks. Those operations we were able to undertake simply didn't measure up to the punch we needed to neutralize the main Japanese bastion at Rabaul.

"And at Wewak, the bases were in the process of being enlarged and improved. Time was on the enemy's side, for he could build Wewak into a massive installation.

"To assure our having a fighter force of sufficient strength—as escort for our bombers over these complexes—it was necessary for us to build forward staging and/or recovery bases. For strikes against Wewak our advance field had to be at Tsili Tsili near Marilinan (this was an inland base developed entirely by airlift and practically under the noses of the Japs at Lae). To strike at Rabaul we built bases on Kiriwina Island.

"General George Kenney made the decision that we should first strike at Wewak. The plan was to fly from our home fields at Port Moresby and Dobodura, hit the targets, and then recover at Tsili Tsili if the fighters lacked the fuel to go all the way home. The advance fields would also be needed for the Port Moresby fighters if the ominous cloud buildups over the mountains became too heavy for us to handle. Our ability to land at Tsili Tsili after the long mission also meant a reduced fuel requirement. This was more important than it may seem at first glance, since all fuel had to be flown into the advance field and then dispensed out of drums to the individual aircraft. I remember times when we had less than one day's supply of food on hand, but fuel had the number one priority for the cargo carried on the many transport planes for which we flew escort.

"Timing of every move and every event was absolutely critical. Looking back at what happpened, I fully enjoy the advantage of 20-20 hindsight; it is difficult to see how the Allied timing could possibly have been any better than it was in those days. From the tempo of the enemy buildup it appeared the Japanese realized they must commit sufficient airpower to wipe out our forward bases. But the Allies consistently were that one critical move just ahead of them.

"Although the first P-39 Airacobras first went into Tsili Tsili on 26 July, the Japs didn't bother to make their first attack until 15 August, which was the day after the major portion of the two P-39 Squadrons of the 35th Fighter Group arrived. On the 16th, the next day after the Airacobras showed up, the Japs struck again. They suffered moderate losses on these two raids but there wasn't that much to cheer about. Our reconnaissance missions indicated they were really building up their numbers of aircraft for the big push against us.

"We hit them first.

"On 17 August we mounted one of our heaviest strikes. Forty-nine B-25 bombers, with an escort of eighty-three P-38 fighters (from six squadrons), went after the four enemy airfields in the Wewak area. The sight we encountered at the two southern strips of Wewak and Boram was almost unbelievable. An estimated 145 aircraft were lined up on either side of the strips, and the majority were being prepared to start engines for a strike against *us*. Meanwhile, there was an additional force of an estimated eighty enemy planes at But and Dagua. After the strike—a devastating sweep by our bombers— Intelligence estimated the B-25s had wiped out 150 out of 225 Japanese planes at the enemy fields.

"Prior to the B-25 strike, fifty-three of our heavy bombers made a dawn raid against these bases. They weren't as effective as hoped for, and the B-25s really did the job. Because of the adequate fighter cover they had over them, they were able to go in low and take out specific targets.

"Because of excellent—and lucky—timing not a single Japanese fighter got into the air. This was the single greatest surprise of the entire mission.

"The next day, 18 August, another heavy strike was laid on. We sent out seventy-four P-38s to cover fifty-three B-25s in an all-out blow at the four airstrips. This time the Japanese were ready with about forty fighters in the air. The P-38s shot down fourteen and the bombers got eighteen more. We lost one P-38 and three B-25s.

"We were now reaping in full the tremendous performance of the P-38. The capability of this airplane to go long distances, to fight it out with the best of the enemy, and to get back was paying extraordinary dividends. These missions jumped the length of P-38 combat sorties from about three and a half hours to almost five hours. (we had had escort missions over four and a half hours before this, but these were scheduled in such a way that if we got into a fight the missions could be reduced in length.)

"During the remainder of August, our strike forces of bombers and fighters continued the program of successfully neutralizing the Wewak bases. At the same time our field at Tsili Tsili went untouched. This set the stage for the seaborne landing at Hopoi Beach (north of Lae) and the airborne landing (west of Lae) at Nadzab on the 3rd and 5th of September. The long endurance of the P-38 played a vital role in these operations in providing cover by flying not only out of Port Moresby and Dobodura but also out of Tsili Tsili.

"We fighter pilots were extremely concerned about protecting the transports carrying paratroopers so close to main centers of Japanese air strength. We expected much more reaction than we actually encountered. But there were other kinds of incidents. Some of us were angry almost to the point of insubordination when an entire squadron of P-38s was assigned to cover three B-17s carrying some of our generals, instead of covering the real and vulnerable attack force.

"During the rest of September, Allied attacks on We-wak continued, allowing not only the capture of all the Nadzab-Lae area but also opening up a move along the Markham Valley, and making available more and more advanced airstrips. The attacks also made a successful operation of the seaborne landing on 22nd September at Finschhafen.

"Now was the time to turn our attention to Rabaul. The airstrips at Kiriwina Island were being completed. On 7 October I flew to Kiriwina and then returned to Port Moresby. At Kiriwina final arrangements were made with the Aussies for the service we would need to get a quick turnaround to enable us to get airborne again in time to join up with the heavies, as they passed over on their way to Rabaul. This was an operation we carried out visually.

"On 12 October we assembled the largest force ever seen in those skies to hit Rabaul. Eighty-seven heavy bombers, one hundred and fourteen B-25s, twelve Beaufighters—and one hundred twenty-five P-38s for cover. Three hundred and forty-nine fighters and bombers! The size of the raid undoubtedly caught the Japanese by surprise. They managed to get only some thirty fighters off the ground into position to intercept. We claimed twenty-six Japanese fighters shot down, as well as destroying another hundred on the ground.

"Our losses were two B-24s, one B-25, and one Beaufighter. This was entirely to anti-aircraft; we suffered no losses to the enemy fighters. On the way to Rabaul the fighters from Port Moresby had turned around at Kiriwina after a 90-minute flight. Opposition on this mission was so light we were able to return all the way to Moresby after a three-hour flight. Later missions, however, were to be far different.

"The plan was to keep hitting Rabaul at every opportunity. But the Japs got a tremendous break when the weather fell apart and storms filled the skies over New Britain. We had to cancel several raids when our weather reconnaissance aircraft reported being unable to get through to the target.

"On the 18th October one group of B-25s, despite receiving the turnaround signal because of weather, pressed on to the Japanese base. They lost three of their number as against thirty-two enemy fighters shot down.

"Finally, on the 23rd October, the weather improved and we started moving again. Forty-seven P-38s covered forty-five B-24s in a strike against Rabaul. The Japanese were stirred up and reacted with a force of at least fifty Zero fighters. We shot down twenty and lost two P-38s— but brought every bomber safely through the strike. My logbook shows my flight from Kiriwina to Rabaul and return at four and a half hours. It was a long and hard fight.

"The next day we went out again, this time with fifty-four P-38s covering sixty-two B-25s to Rabaul. The P-38s hit the Japanese fighters like a falling locomotive—we shot down thirty-five and the bombers got eight more. There were no losses to our strike force—every plane came home. Again, it was a long combat mission. We covered the B-25s by staging out of Dobodura and then had to recover at Kiriwina after another mission of four and a half hours.

"Then we received reports that the Japanese were flying in still *more* replacements to Rabaul . . .

"Next day the B-24 heavies went out again. Sixty-one Liberators covered by fifty P-38s went after Rabaul despite marginal weather. Seventy Nips were up this time, and thirty-seven were shot down. We lost but one B-24.

"For the next three days the weather was very poor. It helped our fighter force. From a figure of some 125 fighters we had dropped to about 50 operational planes. The mechanics worked around the clock to put the others back on the line. The news we received from the States didn't help. Due to the situation over Europe, we were told, we would receive *no* replacements for the next several months.

"On the 29th October we went out again. Fifty-three P-38s covered thirty-seven B-24s, and again we got an intense fighter reaction. We shot down twenty-five fighters (on this mission I got two Oscars, my fourth and fifth kills). Our losses again were kept to nil, although a great many of our planes took heavy battle damage. Attempts to hit Rabaul again on 31 October and 1 November were stopped by poor weather. We were extremely anxious to keep the Japanese at Rabaul occupied on the 1st because this was the day the Third Marine Division landed at Empress Augusta Bay. However, there was no question but that our strikes had taken their toll—the landing went unopposed.

"Somehow the Japanese managed to keep reinforcements flowing into Rabaul. On the 2 November we carried out a most significant raid. Fifty-seven P-38s (every flyable fighter from six squadrons, down to half-strength by now because of maintenance) escorted seventy-five B-25s to the Japanese base. The Mitchells concentrated on the harbor but also hit Lakunai Airfield. The Japanese reacted with over a hundred and twenty-five fighters. The P-38s shot down forty-one and the B-25s got another twenty-seven. We took some losses ourselves—nine B-25s and nine P-38s went down. At least six of the Mitchells were victims of ground fire in the extremely effective strike on the harbor. They hit some thirty ships and sent 114,000 tons of shipping to the bottom. Back at Dobodura one B-25 and three P-38s crash-landed. Many of the returning Mitchells had wounded aboard. Several stopped without taxiing from the dirt strip while their wounded were removed. One B-25 crashed on the metal strip just in front of my P-38, forcing another B-25 to land just over me on the taxi strip.

"We flew to Kiriwina again on the 3rd and 4th November to cover B-24 strikes to Rabaul, but the weather forced us to turn back short of the target.

"The next day we managed a raid coordinated by the Fifth Air Force with Navy planes from Halsey's carrier force. The Navy hit Rabaul at 11:30 A.M. with almost a hundred aircraft—they lost eight and shot down twenty-seven. We arrived at the target fifty-five minutes later with twenty-seven B-24s escorted by sixty-seven P-38s. Only fifteen enemy fighters tried to intercept, and we shot down two. (I got two probables and one damaged; later

my film showed I had shot the canopy completely off one
Zero.)

"We lost one P-38. *This was the only aircraft my
squadron ever lost over Rabaul on all the tough missions
we flew over that target.* Good air discipline had paid off
in a tremendous way. Our one loss was a number two
man shot out of the middle of a flight by a Japanese on a
90-degree deflection shot.

"It was a good thing—it was critical—that we had
this excellent air discipline. Because it wasn't until *after*
the raid that we learned that the Navy had actually carried out their strike against Rabaul. Apparently they were
supposed to be completely out of the area before our
attack. *They weren't.* It nearly precipitated an AAF attack against U.S. Navy planes. On the way in to the target
I saw several planes down low on the water headed southeast. They were in position for a perfect bounce. I stayed
with my assigned mission, and that's where the air discipline came in. Because any other time . . .

"On what turned out to be the last big raid of the
Fifth Air Force on Rabaul, sixty-four P-38s escorted
twenty-four B-24s to the Japanese bastion on 7 November. Fifty Japs intercepted and we shot down twenty-
three. No bombers were lost but five P-38s failed to return.

"A look at the record of seven major P-38-escorted
missions to Rabaul is extraordinary reading:

"On 12 October, we lost two B-24s, one B-25 and one
Beaufighter, for twenty-six Japanese fighters shot down,
as well as another hundred destroyed on the ground. (All
told, through these seven strikes, the number of Japanese planes wrecked on the ground is estimated at several
hundred.)

"On 23 October, we shot down twenty enemy fighters
for a loss of two P-38s.

"On 24 October, thirty-five Japanese planes went down
in air combat. American losses: none.

"On 25 October, the score came to thirty-seven Japanese fighters destroyed. We lost one B-24.

"On 29 October, twenty-five more Japanese fighters were shot down. Our losses: none.

"On 2 November, in one of the wildest fights of all, we lost nine B-25s (six to flak) and nine P-38s, against sixty-eight Japanese fighters destroyed.

"The last raid, 7 November, cost us five P-38s for twenty-three Japanese losses.

"On these seven strikes, the air combat record shows our losses at sixteen P-38s and fourteen other aircraft, as against 234 Japanese fighters shot down in the air. And there is no way of knowing how many Japanese planes fell to the thirty aircraft lost from our forces.

"It's the sort of record that speaks for itself.

"On three days running—9, 10 and 11 November—we staged again to Dobodura, but failed to reach Rabaul. The problem was weather.

"But by then our forces had sufficient facilities and strength at Empress Augusta Bay to provide fighter cover for Thirteenth Air Force strikes against Rabaul, and the Fifth Air Force was able to terminate its campaign against that particular target, and attend to other matters with the enemy.

"The bombers protected from enemy fighters by the P-38s had done a tremendous job. It was a pattern that was to be repeated over and over again on the way back to, and then beyond, the Philippines.

"But for us—the P-38 pilots in the Fifth Air Force—another phase had set in. For months to come, we would be denied replacements of the fighter airplane, the P-38, we all wanted and needed so badly. Without additional P-38s Generals Kenney and Whitehead had to tighten their belts. It was like getting our ability to reach far out to the enemy sliced right in half. In a decision that was a bitter blow to the 39th Squadron of the 35th Group, and the 9th Squadron of the 49th Group, we all lost our P-38s.

"They were given to the 475th Group as replacements for the many losses they had suffered.

"The two squadrons which had led most of the big raids were now to be supplied with the Republic P-47 Thunderbolt. The big Jugs were also scheduled to be sent to the whole 35th Group to replace their P-39s, and, to the 49th Group to replace their P-40s. I'm sure the people flying the 39s and 40s were pretty happy about getting the Thunderbolt, but I can't say the same for those of us who flew the Lightning.

"A few final words about Rabaul, and the tactics we developed and used. Generally, a mission saw the use of two groups of bombers. Whether they were heavies (B-17 and B-24) or mediums (B-25), for each group we provided one squadron of P-38s for close and one squadron for top cover. The other two P-38 squadrons made a fighter sweep three to five minutes ahead of the bombers.

"Usually this lead was alternated between Gerald Johnson of the 9th Squadron, or myself, with the 39th Squadron. We were generally able to contact the major concentration of Jap fighters and keep them too busy to make anything like a coordinated attack on the bombers. We confused the Japanese by staying high over the bomber formation (at approximately 25,000 feet) and about fifty miles from the target we started a shallow descent to about the primary bomber altitude of 18,000 feet. Most of the time we found the Japanese climbing at that altitude. I do not believe they ever realized how much speed we had built up by then. Our superior speed was then used as we yo-yo'd up and down through the concentrations of Zero fighters.

"After our successes with the P-38s and our knowledge that the only sure way to engage the Nip was over his airdromes at a long distance from home base, it is easy to understand why Gerry Johnson and I hated to put our squadrons into what we thought was a lumbering P-47, and what we knew was a fighter of much lesser range than the P-38.

"However, that was our job, and we did what we had to do. But not without incident. As had happened before,

Colonel Neal Kearby had been given the job of convincing us that the P-47 was a better aircraft than the P-38. After a few flights we knew it was a good airplane, but it just couldn't compare with the P-38 for the job that we had to do. And we had two squadrons of very experienced combat pilots who could be talked into changing, but who absolutely could not be fooled about relative performance, no matter what Kearby said. Of course, Neal Kearby could have beaten just about anyone in the air in single combat no matter what he flew. He was that great a pilot. But single combat wasn't the way the air war in the Pacific was being fought and won.

"We had a special meeting called by X Fighter Command where Kearby tried to get us all to agree that the P-47 was a better plane than the P-38. I told him that it just wasn't the truth; I added that I was having no trouble with my pilots in converting to the Thunderbolt.

"Gerry Johnson was another matter. Faced with the same question as to which was the better airplane he wanted to argue the point and he and Kearby got heated up pretty good. Finally Kearby demanded: "Well, how can we settle it? You and I over Port Moresby?"

"When Gerry, who like me was still a captain, hesitated briefly, I jumped in with both feet. "Hell, yes!" I told Kearby. "When?"

"I could see a couple of group commanders—especially mine—about ready to swallow their teeth. Fortunately for me, Colonel Kearby realized it was a pretty foolish challenge, and he more or less said so, and the meeting went on to more practical matters.

"But we all knew—*the P-38 was the airplane.*"

CHARLES W. KING

19.   From the Record

Several times in his narrative Colonel King has referred to a close friend and fellow pilot, Tommy Lynch, who was finally killed by ground fire on a two-man sweep with Dick Bong. At that time Lynch had twenty confirmed air kills. But his real value to his men, as Colonel King has stated forcefully so many times, was Lynch's role as a leader. Among the documents forwarded to me by Colonel King is a special operations and tactics paper that Lynch wrote for his pilots—and that became a bible for fighter operations in the Southwest Pacific. It is not a personal paper, of course, but the man behind the pen comes through in an intensely human—and pilot—fashion.

The document is signed:
>Thomas J. Lynch,
>Captain, Air Corps,
>Commanding.

"RADIO CONTROL

"Radio control is essential for successful operation of more than one flight. Even the single flight is greatly hampered by lack of radio contact.

"A major factor in the value of radio is transmitting information of immediate importance. This factor contributes to the limiting of radio use to essential messages only. Consequently the length of these messages should be as short as intelligibility permits.

"It cannot be overemphasized that, in reporting to leaders, members must use code words and position (e.g., Music Blue Four to Music Leader, etc.). This is extremely necessary, though it may lengthen the message more than the use of personal names. The use of names is very confusing in this area where numerous flights are on the same radio frequency. It cannot be overstressed that the words, low, high or same level, must be included in these messages.

"The clock system should be used for reporting any aircraft (e.g., aircraft at three o'clock low.).

"Unless the reporting pilot can definitely recognize the aircraft in question as friendly or enemy, he should report them as unidentified. The use of the word "bogie" is recommended. The pilot reporting should be extremely careful not to report aircraft as enemy unless he recognizes them as such, or unless the aircraft appear to be making an attack, which action leads the pilot to believe they are enemy aircraft. LIMIT RADIO CONVERSATIONS TO NECESSARY INFORMATION.

"WEATHER

"As weather plays an extremely important part in all flying, it should always be taken into consideration when a mission is planned. In tropical climates weather is very erratic and should be studied and watched carefully on all flights. In planning missions, the range of the fighter aircraft should be considered and a safety margin allowed in case of bad weather.

"It should be left to the discretion of the Squadron Leader or flight leader of the fighter aircraft to determine if the mission should be completed or abandoned to insure the safe return of his aircraft. Bomber formation leaders should be instructed to consider the fighter escort before attempting to go through any bad weather.

"In the following paragraphs it will be impossible to

consider weather in determinging the tactics to be adopted but nevertheless it should always be taken into consideration in planning and executing all missions.

"TACTICS EMPLOYED ON ESCORT OF HEAVY BOMBERS

"Due to the slow speed of heavy bombardment aircraft of the B-17 and B-24 type the escorting fighters are forced to weave considerably to maintain a protective cover over the bomber formation. The squadron leader should maintain a position three to five thousand feet above and on a flight front or slightly behind the leading bomber, weaving back and forth in order to maintain this position. Minimum cruise should be maintained by escorting fighters. In weaving, the flight leaders should maintain position so that an equal distribution of fighter aircraft to the left and right of the bombers is maintained. This can be accomplished by the flights crossing over directly behind the bombers. The flight leader should attempt to maintain positions (as discussed in the meetings on squadron formations). This fighter screen should be maintained until the bombers are on their way home and are out of any danger.

"TACTICS EMPLOYED ON ESCORT OF MEDIUM BOMBERS

"In escorting medium bombers, the same type of formation will be used, but, as the speed of the B-25s and B-26s approximates that of the P-38s it is not necessary to adhere to a weaving formation as described in the previous paragraph. The squadron leader should maintain a position three to five thousand feet above and on a flight front or slightly behind the leading bomber.

"In escorting low-level bombing attacks or strafing attacks it is necessary for mutual protection that the flights be spread over a greater distance in elevation. The lowest flight will maintain a position three to five thousand feet above the bombers, never getting lower than 5,000 feet above the ground, unless making an attack or unless some situation demands going lower. The second, third and fourth flights should be stacked at intervals of 2,000 feet, thus making an interval of 6,000 feet between top and bottom flights. As strafers usually spend quite a length of time over the target making numerous passes at the objective, considerable weaving and turning must be executed by the escorting fighters. During this time formation of any type between flights is impossible, but visual contact should be maintained between the flights. Formation within the flights will be maintained at all times. Radio contact at this time plays a very important part as enemy fighters are likely to be encountered at any time, and the rapidity with which they are reported may determine the success of the mission. All flights must be notified when the strafers intend to leave the area. At this time the formation between flights must be rebuilt and the strafers escorted to a safe distance from the target.

"One of the most important factors on an escort mission is to stress to the flight leaders, element leaders and individual pilots in the formation, the importance of carrying out their mission to the fullest extent possible. Cases have arisen where flight leaders have forgotten that their mission is to protect their charges. Under no circumstances should a flight leader leave his mission in order to make an attack on another target which does not endanger his charge. No definite rule can be set to determine the action to be taken by the flight leader, but it should be stressed very strongly upon him that he has a duty to perform and failure to do so may prove disastrous. The enemy have been known to use a decoy to lure the escort from their charge and at times have practically thrown away aircraft and personnel in order to accomplish this. KNOW YOUR MISSION. Air discipline must be maintained at all times and is a determining factor in many cases as to the success or failure of a mission.

"In the event that the bomber formation is attacked by enemy fighters, the escorting fighters should take action to protect the bombers. This action depends upon the formation and type of attack delivered by the enemy and will be determined by the squadron leader. The situations encountered are variable but nevertheless a plan of action should always be made before the mission. Before the mission is undertaken, the probable situation should be carefully studied and a plan for the mission adopted and carried out as far as the situation permits. Tactics employed by the enemy on former occasions are extremely useful in pre-determining the tactics he will use under similar conditions.

"On a mission against an enemy convoy of transports, it is very likely that a continuous patrol of enemy fighters will be encountered; this fighter patrol is not likely to leave the area surrounding the convoy; therefore, one must consider this factor in planning such a mission.

"On a mission comparable in size to the morning mission of March 3rd during the Bismarck Sea Battle, the following plan is recommended and has proven successful:

"Due to the difference in speed of the attacking aircraft on a mission of this type, it is necessary to establish a rendezvous point. It is essential that all aircraft meet promptly at rendezvous time. On escort missions with B-25s, B-26s, A-20s, Beaufighters and similar aircraft whose speed approximates that of the P-38 it is not necessary to have a rendezvous point away from the base as escort from the base is easily accomplished. When slower type aircraft are involved the rendezvous point should be as near to the target as possible without giving away the mission.

"One squadron of fighters should act as low cover and one as high cover. The bombing attack being at a low level, the low cover should be within three to five thousand feet above the top lead bomber and should stay with them throughout the attack. Until the main flight of enemy fighters is sighted, the top cover should remain with the low cover and the bombers, the main flight of enemy usually being numerically equal to, or greater than one of our squadron flights. The top cover should then move ahead and attack the enemy fighters, engaging them as long as possible and breaking their formation, thus preventing a concentrated attack on our low cover and bombers and providing our bombers with an undisturbed bombing run. As our bombers and strafers continue the attack in waves, it is necessary for our fighters to remain in the area until the last bomber and strafer have left.

"The squadron leader should give a radio signal to have the fighters clear the area. If the squadron leader fails to do this within a reasonable time, contact with him should be attempted by the flight leaders and, if not made, the flight leaders can warn the squadron to clear the area.

"TACTICS EMPLOYED ON OFFENSIVE PATROL

"On offensive patrol the formations as described in previous paragraphs will be used. Here again the situation encountered will be variable; however, a few rules can be made and carried out. Flights should be dispersed to give the maximum protection to everyone involved. In the event that enemy planes are sighted, the squadron leader should determine the action taken. If there are only a few enemy planes (two or three) one flight might be dispatched from the squadron to deliver an attack, providing a definite advantage is held by our fighters. In case a large number of enemy planes of the fighter class are encountered a squadron attack should be delivered providing again that our planes have the advantage. If the advantage is not held by our planes it is advisable to run, and return after a more advantageous position has been reached. After contact is made the fighting will break down into individual combat. In this type combat it is the responsibility of every pilot to take full advantage of the airplane he is flying. The advantages of the P-38 are readily seen and should be used to their fullest extent. Also the advantages of the Zero type fighters are known and should be avoided.

"The P-38 has the advantage of speed and also is equal to the Zero in climb providing a high speed climb at a very shallow flight angle is maintained. Climb at a steep angle and slow speed should never be attempted against a Zero. Above 20,000 feet the advantage in climb favors the P-38. Circle combat and maneuvers of any type should not be attempted. Head-on attacks give the advantage to the P-38 due to the greater firepower and heavier armor. Care must be taken to break away from a head-on pass to avoid mid-air collisions. The Zero pilots do not like a head-on attack and in most cases will not attempt it and will strive to break away soon. But, with the possibility of the enemy pilot being killed, a head-on collision may result if the P-38 pilot does not initiate the breakaway. The P-38 airplane has the ability to pick its own fight and avoid combat at a disadvantage, providing the pilot uses the properties of the plane to their fullest advantage. AVOID CIRCLE COMBAT— AVOID STEEP ANGLE CLIMB—AVOID COMBAT STARTING AT A DISADVANTAGE. Make an attack, clear the area before making a turn, and then return to make another attack; these maneuvers have proven highly successful. The squadron leader should signal by radio when he wishes the squadron to clear the area. Pilots should attempt to stick together and reform with any other P-38s present after initial combat. This gives added protection to everyone concerned.

"TAKEOFF AND CLIMB

"In the event of an attack delivered against any of our installations the tactics used by our fighters will be slightly different than the tactics used on the offensive. The time element is usually the deciding factor on an interception problem. Taking this into consideration the pilots should be highly schooled in getting to their planes and taking off in formation in as short a time as possible. Planes should be dispersed in such a manner that flights can be readily formed for takeoff.

"Pilots should have their equipment in a handy place and transportation for the pilots to get to their planes should be ready at all times. After the planes are in the air it is necessary to organize the formation as quickly as possible; therefore the pilots should be highly trained for this maneuver. In climbing to maximum altitude the squadron leader should use as much manifold pressure as possible without breaking up the formation. In a squadron of sixteen P-38s, 35 inches and 2,800 rpms permits enough throttle play for the formation to remain intact. Above 25,000 feet this will have to be reduced. An indicated airspeed of 160 mph provides for maximum rate of climb and ease of staying in position. The mission of our fighters in this case is to prevent the enemy bombers from making their runs. If it is at all possible the enemy fighters should be avoided completely and strict attention given to attacking the enemy bombers. With a high-speed airplane of the P-38 type this is entirely possible. The head-on attack should be made with the flight coming in at different angles thus making it harder for the bomber gunner to change from one target to the next. If the attack is delivered swiftly and the breakaway completed the enemy fighters can be avoided easily. The initial attack should be designed to break up the bomber formation. If this plan is successful the squadron can then break down to flights and proceed to pick off stray bombers. If the formation is not broken the squadron attack should be delivered a second time.

"CONTACTING ENEMY BOMBERS WITH FIGHTER COVER

"Number One and Two flights should break away to the left, circle back to the left, and make a second attack. Number Three and Four flights should break away to the right, circle back to the right, and renew the attack. In the event that enemy fighters intercept, action should be taken to avoid them or an attack made on them as the situation demands, remembering that the primary target is the bombers. Breakaways after an attack on bombers must be sharp and definite. Skidding and diving away at the same time makes a hard target for the gunner. This combat usually ends in flights being broken up and individual combat ensuing. Pilots should attempt to stick together and reform with any of our planes present. This gives added protection for everyone concerned.

"After a bomber formation is broken, the type of attack delivered on single bombers will be left to the discretion of the flight leader or individual pilot, as the case may be. If a flight of four ships has the opportunity of making an attack on a single bomber a tail attack should be considered. With one element attacking from the left and the other from the right, a very good show may be had without too great a risk to the attacking fighters.

"This type of attack has the advantage of a rapid return to position for a second attack, which the head-on attack does not have. Of course, heavier firepower from the tail may be expected, as well as from the turret. The firepower forward is usually less than to the rear.

"On a head-on attack as well as on a tail attack the breakaway must be sharp and skidding in order to present a poor target for the gunners.

"In the event of attacking a single bomber or formation of bombers with a single fighter, the head-on attack should be used. The rapid rate of closure, the speed of the breakaway, the poor firepower forward for the enemy and the relatively easy shot of the head-on attack are all advantages which should be considered in determining whether to make a tail or head-on attack. The tail attack has the advantages of a slower rate of closure (thus a longer shot) and also an easier shot when the deflection is very small.

"TAKE ADVANTAGE OF ALL OPPORTUNITIES. DO NOT TAKE TOO MANY CHANCES. RE-

MEMBER THE WAR CANNOT BE WON IN ONE DAY. LOOK AROUND—WHAT YOU SEE WON'T HURT YOU. KEEP YOUR HEAD OUT AND USE IT."

THOMAS J. LYNCH

20. One Hundred to One

Some parts of history cannot and never will be told. Too many pilots, caught alone in the sky, have fought battles that would—if they could be known to us—form a memorable chapter in our history. Sometimes the rare event happens. After many years of patiently sorting out the historical record, of studying logbooks and diaries, of interviewing pilots, and of recollections finally being put to paper, an aspect of the war never reported emerges to life. This chapter, the story of a pilot whose name few will ever recognize—Lieutenant William Sells—is one of those rare events. Strange to say, this incident is not reflected in any of our *published* military histories. I scoured every publication known on this matter and found—nothing. Yet the story, the event, is recorded officially.

Lieutenant William Sells was assigned to Port Moresby as a P-38 pilot of the Fifth Air Force. Until taking off on his last mission he had been in combat several times and had shot down one Japanese airplane, with this kill confirmed.

What does not exist in the published records is the fact that Sells—on his last flight—shot down another six Japanese planes, for a total of seven kills. But you will not find his name on the roster of World War II aces, despite the fact that he achieved this coveted status in a single flight.

The case of Lieutenant Sells is a series of unfortunate incidents, all of which occurred during the frenzy of war, and which combined to keep this story shrouded for so many years.

In 1948 this writer was assigned to Headquarters Fifth Air Force in Nagoya, Japan. One of my assignments, which was then to Intelligence, was to research some of the wartime activities of the Fifth that had never seen the light of day. The Yamato Building in Nagoya, which housed the headquarters of the Fifth, had several deep sub-basements in which were stored guns, ammunition, supplies, and the still-secret wartime files of the Fifth. The latter were packed into dozens of foot lockers and crates which had been jammed into a storeroom.

The crates with which I worked were battered and worn. Several crates of records were missing, and so there are gaps in the history of the Fifth that will never be revealed. Unlike the Eighth Air Force in England, the Fifth did not enjoy the solidarity of permanent headquarters and a huge administrative staff. The Fifth was a nomad air force scrabbling from one island base to another as it pursued the Japanese. Its historians hammered out their records often in wet, stinking tents and, too often, abandoned their typewriters and files as the Japanese paid unscheduled visits. The Japanese didn't always miss, and sometimes the bombs scattered the makeshift administrative facilities.

Apparently this is what happened soon after Sells' last flight. From one scorched and blackened crate I extracted sheafs of paper which had suffered from fire. It wasn't difficult to understand what had happened with Sells' records. Soon after his mission, Fifth's headquarters were hit in an enemy raid. The original records were destroyed, and of all the papers relating to the mission of Lieutenant William Sells, perhaps only the scorched carbon which I discovered was all that remained. I will not detail the exhaustive research carried out since then in the Pentagon, the Air University and other historical sources to obtain further details. Only that one piece of carbon paper with scorched edges remained. Even the exact date of the flight was obscured by the charring, and there existed no confirmation of his organization, although it was most likely the 49th Fighter Group. I am not certain of this, of course. The unusually high number of Japanese aircraft in this mission is accounted for by the fact that in this period of 1943 the Japanese were still attempting to knock out Moresby with heavy air strikes. So from the charred files, from other records, from conversations with pilots, I have pieced together as well as can be done the extraordinary, unknown flight of this young lieutenant, who alone, in a P-38, attacked more than one hundred Japanese fighters and bombers.

The mission started without preamble as to what lay ahead. Sells apparently was making a test flight to check out the engines of his P-38, which had been giving him trouble earlier. He climbed out through scattered clouds, running through different power settings until he was satisfied with the results, and then prepared to return to the field.

And then he saw them. Riding through the clouds. Good God! Dozens and dozens of bombers with a heavy escort of Zero fighters. Unnoticed by Allied radar, they were rushing in a wide sweep against Milne Bay, hidden in their approach behind a storm front. They had every chance of hitting the Allied fields without warning.

Sells shouted his alarm by radio. On the ground pilots raced for their planes. But there wasn't enough time for an effective intercept; before the fighters could clear the deck the bombers and Zeros would be on them. Sells, of course, was little more than a bothersome gnat facing a huge swarm. He didn't hesitate. He advanced his throttles, jockeying for additional altitude, then pushing forward into a dive that took him straight for the bombers. Sells made it to the first bomber formation before the Zeros could cut him off. He bored straight at the Mitsubishis and his thumb stabbed the trigger on the yoke. Sells' aim was true. A flaming bomber tumbled through the clouds, shedding debris as it fell.

Sells had the momentary advantage and it was clear he pressed it as hard as he could. The Lightning raced straight at the lead bombers and the formation broke up as Sells plunged through, with Zeros now in pursuit. Sells needed time, enough time to disrupt the flow of the attack, to break up the bomber formations, if possible, so the fighters below might get into the air in time to follow his initial passes. Sells went through the first formation, dove and rolled into a turn and came around beneath a second formation, the bombers lined up before him like geese. His second kill left no doubts; the concentrated buzzsaw fire of the P-38 sliced a wing from a fuselage and the bomber spun flatly through the clouds. That made two.

Sells' initial dive, his diving, rolling turn and up-and-down tactics unquestionably saved his life. The bomber gunners were tracking him, but he was rolling and skidding wildly and the Zeros were so close the bombers had to hold their fire for fear of hitting their own pilots. Again, it was a desperate measure of relief, but it added up to precious moments. Sells went up through the bomber formation in a zoom climb to take advantage of his speed, the Zeros hard after him. Their own numbers became Sells' ally as the Zeros rolled away from collisions. But there were too many and the Lightning was taking a battering. Sells gave the P-38 everything it had, he ran the gauntlet of fire and he was through. For the moment he raced ahead of the Zeros.

Sells dove straight into another formation. Perhaps the Japanese believed he was going to ram, or they thought more than one P-38 was in their midst. Whatever were their thoughts there was no questioning their actions—another formation began to break up as the P-38 rushed against them, and set a third bomber aflame. Three down.

Sells stayed in tight, risking the burst of fire from a Zero that could be the last thing in life for him. He kept snapping out short bursts. Far below, explosions tore the jungle. Some of the bombers were jettisoning their loads and breaking away from their course. Sells didn't see this, of course. Zeros came at him in a head-on pass. A short burst and one fighter exploded. Four down. But the P-38 was taking it from all sides. The fighter shuddered as bullets and cannon shells ripped the metal. The canopy cracked. Blood pulsed through Sells' flying suit.

He stayed in the fight.

They could see the battle now from the ground.

They could see the flames reaching back from the right engine of the P-38.

More flame. A Zero—a gyrating blaze falling.

They watched other Zeros come at Sells. Head-on. A longer burst this time from the P-38, then the thin smoke stopped trailing behind. Sells' was out of ammunition. But ahead of him a sudden explosion. The third Zero, gone. That made six. *No more ammo.*

Sells shoved forward on the yoke and the Lightning dove. Away from the fight. The Zeros followed briefly, turned back to the bombers. Sells eased out of his dive and headed for the nearest field. He was weak now from shock and loss of blood and his airplane was punctured from nose to tail and through the wings, and the engine was still burning. He asked for an immediate landing. But the ground controllers didn't realize how badly he was hurt.

There were still those bombers in the sky, and on the airstrip Aussie P-40s were running for sky. Sells saw a red light flash at him from the ground. *Go around.*

He tried.

The crippled P-38 banked into a wide turn for a second approach to the field. What happened then we will never know. Perhaps by now Sells had lost too much blood. He may have blacked out. Or maybe the battered fighter just gave up the ghost. It could have been the engine, or the control cables. It could have been anything.

Beyond the edge of the field something happened.

The fighter fell off on one wing.

When it hit the ground it exploded.

21. Into the Maw of History

The history of the P-38 throughout the vast reaches of the Pacific for the remainder of the war is essentially a tale of personalized statistics. Whatever problems had been encountered with the airplane in its earlier days were now matters of history; frustrating in memory but committed nevertheless to the past. The early success with this airplane, the extraordinary victory ratio over the Japanese and the ability of the P-38 to fight literally anywhere and under almost any conditions, had been achieved with the first production models, an achievement the reader will recognize clearly is all the more remarkable when considering the rapid performance growth of the later variants. The G models gave way finally to the H, and then the J and L series appeared, and whatever advantages the Lightning provided its pilots over the enemy became even more pronounced. Mechanical headaches, as they were first known, slipped into the past. Shortages of spare parts, never fully alleviated, at the least became a matter with which the men could live. The numbers of P-38s available, although never satisfying the demands of theater commanders, swelled to the point where the Japanese remained consistently on the receiving end. And as companion fighters appeared in the form of high-performance Mustangs and Thunderbolts, and the Navy spread its wings in the form of the Corsair and the Hellcat, the Pacific truly became an American lake. Not, at its best, uncontested, of course, but we were doing the pursuing instead of events being the other way around.

To review, even in the briefest of detail, the day-to-day missions of the Lightning throughout the war's remainder would be to require a document several times the size of this book, and we would soon begin to be sated with the repetition of missions. We know, now, the nature of the machine, its extraordinary success and performance, and there can hardly be a statement more meaningful than that the P-38, despite the lack of numbers desired by the men who commanded the fighters, was *the* airplane that destroyed more Japanese aircraft than any other fighter plane of the United States or its Allies. Colonel Charles W. King, sharing the seat of the tactical pilot with the view of the strategist, has placed in minimum words the essential nature of the P-38's overwhelming role—it gave us the means of deciding when and where and how to fight, and it did so to our advantage, including our pilots' being able to pick fights directly over the enemy's home fields, where he could be caught in grimly disadvantageous positions.

In the area of Guadalcanal, where the initial use of the P-38 had been a matter of confusion and frustration, affairs settled down to the steamroller grinding of war that slowly and inexorably crushed the Japanese. Bitter defense shifted clearly to a mounting offensive in which the P-38 shared the burden of hunting down and destroying the enemy with the Corsairs of the Marines, as well as other fighters of the Army and the Navy. In the early months of 1943, to be sure, maintenance was still a many-headed dragon as effective in delaying operations as were the Japanese and the problems of weather. An example of both elements—cloying maintenance and superb performance on the part of the men and airplanes that survived the gantlet of mechanical problems—is evident in the mission flown on March 28, 1943 out of the Solomons. Here the Thirteenth Air Force had taken root and was working closely on a daily basis with the Marines, with naval air units, and with New Zealanders who fought side-by-side with their Allies. The air campaign was simple enough—a steady whittling down of enemy air strength, supporting ground and sea forces, and protecting Allied bases in Guadalcanal and Tulagi that remained within reach of the reeling, but still lethal, Japanese. The fighters flew as many bomber and direct ground-support missions (if not more) than they did bomber escorts. The nature of the war had changed and the fighters were being used more and more to slug hard at the enemy wherever and whenever he might be found. Especially to be preferred were the fighter sweeps, which came up as enemy targets worth this sort of effort were discovered.

Reconnaissance aircraft late in March indicated that the Japanese were using the Shortland-Poporang area off the southern edge of Bougainville as their principal seaplane base in the Solomons. One group of photos showed no less than twenty-seven seaplanes dotting the water. The next morning a fighter sweep moved out. Before it could really get up steam, mechanical problems crippled the mission. Eight P-38s and eight Corsairs took off. Then engines began to fail. The weather went to hell. One by one fighters started turning back. Of the sixteen fighters that took off *ten* were forced to return to base—seven F4U Corsairs and three P-38s. That left one Corsair and five Lightnings, but Captain Thomas G. Lanphier, Jr., of the 70th Fighter Squadron, pressed on. The six fighters went in against Shortland and Poporang barely fifty feet off the water, tore up the planes in the two bays, and left eight of them ablaze. The flak was heavy but the results nil. On their way home Lanphier caught sight of an enemy destroyer and everyone started in. Immediately the warship began weaving desperately and throwing up a heavy AA barrage. Two P-38s went in first to sweep the decks with their heavy firepower and the guns went silent. Each man then made four passes against the destroyer, concentrating on the thin hull at the waterline. By the time the five P-38s and one Corsair finished the job, the destroyer was wrapped in roaring flames from stem to stern and listing. The only casualty for the entire mission was more chagrin than bruise: Rex Barber (a close friend of the writer) of the 339th Squadron was just a bit *too* enthusiastic going in on the destroyer. and he sheared off the ship's foremast with his wingtip. Barber left *three feet of wing* behind him sailing crazily over the water. Little disturbed by it all, Barber came home and made a normal landing.

The air fighting in the Solomons and to points outward was often a matter of intense combat and then mystifying periods of little or no contact with the enemy. During all of March 1943 only sixteen Japanese planes had been destroyed in combat by *all* air units operating out of Guadalcanal and Tulagi. Then the next month, with a startling suddenness, the Japanese showed up in strength and chomping at the bit to fight, throwing in huge forces at the American installations in the Solomons. The Japanese especially went after transports and merchantmen moving supplies ashore for the American ground forces. On April 1st forty-two American fighters, six of them P-38s, slugged it out with successive waves of Japanese planes. For more than three hours the battles moved across island and ocean and when it ended twenty Zero fighters had been shot down and destroyed, for the loss of six American fighters. The pilots of three planes were picked up within minutes of bailing out.

The Japanese battered their targets with night raids while building strength for further daylight hammer blows. On April 7 they came thundering in again with more than 160 bombers and fighters. Fighter Command on the 'Canal sent up everything that could carry a gun; seventy-six fighters went out in layered stacks. On top were the "flying foxholes," the P-38s, as top cover and spaced below them, at their best fighting altitude, were in order, Corsairs, Wildcats and Airacobras. Before the wide-spread fracas ended thirteen planes had fallen to the AAF fighters and twenty-six more to the Marines. Seven of our planes had been downed; six pilots were rescued and only one was lost.

Two weeks later there took place what the AAF History describes as "one of the most extraordinary interceptions of the entire Pacific campaign." In one of the most celebrated individual battles of the entire *war,* the P-38 proved its magnificent combat reach by being the only airplane that could possibly be sent out after an astonishing target—none other than the supreme commander of the Japanese Navy, Admiral Isoroku Yamamoto. He would be flying on an inspection trip to the Kahili area, and would be there briefly. It was a rare, an incredible chance, and the word was passed: "get Yamamoto."

The story has been told many, many times—by the pilots involved, by historians from every walk of the war, and by the Japanese themselves—in this case, for the first time, in *Zero!*, which I co-authored with Masatake Okumiya and Jiro Horikoshi. The essential facts are that Major John W. Mitchell carried out what is properly described as "flawless timing of the flight," different services worked together as a team so finely knit that it astonished veterans of interservice rivalry, the Japanese, with exact punctuality, kept to their schedule—and the P-38 delivered the performance its pilots demanded of the fighters. It would be a difficult mission for more than distance and the lethal swarming of Zeros from Kahili Field. Allied headquarters was extremely anxious to make the attack appear as if the P-38 encounter with the enemy would be strictly coincidental—a "lucky break." If this could be done then the Japanese might not be led to believe that we actually were able to read their secret code. Eighteen P-38s were assigned to the mission—four in the attack section with Lanphier and Barber and two other pilots, and fourteen Lightnings under Mitchell to provide top cover. The AAF History notes:

Briefing was meticulously done, and every detail was reviewed, for the slightest error in timing would result in failure. The plan called for an overwater wavehugging flight of 435 miles by a circuitous route which would avoid all danger of detection by land-based enemy coast watchers. If Yamamoto followed his schedule punctually—and he was known to have a passion for punctuality—then at 0935 he should be over a point some thirty-five miles up the coast from Kahili.

Two hours and nine minutes after takeoff at 0725, as sixteen P-38s flew in toward the coast of Bougainville barely clearing the water [two Lightnings had been forced to abort], there appeared ahead the enemy almost as if the entire affair had been prearranged by mutual consent. . . .

In the fast and sharp battle that followed, as reported in the official histories, Lanphier exploded one Zero and then shot down one of the two Betty bombers. Rex Barber was tearing up the second Betty. Both planes crashed and were destroyed. By violent evasive action and staying on the deck at full power the P-38s managed to elude their pursuers, hurtling after them like maddened hornets and enjoying the advantage of height. One P-38 pilot, Ray Hine, was shot down—the others all returned safely.

The Official History of the AAF states that Yamamoto was a "victim apparently of Captain Lanphier's guns." I would like to emphasize the word *apparently*. Long after the war, Rex Barber and I went over every tiny detail of this mission, and coordinated his records with those which only I was given, by the Japanese. Intelligence files were opened to me, and Barber and I came to the conclusion that he had suspected all along—that it was just as apparent that Rex Barber shot down and killed Isoroku Yamamoto, and not Tom Lanphier. The issue has been shrouded in uncertainty all these many years (but belongs to another book), but one point was spectacularly clear —the P-38 was giving us the means to carry the air war to the enemy on our terms, and the "impossible" was being made a matter of everyday record.

One of the briefer but equally spectacular feats of the P-38 in the Guadalcanal fighting took place on the night of September 20, 1943. Airfields on Guadalcanal had been taking batterings almost every night by the Japanese, and there was precious little we seemed to be able to do about it. The AAF rushed Douglas P-70 night fighters to the area but they proved useless for high-altitude work. On September 19 a Corsair with radar shot down a Japanese bomber at night over Munda, and it was the next night that Lieutenant Harry Meigs II made the P-38 perform in record fashion. Teaming up with searchlight crews, Meigs within sixty seconds shot down two Betty bombers in a night mission. It was a spectacular achievement, especially considering the conditions under which Meigs flew, but in reality the ability to stop the enemy at night would have to wait for the big, powerful, radar-equipped and heavily-armed Black Widows.

One group of pilots and mechanics in the Southwest Pacific must have long pondered the reports from Europe that the North American P-51 Mustang was the undisputed champion of long-range fighter missions. Nor could they fathom the problems that were being reported of "short-range" Thunderbolts in Europe. And they found it hard to understand the reports of desperate attempts to extend the range of even the Lightnings.

In *1943*—and this was well before the arrival of the long-range P-38J and L models, and the later P-47N series—P-38s and P-47s were modified to carry out missions of range so astounding the reports were, frankly, disbelieved in the European Theater of Operations. The need was to escort bombers striking at the Balikpapan oil fields, a mission many strategists at the time considered impossible. The mechanics didn't feel it was so.

They fitted the Lightnings and Thunderbolts with one 310-gallon and one 165-gallon fuel tank each, enabling the fighters to fly the tremendous route from their base at Morotai to the target, fight at the target, and return—a straight-line distance of 1,600 miles.

On October 10, 14 and 18, B-24 bombers struck with great effectiveness at Balikpapan, accompanied by fighters of the 40th and 41st Squadrons. Any question of the ability of the pilots to engage the enemy successfully after so many hours in the air was dispelled when the Lightnings and Thunderbolts shot more than thirty enemy interceptors out of the air.

The mission of October 14th was even more extraordinary. Lt. Colonel Leonard Shapiro led his P-38s from Middleburg to Balikpapan, a flight of more than 1,900 miles that called for more than nine hours in the air. And this was just the beginning, as the P-38J and L fighters extended their missions to some 2,300 miles, with more than twelve hours spent in the cockpit!

The combat missions of 1,600 miles and 1,900 miles flown in 1943 by the P-38 assumes a strange aspect when we consider the special role of Charles Lindbergh as an advisor in the Pacific during the summer months of 1944. Lindbergh affiliated himself with a major aircraft company and as a technical representative (to bend the term somewhat) he received permission from the Navy Department to tour installations in the South Pacific. He spent time with Navy and Marine outfits, did some flying in the F4U Corsair, and managed to protect himself in a Corsair by chopping up a Zero fighter. Finishing his "advisory tour" with the Marines, he bummed a flight down to New Guinea, arriving at General Ennis Whitehead's headquarters on July 1, 1944. General George C. Kenney, hearing of his arrival, had Lindbergh taken immediately to MacArthur's office, where Kenney arranged for official status for Lindbergh to visit and fly with some P-38 outfits. Kenney reasoned that anyone who could cross the Atlantic in an ancient monoplane ought to be able to teach the P-38 pilots how to extend their range through careful cruise control of their engines. This wasn't simply a matter of hanging bigger drop tanks beneath the airplanes; this was the art of flying polished to a high degree.

Charles Lindbergh spent the majority of his time with the 475th Fighter Group commanded by Colonel Charles H. MacDonald. He flew constantly for several weeks and demonstrated his cruise-control techniques to the combat pilots. Lindbergh had promised to extend the radius of action of the P-38 to 600 miles from base—without adding larger tanks to the airplanes. A 600-mile radius meant a range of some 1,500 miles, since there had to be fuel considerations for starting, runup, taxiing, forming up in the air, climb, reserve for combat, and reserve for landing. Before long the P-38 pilots were talking enthusiastically of getting an 800-mile radius out of their airplanes.

Early in August, operating from the 475th's field at Biak, Lindbergh went along with the other pilots on a "milk-run" escort mission to the island of Ceram. The "uneventful" flight became sticky when a Zero fighter suddenly appeared directly before Lindbergh's P-38— which Lindbergh promptly shot down.

A week later Lindbergh went out again to prove in actual operation the value of his cruise-control methods. Colonel MacDonald, Lt. Colonel Meryl Smith and Captain Danforth P. Miller were the other pilots on the mission to Palau, just over 600 miles north of Biak. At 15,000 feet they circled their target, the main island of Babelthaup, and then went down at high speed to strafe a number of targets. Racing over a Japanese airfield on the way home, Lindbergh was told by radio that a Japanese fighter was on his tail. Fortunately he had some experts with him. They not only shot the Zero off Lindbergh's tail, but added three more fighters to the toll.

The fact that the Lightnings had flown more than the distance promised by Lindbergh was almost forgotten in the excitement engendered by the other pilots back at Biak when they learned of the close call.

Later, a historian of the 475th Fighter Group wrote of Lindbergh's visit and his lectures on cruise control:

He spoke informally on operational technique and engine problems, and fuel economy. However, when he claimed that the current P-38J-15-LO was good for an 800-mile operating radius and 10 hours flying time, it was generally felt that even if the engines could do that, it would be unwise to subject a fighter pilot to missions of such length. Apart from that feature, it was felt that the Lone Eagle made a valuable contribution to our operating procedure.

And the *older* P-38s, a year and more before, were already flying missions with a 950-mile radius. Somebody wasn't getting the word to the 475th ...

They had some great pilots flying the P-38 in the Pacific. Again, as one of the penalties of being unable to record all events, to capture all personal stories, we have little choice but to select representative battles and pilots, as we have done with the men the reader has already met in these pages.

And from history we can put to these final pages the stories of other pilots who flew the P-38 . . .

On June 16, 1943, the 347th Fighter Group scrambled from Guadalcanal to intercept a large strike force of Japanese bombers and fighters heading for the Russel Islands. Twelve P-38s, twenty-one P-40s and fourteen P-39s raced into the air on the intercept mission. One of the pilots flying a P-38 was Lieutenant Murray J. Shubin. At 27,000 feet, in company with three other pilots, he called out the bogies to his flight—some fifty planes about fifteen miles from the west end of Guadalcanal at 23,000 feet. The Lightnings took advantage of their superior height, and Shubin led the flight into the rear cover of approximately a dozen Zero fighters.

Shubin shot down one Zero immediately, and as he pulled up sharply from his attack a Zero lanced upward in a vertical climb before him. Scratch number two for Shubin; the Mitsubishi was a dead-on target. In the brief seconds of the fight the other pilots shot down another two. One P-38 was damaged and the pilot left for home. The three P-38s picked up another group of Zeros; in short order one pilot shot down two Japanese fighters and then broke away with jammed guns. A P-38 escorted him away from the fight, and that left Shubin alone with five very angry Japanese pilots.

It started a fight that lasted for forty minutes.

Shubin chopped a burst into the cockpit of one Zero that seemed to poise in the air, and then flipped and fell away. He didn't have time to study what happened. He managed a neat deflection shot into another Zero, hitting the engine; the fighter loped along, slowing down rapidly, then plunged earthward. There were three more Zeros, and Shubin was having a rough go of it. He dove rapidly, pulled up to get the sudden advantage of a zoom climb into the sun, and came down swiftly after the Japanese fighters. The first two times the Zeros skidded away from his guns, but on the third dive he got in a long burst that tore into the Zero from the prop to the tail.

Shubin shoved the yoke forward and dove for speed. He outdistanced the two remaining Zeros, then went into a high-speed climb in the direction of Savo Island. He was surprised—and delighted—to see the two Zeros head for an island where they circled slowly. Shubin came after them from the rear, fired prematurely and blew his chance. One Zero dove away quickly, the other flashed around in a tight turn and came after Shubin in a head-on run. Shubin fired, passed the Zero, racked the '38 around as tight as it would go, and began a long chase of his prey. He caught it near Savo, and raked the fighter along the fuselage. It dropped into a dive. Shubin started to follow, thought better of it, and ran for home. He could always come back another day.

He had confirmation of two kills—the others were only probables. One of the problems of fighting over water. But unknown to Shubin, Captain F. P. Mueller of G Company, 35th Infantry, had watched the entire fight through binoculars, and watched Shubin shoot down the three Zeros. Mueller confirmed the Japanese fighters crashing. That gave Shubin five confirmed and one probable for the day. Later, fortune smiled again. Ground forces confirmed the probable, and Murray Shubin had racked up six Zero fighters shot down and confirmed destroyed, for a single mission.

Sometimes the good guys didn't make it . . .

Daniel T. Roberts was one of those rare pilots who actually managed to shoot down two Zero fighters while flying that old sick cow known as the P-400 Airacobra. Flying out of New Guinea in the summer and fall of 1942, Roberts' most memorable mission was on 26 August, when he and his flight of six P-400s went over the Owen Stanley Range, and then dove at high speed for the Japanese airstrip at Buna. They caught the Zeros still climbing out and took advantage of their rare position. Danny Roberts shot down two in the fight, which was something of a grand vindication for him.

Roberts was out of action for eight months, and returned to the fold as a captain with the 80th Squadron, now flying P-38s. On 11 April, 1943, Roberts flamed two Aichi 99 Val dive bombers to run his score up to four.

He transferred soon afterward to the 432nd Squadron of the 475th Group and started a brief but dazzling career with this outfit. On 21 August he got into a big scrap with Zeros bouncing the Lightnings, and in the frenzied melee Roberts and another pilot were forced to dive into a pack of Zeros to help out some P-38s in trouble. Roberts got two fighters, but he and his wingman were in trouble. They ran for it, escaping by the simple expedient of going to full power and pulling away from the Japanese fighters.

On 7 September, there was another big and savage fight. The P-38 pilots were hard-pressed through every minute of the battle. Roberts got one Oscar confirmed and two Betty bombers as probables. That gave him seven confirmed kills.

On 17 October, Roberts took command of the 433rd Squadron. He would remain in command but for thirty-seven days of heavy fighting.

On that day, the 17th, Roberts led his squadron in a beautiful intercept of Japanese fighters at 18,000 feet over Morobe and Cape Ward Hunt. Here is his actual combat report:

> After chasing the enemy for about ten minutes, we initiated our attack from dead astern. My first burst brought smoke and a small flame from the Zeke, and as Lt. John Smith, my wingman, and I passed over it, the enemy plane crashed into the sea, one wing first. The pilot tried to jump, but I think he was killed as he was thrown from the plane.

The combat report continues to later events in the fight:

> This Zeke turned violently to the right and to the left until we reached a minimum altitude of 150 feet. The

Zeke failed to absorb the shock from three short bursts and it immediately burst into flames beneath the fuselage.

The Zero plunged into the sea as the "cockpit became engulfed in flames." That made two more for Roberts. The Squadron shot down ten fighters in that combat without loss to the P-38s.

On 23 October, over Rabaul at 20,000 feet:

One flight of the 431st delivered an attack on approximately eight Zeros and when several of the enemy pursued them [the 431st's planes], I flew directly behind a Zeke, giving him three short bursts. As the Zeke turned right I gave him another burst which left his wing very ragged and the plane burning furiously. I then made an attack on another Zeke from quarter head-on, firing a long burst. The Zeke immediately burned, rolled over, and some large object appeared to drop from the cockpit; however, I saw no parachute open.

That made eleven kills.

The next day, the 24th, Danny Roberts shot down number twelve.

On 29 October, number thirteen, another Zero, went down.

On 2 November, over Rabaul, he chopped number fourteen from the air.

Danny Roberts flew his last mission on 9 November 1943, with P-38s escorting B-25s on a low-level mission over Alexishafen. Danny Roberts went after a Hamp, gave it four bursts, watched it explode into flames and crash into the water.

That made number fifteen.

Then fate stepped in.

Roberts went hard after another Zero fighter. His wingman, Lieutenant Dale Meyers, took up position off his right wing. Down low, the Zero cut very sharply to the right. Instantly Roberts racked the P-38 around to keep the Japanese fighter in line with his guns.

His wingman didn't turn fast enough. *Meyers' fighter smashed directly into Roberts' airplane as it swung into the turn.* Both airplanes exploded, and tore into the jungle. There were several more explosions, and then only the columns of smoke, rising as if from funeral pyres. Nobody got out.

It was a hell of a way to go. Danny Roberts left a legacy of thirty-seven days as commander of the 433rd Squadron. In those five weeks, with a loss of only three pilots, his men destroyed fifty-five enemy fighters and bombers in the air. And at a time when maintenance was an act of hysteria, not one P-38 in the squadron ever turned back from a mission for *any* reason.

But Danny Roberts, who was regarded as one of the great aces of the Fifth Air Force, was gone forever.

He was only one of the top P-38 aces to be taken out of the war by misfortune.

Not by an enemy fighter pilot.

September 4th, 1943, was one of these red-letter days for a P-38 pilot with the 80th Fighter Squadron, 8th Fighter Group, Fifth Air Force. Captain Jay T. Robbins flew with the "Headhunters" out of Three-Mile Drome at Port Moresby; the 80th Squadron had gone hard on the heels of the 39th in air kills and was the first squadron to reach 200 air victories against the enemy.

The night before, Robbins and his fellow pilots were briefed on their mission of flying patrol over Allied forces landing at Lae and Salamaua along the northern coast of New Guinea. The transports were sure to bring out the Japanese in strength. They'd be coming down from Rabaul.

Jay Robbins had been in only two aerial combats prior to his mission of September 4th. In his first fight he and another pilot clobbered a Zero. To hell with halfkill nonsense; they tossed a coin. Robbins lost and a small Japanese flag went on the fuselage of the other pilot's airplane. Then came a second battle southwest of Bogadjum, in July 1943, and the neophyte P-38 pilot shot three Zero fighters out of the air in that single melee.

At 5:10 A.M. on the morning of September 4th,

Robbins started his engines. Sixteen P-38s would make up the patrol. At 5:15 A.M. they were rolling down the runway, cutting their turns neatly on climbout to join into formation. Then the pilots adjusted power in the cockpits; 33 inches manifold pressure and 2,850 rpms on the props. An indicated 160 mph for climb. They crossed the Owen Stanleys, went down to land at Dobodura, where they waited until 11 o'clock for the word to take off again. At 8,000 feet they approached Huon Gulf, and the Lightnings spread out. Bottom cover at 8,000 and the top cover at 21,000 feet, level flight with 225 mph indicated airspeed. Then, at 1:45 P.M., a pilot called in: "Bogies —ten o'clock high."

Robbins was the closest and he led his flight of four Lightnings directly at a force of some thirty Zero fighters. Another pilot in his flight called in: "Bogies below." The men glanced down. Five dive bombers at an estimated 12,000 feet, headed for the ships.

Robbins held true for the Japanese fighters. The other P-38s would attend to the dive bombers. It was his job to mess up the top cover of Zeros to give the Lightnings below their chance.

The P-38 pilots went through their motions as if they were on a test drill. Jettison belly tanks. Switch to internal tanks. Gunsights on; the sighting glass came alive in an orange ring with an inner dot. Guns charged.

It wasn't the best of situations. The Zeros were higher. They didn't hold tight formation, however, and that helped. The Japanese pilots were in a loose gaggle, sort of weaving in and out in a lax bunch, everybody eager to take advantage of superior numbers and height to hit the P-38s. Robbins led the Lightnings up in a shallow, high-speed climb. The Japanese threw away even more of their advantage; they turned in various directions, threw away the effect of tight air discipline.

A single Zero came around tight to get on Robbins' tail. To the surprise of the Japanese pilot the big P-38 sucked it in tight, and stayed with the Zero in the turn. They were over 20,000 feet and speed was high, and some of the Zero's nimble maneuverability was lost. Robbins guessed later that this pilot wasn't that familiar with the P-38; confused by the turn, the Zero rolled into a dive and ran away. Robbins' took the most of the advantage. He closed swiftly, lined up directly behind the fighter, and tore holes in the right wing. Flame, then smoke. Another long burst and the wing ripped away, fluttering madly. Score one.

Zero fighters milled about a trapped Lightning. Robbins went in at full power, scattering a few. One Zero came at him head-on. Robbins fired a short burst, broke away hard. No hits. Another Zero took his place in another head-on pass. This time Robbins was dead on. Cannon shells and bullets tore up the engine, gashed the wing, sent smoke pouring thickly back. The Zero spun out, all the way into the water. That made two.

The Lightning shuddered. A Zero hung on Robbins' tail. He couldn't shake him by turning or climbing. Only one way to go now—*down*. More Zeros followed, but the P-38 ran away in the dive. Robbins started bringing her out carefully—to find a single Zero far ahead of him. He closed with tremendous speed, waited for the break, and started his own turn to the left almost at the same moment the Japanese pilot tried to come around in a tight left turn. Close, some deflection, and a short hammering burst. Pieces of airplane broke away from the Zero. Smoke appeared, then the pilot bailed out. Make it three.

The other fighters were there now. Robbins snapped out short bursts to save ammunition. He got a few hits, but nothing lethal. Then he froze. His left engine, coughing, starting to run intermittently. Robbins yelled for help on his radio. No response. The Zeros were trying to cut him off, keep him from being able to run for safety. Several more Zeros began chewing on the P-38. One came in for a head-on pass. Robbins aimed carefully, fired. Tracers appeared. He was almost out of ammunition. The oncoming Zero banked sharply. Robbins fired his remaining ammo. It took the wing off at the root. That made four kills for the fight. Robbins went to the deck and tried to run for it. The engine rumbled ominously. The P-38 drifted away from its pilot; the controls had been shot up and Robbins had to hold her steady with full left rudder. He knew it wouldn't be long before his foot began dancing on the pedal from muscle strain.

He got to 6,000 feet; turning his head he saw two Tony fighters and a Zero hard after him. One moved ahead, turned sharply and came back in a head-on pass. Robbins hit the gun button. One machine gun fired a few remaining rounds; the fighter broke away. Robbins couldn't pull away from the other fighters. The engine just wasn't giving out enough power. He put the nose down. For five thousand feet he dove. It wasn't enough; the Japanese fighters stayed with him, pulled up slowly, got ready for their firing runs. One moved ahead. Another head-on pass. Robbins stabbed the gun tit. Nothing there; but again a brief roar from a single gun. The Japanese fighter took hits, broke away. But they came back and began to chop the Lightning apart. Robbins met every pass by turning into the enemy fighters—unable now to fire.

He skidded and jinked violently to throw off the aim of the Japanese. Enemy cannon shells exploded the radio behind him, hammered the armor plate at his back, tore holes in the wings and fuselage and booms.

There was still a chance. He had some slight altitude and dove to pick up speed. Warships ahead; *American*. Hard to mistake the twin-boomed silhouette of the Lightning. Flak filled the sky behind him.

Robbins thought about what came next. One good engine, one rumbling, about to quit. He could land on the beach or he could give the mountains a try. He gambled, started climbing, his foot on the rudder pedal a limb of growing pain. He kept climbing, fighting her higher and higher. He was at 8,000 feet. He could slip through a mountain pass at 10,000—fighters ahead! Robbins prepared to get the hell out. The P-38 was a wreck. It couldn't do much for him any more.

They were Thunderbolts. Robbins sighed, started climbing again. The P-38 staggered on up to 11,000 feet. He wanted just that extra margin. He slipped across the mountain ridge, immediately started down again. He pretty well had it made now. Over Moresby he hit the gear switch. It stuck; he hit it again. The gear came down slowly, much too slowly. But finally it was down. He brought her around, lined her up carefully, set her down. He stopped, climbed out, slid to the ground, exhausted, his leg aching fiercely.

He told his commanding officer he wanted nothing to do with an airplane for at least ten days. His C.O. nodded. Two days later Robbins was on his way to Australia for leave.

He came back.

Into the P-38.

He ended the war with twenty-two confirmed air kills —one of the nation's greatest aces.

Bob Westbrook was talking to a newsman on Guadalcanal. They were talking about the air kills of fighter pilots, and Westbrook was getting rid of the popular impression of daring aces. "We're all just members of a big team, out here," he said. "We have to be if we want to win this war. We aren't supermen, and no one pilot goes up on a pedestal merely because he shoots down a bunch of Japs. When one of us hits the jackpot, it's partly luck in being in the right spot at the right time, but mainly the work of your wingman and the other boys protecting your tail. We're trained to work together, and that's our one big advantage over the Japanese."

Lieutenant Colonel Robert B. Westbrook, Jr.

Thirteenth Air Force.

On September 28, 1944 this P-38 pilot was on a seven-hour fighter sweep over Kendari in the Celebes. On this day he shot down his sixteenth Japanese plane to stand clearly as the leading ace of the Thirteenth. Eight weeks later he was an ace four times over with twenty confimed kills.

He was one of the few of the top P-38 aces who was then killed in action.

Earlier in these pages we came to know Tommy Lynch through Charles King. Lynch, who was officially credited with twenty kills before ground fire brought about his death, was considered by King to be the single greatest leader of fighter pilots in the Pacific. Had he not lost his life through the freakish move of fate, believes King, Tommy Lynch would have been the greatest fighter pilot of the war.

The leading ace of the United States in World War II was, of course, Richard Ira Bong, with forty confirmed air kills. Like many other top aces, historians who have talked to pilots who flew with these aces know their scores were actually much higher, it being impossible at times to confirm kills that had gone down in mid-ocean.

For a while Tommy Lynch and Dick Bong flew together as a team. Dick Bong during the war described that brief period to Lee Van Atta in 1944:

"The most real fun I have ever had as a fighter pilot was during the three weeks Lieutenant Colonel Tom Lynch and I had our own 'flying circus.' It was an ideal setup—we could fly wherever and whenever we wanted to. We ran into some swell scraps, and the only people we actually had to account to were ourselves.

"Tom and I had come back from a leave in the United States practically together—we'd both been home for two months. Brigadier General Paul Wurtsmith was reorganizing the Fifth Fighter Command at the time and Tom went in as operations officer with me as his assistant.

"Neither of us liked desk work, so we went to General Wurtsmith and asked permission to start flying again. To our considerable surprise, he gave us a free hand—he told us that as long as we kept operations running smoothly we could fly all we wanted to.

"Tom had eighteen victories then. I had the same twenty-one I'd had when I went back to the United States on leave. I was tied with Colonel Neel Kearby then, but after the general gave us permission to start combat flying again I had an edge on the colonel. They had given him an administrative job with one of the air task forces and he was so tied down he couldn't get out at all.

"Tom and I started as a team and we would have stayed that way indefinitely, I guess, if Tom hadn't been lost while we were on a fighter sweep along the north coast of New Guinea. But I'm getting a little ahead of my story—

"The team idea made it swell—neither of us had to ask the other's permission to be gone from the office all day. So we got our own two-man show on the road.

"Some days we would hook on with other squadrons escorting bombers to Kavieng or Wewak or Tadji. Some days we went out on sweeps by ourselves. Often we took the early morning weather reconnaissance job over Wewak in the hope we would pick up some Jap stragglers.

"One day, Lynch and I had hooked on to a flight of P-38s taking Havoc and Mitchell bombers to Kavieng and, coming home after seeing nothing at all, we left the main flight at Makieng. Lynch and I had decided to alternate on passes. If we saw something one day, it was his turn to attack first. If either he or I saw something the next time we were out, it was my turn first. On this particular day it was mine. It was getting on toward dusk and we were just parallel to Cape Hoskins on the northwestern coast of New Britain when I spotted a Jap fighter plane all by itself.

"I judged he was about 12,000 feet. I don't think the Jap pilot ever knew what hit him or if he did, he didn't have long to think about it. I made a 180-degree turn and closed in to about seventy-five yards from his tail. I gave him one long burst and that was enough. He blew up right in front of me. It may sound a little far-fetched, but I was so close to that Nip I had to fly right through a ball of fire which was all that was left of him.

"After our bombers finished with Kavieng there wasn't much use of going back there any more—it was just another Jap ghost base, so Tom and I shifted our attention to the north coast of New Guinea. There were any number of interesting experiences while we were pestering the Japs in that vicinity and several stand out in my mind.

"It made a really nice show. We weren't hurt at all and we figured we made the Japs use up a good supply of antiaircraft shells. Tom felt better about it when they finally got mad, so we went on home.

"Another time, we were giving Wewak the once-over

when we spotted what looked like a bomber converted into a transport. We went down in a screaming dive and Tom made the first pass. The bomber was weaving all over the place as it landed and I think Tom managed to get in some damaging hits. Then I came in and popped away with all guns. The bomber still wouldn't catch fire—at least that's what I thought. But when I pulled up and looked back there was one very nice explosion and flames shot up all around the plane.

"After getting the bomber, we made a strafing pass at a flock of Japs lined up to greet the plane. We figured there must have been a brass hat or somebody important aboard the bomber because these clowns were all nicely lined up right where it was supposed to park.

"With our long-range jobs, we could probably have kept harassing the Nips almost indefinitely if one of those flukes you just can't account for hadn't broken up our 'circus' team.

"It cost me one of my best friends and it cost the Air Force one of its best combat pilots. Tom and I were up on routine sweep above Tadji when we came across three Nip 'luggers' flubbing around in the water off the coast. It looked perfect for a strafing pass and it appeared as if there were fuel barrels on the ships' decks. Tom led us down and we must have been doing a good 300 miles per hour.

"I didn't see any kind of ack-ack and the run was easy —we were only going to make one pass. I was following Tom and when we pulled up I suddenly noticed his right propeller fly off and his engine start smoking.

"Tom made for the nearest shore and just as he approached it he bailed out. Almost right away, his plane exploded. And that's the last I ever saw of him."

Dick Bong, who received the Medal of Honor before his death, first came to the attention of General George C. Kenney when the General dressed him down severely for "looping the loop around the center span of the Golden Gate Bridge in a P-38 fighter plane and waving to the stenographic help in the office buildings as he flew along Market Street" of San Francisco. When the first P-38s went overseas, Kenney personally selected fifty pilots to fly them. Dick Bong headed the list; Kenney apparently hadn't forgotten his own *first solo flight* stunt of flying beneath bridges over the East River of New York.

Bong rose quickly to flight leader, and his squadron racked up an official victory ratio of ten to one over the Japanese. By the time Bong had flown 146 missions, with some 365 hours of combat time, he had chalked up the astonishing tally of twenty-eight enemy planes shot down in air fighting. He was sent home for eight months, much of which he spent trying to get back to the Pacific. In this he succeeded, and as an advanced gunnery instructor who was now officially a "noncombatant," he racked up twelve more kills to reach his final toll of forty.

Dick Bong wrote some advice for other pilots:

From the experience I have gained in individual P-38 combat in this theater against a number of different types of Japanese fighters and bombers, these facts stand out:

Defense against Japanese fighters revolves around the superior speed of our fighters. If you are jumped from above, dive to pick up an indicated speed of at least 350 miles per hour, then level out and start a shallow climb at high airspeed. Generally speaking, a Japanese fighter will not follow you in a high-speed dive; occasionally one does, and if it happens, a turn to the right for ninety degrees will throw him behind. The controls stiffen up excessively in high speed dives, and he cannot follow a sharp diving turn. A turn into the Jap is always effective because they have a healthy respect for the firepower of our planes. An indicated airspeed never less than 250 miles per hour in combat is good life insurance.

Offensive measures go according to the number of the enemy, but they are always hit and run because the Jap can outmaneuver us about two to one. Any number of Nips can be safely attacked from above. Dive on the group, pick a definite plane as your target, and concentrate on him. Pick up a shallow high speed climb and come back for another pass. Single enemy planes or small groups can be surprised from the rear and slightly below, a large percentage of the time. He seems to be blind, or he does not look directly behind him enough to spot you, and your first pass should knock him down.

When he reached his fortieth air kill, the worries of the Pentagon that Bong might be killed in combat brought precipitous action from General Hap Arnold. The word came from Washington: Dick Bong is *ordered* not to fly any more combat and is to return immediately to the United States.

On August 6, 1945, the same day an atomic bomb crushed the Japanese port city of Hiroshima, Dick Bong took off from a California field in a P-80 jet fighter. Moments later the engine cut out. There was a flaming explosion.

He went quickly.

They flew P-38s and they piled up the kills.

George Welch ran his score to sixteen and Washington ordered him back to the States.

Danny Roberts in just eleven weeks shot down fifteen and was killed on November 9, 1943.

Six weeks later, Ed Cragg, also with fifteen, was shot down and killed over Gloucester.

Bob Westbrook shot down twenty and was killed in 1944.

Charlie MacDonald shot down twenty-seven in the P-38. He survived the war as the third-highest ranking ace in the Pacific, and the fifth-ranking ace of the war in all theaters.

Gerry Johnson got twenty-two. He also survived the war. But not for long. On October 7, 1945, just two months after Bong was killed, Johnson crashed in the States and was killed when he hit the ground.

There was also Neel Kearby in that P-47 he insisted was so great. It must have been. He received the Medal of Honor for shooting down six in a single fight with the barrel-chested Jug. He ran his score to twenty-three kills. Then on March 4, 1944, Kearby shot down three more in quick succession to make it twenty-six. He never saw the

Zero that came at him in a three-quarter rear attack and poured a long burst at pointblank range into the cockpit. The big Jug went straight down, into jungle near the Japanese field at Dagua.

And then there was Tommy McGuire.

Another Medal of Honor pilot.

Thirty-eight confirmed air kills in the P-38.

No pilot shot him down.

Ground fire didn't get him.

He tried to save another pilot and died in the attempt.

22. Tommy McGuire

It was the last week of October 1944. The Fifth Air Force, and the entire war, had come a long way, and the center of operations was now the Philippines. The war loomed higher over Japan's front doorstep, but right now here was the action. At this moment it centered at Tacloban Airdrome on Leyte in the Philippines. Fighters were needed desperatly at the field, and now they were in sight. Twenty big Lockheed P-38s getting ready to roost and be prepared at once for any combat that might come at any moment. The jury-rigged control tower signalled the Lightnings they were clear to land, and one by one the twenty pilots in their airplanes went through their motions of power settings, working flaps and gear. The ground crews had been alerted for their arrival and they watched the Lightnings easing toward the pierced steel planking that made up the hurriedly improvised Tacloban strip.

On the ground they saw the Lightnings. No one saw ten Zero fighters break through cloud cover and streak for the Lightnings, now slow, low and with all the garbage hanging loose. Helpless. The Japanese pilots had timed their break beautifully. The Lightnings were set up like ducks for the slaughter.

Almost.

One P-38 suddenly came alive. Inside the cockpit the pilot was moving in a blur. Almost at the same instant he had rammed the throttles forward, hit the gear and flap levers, barked a warning by radio to the other pilots, charged his guns and was working ailerons, rudders and elevator all in a single fluid motion. Surging ahead, the P-38 skidded crazily to the side even as a Zero's tracers flashed where the airplane had been. And then the big Lockheed was coming around, the airplane clean now, accelerating rapidly, and the four guns and cannon boomed out from the nose. The lead Zero stumbled in the air, a wing broke free and the Japanese fighter tumbled wildly into the trees and exploded.

What had been a beautiful trap turned into a den of rattlers. The Zeros whistled low over Tacloban as P-38s skidded and yawed and turned like dervishes as they scrambled for safety. The first P-38 to make the turn and destroy the lead Zero rushed head-on into the remaining Japanese fighters, catching them by surprise, throwing them off their stride. By the time they got their second wind it was too late. The twenty Lightnings were all over them.

Only four of the Japanese got out of there alive. They left six Zeros burning in the jungle near the airstrip. All twenty P-38s came around in the pattern again and eased to the steel planking. The pilot of the P-38 who had sounded the warning and gunned down the first Zero taxied from the runway and cut his switches. Officers and men crowded around his fighter, staring at the rows of Japanese flags stenciled neatly to the nose.

Major Thomas B. McGuire, Jr., of the 475th Fighter Group climbed down from his airplane and stretched. Then he grinned. A little while later his crew chief added a twenty-fifth Japanese flag to the nose of the big P-38.

Today, nearly three decades after that event, it is still disturbing to realize how few people know the name of Thomas B. McGuire, Jr., or have ever heard of the man who was America's second-ranking ace of World War II, who received the Medal of Honor; McGuire Air Force Base in New Jersey was named in his honor, and I suppose if visitors stop to read the plaque commemorating his name, they will nod sagely and, for at least a few moments, they will know and understand. But few people are aware, just as the names of the greats in aviation always slip quietly from the attention of those who are around for the moment.

In this business of aviation, there is always a tried and true question to jar us all. Who was the *second* man to fly the Atlantic solo?

Tommy McGuire enjoyed an almost delirious following among the pilots with whom he flew. He was famed within their ranks for his extraordinary skill, steel nerves, his superb marksmanship. His official record leaves little question as to the bloody, fiery swath he tore through the enemy. But it's the personal element that counts, and those who watched him fly and who were privileged to fly with him have always said that Tommy McGuire could do things with a P-38 that were impossible. They saw these things happen but regarded them with disbelief. His skill with his heavy, twin-boomed fighter was so extraordinary as to defy reality, and he had such faith in himself and his airplane that he never indicated hesitation in plunging into the midst of enemy fighters, to tangle with Zeros in swirling dogfights in which he always managed to prevent the Japanese from using their agility to shoot him down.

Dick Bong, of course, is credited with forty kills and Tommy McGuire with thirty-eight. No one who flew with the Fifth Air Force doubts that each man actually shot down many more enemy aircraft than they were credited with. In referring to Bong's kills, General George Kenney, who was the commander of both Bong and McGuire, made this point clear. "Everyone knew that he had knocked down at least that many more which he had reported destroyed," Kenney said of Bong, "but for which there were no witnesses. They had nearly all been shot down over the ocean, so we could not even find the wreckage to serve as evidence." McGuire's case is the same. Those who flew with him insist he had shot down at least seventy to eighty enemy planes. There were many occasions, these veteran pilots have told me, when they fought high over a solid cloud deck, and McGuire's victims went spinning, smoking, burning and diving forever out of sight, with no way of telling with absolute certainty whether or not he had a kill. "Either we saw the guy get out, a wing come off, or the whole thing explode," one pilot said, "or it went on the record as a probable or damaged."

Little is known about Thomas B. McGuire, Jr. He was born on August 1, 1920, in Ridgewood, New Jersey, and later moved to Sebring, Florida, where he completed high school. From there he went on to the Georgia Institute of Technology. As quickly as he acquired his diploma he shoved it into a bureau drawer, packed his bag, and enlisted as an aviation cadet. The United States wasn't yet involved in any shooting war; Tommy McGuire was convinced the nation would be and he was out to earn his wings before the shooting started. He almost met his own schedule. The Japanese turned Pearl Harbor into a flaming shambles only two months before Tommy McGuire earned his pilot's wings and lieutenant's bars.

His early career as a fighter pilot had little to distinguish him from the ranks of the men with whom he flew. For a while he served in the United States. Fretting over this enforced inactivity, he badgered his superiors for overseas duty. It took more than a year to get his way, and it wasn't until March 1943 that he received orders to ship out to Alaska. But it had been a year well spent. As he acquired time and experience in different fighter aircraft, "something" began to happen to McGuire. He had what other pilots called "the touch." Always an excellent pilot, he emerged from the excellence other men shared to fly with a noteworthy sensitivity and perfection. He greeted his orders to move to Alaska with a whoop of joy heard for a mile.

The joy slowly ebbed in the fierce winds, cold, wet and fog of the Aleutian chain. He faced three basic problems—the weather was lousy, the Japanese elusive, the combat almost nil. McGuire started rocking the boat again, asking for, pleading and demanding to be sent to a fighting zone. He got his wish. He was told to report to the 49th Fighter Group of the Fifth Air Force in the Southwest Pacific.

Here, the problem was somewhat different. The weather was fine (compared to Alaska), and it was hot, and the Japanese were as thick as flies. Some of Japan's best pilots were willing to mix it up over New Guinea and their own fields of Buka, Buna-Buna, Rabaul, and others.

The 49th Fighter Group, as we have seen, was delighted to oblige the men in the Zeros. The name that went to everyone's lips was that of Dick Bong, brilliant P-38 pilot who became a flight leader in the Flying Knights Squadron. Bong was knocking down Japanese fighters with a daring and skill that splashed his name across front pages throughout the States.

Except for those who flew and fought in the Pacific, and those who maintained the airplanes for their pilots, no one seemed to know of a guy named McGuire. Unpublicized in the States, his toll began to creep up slowly behind that of Dick Bong. And what even fewer people knew was that Bong and McGuire often flew with one another (as Bong had flown with Tommy Lynch) as a team, and their competition for kills slowly built to a daily challenge. When the two pilots were separated and each flew missions on his own, the entire Fifth Air Force sweated out the latest reports on each man. Tommy McGuire, however, seemed destined to remain about eight kills behind the score of Dick Bong, for whenever McGuire returned to his home field with fresh scalps, he discovered to his chagrin that Bong had done just about the same thing, and they were still separated by those eight kills.

At this point a mystery enters the career of Tommy McGuire, and to some extent it apparently explains why so few people were aware of his name or his exploits. As we have noted before, especially in the chapter regarding Lieutenant William Sells and his solo attack against a force of a hundred enemy planes, many of the official records of the Fifth Air Force were destroyed in enemy bombing raids, and the details of McGuire's combat, as he progressed to an ace several times over, have vanished into the windblown dust of history that must forever elude us. We do know, of course, that he transferred from the 49th to the 475th Fighter Group. Then came the summer of 1944. American forces pounded the Philippines and our troops went ashore. The enemy had been hurt but we discovered quickly the Japanese could still fight and were determined to fight just as fiercely as they could—which was a mite considerable. The ground troops sent out loud cries for airpower right there in the Philippines with them. Engineers carved out strips anywhere they could level the ground. One of those strips was Tacloban, where the runway was made up of the inevitable pierced steel planking.

The Fifth Air Force hadn't seen fighting like this for a long time, for the Japanese were determined to give ground as slowly and bloodily as they could before the grinding erosion of our advances. Almost every morning Japanese fighters raced low over the primitive airfields, strafing and bombing anything that even resembled a target. Their attacks were carried out with great courage and skill, and physical training at the fighter bases consisted largely of P-38 pilots rushing over the ground and diving headlong into ditches and foxholes. The P-38 pilots lived in conditions even more primitive than their runways. Tents, cold food, lack of water and medicine, and above all, seas of mud.

All through November 1944 the Lightnings were kept hard at their tasks. Dick Bong kept adding to his score, and McGuire stayed grimly behind—always that frustrating eight or nine kills behind in the official tally.

By December 1944, Tommy McGuire had twenty-eight Japanese flags painted on his airplane. He was well ahead of Jay Robbins. Bob Westbrook had twenty and he was killed this same month—December 1944. Neel Kearby had been killed. Gerry Johnson and Charlie MacDonald were well up on the scoreboard but Tommy McGuire was well ahead of *them*. There was just Dick Bong.

The first week of December 1944 loomed ominously for the American forces in the Philippines. The Japanese gambled heavily and they bulled a big convoy through our Navy to pour fresh troops into the Philippines. The American plan was to cut deeply into the Japanese ground defenses by setting up a new landing at Ormoc Bay in northwest Leyte.

This same week found the 49th and the 475th Groups separated. The 49th, with Dick Bong, flew from Tacloban, but the 475th was transferred to a miserable jungle strip at Dulag. Here the Group flew with its 431st, 432nd and 433rd Squadrons. Leading the Group was Charlie MacDonald, who at the time had twelve kills (and would get twenty-seven by war's end). Tommy McGuire commanded the 431st Squadron, his big Lightnings clearly distinguished by brilliant red spinners.

After settling down in their jungle hellhole, the pilots of the 475th received their assignment—protect the American convoy transporting the 77th Division to its landings in northwest Leyte. McGuire would fly low cover with the 431st, and the other Lightnings would take up medium and high cover positions.

On December 7, 1944, almost as if to celebrate Pearl Harbor three years earlier, the Japanese hit our forces with just about anything and everything they could get into the air. The P-38s of the 475th met them head-on.

And somehow, despite their new isolation by flying from different fields, Dick Bong and Tommy McGuire ended up flying side by side in the huge melee. Their primary task, as was that of all the pilots, was to keep Japanese planes away from the thin-hulled troopships far below. They wheeled in wide circles over the beachhead, turning quickly into any threatened attack. Several times the Lightnings mixed it up with the enemy, smoking and chewing up Japanese fighters, but breaking off the engagements early to stay over the troopships rather than pursue enemy aircraft.

Bong and McGuire proved the effectiveness of their team. Bong flamed a Japanese bomber with a single burst at long range. Almost immediately afterward, McGuire saw a Zero on the deck going in for a strafing run on the ships. He stood the Lightning on her nose and went for his quarry. For an instant the ocean boiled from his guns and cannon, then the concentrated firepower poured into the cockpit and the fuel tanks. The Zero disappeared in a blinding flash.

Grinning that he had at least maintained pace, McGuire poured the coal to the Lightning to climb back into the fray. He arrived just in time to see Bong pumping bullets and cannon shells into a fighter, methodically chewing it into pieces that sprayed back from the stricken plane. The Zero began to shred, and soon it was breaking up into big chunks as it tumbled all the way into the water.

It was quite a day. The P-38s came home with some casualties, but the losses were lower than anyone had dared hope for. Behind them the sea and jungle had swallowed the wreckage of no less than sixty-four Japanese fighters and bombers. And the other aces, fast climbing the totem pole, had done pretty well for themselves. Charlie MacDonald and Gerry Johnson had each shot down three planes.

But everyone else centered their interest on Bong and McGuire. Bong was up to thirty-eight kills and Tommy McGuire was still his exasperating eight kills behind with a tally of thirty.

Eight days later, four P-38s took off from their Leyte fields and cruised over the ocean on a free-flying rat hunt. In one Lightning cockpit sat Dick Bong, his wingman tucked in close behind and to the right. In the other lead fighter was Tommy McGuire, followed by his wingman.

McGuire was first to grab the advantage. Well ahead of the Lightnings and slightly below were two Japanese fighters. Instead of using radio, McGuire signalled by hand to his wingman. Suddenly, his P-38 shot forward, the wingman close behind.

McGuire hit the trailing Japanese fighter with deadly aim. He came in swift and sure, his guns and cannon working like a giant buzzsaw. The Zero vanished in a dazzling fireball.

Now! McGuire kicked hard rudder and slammed the yoke to the left. The second Japanese fighter broke sharply, and the pilot was clawing around in a tight turn to get onto the tail of the attacking P-38. McGuire was ready, waiting for the maneuver; the Lightning skidded and McGuire had a deflection shot. He aimed, pressed the gun tit.

Before he could fire, the Zero showed streaks of flame. Moments later, as Bong's P-38 closed in with short bursts of fire, it exploded into gyrating chunks.

Two days later, on December 17, Dick Bong closed to point-blank range to score his fortieth kill.

McGuire still had thirty-one.

But that was the end of the combat road for Dick Bong. Hap Arnold studied the 146 missions and 400 hours of combat time of Dick Bong and ordered him home. Pending his return to the States, Bong was grounded from any further combat missions.

Now the field was wide open for McGuire. Could he end the jinx of always trailing Dick Bong? He took to the air the next morning like a big cat thirsting for blood.

Well, Bong was out of the air but his jinx remained. The savage fighting had depleted the Japanese ranks. The Navy and Marines joined with the AAF in ripping Japanese fields to turn them into junkyards. McGuire flew mission after mission without even sighting an enemy plane. His patience stretched thin but his feelings availed him little.

The Japanese refused to come up and fight. The Tacloban area was fast becoming off limits to all Japanese warplanes.

Then reconnaissance planes brought home pictures that revealed feverish airfield construction in Mindoro. Working around the clock the Japanese hacked and gouged strips from fields and jungles. They flew in their replacements at night, hid the planes by day until they could build up strength. The AAF prepared to hit the enemy where he lived. The new campaign began on December 22.

Two hundred fighters and bombers went after the new Japanese fields. It was a slaughter. Strafing and bombing runs were carried out at treetop level. Fighters raced up and down the runways shooting at anything that moved or cast a shadow. The Japanese were caught flat-footed. Only nine of their fighters made it into the air. Brave pilots against those odds, but they didn't stand a chance. They were climbing from their fields, hanging on their props, when the American fighters hit them with a plunge through line center. Eight out of the nine planes went down within seconds. The sole survivor hit the deck and managed to run safely from the scene. On the ground, no less than 125 fighters and bombers had been destroyed. We didn't lose a plane.

The day following, the 23rd, the Japanese reacted with somewhat more alacrity. Improved response didn't appear to help. The low-level strafers and bombers clobbered another fifty-eight fighters and bombers on the ground. But the Japanese were prepared to exact some toll from the American strike force, and they met the incoming planes with their own fighters at medium altitude. As the low-level raiders streaked for their targets the Japanese fighters peeled off to catch them at a disadvantage.

They never made it. A high cover of P-38s—most of them equipped with dive brakes by this time—plummeted from above to plow into the Japanese planes. It was a slaughter. The Japanese managed to down one P-38 and kill its pilot, in the process having thirty-three of their number shot out of the air.

But Tommy McGuire came home empty-handed—and baffled and frustrated.

The 431st Squadron moved on to a new field at Mindoro. On Christmas Day the Fifth Air Force laid on a heavy strike of B-24 bombers against Mabalacat Airdrome, and McGuire volunteered to lead fifteen P-38s as escort.

Seventy Japanese fighters rose to contest the Liberators and their small number of escorts. Of this number, twenty Japanese planes went after the bombers and the others climbed after the Lightnings. The American force was crossing Luzon when the Japanese fighters swarmed like angry hornets into their midst.

This time nothing was going to interfere with McGuire's determination to come to grips with the enemy. Under his direction the P-38s broke away from the bombers in a curving attack to hit the superior force of Japanese planes head-on. McGuire rolled away from the opening fire of several Zeros and suddenly horsed the yoke back into his stomach. His P-38 shot skyward and as she went through the zoom he came around sharply against a formation of three enemy fighters. The Japanese were not caught sleeping; the Zeros cut tightly in turns to make a head-on pass at the Lightning. McGuire took dead aim on the center Zero, hammered out a burst into the engine. The Zero exploded; his wingmen dove away to the sides.

Wisely, McGuire decided against a diving pursuit. Too many Zeros still about and above him and he could be boxed if he left the P-38s still in the immediate vicinity. Instead, he broke sharply to the left himself, cleared the area and saw three Zeros hard after the bombers.

Now was the time to use his altitude. He went to full power and dropped the nose, the P-38 swiftly picking up speed. He closed the distance quickly, lined up on the trailing Zero, went in dangerously close and fired. A wing snapped away from the Japanese plane even as his bullets and shells chewed into the cockpit. The wreckage flipped wildly earthward.

That made two . . . Glancing about him, his head on a swivel, he saw a P-38 weaving and skidding wildly to shake off a Zero clinging to its tail, snapping short bursts into the American fighter. Again McGuire went to full emergency power trying to get there in time. He came in from the rear in a sliding turn and set up a long burst. He caught the tanks neatly and the Zero erupted in flames.

Tommy McGuire returned to Mindoro and climbed from the cockpit with three fingers held high. At long last he had broken his "jinx" of always being eight behind Bong. His crew chief wasted no time in adding the three Japanese flags to the fuselage. That made a very satisfying thirty-four.

The next day McGuire was back in the thick of the fighting as he led his squadron on another escort mission. The Liberators were out to wreck what was left of Clark

Field near Manila, and twenty Zeros came up to argue the point. To McGuire's consternation the Zeros got past the escort to hit the bombers. One B-24 took a bruising from several Zeros; the crippled bomber sagged away from the formation, attracting every fighter in the immediate vicinity. McGuire saw six Japanese fighters hard after the B-24, and he dove with all the speed he could get from his Lightning, trying to protect the cripple. The maneuver exposed him, quite deliberately, in fact, to the Japanese fighters, but he considered the risk well worth the candle. The Zeros cut in hard after McGuire, and at precisely the right moment, the only moment of perfect timing, the P-38, moving with high speed, rolled into a sudden turn. At that speed the Zero fighters couldn't hack their tight turns, and there was enough time for McGuire to get in a long clean burst. A Zero went up in flames.

One Zero broke away from his attack; the other four boxed him in. A Lightning caught in this situation could usually dive away from trouble. The Japanese pilots anticipated this move, and two Zeros were already diving to catch the P-38 in a crossfire before it could pull away. McGuire sized up the situation, knew he had some pros on his hands, and decided this was the time to break the rules. He went to maneuvering flaps and the big fighter came around in a tight turn, deliberately accepting a mix-it-up dogfight against the Japanese.

The unexpected maneuver paid off. McGuire's airplane was suddenly where the Japanese never expected it to be, and before they could break away McGuire had torn a Zero into flaming wreckage. A second fighter broke away from his guns, but now the two Zeros that had started down in anticipation of his dive were climbing steeply to finish off the P-38. These *were* pros; McGuire watched the Zero that had broken away coming around in a tight turn to flank him. He had his opening and McGuire took it; he snapped in the flaps, stuck down the nose and ran for safety. He was away from the box before the Japanese could get in a shot.

He cleared his area and started up again, a shallow

fast climb to regain his formation which was weaving above the B-24s. He kept looking about him, rolling gently from side to side, and he saw three Zeros climbing in a loose formation. Well below him. Plenty of room to make his move. The yoke went forward and as the nose dropped McGuire rolled into his dive. The Japanese, quite clearly, never saw his approach. The Zeros held their loose formation as McGuire plunged from above. He set up his target, held down a burst slightly longer than normal for him, and a Zero exploded. No time to stick around; McGuire went through the wreckage like oats through a goose, out of range before the Japanese pilots knew what had happened.

Three for the day was *enough*. McGuire rejoined his fighters. They escorted the B-24s through their run and started home. A half-dozen Zeros climbed toward the formation. McGuire eased out of position into a dive, bounced the Japanese fighters, killed the pilot of one, and was gone, his speed leaving the other Zero pilots frustrated. They broke off their attack.

That made four for the day. Seven in two days. All fighters. And Tommy McGuire was up to thirty-eight, only two behind Dick Bong.

Tomorrow could be the day . . .

It wasn't. The next morning, General Kenney ordered McGuire grounded. No further combat missions until the order was withdrawn. McGuire was stunned. He complained bitterly. The general insisted he was tired and needed a rest. McGuire complained he had never felt better. "Besides, I'm only two behind . . ."

That was the whole point, the general explained. Dick Bong would be on his way home in just a few days. He was to be awarded the Medal of Honor for his all-time victory toll of forty airplanes shot down in combat. The nation was primed to receive Bong as the top-scoring ace of the war.

Kenney told McGuire that if he went out on a mission he would most likely "knock off another three Nips and spoil Dick's whole party. He said it would certainly be strange to have Bong come home to all that fuss, and be greeted as the Number *Two* ace of the country.

Even as Kenney ordered him out of the air for a few days, the recommendation had gone through to award Tommy McGuire the Medal of Honor for his exploits on the 25th and 26th of December, for his seven kills, and for often deliberately exposing himself to danger.

For the next several days, McGuire remained on the ground. He took the time to spell out the lessons he had gleaned in combat against the enemy, hoping the information would improve the combat skills of other fighter pilots.

"On individual combat tactics," he told them, "aggressiveness is the keynote of success. A fighter pilot must be aggressive. The enemy on the defensive gives you the advantage, as he is trying to evade you, and not to shoot you down. Never break your formation into less than two-ship elements. Stay in pairs. A man by himself is a liability, a two-ship team an asset. If you are separated, join up immediately with other friendly airplanes. On the defensive, keep up your speed. A shallow, high-speed dive or climb is your best evasive action against a stern attack. You must never reverse your turn; that is asking for it. Try to make the Jap commit himself, then turn into his attack.

"At minimum range your shots count and there is less chance of missing your target. On deflection shots, pull your sight through the Nip. Most shots in deflection are missed by being over or under rather than through incorrect lead.

"Always clear yourself before and during an attack. It is always the one you don't see that gets you. On long-range missions especially don't chase a single out of the fight; he is probably trying to lure you away from the scrap. Your job is to provide cover for the bombers."

Above all, Tommy McGuire told the other pilots, there are three cardinal rules for men flying the P-38:

1. Never attempt combat at low altitude.

2. Never let your airspeed fall below 300 miles per hour, because at 300 mph or better the ailerons of the Zero become extremely hard to move and their maneuverability suffers.

3. Never keep your wing tanks in a fight.

On January 6, 1945, General Kenney received news of Dick Bong's safe return to the United States. He told McGuire he was now free to return to combat.

The next morning McGuire roared off his home field with three other P-38s close behind. The Lightnings each carried two 160-gallon tanks beneath their wings. McGuire set his course for Los Negros Island where there was a Japanese fighter strip. His plan was to come in at 2,000 feet, and be in a perfect position to bounce any fighters taking off. Near their objective the Lightnings went in low, beneath a deck of broken clouds above them.

It happened without the slightest warning. Tracers flashed past the P-38s. *A single Zero* whipped from the clouds in a classic bounce, a swift, shallow dive, counting on surprise and audacity to catch the Lightnings unawares. In this move the Japanese pilot succeeded.

What no one knew until well after the war (when records were examined and the Japanese pilots interviewed) was that the man flying the Zero was one of Japan's greatest fighter pilots, Shoichi Sugita, who reached a score of some eighty kills before he met his own death. Sugita came down beautifully.

Only the combat experience of McGuire saved the moment as Sugita opened fire. Immediately, McGuire broke into a vertical bank, coming around in a steep turn, calling for the other pilots to do the same. The four P-38s slid into a Lufberry Circle, snaring Sugita inside.

Any other pilot would have been boxed in, caught, unable to excape. Sugita was no ordinary man at the controls. He broke sharply to the left to get out of the trap, but McGuire kept the P-38s grinding around and around in the Lufberry. The formation with the Zero in its midst dropped down to only 200 feet above the trees, with Sugita still trying to break free without being caught in a crossfire.

There was no going lower. The P-38 formation scattered, flashing low over the trees. It was a fatal mistake.

Before the Americans could counter the move, the Zero clawed around in an impossibly tight turn. Sugita wasted neither time nor motion in battle and he fastened onto the tail of a P-38. The pilot skidded and maneuvered frantically, but there was no getting away from Sugita in this kind of fighting.

The P-38 pilot shouted for help, and McGuire, unthinking, responding to that plea, rushed to his aid.

At that moment Tommy McGuire violated not one, but all three of his cardinal rules of combat.

He was at minimum altitude.

His speed was well below 300 miles per hour.

He still had his heavy wing tanks—which, among other things, raised his stalling speed.

The big Lightning responded instantly to McGuire's bidding. Working hard rudder and full aileron, McGuire snapped the P-38 into a hard, vertical turn.

It was too tight and too steep for low speed, high drag and heavy weight. And there was no room below. The Lightning staggered suddenly as though it had rammed into an invisible wall in the sky. No Japanese plane was near McGuire. No Japanese gun or cannon fired at him. But he had been snared by the inviolable laws of aerodynamics.

In that tight turn, the lift over his wings burbled. The smooth flow of air so critical to flight at his speed and in that maneuver swirled and eddied. Almost instantly the P-38 was into a high-speed stall.

There was only one way to go. The Lightning flipped crazily over on one wing, control wrested from its pilot. If he had altitude below him McGuire would have fallen, brought the fighter out of its plunge as he regained lift.

There wasn't room. The Lightning snapped over on

her wing. Almost in the same instant it plunged into the jungle.

A blinding sheet of flame erupted through the trees. Tommy McGuire was dead.

23. Satan's Angels

Throughout the past several chapters we have encountered different pilots of the 475th Fighter Group in combat—Danny Roberts, Tommy McGuire, and others. In truth, however, the 475th has been included in many combat actions without specific identification as such, because the situation described, especially those by Charles King, often referred in generalities to large fighter forces of the Fifth Air Force, notably the P-38s. What took place, however, in those descriptions included the 475th in all but name.

Now, that has been a serious problem if you're a member of *Satan's Angels,* the 475th Fighter Group, and its three squadrons, the 431st, 432nd, and 433rd, with the call sign names of Hades, Clover and Possum. (The 80th Fighter Squadron tagged along as part of the 475th Group for slightly less than ten weeks, from December 13, 1943 to February 24, 1944. Otherwise, the history of the 475th stays exclusively with Hades, Clover and Possum Squadrons.)

The problem is that history and our contemporary historians have buried the story of the 475th Fighter Group in the surging backwash of the sea that pounded the Japanese into a broken fighting force and a defeated nation. There are, likely, many reasons for what has become a glaring omission in the documents of the air war in the Pacific, but the members of the 475th would doubtless disagree with *all* of them. Although there is much *mention* in such official documents as *The AAF in World*

War II, there is little substance. Other fighter organizations, especially those of the European and Mediterranean theaters, abound in detail, a reality in direct proportion to their substantial wartime administrative staffs.

Especially to the reader of this book this is a sorry omission, for the 475th Fighter Group not only produced such aces as Tommy McGuire (thirty-eight kills), Charley MacDonald (twenty-seven kills), Danny Roberts (fourteen kills), and others, but also it was the only *all*-P-38 fighter group to fly during the war. Other groups, of course used the Lightning, but never did they both start and end the war in the P-38.

Carroll "Bob" Anderson, who flew with the 475th (and who provided the material for the report on Danny Roberts) emphasized this point. "It was in the Pacific that the P-38 was at its absolute best," he wrote me, "and it was with the 475th, the only group activated in the Southwest Pacific Area, and the only group to use P-38s from the beginning of its combat tour to the end of hostilities, that it saw its greatest hours.

"The 475th shot down 551 enemy aircraft (that doesn't count the Zero Lindbergh got with us), and this is the highest of any group of pilots flying the P-38 in combat. Now, the 49th Fighter Group, which operated a great deal longer than we did, had more kills, but they collected theirs in a variety of fighters that included such machines as the P-40 and the P-47 in addition to the P-38, and they certainly had many more planes than did the 475th."

Bob Anderson in another letter noted: "I think it would be correct for me to say that most of us World War II types who were with the 475th have hoped, down through the years, that if someone were to write about the P-38, he would discover the 475th and tell the story of that one group that used this fighter to its greatest advantage . . . After having purchased everything written about the Lightning since the war, and after having virtually nothing in the way of results except the same general rehash of old Lightning data, with little or nothing about Satan's Angels, we all looked forward with great expectation to your book. . . ."

Now, earlier in these pages Charles King provided us with great detail about teething troubles with the first P-38s that arrived in Australia and the Southwest Pacific. This was, of course, an advantage for the 475th, which was not formed until May 14, 1943, in Australia. In April 1943, when the decision to form the 475th was finalized, the total P-38 strength in the Fifth Air Force consisted of only three squadrons: the 80th of the 8th Fighter Group, the 39th of the 35th Group, and the 9th of the 49th Group (Charles King's outfit).

The 475th was formed as an all-P-38 outfit under Major George W. Prentice, who until then had been commander of the 39th Squadron flying P-38s with the 35th Group. The new pilots used Amberly Field, close to the supply depots on the outskirts of Brisbane, as their official station of activation.

The 475th spent three months whipping itself into shape and early in August 1943 started out for New Guinea by C-47 transport planes and, for the ground echelon, Liberty ships. By August 11 the 431st and 432nd Squadrons were flying from the Port Moresby area—the 431st at 12-Mile Strip and the 432nd at Ward's Drome. On August 16 the 433rd Squadron moved into Jackson Drome.

It was also on August 16 that the Group made first contact with the enemy. Pilots of the 431st escorted transports to Tsili Tsili and ran into two dozen Japanese fighters and bombers. In their first blooding the Lightning pilots shot down twelve enemy aircraft for a loss of two P-38s—an auspicious six-to-one curtain raising for what was to follow.

Many of the 475th's pilots flew with the P-38 drivers from other groups, notably the 49th (as Charles King has related), in missions against the powerful Japanese base at Wewak. Sixteen missions, with a total of 257 sorties, were flown against Wewak. The missions were more than mere statistics. The 475th pilots were relatively inexperienced, still learning the fine tricks of actual fighting, but learning their art with an incredibly skilled hand. During those sixteen missions the 475th pilots shot down forty-one enemy fighters and bombers, for the loss of but three

P-38s. It was one-sided victory column that would be repeated for the next two years.

The 475th continued moving up against the major Japanese strongholds, and the pilots became familiar with Wewak, Hansa Bay, Saidor, and Cape Gloucester on New Britain. They supported landings near Lae; in September they were covering the paratrooper strike against Nadzab, flying mixed formations with Lightnings from other groups. The names went up one after the other on the Group's scoresheet—Madang, Salamaua, Lae, Kaiapit (up the Markham Valley), Finschhafen . . . On September 22, at Finschhafen, the 475th racked up one of the brightest moments in its history. The 432nd Squadron had a sixteen-plane patrol in the air, of which twelve P-38s were covering Allied landing operations. Ten bombers and thirty fighters staged against the invasion force, and the P-38s moved swiftly to cut them off. Led by Captain Fred Harris, the first flight of four Lightnings went down in a fast diving attack to scatter the Japanese formations. Right behind Harris were eight more P-38s, and the maneuver went off like clockwork. The Japanese broke their air discipline and the Lightnings hit them like runaway locomotives, shooting down seven bombers and eleven fighters —eighteen enemy planes destroyed for the loss of one American pilot and two Lightnings.

After several more weeks of staging against Japanese targets, flying patrols, escorting bombers, flying sweeps against targets of opportunity, the pilots of the 475th were briefed for the first missions against Rabaul. Again, many of these missions have been described by Charles King, whose squadron often flew with the squadrons of Satan's Angels. On October 12, fifty-five P-38s from the 475th made up part of the force of some 300 American fighters and bombers (the fighters staging through Kiriwina) that struck Japanese airfields at Rabaul. Only two Japanese fighters intercepted; both were shot down by 475th pilots, who spent most of their ammunition on the deck, shooting up airfield installations. Many more missions followed against the Rabaul installations.

But it wasn't only a matter of going out against the

enemy—the Japanese could and at times did turn the tables. On October 15 the controller at Oro Bay, New Guinea, flashed a radar warning report that a large force of enemy aircraft was moving toward the Allied base at Dobodura. The warning blared across the field. Those P-38s on alert had their engines running within seconds. As quickly as the pilots strapped in and closed their canopies the big twin-boomed fighters thundered from the runway into the air. Behind them the field was controlled pandemonium. Pilots were coming from all directions. The main camp was a good distance from the airstrip, and the 475th pilots tumbled and ran from their tents there to race for the airfield in everything that had wheels. Charley MacDonald and Bill Ivey set an unofficial jeep record from a standing start as they raced for the strip. MacDonald and Ivey never got to their own fighters; they grabbed the first two P-38s in sight (from the 433rd Squadron) and raced into the air. A total of fifty-one Lightnings of the 475th managed to take off before the Japanese—now identified as a force of sixty planes—came into contact. Fighters were still climbing, pilots pounding their twin throttles, as the battle was joined high over the airstrip. The ground crews were delighted to see, for the first time, the big Lightnings in action. Until this moment the planes on which they labored took off to disappear into the distance and, hopefully, to return again. Now they witnessed the action firsthand, cheering madly as the Lightnings sailed into the enemy formations. Fifty-one of the big P-38s against only sixty enemy airplanes was the beginning of an immediate disaster. The ground crews watched—and confirmed—thirty-six Japanese fighters and bombers plunging from the skies.

Losses to the 475th—*none*. (Five Lightnings were damaged; all landed safely.) MacDonald and Ivey withstood with grins the angry screams about their having stolen two P-38s: each pilot shot down two enemy aircraft.

Two days later, undaunted, the Japanese came back for more. And once again the 475th was there in force, shooting down eighteen enemy aircraft. Only one P-38 was lost and *not* to the Japanese. The Lightning pilot shot down three Japanese planes, one after the other in quick succession, and was then set aflame by friendly anti-aircraft guns. Spitting mad, the pilot, a young lieutenant, bailed out—his name was Thomas B. McGuire, of the 431st Squadron.

Many of the major air engagements, however, were fought over Japanese territory. On November 2 the 475th escorted Marauders against Rabaul, and ran into a hornet's nest of new pilots and planes sent down from Japan. Badly outnumbered, the 475th pilots shot down nineteen Japanese fighters. They lost five—and the pilots. The 475th considered the fight a defeat.

Up until mid-December of 1943, the 475th flew twenty missions (322 sorties) to Rabaul and in the process destroyed sixty-two enemy fighters and bombers (mostly fighters). Seven of the big twin-boomed P-38s were shot down during these missions, and two pilots of the seven managed to escape from enemy territory to work their way to Australia.

The 475th had lost only seven fighters in combat, but it had also taken a mauling in terms of battle damage. Some fighters returned so badly shot up they were listed as unfit for further service. Others had crash-landed, and all the wearies and the wrecks were promptly cannibalized for spare parts and equipment. Notwithstanding the day-and-night efforts of the ground crews the Group suffered a loss of 30 per cent in available aircraft for combat. The Fifth Air Force decided the 475th *must* be up to strength, and the word was passed down the line to transfer the P-38s of the 9th Squadron, 49th Group (see the chapter on Charles King), and the 39th Squadron, 35th Group, to the ranks of the 475th.

In early November the Group lost Danny Roberts, who, at the time of his death, was the ranking ace of the 475th with fourteen kills.

Supporting the invasion of New Britain, which began December 15, 1943, the Group shot down another nineteen enemy planes. Then came the invasion of Arawe with the Marines going in to the beaches, and the 475th overhead. On D-Day, December 26, Tommy McGuire, now a captain, shot down three enemy planes attacking the invasion fleet (other pilots shot down ten more). This put McGuire into lead position as the Group's ranking ace, a lead never to be relinquished.

Two more weeks passed before the 475th again tangled in the air with the enemy. Colonel MacDonald led a six-plane sweep to Wewak, and the Lightning pilots had fast second thoughts when forty Japanese fighters swarmed into the air after them. Against those odds, MacDonald figured discretion had precedence over valor—but not until he creamed a Tony for his tenth kill on the way out of the area. The news of the powerful Japanese fighter force galvanized the 475th into a return visit. On January 18 all three squadrons of the Group, as well as additional Lightnings of the 80th Squadron (8th Group) swept against Wewak and Boram. The expected devastation of the enemy did not take place. The records are hazy as to what interfered with the scalping plans of Satan's Angels, but of the forty Japanese planes that rose to do battle, only four were shot down. No P-38 losses for the day.

By the end of the month the Fifth Air Force was taking new stock of its battle lines. Comparative quiet had fallen across the skies of New Guinea and New Britain, and there seemed little question but that Japanese airpower in this area had suffered so badly it no longer posed a major threat to Allied operations. The long and short of it, grumbled the 475th, was that "we can't find the enemy and he won't come up to fight." Since beginning operations in August 1943, Satan's Angels, the neophytes of fighting in the area, had managed to fly 557 combat missions consisting of 6,069 sorties, and had shot down a *confirmed* total of 285 enemy fighters and bombers.

By the end of February 1944 the Lightning pilots of Hades, Clover and Possum Squadrons were fairly screaming for action. During the entire month they encountered the enemy in the air only *once*, on the 3rd, when Lightnings of the 431st Squadron ripped into the first enemy planes they'd seen in weeks and shot down six. The month went by with, for the most part, routine patrols over New

Guinea. The pilots hoped for action on the 11th when the Lightnings escorted Liberators to Kavieng, New Ireland, in their longest overwater flight (816 miles) to date for fighters in that theater. Japanese fighters failed to show. The Group flew another eleven missions to the same target during the month and again failed to rouse the enemy.

It was time to move forward from Dobodura, and after preliminary moves, the 475th shifted to a new base. The 433rd Squadron went to Finschhafen on February 26, and in late March 1944 Group Headquarters and the 432nd moved on to Nadzab, with the other two squadrons joining them within a few days.

During the same month the 475th received new P-38s that greatly extended their range, and launched a series of fighter escort missions to Hollandia. On March 30 the 431st and 432nd Squadrons, along with the 80th Squadron of the 8th Group, shepherded three B-24 groups to the new target that had never seen Allied fighters overhead. The B-24s bombed with great accuracy, the 80th Squadron P-38s dove into the few intercepting Japanese fighters, and the pilots from the two squadrons of the 475th grumbled unhappily—they failed to tangle with a single enemy fighter.

On April 1 it was Hollandia again—and again unfired guns. But on April 3 the Japanese took to the air with blood in their eye, and the pilots of Satan's Angels went after them with a vengeance. Fifteen Japanese fighters went down—three to the guns of Joe Forster who was cutting combat teeth for the first time.

Missions of this type continued, interspersed with strikes against ground forces and shipping. But the air action had dropped once again to a new low, and there was little to keep the pilots happy in terms of mixing it up with the enemy.

The Japanese enemy, that is. Then came the disaster of Bloody Sunday, and the grim reminder that a pilot always fights enemies on all sides. This was April 16, with the Group returning from another mission to Hollandia. The Lightning pilots ran into violent storms—

towering cumulus, tremendous rains, clouds from the deck to more than 40,000 feet, severe turbulence.

Eight Lightnings, and six of the pilots, vanished. Satan's Angels had suffered its worst loss of the entire war—more men and aircraft lost in a single flight than they would ever suffer in a single combat at the hands of the enemy.

In mid-May the group shifted to their new field at Hollandia. Bomber escort missions, strikes against shipping and ground forces, and long patrols characterized the missions flown in ensuing weeks—and with mostly "no shows" by the Japanese. Enemy air resistance was described officially as "feeble," and the Lightning pilots were chafing at the bit.

But in October the tempo changed. American forces stormed the Philippines. The 49th and 8th Fighter Groups went north, and the pilots of the 475th screamed when their planes were ordered transferred to the 49th and 8th to keep them at full strength. On November 1, in fact, pilots of the 431st Squadron were *ferrying* their Lightnings to the 39th Fighter Group at Tacloban, Leyte. Leading the 431st in was Tommy McGuire—who was held in the air when the Japanese attacked suddenly. That was the day McGuire chalked up number twenty-five for confirmed kills.

Several days later the 475th moved into Dulag in the Philippines and was back in action. During the next two months Satan's Angels pilots were back in the thick of fighting, flying mainly escort and intercept missions with very heavy enemy air opposition. On Christmas Day the Group held a celebration—victim number 500 had gone down.

Two weeks later a black pall descended on the Group—the impossible had happened. Tommy McGuire, with 38 kills to his credit, was killed. As we saw in the previous chapter, this tragedy occurred after a steady sweep by McGuire to bring his score to thirty-eight, making him the nation's second greatest ace.

Now, the official record of what happened with Tommy McGuire stands as it is written in the preceding chapter. But more can be added. It took a long time to ferret out the details, and it is a rather extraordinary tribute to the skill of the Japanese pilot involved (later identified as Shoichi Sugita), a tribute from the men who flew the P-38s.

Officially, as the story has been maintained in the records all these years, Sugita bounced the four Lightnings led by McGuire from a superior position by breaking from cloud cover. I had always assumed this to be so; after all, this was the way it had been reported and the way it seemed. But after talking with several pilots of the 475th a familiar pattern reappeared. Official histories are often happenstance creations. Men far removed from the scene receive squadron and group reports. The reports, to them, leave something to be desired, or perhaps several pages are missing from a particular document. Whatever happens, the facts become altered. Not distorted deliberately, not propagandized, but they are sometimes "convenienced," to use an awkward phrase. This seems also to be the case with the death of Tommy McGuire. The basic facts are correct. Four P-38s, down low, and a single Zero fighter against them. A pilot in trouble, McGuire clawing to the rescue and stalling, then crashing. All of this correct. But there are other, vital changes. The reader is asked to recall the story as it is recorded officially.

The four P-38s were on a sweep, still with belly tanks on, when they saw the Zero. But it wasn't the Japanese pilot bouncing the four P-38s. Instead, the Zero was ahead and to the side. *And he was lower than the P-38s.*

The immediate response when getting set to tangle with the enemy is to drop your tanks. It was a long-standing cardinal rule. The other pilots waited for McGuire to give the order. McGuire didn't. Not because he forgot. The four fighters were out hunting scalps, pure and simple. McGuire had thirty-eight kills. A few more and Bong would be in the records as number two. McGuire would be the new leading ace; it was all set for him to be ordered out of combat then. The word was he would receive the Medal of Honor and be sent home. Pretty much the same pattern as Bong.

Enter another factor. The tremendous skill and confidence of McGuire. The four Lightnings still had plenty of fuel in the belly tanks. They wanted a long and effective "killing" sweep. Dropping the tanks now meant cutting short on the mission. Add it up. Four Lightnings against a single Zero that was *below* the American fighters. They moved in to scratch the Zero.

Absolute hell broke loose. Nothing they expected to took place. Before anyone could realize what was happening the Zero flashed in like a rapier. Sugita was swift, brilliant, and a beautiful gunner. Just like *that*, the pilots told me, a P-38 went down, torn to pieces by cannon shells. Instantly Sugita flicked through a roll and was after a second Lightning, guns hammering. The big P-38s, low, heavy, flying slower than they should have been, were in perfect position for Sugita. The radios exploded with shouting. The victim under Sugita's guns shouted for help. The rest of it we know. McGuire violated all his own rules of combat trying to save the other pilot. He racked the 38 around in a tight turn, wings almost vertical. Too tight, too slow, too low—the Lightning stalled as if hitting a brick wall and snapped over on its wing, plunging for jungle. McGuire in that brief period *righted the fighter, was pulling out.* Not enough room. A sheet of flame marked the end.

In February the 475th moved to Mindoro to begin support of ground operations on Luzon. In March they moved again, this time to Clark Field near Manila. In April 1945 they again shifted to a new field, Linguyen, Luzon. For the rest of the war they flew mainly ground support and long escort missions, the latter including targets in China, French Indo-China, and Formosa. By now aerial opposition had dropped by a drastic margin and the opportunities for combat were almost nil.

During their nearly two years of combat the 475th flew 3,042 missions (21,701 sorties) and shot down 551 Japanese aircraft—plus one more shot down by Charles Lindbergh.

Total losses were fifty-six Lightnings to the Japanese—a ratio in combat of almost ten to one in favor of the P-38s. A record that requires no further comment.

Bob Anderson, who supplied much of the material on the 475th for this book, must have been one of the most frustrated pilots in Satan's Angels. He could apply at least for the position of the second most frustrated pilot. He explained that "in 340 combat hours I saw precisely one enemy plane shot down. I was the sixteenth of thirty-two airplanes chasing it. It was a Pete floatplane, and the seventh kill for Major Warren R. Lewis, over Noemfoor Island. I *never* saw enemy fighters or bombers. But I think Captain Kenneth Ralph tops even me. Kenny flew more combat hours than any other pilot in the 433rd Squadron and more than most pilots in the other squadrons, and in all that time he never saw an enemy plane of *any* type and, of course, never fired his guns at anything that flew. Some of us just didn't live right. *Or maybe we did*; we lived through it. But Kenny's 'record' was really incredible —something like 650 combat hours without ever *seeing* an enemy plane. . . ."

PERSONAL

Just as Charles King opened for us pages of air combat history which have never seen print, so Bob Anderson has done the same with the 475th, the exclusively P-38 air group. He gives us a rare insight into the years gone by.

"Most of the old-timers," Bob Anderson wrote, "will tell you that the 475th, Satan's Angels, which received its name about April of 1944 when based at Nadzab in the Markham Valley, was organized in June 1943, when in fact the orders for establishing the new outfit were first put out the month before.

"The Group came to life at Amberly Field near Ipswitch, Australia, which was the nearest city of any size. It was an area of gentle rolling hills covered with oak and gum trees and quite a bit of eucalyptus. Most aircraft were assembled nearby at a place called Eagle Farms. Primarily, the Group received P-38H models, although the diary of the 432nd Squadron noted, and not too happily, that their first airplane was a P-38G. The Group was formed in the middle of the Australian winter and at night nearly everybody damned near froze to death, although the days weren't too bad.

"Now, this was General George C. Kenney's own group, almost his personal group, and there should be no misunderstanding about this. He had cajoled and pleaded with Hap Arnold for months for an outfit made up *only* of P-38s. As you are well aware, the 8th, 35th and 49th Fighter Groups each had one squadron of P-38s. And as you are also aware, the attrition rate alone was sufficient to reduce the effectiveness of the outfits to just eight or nine planes per squadron airborne, which really was less than the muscle these outfits needed to really take it to the Japanese.

"Kenney knew he couldn't fulfill his obligations to MacArthur until such time as all our bombers could make the long flights to such targets as Rabaul, Wewak, Kavieng, and the Admiralties, with escort by fighters going all the way. There was only one fighter at the time that could do the job and that was the P-38. For a long time Arnold resisted Kenney's outright pleas, pointing out with considerable accuracy and justification that all Lightnings were needed just as desperately for the ETO and North Africa. But Kenney never quit; he kept bugging Arnold until he got through. Arnold finally told Kenney: 'Okay, George, you get the pilots and the crewmen to form a group, and I'll send you the hundred P-38s.'

"Kenney fired his answer right back. 'I've got the people. Send the airplanes!' And Arnold sent them, via ship to Brisbane where they were offloaded and then assembled at Eagle Farms.

"Now, let's grab reality by the hand. Forget the official records and what they say about how we staffed the 475th. Hardly any of it is true. The truth is that Kenney *didn't have the people to form the 475th.* Now he showed his true light, that he was never one to hide under a bushel his ability to improvise. Orders went out to pull men from the 49th, 8th and 35th. Major George Prentice of the 35th got the call to head up the new group, and the group got a fine man and an outstanding leader at its helm. He was later killed. Frank Nichols from the 49th was the C.O. of the 431st Squadron (call sign *Hades*). Captain Frank D. Tompkins led the 432nd (call sign *Clover*), and, Major Martin Low headed the 433rd (call sign *Possum*).

"Let me get back to General Kenney. He didn't have the men, but he already had some tradition in his outfit that they were professional scroungers from the word go— and that meant from the commanding general down to the lowest enlisted ranks. The word went out that 'this is the Old Man's outfit so don't send your foul-ups.' As a consequence, the three contributing fighter groups did indeed send some of their best people. The C.O.'s of each squadron were given the opportunity of picking their own key men, regardless of the effect it created on the supplying groups. Thus the 475th started business with excellent leadership and some truly seasoned fighter pilots.

"The balance of the pilots were fresh kids from the States, so the group became a melting pot of experienced and partially experienced pros who were eager but knew the ropes, and a bunch of eager-beaver yardbirds who knew nothing but were feisty and game for anything. Everybody from the lowest enlisted man to the officer of highest rank had something to prove. *There were no traditions for the 475th Group*. It had to build even these from scratch. There was considerable good-natured rivalry between the squadrons, but the group never permitted this friendly contention to get out of hand.

"Kenney went so far as to drag cooks out of the bush. Anybody who looked as if he could cook or type or just plain wipe down an airplane was suddenly transferred to the 475th.

"Tommy McGuire showed up, scrawny and underfed as usual, and was assigned to the 431st. A few years ago Frank Nichols told me, 'I took a look at this scrawny kid and tried to get rid of him, but none of the other flight leaders would take him, so I was stuck with him. How'd I know he was going to become America's second greatest ace?'

"McGuire was constantly hanging around the armament men as they boresighted the Lightnings. When his plane was boresighted, he spent hours with the gun people, checking the range and the firing effect. The armament people grew to know and respect him because he really was interested and really did want to know about the guns. Even at that time there was a certain no-nonsense attitude about him. McGuire immediately exhibited an aggressive posture and when he flew the P-38 it was as if he had strapped it on. When his body moved, the Lightning simply went in that direction. As you know so well, the only time he failed to handle his plane properly was the day he was killed. His confidence was such that he thought that the four P-38s flying patrol that day certainly could handle one lone Zero, but the Japanese turned out to be one of the great pros at a time when the pros were really scarce in the Japanese air ranks. You know by now, also, that McGuire had righted his plane before he hit, but it was too late.

"The combat reports of Weaver and Thropp both indicate that the Japanese pilot's guns never hit McGuire. In fact, Sugita, as it seems to have been, never even took a shot at Tommy. Small consolation. The 431st was in a state of shock, because an aura of invincibility had been built up around McGuire. He was such an expert in the plane, everyone sort of believed nothing would ever happen to him. It is a credit to Pappy Cline, as an outstanding officer and a man, that he was able to take over as C.O. after McGuire's death and bring the squadron back to its former peak.

"There are some incidents pertinent to the records both of Satan's Angels and the P-38. Joe Forster of the 432nd flew what we believe was the longest overwater single-engine mission when he had an engine shot out over Balikpapan, Borneo, and then flew 840 miles on one engine to Morotai.

"Under Captain Danny Roberts, about whom you've

written, the 433rd Squadron in thirty-seven days shot down fifty enemy planes with the loss of but two pilots, a victory record and ratio that staggered us all. Because of the P-38s of the 475th, Kenney was able to hit Rabaul in November and December of 1943, *in force,* and interrogation of Japanese officers after the war pointed out that the Japanese well remembered those raids and the extreme damage done, in spite of our exaggerated records of shipping sunk.

"When the 475th is considered in context with MacArthur's movement back to the Philippines, surprisingly, it becomes a key factor. Kenney could send out his bombers with the protection they needed to hit the Japanese targets straight up the coast of New Guinea. The Fifth Air Force, under cover of Lightnings, flattened every enemy base between Moresby and the Philippines, and the Lightnings of the 475th were always in the vanguard. When the groups moved up, the 475th was always second in movement, usually ahead of the 8th and 35th, but usually behind the 49th. The 49th was of course the oldest group in seniority and was entitled to the front move, but when Kenney's bombers had to reach way, way out, we were the ones who did it. This, of course, sounds like ego coming forth and, in fact, there is a collective ego in these words. But it is less ego, really, than the urgent desire to at last attempt to tell the facts about the one and only P-38 group in the whole damned United States Army Air Force anywhere in the world. And the only outfit that actually did the job the P-38 was really capable of doing.

"We lost, in all the time we flew, exactly twenty-seven men in combat to the enemy, and that is absolutely astounding when you consider the confirmed 551 air kills Satan's Angels scored. We met some of the very best the enemy had to offer in the way of pilots and planes. Incidentally, we do not count in our totals the Zero shot down by Colonel Lindbergh.

"All during the early stages of that air war—as you have documented so thoroughly—it was really a matter at Port Moresby of 'Katy, bar the door!' The same for

Darwin, too. The Fifth Air Force was hanging in there literally by its nails and by raw courage. We were so woefully unprepared it was a matter of criminal failure. When I came through Amberly Field I learned, and fast, that we had kids in fighters who had never fired their guns at a ground target or a tow sleeve. Some had only five or maybe seven hours in P-40s, so you can imagine the shellacking they took just trying to fly their airplanes cross-country without the Japanese hammering at them.

"When the three squadrons of the three fighter groups in action became P-38 outfits, the balance of power in favor of the Japanese was checked. But Kenney still didn't have the muscle to take the offensive against the Japanese, and that's what all the yelling was about for P-38s for the 475th Fighter Group. In the final analysis, we made the difference.

"Finally, at long last, there is a really competent author who is interested in Satan's Angels. I thought I'd never see the day . . . when we would all see in writing the story of the one group that truly proved the worth of the Lightning."

Sure it's a matter of competence.

When you let people like Bob Anderson tell it in his own words.

24. Final Critique

Sure, the war was over. The P-38s grabbed the honors when they escorted the Japanese surrender mission to Ie Shima. Not long after, despite orders that no American planes were to fly over Japan, two P-38 pilots encountered mysterious "engine trouble" and had to "force land" at a Japanese fighter base in the home islands. The chance was too great to miss. The pilots didn't know what to expect. It sounded like a good idea, but now that they were *there* . . .

The Japanese met them with candy.

A few months later there was another sight to behold. It was January 1946 and the AAF had a problem on its hands. What to do with all the thousands and thousands of spanking new combat planes for which it really didn't have any need? Pilots flew them into Kingman, Arizona, where the Pentagon declared them surplus.

Seven thousand five hundred of them.

Including more than 500 brand-new P-38s.

Now, just try to picture this scene in your mind.

More than *500* Lightnings. Think back to when fifty P-38s meant all the difference in a combat theater. And here they were, just waiting to be bought, with full tanks and equipment.

Buy yourself a gleaming, beautiful, perfect Lightning for precisely $1,250.00.

Tony LeVier bought one. He flew it back to Burbank where his fellow pilots, engineers, and mechanics acted as if they'd never seen one of these things before. Well, in a way it was true, because they'd never seen a *personal* P-38. Tony and his friends stripped the big Lightning. He figured to do air shows in the bird and maybe get into some racing.

He painted his ship a bright red and he put on aerobatic demonstrations that brought crowds to their feet cheering hoarsely. He did vertical dives for low-level high speed passes. He did vertical climbs, aileron-rolling on the way up. Then he did vertical dives, aileron-rolling on the way down. He leveled off and did a square loop with rolls on the straight sides. Out of this he went through a cuban eight, then an aileron roll in level flight, a wide circle doing some more aileron rolls, and broke out into a speed climb to altitude. From here he did a dive with one engine shut down and the prop blades feathered, and then aileron-rolled the ship in level flight. He did inverted reversements, he demonstrated unfeathering and restarting in the air. He went through dives and climbs, feathering one as he dove and climbed. Then he chandelled, and with one feathered, dropped his gear and flaps and landed with the dead engine. That last one was too tame, so he changed the show a bit, going for altitude, where he feathered *both* engines.

On the way down he did a series of aerobatic maneuvers and landed deadstick.

Precision landings, parking the bird right where he said he would before he took off.

He added a few more details. Takeoff was one of them. He got off the runway, tucked up the gear and flaps, held down the nose until he was at the end of the runway. He pulled up into a loop; at the top he half-rolled and roared down the runway in the direction opposite to that of takeoff. Then he developed a new grand finale.

Let Tony tell it:

"Down I came, picking up speed, and when it seemed I would fly into the ground I pulled up and over in a half roll. Back up I went again. Then both propellers stopped turning and down I came once more in a nearly vertical dive. At the last moment the nose came up and at three hundred feet I pulled out of the dive and went around and landed. I could see by the look on the faces around me that the act went over well, and I felt really proud, especially of the P-38."

Well, Tony had come a long way in the P-38. But then, when you stopped to think about it, the P-38 had come its own long trip since the first prototype took to the air and thrilled everyone involved with its tremendous promise.

Every now and then the promise of a new venture is fulfilled.

That's the story of the P-38. A stirring fulfillment with heartbreaking moments but without apology. You can't argue with a record. It stands by itself.

Earlier in our story we were introduced to Arthur W. Heiden, a former P-38 pilot with considerable training and combat experience in the airplane. As well as with other fighters. If you will recall, Art Heiden is one of the reasons this book came to pass. But Art wasn't getting off the hook that easily. I wanted a special kind of wrap-up for this book, a final critique, and I asked Art to deliver. He did, and I believe his words add the perfect closing touch to the story of the P-38.

Now, these are his words. His story. His vital contribution to understanding what this airplane was all about. Art Heiden recalls:

"Like so many who were involved with this airplane, I have particular impressions, memories and very strong opinions. But I cannot, and I don't, pretend to be any kind of authority. I'm confident that you especially can overcome this sort of difficulty and give an honest analytical history of the P-38.

"Among other things, you asked for my commentary as an instructor and here, I believe, lies the source of such divergent opinion of the P-38. A case of getting smart too late.

"From this point of view, I will make the analogy that

the quality of multi-engine training during World War II bordered on the ridiculous. I am convinced that with training methods now in use we could take most of today's private pilots who might be about to fly the Aztec or Cessna 310, and in ten hours, have a more confident pilot than the ones who flew off to war in the P-38.

"A P-38 pilot usually got his training in two ways. The first way, of course, was twin-engine advanced training, in Curtis AT-9s, which had the unhappy feature of having propellers you couldn't feather. After sixty hours of this, the student received ten hours of AT-6 gunnery, although he might also get his gunnery training in the AT-9, since AT-6s were sometimes in short supply.

"At this point he had his chance to fly the RP-322 for another twenty hours. The 322, as you know, was the British version of the airplane, and they came with assorted equipment and things on them that nobody could predict. Upon graduation from the RP-322 he was assigned to a P-38 Replacement Training Unit (RTU) or an Operational Training Unit (OTU) for 100 hours or more fighter training. A second way to get into the P-38 was to transition from single-engine fighters. In this event, someone probably took him up in a multi-engine transport or bomber and demonstrated engine shutdown a couple of times—after skimming the tech order, a blindfold check, and then ignoring entirely the checklist (not for *real* fighter pilots!), he blasted off. More than one neophyte has described his first "launch" in a P-38 as being hit in the ass with a snow shovel.

"Either method of training, probably, made little difference as neither guy knew that much about multi-engine operations and procedures. True, he had been warned about the magic number of 120 miles per hour—his V_{mc}, or minimum single-engine control speed. He had swam in the glue during a couple of prop featherings while in formation with his instructor. He was, also, warned never to turn into a dead engine, never to put down the gear until he had the field made, and *never* to go around with one caged. That was about it—until shortly thereafter the old Allison time bomb blew up, and he was in business the hard way. Right on takeoff.

"Some people lucked out if the runway was long enough. Some overshot or undershot and they bent the whole thing. Some tried a single-engine go-around anyway, usually with horrible results. Such happenings would make a son of a bitch out of *any* saint.

"Tony LeVier's spectacular demonstrations were an attempt to rectify all these problems, but the damage had been done. The Air Corps, as far as I knew, never did change its P-38 training.

"There were other weird things, ridiculous things, to rob the confidence of the trainee as well as the combat pilot.

"Wartime priorities demanded that 91-octane fuel be used in training. This was all right until some guy exceeded 44 inches manifold pressure. Then holes suddenly developed in his pistons which, of course, were needed to keep things going.

"The idea that only one generator was all that was needed, no doubt, eliminated more P-38 pilots in training and in combat than any other single cause. There was a paradox here that the tech order didn't mention. Those old Curtis Electric props without the generator on the line would feather-up—kind of take a rest. Also, if you took off with a low battery the silly things would run away with themselves. Maybe the props were just trying to figure it all out, like what they should really be doing, but two feathered or two runaways made a good and exciting day.

"The guy who bought the extra generators and solved this problem should have received a weekend pass to Picadilly.

"RAMIFICATIONS

"The situation that set up the Eighth Air Force P-38 pilots for their biggest surprise was the equipment used in training (P-38E, F and G variants), and, to a degree, the tactically orientated instructors who had returned from

Africa and the Pacific. It is difficult to overestimate the emotional and the psychological factors here. All this had such an impact on our men that most pilots going to England were asking for assignment to the Ninth Air Force so they could work at low level. Their level of confidence, because of their own training and what was being dinned into them from combat-experienced men from Africa and the Pacific, gave them the great urge and desire to stay down low with the P-38 over Europe. These pilots had never been much above 20,000 feet, if they ever reached this height, and they knew little if anything at all about altitude operations and flying long-range bomber escort.

"Now, this isn't one of the brightest chapters of the P-38. But as you and I agreed from the outset, our primary interest lies in a wholly objective viewpoint, and *every* airplane has one cross or another to bear. What happened in the early days with the P-38 in England, unquestionably, is that time when burdens were the greatest and hearts were heavy.

"These new pilots made their attempts to go to altitude. This is what the curriculum called for and they gave it their best, but those early airplanes, the way they were set up, just wouldn't make it. There were disastrous incidents of ignition breakdown because of high-tension ignition leakage. The oxygen systems were woefully inadequate. This is what they put into the airplane and the pilot in the cockpit was stuck with what he had. It just wouldn't do the job. No one liked 30,000 feet anyway. There had been no training for it. There had never been any need for it. It was too cold and the windows frosted up.

"All this piled up on the Eighth Air Force pilots, but there they were at 30,000 feet plus and sixty below zero. It was miserable.

"Then things really started to come apart. Now, suddenly, superchargers were running away. They were blowing up engines on the basis of one engine blowup *every seven hours*. Intercoolers were separating the lead from the fuel and the result was lowered octane. Hands and feet were freezing; pilots were calling their airplanes airborne ice wagons and they were right. Frost on the windows got thicker than ever. The most disgusting of all was the leisurely way the German fighters made their getaways straight down.

"Despite these revolting developments, the pilots of the Eighth knew they could outturn, outclimb, outrun and outfight anybody's airplane in the air so they set about rectifying their problems.

"Every one of these problems was solved with the introduction of the P-38L.

"Let me repeat this again and again. It can never be emphasized too strongly. It makes up the gospel word. The P-38L. Now *there* was *the* airplane.

"*Nothing, to these pilots, after the hard winter of 1943-44 could be more beautiful than a P-38L outrolling and tailgating a German fighter straight down, following a spin or a split-S or whatever gyration a startled, panicked and doomed German might attempt to initiate. You just couldn't get away from the P-38L. Whatever the German could do, the American in the P-38L could do better.*

"It was easily among the greatest fighting machines ever made.

"INTO THE MACH

"However, no one knows better than you, who have followed the P-38 through every week of its teething pains, that the P-38L was the result of much effort along the way.

"In the early days of the Lightning, compressibility training (which we had whipped in the P-38J-25-LO and all subsequent models) was conducted by firsthand observation of the results. Of course, after we ran into any incidents, a Lockheed tech representative such as Jimmy Mattern came around to see if anything was new. That's one way to learn . . .

"My first information, other than hearsay, came at San Diego one day when an instructor got an oxygen disconnect, passed out, and with Lieutenants Jordon, Fiebelkorn and Butler in trail, went vertical. The instructor came to later and, still groggy, jumped. Jordon also jumped, after tail separation, but his wildly gyrating P-38 cut him in two while he was in his chute. The biggest piece of the airplane landed flat in the streets and expended itself shooting up the city while sections of Lieutenant Jordon hung about on the wires. Lieutenant Earnest C. Fiebelkorn (who was to become the leading ace of the 20th Fighter Group) pulled as hard as he could on the yoke, rolled all the nose-up trim into the bird he could get, and managed to land the spectacular remains back at North Island.

"Lieutenant Ival Butler (later to disappear over the North Sea) as Tail-End Charlie just couldn't keep up with the others, said to hell with it, and came home. Compressibility had come to be regarded as a very bad thing.

"The P-38 design had another interesting tendency. Cadet James McGovern (the same man who would become famous as Earthquake McGoon McGovern of China and Dienbienphu) was a man who believed in following his first impulses, and he demonstrated this to us (often) during training. He also demonstrated a tendency of the early P-38 we didn't like—the urge for the airplane to tuck under its nose in a dive as speed increased. The RP-322 we flew was lighter than the combat P-38. This changed its characteristics. It would reach terminal velocity (where it just couldn't go any faster) before it got into the shock stall of the Mach regions. Which meant that it didn't get into compressibility quite as fast as the heavier combat fighters we flew later.

"But it sure tucked under. The nose just went down, then tucked back, and there you were in inverted flight. These results were not what McGovern had in mind when he did a screaming vertical dive in the RP-322. The nose tucked under, McGovern cursed and yelled, but it didn't do any good. The canopy caved in and damaged his head enough for considerable hospitalization. This was, also, the first case of severe redout (blood rushing to the head) I had observed.

"McGovern, naturally, convinced the accident people that the damned canopy had just come off in the traffic pattern, so this bit of vital information he gained in his dive did not get into the literature of possibilities with the RP-322. Mac did advise a few intimates not to dive that bear too fast or it could get mean. The word was out.

"THEN, LATER . . .

"To the best of my memory and knowledge, it wasn't until the last half of 1944 that fighter training took a major upturn. Don Blakeslee had taken over the Third AAF Fighter Gunnery and Instructors School in Florida; the pretense of a 5 percent qualifying gunnery score was now above 20 percent. There was an instrument school at Byron, Texas where something tremendous was happening. Fighter Training schools were getting a sudden influx of enthusiastic new blood from the ETO, who were eager, dedicated and insisted on telling old maids, senators and mossbacks in the training command to go to hell. Training bases were commanded by leaders like Colonel Chesley Peterson (Eagle Squadron) who had the guts to back up the instructors.

"Combat-capable trainees were being turned out and they were staying alive as combat pilots and becoming leaders. Previously it was all right to die in combat but not to get roughed up in training. What a record those guys made that last year of the war. The training and the airplanes had mostly been de-bugged.

"A fighter pilot job had become the most exciting, rewarding and inventive work to be had.

"For perspective it must also be remembered that two other significant events had taken place in training. Theater indoctrination at Goxhill in England had received the same enthusiastic overhaul as had happened in the States. The most important of all may have been the training units set up by the combat organizations themselves. Here it was possible to up-date training to the latest information and for individual commanders to put their special stamp on things and to develop new tactics.

"But—and this is a giant, towering BUT—this was all for the P-51 pilots.

"What would have happened if the P-38 pilots and their units could have been blessed with this same wonderful opportunity?

"MAXIMUM EFFORT EQUALS A HAIRY DO SHAKY EFFORT

"P-38 units from the moment of going on initial operational status were committed to MAX EFFORT. No two ways about it. No time to shake things out, to discover your problems. You got there and *zap,* you were in up to your eyeballs. This meant that everything flyable went and everything that still had wings would be made flyable. No matter what. This in effect was the same as demanding, by direct order, that everyone and everything must have, immediately if not sooner, 100 per cent combat capabilities. Like Casey Jones, the pressure was all the way up without any margins.

"The greatest story of combat may be in the efforts of the ground crews and how they reacted to impossible situations. The spirit and morale of these men could well have been the deciding force that kept the young pilots going when there appeared to be no tomorrow. These ground crews working under pressure, seven days a week, all night long, outside in the snow and cold, and with overseas duty to the duration of the war, turned in one of the most amazing stories of enthusiastic competition, ingenuity, improvisation and spirit that might be imagined.

"Colonel Cy Wilson, commanding officer of the 20th Fighter Group, helped keep the fires burning in his own way. He stayed up with them each cold and wet night encouraging his men, serving hot coffee, and helping them out with thorny problems. Wilson needed transportation. So he just stole a motorcycle from the M.P.'s and dared them to take it back. If an airplane part wasn't available he would help steal it. He was with his kind and he knew it, for when the planes were out flying, these crews were scrounging and stealing.

"The ground crews stationed themselves along the runway when a mission departed or returned. They equipped themselves with fire axes which weren't for rescue purposes. If an airplane crashed, the race was on. They were chopping it apart for parts before it stopped sliding.

"Each crew had its own cache of parts secreted somewhere. Cellars were dug and concealed in a fashion that would have shamed Al Capone and Dutch Schultz. Habits formed from prohibiton paid off handsomely.

"Crew chiefs were like hawks scrutinizing their pilots. Those pilots had better do things right or that old sergeant was sure to grab him by the short hairs and give him the message. Many a pilot found himself helping change an engine or making some other repair if the crew chief had the slightest idea it might help prevent a problem. There were no pilot protests as Colonel Wilson or a squadron commander was always there looking over the shoulders of the crew chiefs. If a pilot aborted, he found himself researching the subject in depth and giving extensive lectures to the other pilots.

"These crew chiefs were a very caustic group. They called it as they saw it. Their remarks were blunt. "Jesus, that was a sorry landing . . . Sir." Or: "Who was that miserable bastard flying Red Three today . . . Sir?"

"They wouldn't speak for days if the tape was still on the gun muzzles after a mission, but a victory by *their* airplane made them turn wild. All wages must have gone into the lottery at the NCO mess.

"Engines were changed and severe battle damage was repaired overnight. No pilot had an excuse not to be on the next day's mission. This was MAXIMUM EFFORT, and this was the organization built around a fighter pilot to lift and carry him into combat.

"THEN THERE WAS LEADERSHIP

"In the early days—which would be immediately after the Schweinfurt Disaster of October 14, 1943—fifteen German fighters faced every one of the P-38s of the 55th and 20th Fighter Groups as they went on full operations. Both groups suffered heavy losses. For a while Colonel Barney Russel's 20th Group approached losses of nearly 100 per cent—*due largely to mechanical difficulties*. This was especially significant as leadership was decimated and, under the operational circumstances, leadership was the most critical item to the men who were facing 1,500 German fighters with but 100 untried pilots and airplanes.

"I personally joined the 79th Squadron of the 20th Fighter Group on February 11, 1944. This was an *experience* from the beginning. No one would spot you over one mission in that outfit. They ran through pilots like oats through a goose. All the pilots on operations looked like they had a severe case of pink-eye (from bright sun and poor diet). It reminded you of some weird movie. To make things more dramatic the 79th lost a whole section of eight airplanes the day I came into the squadron.

"Colonel Montgomery, the Deputy Commander, and seven others of the 79th failed to return that day. A bunch of Me-109s had forced them into a defensive fight that lasted beyond their fuel limit. Realizing this, they simply stayed and fought until they had shot all their guns dry, then ran back into France as far as they could fly, and bailed out. Montgomery, with a broken leg, and several others, successfully evaded through Spain. They didn't lack for spirit.

"Hence (before the men returned), the 20th Group and the 79th Squadron particularly should have been at an extremely low morale status. But even though they were badly shattered and physically exhausted they were still very tenacious and full of fight. This isn't from any handy-dandy squadron history. Its personal, and shared, observation.

"Captain Jackson, 79th Commander until after the next mission, made the new wingman job perfectly clear. "No one, but *no one*, will leave his leader." In such an event we were assured we would receive the prompt attention of Captain Jackson's personal guns. In today's view this may sound a bit harsh, but at that time, this blunt advice was entirely necessary to make an irrevocable point. German air leaders later verified this tactic as the single overriding factor that saved the earlier Allied fighters from total decimation.

"Increasing numbers of fighter units went operational, Big Week came and went, and now the German fighters were in trouble and as hard-pressed as the earlier Allied bombers and fighters had been.

"Colonel Russel held the badly mauled 20th together with all its mistakes and disasters. Colonel Rau now became Group C.O. with Colonel Cy Wilson as his deputy. These two gave a combination of intellectual and dynamic leadership that would prove to be on a par with that of Zemke's 50th and Blakeslee's 4th Groups.

"IN COMPARISON

"Erroneously, we are always trying to categorize everything. We have to believe something is best, then build a myth around it. Democrat or Republican; Ford or Chevy; Beech, Cessna or Piper—I suppose the choice and the myth in some way is our security blanket. To say which gets too complicated. Any airplane you mention at a World War II fighter was the best is a bit ridiculous. It particular time, in a particular model, might generally meet this criteria. A certain plane in a certain model, one certain day and at a certain area might be considered best.

"If you flew a Zero or an Me-109E or a Spitfire V in December 1941, you might feel you had the best airplane. Six months later, a new airplane or a new modification to an old one might be better. All first-line fighters went through extensive modernization and modification that kept them up with the situation.

"The impact on thought and doctrine is the important thing. Battles lost or won do not necessarily win a war.

"It seems people resist changing their security blanket, but a good sales job helps. Blakeslee sold the 4th Group on changing from P-47s to P-51s and they transitioned on the way to the target. The 5th Group just refused to adapt to that "hole in the radiator thing." Cy Wilson recognized the problem and sold the 20th on getting out of those milk trucks. I've seen combat-experienced instructors refuse to give up their trusted P-40s for the Whiz Kid P-51.

"Any comparison must be confined to a particular model. A Lightning I, the RP-322, only *looked* like a P-38F. A P-38F was no P-38H and a P-38L was an entirely different animal from anything else in the sky.

"An engine change in a P-40 or a P-51A from an Allison to a Merlin made that airplane something else again.

"A propeller change on a P-47 was a difference like day and night. An Me-109E was no Me-109G. An individual supercharger change made some birds perform like different machines.

"Everyone who talks about fighters always has to get into the dogfight thing and which one could turn the best. As any student pilot knows, turning radius is a direct function of the speed. So the airplane with the lightest wing loading had the lowest stall and would turn better. The turning radius was variable even to the load carried by a particular airplane. An airplane with a light pilot, low on fuel and ammunition, might stall 20 miles per hour slower than it would with a large pilot, heavy on fuel and gun belts full. An Me-109 or FW-190 set up with heavy cannon to destroy bombers was something different from the same airplanes with lighter armament. Something like using a football guard to ride in the Derby. To turn shortest the airplane simply had to be slowed up more than the other; the closer the stall the shorter the turn. Then if the guns were fired he lost 10 to 20 miles per hour and a spin or worse resulted.

"Generally speaking, all first-line fighters stalled within a range of 20 mph of each other so it was a close margin when talking about turning radius. Some had advantages of more power, wing slats and good usable flap systems.

"A good pilot in a light Me-109 that could hang his plane on the prop, properly use his slats and with the *Luftwaffe Stomp*—the stall turn—might well have been the terror of all the skies. Few were that good or that cool.

"A plane that had more power and could stay above the other had an advantage over the lower and shorter-turning plane.

"Some fighters such as the P-38, P-51 and Me-109 had a good usable flap system that gave a definite advantage simply by lowering the stall speed. The special combat flap system in the P-38—the Fowlers snapping back to 8 degrees—was very useful. And then there were airplanes like the P-40, on which the flap system was so clumsy that to my knowledge its use was seldom attempted for combat purposes.

"Yet there are other points to consider. Despite its atrocious flaps, low-altitude Allison engine and stiff controls, the P-40 had beautiful flight characteristics. With strong legs and the senses to keep the ball centered, a pilot could fly the old beast in the stall without problems. A P-51 was a different matter. With its sensitivity and wing design, an insensitive pilot could have spin trouble.

"Some describe the P-47 as the Cadillac of fighters. This was something of the sensation it gave me. With its comfort, silky sewing machine sound, minimal vibration, and fantastic control response a pilot was completely seduced. The whole airplane seemed to be the arrow behind that big Pratt & Whitney. A P-47 pilot had to keep his mind on the engine if he was to alter course from where it was pointed. An impatient jerk on the elevators didn't change its flight path. The old P&W kept right on going and the pilot found himself and the rest of the airplane auto-rotating around and around behind it. He learned to gently start the engine moving in the desired direction.

"Any pilot who has found himself stalled out in a dog-fight below the treetops in a P-38 will always remember those beautiful stall characteristics and power available. His only desire is to take on all the single-engine fighters in the world at fifty feet and settle the arguments. (Balanced torque and P factor resisted the onset of auto-rotation.) The P-38's flight characteristics had to be great; its cockpit comfort was miserable. *The climb in the P-51 was a disappointment after the P-38L which could get to altitude nearly twice as fast.*

"With the exception of the P-39 design, all the World War II fighters had good, safe characteristics. True, all would enter spins or snap maneuvers without much pro-vocation but, like today's general aviation airplanes, really all you had to do was to let go, and they recovered by themselves. Although intentional spins were prohibited, oc-casionally someone would deliberately hold one into a spin for an extended period. This could get vicious. I'm sure it wasn't repeated by the same individual.

"Instructors in the P-40 and P-51 at Tallahassee in Florida would deliberately introduce the trainee to some rather violent maneuvers. During acrobatic training, the student was asked to do Immelmann turns from level flight and cruise throttle situation. In the clean P-51 this would not be too difficult, but in a P-40 it was interest-ing. The idea was that this made an excellent simulated combat maneuver, that it took some skill to accomplish, and the results of a bad maneuver were more difficult to produce any other way.

"It usually took a new trainee two or three times to get on top of the Immelmann, but in the meantime he had entered inverted spins and other tumble-pendulum gyra-tions. The point is he couldn't do much about the situation anyway, so he *had* to sit back and let the airplane fly itself out. Thus, he learned that when inverted, excessive forward stick and simultaneous aileron application pro-duced weird results.

"COMBAT TO ME

"In the P-38, in the ETO, it was a defensive war when I arrived. Too few P-38s for the job they were being asked to do. As simple as that. When one is on the defensive his attitude is always totally directed to staying alive. Shape up formation . . . ward off attacks . . . drive off the attacker . . . maintain air discipline . . . be sure you're in the right position at the right time . . . don't leave a defensive gap. By nature, the defensive position is depressive, and it must be a credit to the bomber crews and the P-38 pilots to have operated under it.

"Shortly before the P-38s were exchanged for P-51s we started wearying of the defensive nature of our fighting, and started to do something about it. Soon after we were in the Mustangs the whole attitude of Fighter Command had shifted to a more aggressive attitude. This took place while we were still in P-38s, but the process takes time, and after people were getting settled in the P-51, the whole war changed to an aggressive situation. This is more compatable with nature. Somewhat to Zemke's and Blakeslee's credit they understood this, and when they came into command, they refused the defensive position. It caused the fur to fly a bit at Headquarters, but the two men were adamant, and these commanders developed their battle tactics around a totally aggressive approach.

"Again I must return to the point, used by both sides, where a few Germans could render a large escorting force of allied fighters ineffective by simply staying higher and continually threatening by bouncing and zooming back up out of range. On many occasions the situation was reversed when a large gaggle of German fighters were discouraged by a small number of our fighters.

"I have experienced both situations. J. D. Bradshaw and I, on our last mission, mostly by accident discouraged from forty to sixty Me-109s preparing to attack our bombers. We were simply staying a couple of thousand feet above them, calling for aid (which never arrived). The

German leader didn't like the situation and went elsewhere with his mob.

"But another time was a disaster. Our Group was trying to escort two boxes of bombers that were separated by a ten-minute interval. The lead box was five minutes early and the second box was five minutes late. A small force of Me-109s kept us on the defensive while Me-110s, Me-410s and Ju-88s rocketed sixty bombers out of the air.

"An aggressive commander, in this situation, would have committed a like force to engage the Me-109s instantly, and went on about his business, even if it cost him the committed force. Here survival of the species was at the wrong time and the wrong place. More bombers could have been saved than fighters lost.

"THEN THERE WAS WEATHER

"Weather in combat was a defensive element with a like effect on pilots. Winter, spring, summer and winter again of 1944 in Europe was no joy. Mission departures were not uncommon with zero-zero conditions and no alternates except the full range of the airplane or diving over the side. Formation instrument climbouts nearly every damned day. Climbouts were made to as high as 34,000 feet without ever seeing even a glimpse of the sun. Formations would become scattered and all this rendered combat rather ineffective. DF (Direction Finding) Steer Approaches were made to whatever ceiling then prevailed. There was no approach radar. There was no precision instrument landing systems. The effectiveness of these procedures was in the simplicity of the thing. With one airplane, 200 feet for a ceiling and a half-mile visibility is one thing. With three on your wing it is a monstrously different matter.

"Air combat usually is *sudden*. There is seldom time for a staff meeting. The thinking and the reactions have to be developed somewhere else. Mistakes are made. Afterwards there is always the critique.

"There is panic on the radio. The sky is empty one second but the next moment may be filled with roaring engines and blazing guns. Victory goes to the most explosively aggressive. There is the old saying that the best defense is a good offense. *Believe it to be true.* It is considered an accident to be shot down by the guy you saw. Adrenalin blasts through the veins, seconds seem like hours; unless there is a chase, it is over as rapidly as it started. Strangely the fight has gone down, not up. It may have started at 30,000 feet and ended among the trees.

"Stay above your opponent.

"Break him down in the stall.

"Then get on him.

"THE HARD PART OF COMBAT

"Combat was the call at three or four in the bloody morning, the vomit and the cigarette for breakfast (nervous stomach and the green powdered eggs), the truck ride to briefing, ready-room and to the planes. Once in the air you were alive and ready. Then the thawing of frostbite on return.

"THE GOOD PART OF COMBAT

"Combat was also the medical whiskey on return, the big spam sandwich and coffee at debriefing. There was the unwinding in a tub of hot water, falling asleep until it got cold. There was the scotch ration at the club. The one day in nine months when the sun shined all day. The plans of the Society for Two for the protection and welfare of Bradshaw and Heiden. The friendly English babe who used the club bar for the sole support of her massive mammary glands and numerous gin and oranges. There was the blackout and the fog. The pub crawling, and busting your ass—in the dark—on a goddamned bike. "Lilli Marlene" in the dark . . .

"THE PEOPLE

"In every outfit there are irrepressible spirits. The impulsive who live to enjoy life. Strangely enough some of these are fantastic combat pilots, and they enjoy it. They are usually natural leaders and just as often are not entirely trusted because of their impulsive traits. Rules, they believe joyously, are made to be broken.

"At Kingscliff probably the prime example was Earnest C. Fiebelkorn, the number one ace of the group. He accomplished this even though he spent half his time off flying status for some infraction of the rules.

"Jack Ilfrey was molded from the same bronze, and he was the number *two* ace of the group. Ilfrey made the phenomenal distinction of being promoted to major and the very same day being broken to second lieutenant. Then promoted, a grade at a time, back to major within a week.

"His list of activities are long. They include taking out an Me-109 with his wingtip for a confirmed kill. While afoot and alone, after being shot down, he ended up with—and helping—the German Army that was facing Caen. Another audacious event was his landing for fuel in Portugal, then escaping internment with his airplane.

"DECISION

"We go back to my original letter to you. There are so many facets, so many myriad factors involved in judging an airplane. As for judging the P-38, there's no question. The record speaks for itself. We've been talking about one of the great airplanes, one of the great fighters, one of the greatest weapons of all time."

ARTHUR W. HEIDEN

Epilogue

This is something I have pursued for more than twenty-five years. The kind of story that raises the hackles on the back of your neck. There's an immediate urge to dismiss it as preposterous, impossible.

Because it *is* preposterous and impossible. Yet the records are there. A document that tells what happened in deliberately cold and official terms. A field in North Africa during the war. An event that took place that was so impossible the commanding officer at the airfield demanded, and got, the signatures of hundreds of witnesses who saw the whole impossible incident. The writer insists on nothing, makes no claims as to truth or impossibility. This is what happened. As it happened. As it was seen and sworn to by hundreds of ground crewmen and pilots, enlisted men and officers.

A flight of P-38s had gone out on patrol. They left to cross the Mediterranean. They mixed it up with German fighters and there was a brief scrap. When the P-38s reformed one airplane was missing. No one could recall, in the furious melee, watching him go down. They looked around, then they started home.

They arrived back at their field in North Africa. The one pilot who failed to return was listed as missing in action. Not yet, though. Not until his fuel ran out. Not until there wasn't even a glimmer of a chance.

The clock ticked slowly. Then, beyond the point of any fuel. Another two hours went by. They put his name on the list of missing.

It happens. That's war.

Then the air raid alert sounded. Radar picked up a single aircraft, unknown, coming in toward the field at fairly low altitude and high speed. Anti-aircraft guns started tracking. Some pilots ran for their planes.

Then they saw the intruder. A P-38, alone. Coming in along a shallow dive, engines thundering. It failed to respond to radio calls. There was no response to flares fired hurriedly into the air.

A strange approach; that flat and unwavering dive. The P-38 crossed to the center of the field.

Suddenly the airplane seemed to stagger. It fell apart in midair, a tumble of wreckage falling toward the ground. No flash of fire, no explosion. Just that startling breakup of machinery.

They saw a body fall clear of the wreckage. Pilots muttered, called aloud their thoughts without thinking. Then a parachute opened. Silk blossomed full. But the body hung limp in the harness.

Close to the wreckage, the pilot collapsed. No one saw him move. The crash trucks raced to the scene.

Those who came later saw their friends stunned, disbelieving, shaking their heads. They talked about it through the night. The next morning the light of dawn hadn't changed a thing.

It was impossible.

The fuel tanks of the P-38, the same airplane that was hours beyond any possible remaining fuel, were bone dry.

They had been dry for several hours.

The pilot whose parachute opened, that lowered him to his home field, had a bullet hole in his forehead. He had been dead for hours.

Impossible.

But it happened.

And no one knows how.

A NOTE FROM THE AUTHOR

It isn't always an easy matter to add this sort of correction to a book in which the author has held no small pride as to its accuracy, based on some backbreaking research and effort. But we can't always be right—even if we must always strive to do so. In this story of the P-38, because of the complexity of research areas to be covered, it appears as if the writer committed some errors. In timing, one might say, if we wish to use dates in that respect. It would have been an easy matter simply to correct the copy after the errors were brought to my attention. Somehow I feel this misses the spirit of the thing. After all, while I find my name listed as author of *FORK-TAILED DEVIL: THE P-38*, it is sort of an extraneous claim to credit, since without the help of hundreds of people, the book would never have been possible. Thus this addition to the copy, which was brought politely if not forcibly to my attention by Carroll R. Anderson, known to his many friends as Andy, and an individual you find, of course, in these pages as a P-38 pilot, member of the 475th Fighter Group, and a most remarkable human being who was of tremendous help in writing the book. In essence, I was politely but most effectively chewed out by Andy Anderson, and I'm grateful for his attention. What he wrote, in part from a very long letter in which we discussed several projects, contains within itself that beautiful touch of actuality from the man who has been there, and although the chastisement is something I'd rather not have found so necessary, well, when you're corrected in this manner by such as Andy Anderson, you can make mistakes and come up roses. Andy wrote me:

"Incidentally, I hate to tell you this, but you made a beauty in the P-38 book, and I hadn't the heart to tell you this, but I've just got to do it. Martin, you goofed when you referred to missions going out in 1943 to the length of the distances we flew *in 1944*. The missions to which you refer as having occurred in 1943 in fact did not happen until the year following. Your staff advised you incorrectly on the dates in question. Point of fact: All of the New Guinea coastline from Sio and the Admiralty Islands *westward* to the Philippine Islands was Japanese territory in 1943, and not until October and September of 1944 did we first reach Hollandia, and then Noemfor and Biak Islands, from which all of those long-range missions were flown. And, all fighter missions, incidentally, exactly because Mr. Lindbergh taught us how to do it. Make no mistake about this. *No missions of that nature were flown in 1943.*

"I don't know what if any good this information does for you, but what I am writing is accurate, and it is correct. I've received a number of letters from our chaps chiding you about that mistake. My old friend, John Tilley of the 431st, who designed the Red Devil insignia for the 431st when we were at Nadzab, wrote an especially humorous letter to me wanting to know about our mutual use (with the Japanese) of their airstrips so we could fly those long missions from our sector of New Guinea to Balikpapan and to the Celebes. John's tongue was really in his cheek. Jack Purdy had comment, too.

"Personally, I didn't make those missions. I went to see Wilson, who was then our CO, and asked permission to make at least one of the flights, but he refused me. Our old CO, Warren R. Lewis, had arranged for my trip home, and Wilson wasn't about to have me killed just before leaving for home. It would have been his proverbial ass. I was still eager, and I knew it was my last chance to get into a fight. No chance.

"Our group, along with the others, including the Jug outfits, staged from Gama strip at Morotai Island to Balikpapan. And although your timing is wrong, those missions more than anything else were the product of Mr. Lindbergh's efforts on our behalf, and proved conclusively why we have never felt that the P-38 had to take a back seat to the Mustang with respect to range. We knew we flew farther than they did. *In 1944,* Martin, for the very first time. *Not in 1943.*

"Hell, I flew farther than the P-51s way back in February of 1944 when we flew from Dobadura to Kavieng, New Ireland. That was the longest bomber mission flown under fighter escort of the war up to that point. I forget how far we went, but it was one hell of a long way. Another example: on the 15th February 1944, when we escorted the 38th, 345th and 3rd attack group to Kavieng, my squadron flew from Dobo up to the Vitaiz Straits, around Cape Gloucester to Sand Island, back to the area below Kavieng, then back up to Kavieng and over it while the bombers unloaded and finally straight across the island of New Britain back to Dobadura. Some of the B-25s and A-20s were forced to return to Finschafen for fuel and Dick Ellis of the 3rd Attack crash-landed at the newly hacked out American strip at Cape Gloucester.

"Sorry to catch you like this, but perhaps it's better if I tell you this way than getting it from some heckler. Perhaps you can get it changed in future editions."

Well, okay, fellas, there it is in black-and-blue. I stand corrected and chastised and *now* the dates are straight!

When I wrote the above material, quite willing to do whatever was necessary to get John Tilley's tongue out of his cheek and back into its proper place, I had expected to add just this corrective story and have done with it. But then as the copy was being readied for mailing to my publisher, a letter came in from a man with the name of Carl D. Camp. A fellow with an extraordinary record as an aerial gunner, and a gunner with an extraordinary viewpoint of the P-38 in World War II. Excerpts, with Camp's kind permission to use this material, are presented for further in-depth study of the Lightning. Camp wrote me:

"I was in the AAF from a year before Pearl Harbor until the end of World War II as an enlisted bombardier and aerial gunner and my experience with and knowledge of the P-38 is from that angle. I first saw it in the spring of 1941 at Chanute Field while a student mechanic, and although I and all my fellow students immediately recognized its beauty and potential, it was not until I was fighting for my life in New Guinea in 1943 that I realized just how fine an airplane it was.

"That it played a major role in keeping my kind alive you very adequately explained, but not even you can properly portray with written words the wild joy and relief that we gunners and other crew members experienced when the Lightnings arrived to kill or chase away the hard-pressing Zekes, thereby restoring our hope of living one more day. Although few of us ever had the chance, we often spoke of how we would honor any P-38 pilot that happened into our acquaintance either then or at any other time in the future.

"You told of P-38 pilots in Europe complaining of the plane's easy recognition as a drawback. To Pacific gunners and probably their European counterparts it was exactly the opposite. No P-38 was ever mistaken for an enemy. None ever caused us near-heart failure as did other friendly but not instantly identifiable fighters that suddenly popped out from a cloud while we were bound for the target. The cumulative strain of those encounters surely had subtracted a year from our lives—from all of us who survived. To my knowledge no P-38 in our theater was ever mistakenly fired at by some Jap-spooked and flak-happy gunner. Every other type, including twin-engine bombers and attack ships, was a sometime victim of such recognition problems.

"You explained that the loss of 5th Air Force records resulted in very little being written about that area in comparison to European and African operations. Another puzzlement to me is that at the time, we bomber people heard nothing of the fighter aces that lived near us on the ground and flew even nearer in their very successful efforts to preserve and protect us. That is, with the exception of Dick Bong. I still consider myself privileged to have seen him often and to have spoken to him once for a few moments. The rest I only learned after the war when I had time to read accounts and histories of 'my' war.

"Bong was both a disappointment and a joy for a gunner to speak to. A disappointment because he turned out not to be a god as we thought him previous to meeting him. In fact, he was very ordinary appearing as a person, in comparison to the image we had of him. He gained back all and more of any lost image in our eyes by not being a god when he told a bunch of us gunners that fighter pilots were only very lucky people to have such an easy job and that he couldn't understand how we put up with our problems. He admitted to respect and admiration of men like us who could swing a waist gun or turret for long hours in a hostile, flak-filled sky over even more hostile terrain, endure the cold, hunger, great fear and, worst of all, personally witness the gory deaths of our comrades and, incredibly, do it time after time until death or the end of the war released us. At that time, MacArthur had abolished the tour-and-return system for bomber crews and we were there forever. Our morale was naturally low but Bong served to raise it quite a bit with his slant on the subject. He made it plain he considered us all fellow warriors of equal importance in that deadly game. We left him feeling that we would cut our wrists and give him our blood if he needed it.

"One . . . maximum effort was my crew's second mission and first strike. I was on most of the subsequent strikes made in October and November and saw several B-24s and B-25s go down, but as stated by King (in your book), few were lost to enemy aircraft. The P-38s were too aggressive. I shot down a Zeke with the only clear, close chance I had during all that period. We saw plenty other Zero fighters at close range but all had one or more P-38s hot on their tails, hardly aggressive, as they sped through our formations trying to shed the P-38s that boxed them.

"I read all your books that I am able to obtain and hope one day to pick up one written on the B-24 in such style as you treated the P-38. If you ever take on that project and think it to be of possible use to you, I offer what information is in my journal and, as well, my log and my photo album."

Mr. Camp, thanks for your letter and as to that offer of help on a B-24 book, you're on. You'll be hearing from me. The book is already in the works for Ballantine Books.

A third and final letter absolutely requires *public* response. In March 1972 I received a letter from William B. Mills of North Carolina. Writing to Mr. Mills personally would satisfy his most courteous letter and his requests, but it might not do justice to a point he has brought up to me, and, in all fairness to all concerned, it is my belief that response in these pages is justified fully. Again, I will be excerpting from the letter. Mr. Mills wrote:

"I have just finished reading FORK-TAILED DEVIL, the story of the P-38, and was extremely pleased with your research. I suppose what was so different was the story of the boys who tried to ferry the '38s over the Atlantic. The reason for this is that most all books and magazines have articles on the combat aspects in great detail, which I have been reading about most airplanes and pilots for years. The Atlantic crossing was a different twist.

"BLACK THURSDAY was an excellent book and, accompanying this letter is an order for FLYING FORTS, SAMURAI!, and, ZERO! I already have THUNDERBOLT!

"I was especially interested in FORK-TAILED DEVIL because of your references to Benjamin Kelsey, the pilot who busted the first P-38. I couldn't help but get the impression that you felt Kelsey was sort of on the lower part of the totem pole as to his abilities as a pilot, his judgement, and in general, him. I am curious as to whether you have ever met or discussed any aviation aspects about any airplane ever flown or tested by Kelsey. Possibly you have and possibly Kelsey was the one who told you and admitted his errors?

". . . . because I have heard so many, many, many comments from my brother about the intelligence, abilities, know-how, flying proficiency, etc., that it was quite hard for me to believe or digest your comments on Kelsey without standing up to protest because you didn't have Kelsey's side of the story. It is sort of like saying Richard Bong wasn't such a good pilot in shooting down forty Japs because of a superior airplane only, because some of those times flak, lucky hits, mechanical trouble or an excellent Jap flier was to be reckoned with sometimes. You know what happened to Thomas McGuire and George Preddy. Preddy was shot down Christmas Day over Europe by our own anti-aircraft guns. He had over twenty-five to his credit. This was the year 1944.

"Drop me a line. I would be extremely interested in hearing from you with comments. I am sure Kelsey would be glad to talk to you about any aviation matters just by calling him cold and arranging an interview. Ask him about most of all the World War II American fighters he has flown and also the B-19, and his escapades in this plane."

Now, of the three letters from which I've just excerpted material, two of them—at least the parts printed here—clearly represent questions and/or criticism of the writer. There's a tendency on the part of those who prepare historical documents to defend at the slightest flareup whatever accuracy they insist lies within their copy.

Well, this writer makes every attempt to capture that accuracy. Many times different opinions by different pilots in the same place at the same time produce a variety of responses, and the writer is stuck. He can show both viewpoints (which is really the only way) or take a choice and commit to one particular conviction.

In the case of Ben Kelsey, let me state unequivocally that I was remiss in *not continuing an evaluation of the incident in which Kelsey lost the XP-38 on its first transcontinental flight.*

First, I did make the attempt to find Kelsey (who lives nearby, as it turns out) but failed to do so when the book was being written.

Second, it was the opinion of at least two P-38 pilots that Kelsey showed every evidence of pilot error in the loss of the XP-38.

Third, *I committed the cardinal sin of not going to pains to explain that it was Ben Kelsey in that airplane, and no one else, and whatever else we might feel on the matter, only Kelsey is fully aware of what happened—and the Air Corps at the time, and later, never felt criticism was in order. That speaks for itself. You do not lose the hottest fighter in the country and escape being raked over the coals if the brass is convinced you pulled the plug the wrong way. I didn't say that in the copy and I should have done so and for this I quickly offer apologies to Ben Kelsey.*

Fourth, I've been flying for 27 years, and anyone who's tooled around in the variety of machines in which I've found myself knows, beyond all question, that the best of the airplane drivers get into situations where human skill is negated by mechanical or other problems. This pilot-error syndrome, of which the FAA today is so fond in using to explain the unexplainable accident, is, frankly, a thorough pain in the ass. 20-20 hindsight is great but rarely satisfactory when the pilot is dead and his iron bird has been rolled up into a crumpled metal ball.

Fifth, I have seen Ben Kelsey fly through the years, and his record is not excellent—it is extraordinary and it is brilliant, and I'd like this moment, on this page, to say so, and to repeat that apology for any misleading conclusions to which I may have led the reader.

MC